Vereinigung für Recht und Gesellschaft
Law and Society

– vormals Vereinigung für Rechtssoziologie –

Herausgegeben von
Prof. Dr. Susanne Baer, Prof. Dr. Kai-D. Bussmann,
Prof. Dr. Gralf-Peter Calliess, Prof. Dr. Susanne Karstedt
und Prof. Dr. Matthias Mahlmann

Band 9

Julia Gebhard

Necessity or Nuisance?

Recourse to Human Rights in
Substantive International Criminal Law

Nomos

The Deutsche Nationalbibliothek lists this publication in the Deutsche Nationalbibliografie; detailed bibliographic data are available on the Internet at http://dnb.d-nb.de

a.t.: Hamburg, Univ., Diss., 2017

ISBN 978-3-8487-4427-5 (Print)
978-3-8452-8644-0 (ePDF)

British Library Cataloguing-in-Publication Data
A catalogue record for this book is available from the British Library.

ISBN 978-3-8487-4427-5 (Print)
978-3-8452-8644-0 (ePDF)

Library of Congress Cataloging-in-Publication Data
Gebhard, Julia
Necessity or Nuisance?
Recourse to Human Rights in Substantive International Criminal Law
Julia Gebhard
296 p.

ISBN 978-3-8487-4427-5 (Print)
978-3-8452-8644-0 (ePDF)

1st Edition 2018

Preface and Acknowledgements

This book is based my doctoral thesis at the University of Hamburg. It was written between 2009 and 2015 and updated in October 2017. More recent legal developments could unfortunately not be taken into account.

The research on which this book is based, as well as the writing itself, could not have been made possible without a multitude of different people and institutions which provided me with incredible research opportunities and environments, criticized and encouraged my research with their feedback and granted me their time to answer all my questions.

First and foremost, I owe my gratitude to my supervisor, em. Prof. Dr. Dr. h.c. Rüdiger Wolfrum for believing in my work, providing me with freedom and time to research while working as a researcher at the Max Planck Institute for Comparative Public and International Law and for supporting me on numerous occasions on which my research took me outside the library and outside of Heidelberg. For his thorough report, kind words and valuable suggestions, I would also like to thank my second supervisor, Prof. Dr. Stefan Oeter.

One of the opportunities which Prof. Wolfrum provided me with was to conduct my research as part of the International Max Planck Research School on Retaliation, Mediation and Punishment (IMPRS-REMEP). I want to thank Prof. Dr. Dr. h.c. mult. Hans-Jörg Albrecht and Prof. Dr. Günther Schlee for their investment in this interdisciplinary research group which offers its students a unique environment to test and develop their research. Thank you, Prof. Dr. Anja Seibert-Fohr, for your guidance and your feedback. Furthermore, I would like to thank Prof. Dr. Günther Schlee and the Max Planck Society for the generous financial contribution towards the publication of this work. Thank you, Dr. Carolin Hillemanns, for the smooth operation of our group and for all your support and encouragement throughout the years.

I would like to thank the FAZIT-Stiftung for granting me a scholarship enabling me to concentrate on finalizing my dissertation.

The libraries of the Max Planck Institute for Comparative Public and International Law in Heidelberg, Germany, the Max Planck Institute for Foreign and International Criminal Law in Freiburg, Germany and the Central European University in Budapest, Hungary and their excellent, helpful and welcoming staff I thank for unearthing every publication I was looking for and for extending kind words. I am furthermore grateful for the support received by Prof. Dr. Michael Anderheiden and Prof. Dr. András Jakab while finalizing my thesis in Budapest.

The insights that this book provides would not have been possible without the judges at the International Criminal Court and the International Tribunal of the Former Yugoslavia who agreed to answer my questions and let me in on their thoughts regarding the significance of international human rights law on their work while working as a Visiting Professional at the ICC in 2010. I owe particular gratitude to the late Judge Hans-Peter Kaul for accepting me as a Visiting Professional and for his curiosity and interest in my research. Furthermore, I am grateful to Xabier Agirre Aranburu, Eleni Chatidou and William Rosato for discussing my research and for the opportunities and the support extended.

I thank Professor William Schabas for inviting me to Galway and guiding my research in more scholarly sound and realistic ways when it was still at the very beginning and Professor Gudmundur Alfredsson, for his enthusiasm for this project and for irregularly checking in and inquiring about its progress.

I want to thank the editors of "Recht und Gesellschaft – Law and Society" for their decision to accept my research within their series. In particular, I am grateful to Prof. Dr. Susanne Karstedt for her support and her comments on the empirical part of this book.

Over the years, I had countless discussions, got so much excellent and honest feedback and the support without which this book might have never been finished. I am indebted to Andreas Armborst, Stephanie Berry, Berit Beyer, Kristina Blohm, Olivia Danai, Mikael Ekman, Julia Breslin Foster, Kiyomi von Frankenberg, Andrea Furger, Johannes Fuchs, Anne Giebel, Jenny Grote-Stoutenburg, Mayeul Hiéramente, Julia Kasselt, Nandor Knust, Mandana Knust Rassekh Afshar, Björn Länsisyrjä, Sally Longworth, Polina Levina Mahnad, Sigrid Mehring, Ulysses Moreira Formiga, Carse Ramos, Isabel Röcker, Jennifer Schuetze-Reymann, Christina Sell, Inga Švarca, Helena Sunnegårdh, Alice Thomas, Diana Trimiño and Johann-Christoph Woltag.

In particular, eternal gratitude to Berit, Diana, Jules, Johannes, Kristina, Sally and Ulysses. Your love, friendship and support have many times saved my sanity and made my days and will surely continue to do so in the future. Thank you.

To my parents, Angelika and Heinz Gebhard, and to Felix, I am grateful for all the love and encouragement, for always being there in any moment of need, for having my back and for putting things into perspective, not only, but also, during the course of this project.

Finally, to Csaba, thank you for your love, your unwavering and enthusiastic support, for cheering me on and for believing and living in an equal partnership. And to Levi, for being with us, himself and a part of us.

Table of Contents

Introduction

I. Approach and Conceptual Framework

1. Overview of the Research Topic

The starting point of this research is the following: crimes under international law are, partly with the exception of war crimes, defined broadly and construed in a vague manner in the respective statutes of international criminal courts and tribunals.[1] As a practical consequence, it is up to the judges to fill the gaps left in the statutes by taking recourse to extra-statutory law. The nature and the hierarchy of these sources are stated in Article 21 Rome Statute of the International Criminal Court ('Rome Statute') for the Interantional Criminal Court ('ICC'), wheras for the ad hoc and hybrid tribunals, the sources are enshrined in the more general provision of Art. 38 Statute of the International Court of Justice ('ICJ Statute').[2] The application of extra-statutory sources and the interpretation that this application inevitable requires can lead to legal uncertainty and to the unequal application of the law within the same court or tribunal. While this is a problem with which all courts and tribunals applying international law are faced, international criminal courts and tribunals encounter this dilemma in an aggravated form because, as criminal courts, they have to adhere to procedural guarantees and fair trial standards. Applying extra- statutory sources, they run the risk of violating one of the cornerstones of the right to a fair trial, the principle of legality.

Hence, this book looks at one of the major external sources consulted by judges, namely international human rights law, in the context of this conflict. The book consists of three major parts: first, the dogmatic analy-

---

1 See Arts 6-8 Rome Statute of the International Criminal Court ([adopted 17 July 1998, entered into force 1 July 2002] 2187 UNTS 90); Arts 2-4 Statute of the International Criminal Tribunal for Rwanda (UNSC Res 955 [1994] [8 November 1994] SCOR 49th Year 13) [Rome Statute]; Arts 2-5 Statute of the International Criminal Tribunal for the Former Yugoslavia (UNSC Res 827 [1993] [25 Mai 1993] SCOR 48th Jahr 29).

2 Statute of the International Court of Justice (adopted 26 June 1945, entered into force 24 October 1945) 145 BSP 832.

sis of the differing doctrinal architecture of international criminal law and international human rights law and resulting problems in the application of international human rights law in substantive international criminal law; second, the analysis of case law to establish how various bodies of international criminal law have dealt with these problems and in which areas judges are most forthcoming in their reference to international human rights law; and third, the attitudes of judges concerning the relationship of international criminal law and international human rights law, the resulting interpretative practices in their decision and judgments and the factors which influence to what extent a practitioner is open to any form of reference to human rights law.

The thesis employs two major methodologies. A larger part of the research consists of doctrinal legal analysis of statutes, treaties, decisions of judiciary bodies both in the fields of human rights law and international criminal law, as well as various international soft law instruments. This is supplemented by a qualitative study of the interpretative practices of sitting judges of international criminal law courts of human rights laws, based on interviews.

The issue of broadly constructed and vague legislative texts is not unique to international criminal law. Many domestic criminal codes also include crimes the definition and elements of which are not apparent when solely consulting the letter of the law and require clarification. However, the problem is particularly pressing in modern international criminal law as an area of law still in its buildup-phase, an area which is frequently criticized as susceptible to the influence of international politics. The perimeters of many crimes often remain vague and unclear, due to fragmentary codification as well as the temporarily and substantively limited number of practical cases of application.

This vagueness in content is highly problematic regarding the principle *nullum crimen/nulla poena sine lege*, one of the most fundamental principles to be adhered to by a State or institution based on the rule of law. According to this principle, an act can be punishable only on the basis of a legal act and a person may not be punished arbitrarily and without sufficient legal basis.[3] For criminal law, including international criminal law, this implicates that at the time an act occurred, a written or unwritten norm

3 Erkin Gadirov und Roger S Clark in Otto Triffterer (hrsg) *Commentary of the Rome Statute of the International Criminal Court* (2nd edition CH Beck 2008) 506.

has to establish its categorization as a crime for a person to be punished accordingly.[4]

In order to define crimes 'with the clarity, precision and specificity required for criminal law in accordance with the principle of legality (*nullum crimen sine lege*)'[5] the ICC, pursuant to Art 9, introduced the Elements of Crime.[6] These help the Court in the interpretation and application of the crimes enlisted in Arts 6-8 Rome Statute. Judges at the International Criminal Tribunal for Rwanda (ICTR) and the International Criminal Tribunal for the Former Yugoslavia (ICTY) cannot take recourse to such elements according to their statutes.

Even though the introduction of Elements of Crimes at the ICC signaled awareness and a positive development, the Elements of Crime can only partially provide legal certainty to the practitioners and the subjects of international criminal law, because they are, again, phrased in a rather broad manner. For this reason, the judges at the ICC will continue to have to consult external sources of law for the interpretation of crimes.

Hence, judges at international criminal law are often faced with a dilemma as, by adhering to the principle of *nullum crimen sine lege* and clearly defining the punishable acts in question, they might overextend the letter of the law, when they take recourse to conventions or legal concepts outside their own statures. In principle, judges at the ICC and other international criminal courts and tribunals are entitled to consult sources outside their statutes. When doing that, they have to respect the sources of international law pursuant to Art. 38 Statute of the ICJ (for the ICC Art. 21 Rome Statute, which also establishes a hierarchy of the sources).[7]

Apart from looking at the application of existing conventions and treaties in the specific case, judges will also consider customary international law. Due to the fragmentary codification of international law, customary international law, is of particular importance to judges at interna-

---

4 See eg Gerhard Werle *Völkerstrafrecht* (2. Auflage Mohr Siebeck 2007) 44; fundamental regarding nullum crimen sine lege in international law: Otto Triffterer *Dogmatische Untersuchungen zur Entwicklung des materiellen Völkerstrafrechts seit Nürnberg* (E. Albert 1966) 124.

5 Summary of the Proceedings of the Preparatory Committee on the Establishment of an International Criminal Court 25 March – 12 April 1996 UN Doc A/AC.249/1 (7 May 1996) para 13.

6 Elements of Crimes (9 September 2002) Doc ICC-ASP/1/3 (Pt. II-B).

7 Statute of the International Court of Justice (adopted 26 June 1945, entered into force 24 October 1945) 145 BSP 832.

tional courts and tribunals. A norm of customary international law is generated through State practice in the in the belief that the act in question is legally binding (*opinio juris*).[8]

In order to determine these two elements, it is common practice to examine, *inter alia*, the acceptance of specific standards of international law within the international community. These standards cannot only be extracted through legally binding conventions or treaties, but can also be deducted from jurisprudence, decisions of treaty bodies or the UN General Assembly.[9]

With respect to international standards relevant to the work of international courts and tribunals, the reference to human rights law, especially, seems obvious and even self-evident as international criminal law and human rights law hold common roots and complement each other.[10] Practically all relevant crimes under international law also contain violations of international human rights law and can be systematized accordingly.[11]

---

8 See eg Malcom N. Shaw *International Law* (6. Auflage Cambridge University Press 2008) 72 ff.

9 See eg *Prosecutor v Delalić et al (Judgment)* IT-96-21 (16 November 1998) paras 453 ff; *Prosecutor v Furundžija (Judgment)* IT-95-17 (10 Dezember 1998) paras 160 ff; *Prosecutor v Kvočka (Judgment)* IT-98-30 (2 November 2001) paras 137 ff; *Prosecutor v Krnojelac (Judgment)* IT-97-25 (15 März 2002) para. 186; *Prosecutor v Kunarac (Judgment)* IT-96-23 (Juni 2002) paras 469 ff.

10 The tribunals also were faced with the problem that a treaty provision to which the parties wree bound or which was part of customary international law provided for the prohibtion of a certain act, but not necessarily for its criminalization. For this reason, the tribunals then had to look at customary law to define the circumstances under which a prohibited act triggered penal consequences: see *Prosecutor v Galić (Appeal Judgment)* IT-98-29-A (30 November 2006) para. 83.

11 It was this knowledge that led the States negotiating the Rome Statute to include several so-called 'treaty crimes' in the Statute (as modalities of crimes against humanity or war crimes), crimes which were listed as violations of international human rights law in the respective human rights instruments but were, up until then not to be found in the statutes of international criminal tribunals; see See Andreas Zimmermann 'Article 5: Crimes within the jurisdiction of the Court' in Otto Triffterer (ed) *Commentary on the Rome Statute of the International Criminal Court* (2nd ed Beck Munich 2008) 129-142, 130-131; see also Anja Seibert-Fohr *Prosecuting Serious Human Rights Violations* (OUP Oxford 2009) 1ff; Alette Smeulers and Fred Grünfeld *International Crimes and Other Gross Human Rights Violations* (Nijhoff Leiden 2011); Gerhard Werle ‚Menschenrechtsschutz durch Völkerstrafrecht' (1997) 109(4) Zeitschrift für die gesamte Strafrechtswissenschaft 808-829; Carsten Stahn ‚Internationaler Menschenrechtsschutz und Völkerstrafrecht' 82 (3) Kritische Justiz (1999) 345-355.

The area of conflict between the need to consult international human rights law as an external source and the need to adhere to the principle of *nullum crimen sine lege* are the subject of this book. The common roots, but also the substantive differences between the areas of human rights law and international criminal law, which allow for recourse to human rights law only under specific, dogmatically well-justified and defined conditions, will be explored. The work scrutinizes the advantages as well as the dangers that such recourse entails. It highlights the preconditions under which human rights law is most likely to be referred to in a coherent and methodologically sound manner. As such, the project seeks to contribute to the dogmatic understanding of international criminal law and its dynamic development.

2. Approach and Demand for Research

As examined in the following, the current practice in jurisprudence is characterized by a condition of legal uncertainty in which dogmatic ambiguity led to a situation where similar acts are at times evaluated differently by different Chambers of the same court or tribunal, leading to an unequal legal categorization of the acts in question. This problem has presented itself, for example, in the categorization of torture as a crime against humanity before the ICTY. Whereas one Chamber required the perpetrator to be a State official or at least having acted with the consent or acquiescence of a State official, another Chamber of the same tribunal deemed this requirement not necessary for the definition of torture under international law.[12] Pointing out these ambiguities, their causes and consequences, contributes to the unification of international criminal law and therefore its legal security. Furthermore, the project explicitly focuses on substantive international criminal law and its interconnection with human rights law. The connection between these two fields is currently underresearched, as priority, in legal research as well as in practice, is often given to the importance of 'procedural' human rights law, in particular, to safeguarding the rights of the accused. While this is no doubt a vital part of applying international criminal law and its violations endanger the the credibility of the

12 See *Prosecutor v Delalić et al (Judgment)* IT-96-21 (16 November 1998) para 473 and *Prosecutor v Kunarac (Judgment)* IT-96-23 (22 February 2001) paras 488-96; see in detail at Part Two Chapter One I. 1. b. and f. below.

field as a whole, the Rome Statute brings about numerous legal innovations with regards to substance. Hence, recourse to extra-statutory sources will be inevitable for judges in the future. Thereby, the ICC, as the single permanent court in the field of international criminal law, has the unique opportunity to counteract fragmentation of the practical application of the law and focus on the development of coherent jurisprudence. This research project points out the preconditions for such development.

II. Scope and Methodology

This book aims at answering the following central research questions:

- How do substantive international criminal law and human rights law relate to each other and how does this relationship allow for or preclude recourse to international human rights law in substantive international criminal law?
- Under which circumstances (status of a specific concept under human rights law, status of a specific crime under international and/or national criminal law, composition of chambers etc.) and within which dogmatic framework do judges of international criminal courts and tribunals refer to international human rights law?
- What are the factors (professional background, legal system in which the judge was educated/was acting professionally) that determine if and how judges refer to international human rights law?
- What are the conditions under which it is appropriate for judges of international courts and tribunals to refer to human rights law and what are the benefits of such reference?

According to the hypotheses underlying this research project, recourse to international human rights law is necessary and helpful for judges in international criminal tribunals due to a variety of reasons:

- International criminal law and international human rights law have common roots; international criminal law developed, in a large part, out of the human rights discourse. However, the differences in scope, the scenarios covered, the actors, addressees and the general framework of a penal system versus a rights- based system do often allow only for limited recourse.
- Reference to international human rights law is often indispensable for judges who have to shed light on the scope of a certain crime under

customary international law, highlighting *opinio iuris* and State practice in a certain area of human rights law. This is due to the area of conflict between the broadly sketched definitions of crimes under international law on the one hand and the judges' obligation to adhere to the principle of *nullum crimen sine lege* on the other hand. Recourse to human rights law is more likely in areas of human rights which are well-established and governed by 'robust' conventions rather than soft law. For crimes which have a counterpart in national criminal legislation, human rights law is more often consulted.

- Experts in public international law are more open to the application of extra-statutory law in general and human rights law in particular.
- Reference to international human rights law strengthens legal arguments and the persuasive power and therefore raises the legal weight of judgments in an area of law which continues to be under construction by drawing from a field of law which offers a sophisticated and well-established convolute of legal dogmatic theory and jurisprudence.
- Reference to international human rights law is a suitable tool for judges to determine the content of a crime under customary international law. However, currently, recourse to human rights law often appears as a necessary box to be ticked in judgments without a deeper understanding of the legal concept in question. In the absence of streamlined international criminal law education, a balanced composition of the Chambers, taking into account various backgrounds, as well as continuous training for judges is advisable.

Generally, reference to human rights law offers international courts and tribunals the opportunity to benefit from decades of work and experience of international human rights courts and committees and their jurisprudence.

This book focuses on the influence of international human rights law on the development and practical application of *substantive* international criminal law. While the majority of scholarly research in the area concentrates on the application of human rights law in procedural international criminal law, in particular the right to a fair trial,[13] this work examines why and how human rights law can be and is used in substantive law in

13 See recently eg Jessica Almqvist 'Complementarity and Human Rights: A Litmus Test for the International Criminal Court' (2008) 30 Loyola of Los Angeles International and Comparative Law Review 20 (2008) 336-366; Segun Jegede 'The

order to define crimes under international law. However, procedural international criminal law and how it is influenced by international human rights law will be also touched upon for two reasons: the first reason is that the two concepts are frequently blurred in the approaches of the persons applying the law as well as in academia. When one asks the question of recourse to human rights law in international criminal law, most of the practitioners interviewed were zooming in on one of the two aspects, procedural or substantive, dismissing or disregarding the other. The second reason why it is impossible to delve into substantive law without having first considered the rules regarding the application of human rights law in procedural matters is that both set of rules are intertwined and frequently misunderstood even by the practitioners. It is important to disentangle the provisions and rules of international law allowing recourse to human rights law in international law and scrutinize which type of recourse, procedural or substantive, they allow for.

The work will not deal with the issue of deterrence of crimes and the potential use of human rights law to further any deterrent effect of international criminal law. This limitation is set despite the repeated (self-) assertion of international criminal *ad hoc* tribunals of their work contributing to the prevention of conflict and crime under international law.[14] Apart from exceeding a feasible scope of a research project, the issue of deterrence is

Right to A Fair Trial in International Criminal Law' in Chile Eboe-Osuji *Protecting Humanity: Essays in International Law and Policy in Honour of Navanethem Pillay* (Nijhoff Leiden 2010) 519-548; Manoj Sinha *International Criminal Law and Human Rights* (Manak Delhi 2010); Thomas Kruessmann (ed) *ICTY: Towards a Fair Trial?* (Vienna Neuer Wissenschaftlicher Verlag 2008); Damien Scalia 'Long-term sentences in international criminal law: Do they meet the standards set out by the European Court of Human Rights?' (2011) 9(3) Journal of International Criminal Justice 669-687; Rebecca Young '"Internationally Recognized Human Rights" Before the International Criminal Court' (2011) 60 International and Comparative Law Quarterly 189-208.

14 Eg *Prosecutor v Aleksovski (Appeal Judgment)* IT-95-14/1 (24 March 2000) para. 185; *Prosecutor v Delalić et al (Celebići Case Appeal Judgement)* IT-96-21-A (20 February 2001) para. 806; *Prosecutor v Todorović* (Judgment) IT-95-9/1-S (31 July 2001) paras 28-30; *Prosecutor v Krnojelac (Judgment)* IT-97-25 (15 March 2002) para. 508; *Prosecutor v Furundžija (Judgment)* IT-95-17 (10 December 1998) para. 288; *Prosecutor v Erdemović (Sentencing Judgement)* IT-96-22-T (29 November 1996) para. 64; *Prosecutor v Hadžihasanović et al* (Judgment) IT-96-22-T (29 November 1996) para 64; *Prosecutor v Perišić (Judgment)* IT-04-81-T (6 September 2011) para 2204; *Prosecutor v Ntakirutimana (Judgment)* ICTR-96-10 and ICTR-96-17-T (21 February 2003) para 882; *Prosecutor v*

a controversial subject, it is hard to measure and many doubt the existence of any deterrent effect of international criminal law altogether.[15] As the author of this study is a public international lawyer by training, the subject will generally be approached from the entry point of public international law in general and international human rights law in particular. Ultimately, the study aims at pointing out synergies between the two areas and seeks to narrow the gap that often prevents further synthesis.

Niyitegeka (Judgment) ICTR-96-14-T (16 May 2003) para 484; *Prosecutor v Rugambarara (Judgment)* ICTR-00-59-T (16 November 2007) para 11; *Prosecutor v Ntawukulilyayo (Judgment)* ICTR-05-82-T (3 August 2010) para. 463; *Prosecutor v Kalimanzira (Judgment)* ICTR-05-88-T (22 June 2009) para. 741; the ICC lists deterrence as one of its goals in the Preamble to the Rome Statute but has been remarkably quiet about the presumed deterrent effect of its work and has not referred to deterrence in its so far only two judgments *Prosecutor v Thomas Lubanga Dyilo (Judgment)* ICC-01/04-01/06 (14 March 2012) and *Prosecutor v Mathieu Ngudjolo (Judgment)* ICC-01/04-02/12 (18 December 2012).

15 See further Payam Akhavan 'Beyond Immunity: Can International Criminal Justice Prevent Future Atrocities?' (2001) 95(1) American Journal of International Law, 7-31; Payam Akhavan 'Justice in the Hague, Peace in the Former Yugoslavia? A Commentary on the United Nations War Crimes Tribunal' (1998) 20(4) Human Rights Quarterly, 737-816; Mirjan Damaška 'What is the Point of International Criminal Justice?' (2008) 83 Chicago-Kent Law Review 329-369; Hunjoon Kim and Kathryn Sikkink 'Explaining the Deterrence Effect for Human Rights Prosecutions for Transitional Countries' (2010) 54(4) International Studies Quarterly 939-963; Julian Ku and Jide Nzelibe 'Do International Criminal Tribunals Deter or Exacerbate Humanitarian Atrocities?' (2006) 84(4) WashingtonUniversity Law Review 777-833; Christopher W Mullins and Dawn L Rothe 'The Ability of the International Criminal Court to Deter Violations of International Criminal Law: A Theoretical Assessment' (2010) 10(5) International Criminal Law Review 771-785; Robert D Sloane 'The Expressive Capacity of International Punishment: the Limits of the National Law Analogy and the Potential of International Criminal Law' (2007) 43(1) Stanford Journal of International Law 39-94; Immi Tallgren 'The Sensibility and Sence of International Criminal Law' (2002) 13(3) European Journal of Public International Law 561-595; David Wippman 'Atrocities, Deterrence and the Limits of International Justice' (1999-2000) 23 Fordham International Law Journal 473-488; Danilo Zolo 'Peace through Criminal Law?' (2004) 2 Journal of International Criminal Justice 727-734.

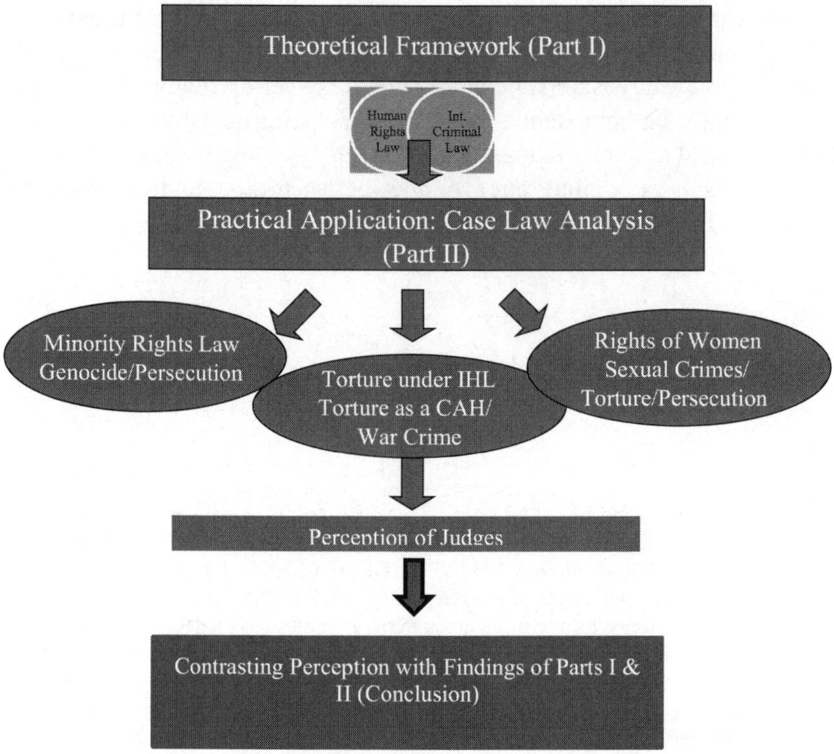

The study is divided into three broad parts which broadly correlate to three different methodological approaches. Traditional analysis and interpretation of positive norms as well as literature exegesis lay the theoretical framework of the research project in Part One. Starting from case law analysis, an inventory of the use of human rights law in substantive international criminal law is created in Part Two regarding the areas of the prohibition of torture, minority rights and sexual violence. Together with the empirical part (Part Three) consisting of interviews with judges at the ICC and the ICTY, this deductive deficit analysis illustrates the perception practitioners in international criminal law have of the relationship between human rights law and international criminal law. Furthermore, it shows how their respective perception shapes the willingness of the judges to refer to human rights law in their jurisprudence and points out which dogmatic considerations are undertaken. Thereby, the study points out to what degree a recourse to human rights law is likely in the future of international criminal courts and tribunals. It further illustrates under which conditions such recourse is appropriate and helpful for the practical application of international criminal law.

Part One: The Relationship between International Criminal Law and Human Rights

Chapter One: Introduction

The relationship between substantive international criminal law and human rights is, despite the continuously academic and non-academic interest in both disciplines, not conclusively established. There are two main reasons for this: the first one is that none of the two areas is clearly and exclusively defined and delimitated in the first place. The term 'human rights' can cover a plethora of rights and claims like the right to physical integrity and the right to liberty, to fair trail guarantees, minority rights, economic, social and cultural rights and the generally non-enforceable so-called third generation rights.[16] They are mostly rights that protect the individual from an excess of authority from the State, but additional to respecting the individual's human rights, the States' role is also to protect and fulfil the right, meaning to facilitate and provide them vis-à-vis the individual.[17] International human rights law encompasses rights, for example rights protecting life, physical integrity, freedom of movement, minority rights, the mass violation of which are under certain circumstances considered to be crimes under international law and can trigger international criminal proceedings. Hence, there is a clear connection, but no concluding answer, as to the relationship between the two disciplines.

---

16 The umbrella term "third generation rights" is in itself ill-defined and covers many different concepts. What unites them is their general non-enforceability as well as their complex nature (which is why they are also referred to as 'composite rights'), see Theo van Boven 'Categories of Rights' in Daniel Moeckli, Sangeeta Shah and Sandesh Sivakumaran (eds) *International Human Rights Law* (OUP Oxford 2010) 173-188 at 178; for the multi-faceted concept of 'human rights' see also Laurence R Helfer 'Forum Shopping for Human Rights' 148 University of Pennsylvania Law Review (1999) at 285-400 at 298: 'The corpus of international human rights law does not exist in a single, comprehensive treaty, code or statute. Rather, the rights and freedoms it enshrines are found in a complex web of overlapping global, regional, and specialized agreements, many of which contain identical, related, or even conflicting substantive standards'.

17 See eg Manfred Nowak *U. N. Covenant on Civil and Political Rights: CCPR Commentary* (N. P Engel Kehl 2005) at XX-XXI.

Equally, the notion of international criminal law encompasses not only conduct which is deemed criminal, but also establishes the principles according to which a person can be held accountable for such conduct, the procedure regulating who can investigate and judge such crimes, as well as procedural frameworks for international criminal proceedings that take into account the proper handling of evidence and the rights of all the participants of the proceeding, including the accused person.[18] International criminal law is therefore, broadly speaking, made up of two large set of rules, substantive and procedural ones. The same is true for human rights law as an umbrella term for very different sets of rights, including minimum standards that an individual is entitled to in court proceedings.

This leads to the second reason for the non-conclusive establishment of the relationship between international criminal law and human rights law: due to the broad concepts used, the discourses regarding the commonalities and differences of the two disciplines get increasingly inaccurate and confusing. Scholars and practitioners talk at cross-purposes because they do not have a common understanding and definition of the areas in question and are essentially discussing different subjects:

- One group, and that includes most scholars debating the relationship between international criminal law and human rights law, examines the relationship between international criminal law and human rights law in terms of the substantive interconnectedness of the two: how international criminal law emerged from, was a by-product or the logical last step of, the evolution of human rights.[19]
- The other group, including most of the practitioners interviewed in the course of this research project, have, at first glance, little regard for this question they see as a rather academic problem.[20] In theirday-to-day work, what seems more pressing or immediately relevant is how human rights relate to the procedural aspect of the trial, *inter alia*, how can the rights of the accused be consolidated with the needs of victim protection. This is a logical consequence of international criminal pro-

18 Antonio Cassese *International Criminal Law* (2nd edition OUP Oxford 2008) 3.

19 See below Part One Chapter Three I. eg M. Cherif Bassiouni 'The Proscribing Function of International Criminal Law in the Process of International Protection of Human Rights' (1982-3) 9 Yale Journal of World Public Order 193-216; Carsten Stahn 'Internationaler Menschenrechtsschutz und Völkerstrafrecht' (1999) 3 Kritische Justiz 343-355.

20 See Part Three Chapter One III. below.

ceedings that take, compared to many national criminal trial, a very long time during which most of the human rights related issues that need to be addressed concern procedural aspects including the length of detention, the degree of victim participation, disclosure of evidence, witness proofing etc.

When discussing the 'use' of human rights law in international criminal law, one must thus first identify which of the two scenarios in question one is faced with, as they both entail very different practical consequences triggered by different legal provisions and questions. Hence, there are two basic conceptual differences that are not sufficiently distinguished with regard to their influence on the development and practical application of international criminal law:

– The first is the influence of human rights law on procedural international criminal law. Those are the rules that safeguard the accused's right to receive a fair, an independent, transparent and expeditious trial which provides for an equality of arms between the parties. Fair trial guarantees containing minimum standards for criminal trials are contained in all major human rights conventions[21] and are a part of customary international law.[22] In the area of international criminal law, the role and influence of international human rights law is much more prominent than in domestic jurisdictions, in which national constitutions often provide for much more efficient mechanisms of individual protection. As these mechanisms are absent in international law, human rights law comes to the forefront to fill the gaps. One of the most crucial, elementary fair trial standards is the principle of legality, made

---

21 Art. 10 and 11 Universal Declaration of Human Rights (UNGA Res 217 A [III] [10 December 1948] GAOR 3rd Session Part I Resolutions 71); Art. 14 International Covenant on Civil and Political Rights (adopted 19 December 1966, entered into force 23 March 1976) 999 UNTS 171; Art. 6 Convention for the Protection of Human Rights and Fundamental Freedoms (Council of Europe signed 4 November 1950, entered into force 3 September 1953) 213 UNTS 221; Art. 8 American Convention on Human Rights (signed 22 November 1969, entered into force 18 July 1978) 1144 UNTS 123 (Pact of San José); Art. 7 African Charter on Human and Peoples' Rights (adopted 27 June1981, entered into force 21 October 1986) 1520 UNTS 217 (Banjul Charter).

22 Patrick Robinson 'The Right to a Fair Trail in International Law, with Specific Reference to the Work of the ICTY' (2009) 3 Berkeley Journal of International Law Publicist 1-11 at 5.

up of the two basic rules *nullum crimen sine lege* (no crime without law) and *nuella poena sine lege* (no punishment without law).[23] This standard plays a vital role in the assessment of the second and more complex concept:

– The relationship between human rights law and substantive international criminal law. Examining this relationship means nothing less than examining the roots of the evolution of international criminal law. What is substantive international criminal law made of? What is the common denominator of the actions we label crimes under international law? What is the essence of genocide, crimes against humanity and war crimes? These questions are so fundamental because international criminal provisions are vague, their written definition, if any, leaves the need for judicial interpretation. If international criminal law is indeed, as argued by some, the logical result of an evolution of human rights, human rights law is an obvious place for judges in international criminal cases to turn to when they seek to fill the gaps left open by the statutes to the international courts and tribunals they operate in.

However, the judicial interpretation of a crime by way of consultation of substantive norms outside the ones written in the statute in which the crime is contained can undermine the defendant's basic rights to a fair trial. To put it differently and perhaps more strikingly, the application or interpretation of substantive human rights law in criminal matters might violate the defendant's human rights. In this case, the whole essence of what courts in general and international criminal courts and tribunals in particular are, what they stand for, is endangered, for if a court who is to uphold law and justice violates human rights itself, it has essentially failed.[24]

This book will concentrate on the role of human rights in substantive international criminal law. However, as demonstrated above, substantive and procedural international criminal law are interlinked and an incorrect application of one will have obvious consequences on the other. In order to grasp the parameters, guarantees and limitations of the application of human rights law in substantive international criminal law, the understand-

23 Claus Kreß 'Nulla poena nullum crimen sine lege' in Rüdiger Wolfrum (ed) *Max Planck Encyclopedia of Public International Law* 2nd ed (OUP 2012) vol VII 889-899 at 889.

24 See also Daniel Sheppard 'The International Criminal Court and "Internationally Recognized Human Rights": Understanding Article 21(3) of the Rome Statute' (2010) 10 International Criminal Law Review 43-71, 59.

ing of human rights in procedural international criminal law is a necessity. The following chapters will hence first outline the relationship between human rights law and procedural international criminal law, followed by the connection between human rights law and substantive international criminal law. This part elaborates on the similarities and the differences of the two fields of law. Once the extent to which human rights law can be useful in international criminal law is established, the thesis will discuss what authorizes the courts and tribunals to use human rights law. This includes a discussion of *nullum crimen sine lege* in international criminal law and the potential clashes of this basic principle of human rights law with the application of human rights law in substantive international criminal law.

Chapter Two: Human Rights Law and Procedural International Criminal Law

'Procedural' human rights law to be applied by international courts and tribunals are, first and foremost, the rights of the accused person. All modern international criminal courts and tribunals explicitly refer to the rights of the accused, albeit to a differing degree of sophistication. The ad hoc and hybrid tribunals, as well as the ICC, all dedicate an article to the rights of the accused during preparation and trial phase.[25] All these provisions are explicitly modelled after Art. 14 ICCPR[26] and only slightly adapted to fit the needs of an international criminal legal context. Other 'procedural'

---

25 See Art. 21 ICTY Statute; Art. 20 ICTR Statute; Art. Art. 17 SCSL Statute; Art. 16 STL Statute; Art. 35 Law on the Establishment of Extraordinary Chambers in the Courts of Cambodia for the Prosecution of Crimes committed during the Period of Democratic Kampuchea (27 October 2004) S/RKM/1004/006 http://www.eccc.gov.kh/sites/default/files/legal-documents/KR_Law_as_amended_27_Oct_2004_Eng.pdf (31 October 2017); see also Art. 67 Rome Statute.

26 International Covenant on Civil and Political Rights adopted 19 December 1966, entered into force 23 March 1976) 999 UNTS 171; for the ICTY see Theodor Meron 'Human Rights Marches into New Territory: The Enforcement of International Human Rights in International Criminal Tribunals' Fourth Marek Nowicki Memorial Lecture (28 November 2008) <http://web.ceu.hu/legal/pdf%20documents/Nowicki/Meron_Enforcement%20of%20HRwarsawnowicki13nov 08.pdf> (as last accessed on 10 June 2013; speech no longer accessible online); 'Report of the Secretary-General Pursuant to Paragraph 2 of Security Council Resolution 808 (1993)' UN Doc S/25704 para. 106.

human rights guarantees, taking the example of the Rome Statute as the most detailed and elaborate of the Statute are Art. 20 (*ne bis in idem*); Art. 22 (*nullum crimen sine lege*); Art. 23 (*nulla poena sine lege*); Art. 24 (non-retroactivity); Art. 26 (exclusion of jurisdiction over persons under eighteen); Art. 64 (2) (Trial Chamber as the organ that must ensure a fair and expeditious trial); Art. 66 (presumption of innocence); Arts 81-84 (right to appeal); Art. 85 (right to compensation in cases of unlawful arrest of detention).

These provisions give guidance to the chamber on how it shall conduct proceedings in a way which guarantees a fair trial for the accused. The ICC has taken ample opportunities to examine the human rights of the accused in international criminal proceedings in the course of its first, now-completed, trial against Thomas Lubanga Dyilo. When issuing the first of its two stays of proceedings the Court's Trial Chamber referred extensively to international human rights law regarding the right to a fair trial, more specifically the scope of the prosecution's obligation to disclose exculpatory evidence to the defence.[27]

Human rights law has also been used by the ICC to outline the scope, rules and limitations of victim protection and has already been used to

---

27 *Prosecutor v Thomas Lubanga Dyilo (Decision on the consequences of non-disclosure of exculpatory materials covered by Article 54(3)(e) agreements and the application to stay the prosecution of the accused, together with certain other issues raised at the Status Conference on 10 June 2008)* ICC-01/04-01/06-1401 (13 June 2008); para. 58 refers to fair trial provisions in Art. 14(1) ICCPR, the Art. 11(1) UDHR and Art. 6 ECHR; paras 77-81 analyses ICTY and ECtHR jurisprudence regarding the prosecution's disclosure obligations; paras 82-87 deals with the role of the judges in determining whether or not the disclosure obligations have been met. The second stay of proceedings following the refusal of the prosecution to reveal the identity of one of its intermediaries did not include such direct references to human rights instruments outside the Rome Statute, see *Prosecutor v Thomas Lubanga Dylio (Decision on the Prosecution's Urgent Request for Variation of the Time-*
Limit to Disclose the Identity of Intermediary 143 or Alternatively to Stay Proceedings Pending Further Consultations with the VWU) ICC-01/04-01/06-2517 (8 July 2010); for a comprehensive analysis of the use of regional human rights jurisprudene by the Court in Lubanga see Annika Jones 'Insights into an Emerging Relationship: Use of Human Rights Jurisprudence at the International Criminal Court' (2016) 16 Human Rights Law Review, 701-29.

clarify the unique victim participation procedure before the ICC.[28] The ICTR and the ICTY have both referenced international human rights law in interpreting what rights a person accused before any of their tribunals is entitled to.[29]

On what legal basis could the *ad hoc* tribunals and the ICC invoke these extra-statutory instruments?

I. Ad Hoc Tribunals

When referencing human rights law in a procedural context, the ICTY and the ICTR, unlike the ICC, could not take recourse to a provision outlining their applicable law (for a detailed analysis of the ICC's rules on the law applicable see Part One Chapter Three II. 2 below). Due to their *sui generis* nature, due to its establishment through UN Security Council Resolutions, it is at times cumbersome to determine which standards they are

---

28 Further William A Schabas *The International Criminal Court: A Commentary on the Rome Statute* (OUP Oxford 2010) 399-400; eg *Situation on the Democratic Republic of the Congo (Decision on the Applications for Participation in the Proceedings of VPRS 1, VPRS 2, VPRS 3, VPRS 4, VPRS 5 and VPRS 6*) ICC-01/04 UN (17 January 2006); *Prosecutor v Thomas Lubanga Dyilo (Decision on Victims' Participation)* ICC-01/04-01/06-1119 (18 January 2008) para. 35; *Prosecutor v Jean-Pierre Bemba (Fourth Decision on Victims' Participation)* ICC-01/05-01/08 6/39 (2 December 2008) para. 16; instruments referred to varied from the Convention on the Rights of the Child ([adopted 20 November 1989, entered into force 2 September 1990] 1577 UNTS 3) to soft law documents such as Commission on Human Rights 'Basic Principles and Guidelines on the Right to a Remedy and Reparation for Victims of Gross Violations of International Human Rights Law and Serious Violations of International Humanitarian Law' ([19 April 2005] ESCOR 61st Session Supp 3, 136); UNGA Res 40/34 'Declaration of Basic Principles of Justice for Victims of Crime and Abuse of Power' ([29 November 1985] GAOR 40th Session Supp 53, 213).

29 *Prosecutor v Akayesu (Appeal Judgment)* ICTR-96-4-A (1 June 2001) para 117; *Prosecutor v Kajelijeli (Appeal Judgment)* ICTR-98-44-A-A (23 May 2005) paras 209-212, 224-230, 251-255; *Prosecutor v Kambanda (Appeal Judgment)* ICTR-97-23-A (19 October 2000) para 33; *Mugenzi and Mugiraneza v Prosecutor (Appeal Judgment)* ICTR-99-50-A (4 February 2013) paraas 7 an 10; *Prosecutor v Furundžija (Appeal Judgment)* IT-95-17/1-A (21 July 2000) para 69; *Prosecutor v Milutinović et al (Decision on Dragoljub Ojdanic's Motion Challenging Jurisdiction–Joint Criminal Enterprise)* IT-99-37-AR72 (21 May 2003) para. 9, *Prosecutor v Tadić (Appeal Judgment)* IT-94-1-A (15 July 1999) paras 43-51
Prosecutor v Vasiljević (Judgment) IT-98-32-T (29 November 2002) para 197.

bound to.[30] This has led to a particular dogmatic vagueness in the application of law outside the Statute, both in the procedural and substantive sense. As international criminal law is a part of public international law, the *ad hoc* tribunals are generally bound by the same sources of law as any other area of public international law, the ones enlisted in Art. 38 ICJ Statute.[31] The rights of the accused are outlined in Art. 21 ICTY Statute and also in Art. 20 dealing with fair and expeditious trial. The ICTR covers substantially the same rules in Art. 20 and Art. 19 of its Statute respectively. As the tribunals are not given the guidance of a specific list of sources applicable, the tribunals seem to be overly cautious not to overstep their legal boundaries. This, paradoxically, leads to a watering down of the standards of applicable law in many instances before the *ad hoc* tribunals: as the tribunals tread carefully as to not exceed their mandates, they seem to circumvent, in many cases, a discussion whether they apply a certain external provision as (customary) law per se and retreat to the safer notion of using the provision as a 'interpretational guidance' or 'inspiration' for the court without properly discussing the basis of such an application as 'guidance' (see Part One Chapter Three II. 2. C. below). In the end, whether a provision is applied as part of customary international law or as 'inspiration' does usually not change the outcome of the Chamber's reasoning. 'Inspriration' and 'guidance' allow the court to use concepts the legal basis of which is not entirely established in circumvention of dogmatically sound discussions about what authorizes the respective tribunal to apply the standard in question. A thorough examination of the status of the applied law or concept as well as convincing proof of why the specific

---

30 The ICTY was established pursuant to UNSC Res 808 (1993) (22 February 1993) SCOR 48th Year 28; the ICTR UNSC Res 955 (1994) (8 November 1994) SCOR 49th Year 15; see also eg Christiane Kamardi *Die Ausformung einer Prozessordnung sui generis durch das ICTY unter Berücksichtigung des Fair-Trial Prinzips* (Springer Berlin 2009); Jacob Katz Cogan 'International Courts and Fair Trials: Difficulties and Perspectives' (2002) 27 Yale Journal of International Law 111-140 at 116-8.

31 Alexander Zahar and Göran Sluiter *International Criminal Law: A Critical Introduction* (OUP Oxford 2008) 277; see also *Interpretation of the Agreement of 25 March 1951 between the WHO and Egypt (Advisory Opinion)* [1980] ICJ Rep 73, 89-90: 'international organizations are subjects of international law and, as such, are bound by any obligations incumbent upon them under the general rules of international law'.

standard is (or is not) considered to be applicaple to the court and tribunal in question is thereby avoided.

This is a regrettable and at times dangerous neglect. The ICTY has justified its reference to the ICCPR by stating that the fair trial rights in the ICTY Statute are based on the ICCPR, which, in turn, based the provisions on fair trials in the ECHR.[32] The Secretary-General's Report which proposed the ICTY Statute stated that it was 'axiomatic' that the ICTY fully respected international standards regarding the rights of the accused and shared its view that 'such internationally recognized standards are, in particular, contained in article 14 of the International Covenant on Civil and Political Rights'.[33] The ICTY jurisprudence seems to not feel the need to delve into a discussion about the content of customary international law in this are and regards Art. 21 ICTY Statute as awarding a greater scope of protection than Art. 14 ICCP as Art. 21 also covers the pre-trial phase.[34]

The court is, however, concerned with the interpretation of fair trial provisions in international legal treaties by international judicial bodies (such as treaty bodies and regional human rights courts), which it sees not as binding,[35] but holds that the provisions and their interpretation have to be adapted to the 'object and purpose' of the statute and its unique context.[36] This might make sense as far as the interpretation of the legal provision is concerned. The treaty bodies' jurisprudence is not binding in itself but provides authoritative interpretations of the binding texts. The relevance of judgments of regional human rights courts beyond their direct binding force on the parties to a specific case is subject to much discussion

32 Christiane Kamardi *Die Ausformung einer Prozessordnung sui generis durch das ICTY unter Berücksichtigung des Fair-Trial Prinzips* (Springer Berlin 2009) 148.

33 UNSC 'Report of the Secretary-General pursuant to Paragraph 2 of Security Council Resolution 808 (1993)' (3 May 1993) UN Doc S/25704 para 106; see also Theodor Meron 'Human Rights Marches into New Territory: The Enforcement of International Human Rights in International Criminal Tribunals' Fourth Marek Nowicki Memorial Lecture (28 November 2008) <http://web.ceu.hu/legal/pdf%20 documents/Nowicki/Meron_Enforcement%20of%20HRwarsawnowicki13nov 08. pdf> as last accessed on 10 June 2013; speech no longer accessible online.

34 *Prosecutor v Tadić* (Decision on the Prosecutor's Motion Requesting Protective Measures for Victims and Witnesses) IC-94-I-10 (10 August 1995) para. 25.

35 Christiane Kamardi *Die Ausformung einer Prozessordnung sui generis durch das ICTY unter Berücksichtigung des Fair-Trial Prinzips* (Springer Berlin 2009) 148.

36 *Prosecutor v Tadić* (Decision on the Prosecutor's Motion Requesting Protective Measures for Victims and Witnesses) IC-94-I-10 (10 August 1995) para. 26.

in international law.[37] They might in any case be an indication of existing customary law. The question at hand is whether existing customary law, in the area of human rights or otherwise, is binding as such to the ad hoc tribunals.

One argument that the ICTY, in particular, invokes to counter such an obligation to apply customary international law in the area of fair trial rights, is that the ICTY Statute, pursuant to Art. 22, obliges judges to provide for the protection of its witnesses and victims. Article 21 ICTY Statute also states that the right to a fair and public hearing is subject to Art. 22.[38] This follows a tendency at the ad hoc tribunals to pay lip service to the importance of international human rights standards before international criminal tribunals but actually wanting 'full authority to determine when it wants to comply with the ICCPR'[39] or other international instruments applicable to it. Instead of a dogmatically sound examination of whether, in fact, the respective instrument is applicable to the ad hoc tribunal and accordingly applying or disregarding it, the tribunals' approach is often characterized by an element of 'yes, but'. One argument, which factually always limits the scope of protection of international human rights instruments,[40] is that the tribunals operate in unique situations of mass violence and thus in a different legal context.[41] The strength of this argument is, however, at least questionable. It is the events that triggered

---

37 Art. 46 ECHR, for example, states explicitly that the judgments are binding on the parties of the case in question, but do not state that the judgments have an effect *erga omnes*; see, e.g. the speech of Boštjan Zupančič, judge of the ECtHR entitled ,The Binding Nature of the Judgments of the ECHR and the Universality of Human Rights' (14 April 2014) available at http://www.cd-n.org/index.php?the-binding-nature-of-the-judgments-of-the-echr-and-the-universality-of-human-rights (31 October 2017).

38 *Prosecutor v Tadić* (Decision on the Prosecutor's Motion Requesting Protective Measures for Victims and Witnesses) IC-94-I-10 (10 August 1995) para. 26.

39 James Sloan 'The International Criminal Tribunal for the Former Yugoslavia and Fair Trial Rights: A Closer Look' (1996) 9(2) Leiden Journal of International Law 479-501 at 488.

40 Göran Sluiter ,Human rights protection in the ICC pre-trial phase' in Carsten Stahn and Göran Sluiter (eds) *The Emerging Practice of the International Criminal Court* (Nijhoff Leiden 2009) 459-476, 461.

41 *Prosecutor v Kunarac (Judgment)* IT-96-23 (22 February 2001) para 470; *Prosecutor v Kunarac (Appeal Judgment)* IT-96-23 & IT-96-23/1-A (12 June 2002 paras 142-148; see also eg *Prosecutor v Haradinaj* (Judgment) IT-04-84-T (3 April 2008) para. 127; *Prosecutor v Mićo Stanišić (Judgment)* IT-08-91-T (27 March 2013) para 47.

the tribunals' jurisdiction, not the tribunals themselves that manoeuvre in environments of mass violations. It is the situations themselves, which might constitute a national emergency in which derogations from some rights might exceptionally be allowed. The Rwandan armed conflict ended in July 1994, the ICTR was established in November the same year.[42] It is true that the ICTY was established in May 1993, when the armed conflict in the former Yugoslavia was still on-going. Nevertheless, the court did not start its investigations until July 1994 and the large majority of suspects was investigated, indicted and tried long after the Dayton Agreement. Naturally, this did not necessarily mean that threats to witnesses and victims were eliminated alongside the cessation of the conflict. However, it put the tribunals, which were geographically removed from the crime scenes, in a position not unlike the one many post-conflict States face in the aftermath of mass crimes or a situation like it occurs in large, high-profile criminal investigation involving gangs or other organized crime able to jeopardize the safety of victims and witnesses. These are precisely the kind of situations in which fair trial rights are especially important, to fend off accusations or tendencies of victor's justice and revenge. They are no situations that require any adaptation to a perceived uniqueness of international criminal law and the environment in which it operates.

II. ICC

1. Art. 21 (3) ICC

In order to provide a clearer guidance of the applicable sources and to avoid some of the ad hoc tribunals' dogmatic mishaps, the Rome Statute, as the first international criminal law forum ever, contains a list of the applicable law in Art. 21 Rome Statute. It also can take recourse to a provision that explicitly enables the court to apply some procedural human rights law. Art. 21 (3) Rome Statute reads

> ' [t]he application and interpretation of law pursuant to this article must be consistent with internationally recognized human rights, and be without any adverse distinction founded on grounds such as gender as defined in article 7,

---

Kunarac, para. 488; see also *Prosecutor v Furundžija (Judgment)* IT-95-17 (10 December 1998) para. 162.

42 See ICTR UNSC Res 955 (1994) (8 November 1994) SCOR 49th Year 15;.

paragraph 3, age, race, colour, language, religion or belief, political or other opinion, national, ethnic or social origin, wealth, birth or other status'.[43]

Art. 21 (3) Rome Statute 'provides a standard against which all the law applied should be tested'.[44] This has been affirmed by the ICC Appeals Chamber when it stated that '[h]uman rights underpin the Statute; every aspect of it [...]. Its provisions must be interpreted and more importantly applied, in accordance with internationally recognized human rights; first and foremost, in the context of the Statute, the right to a fair trial'.[45] Art. 21 Rome Statute imposes a hierarchy of sources unknown to Art. 38 ICJ Statute. Art. 21 (3) Rome Statute is on the top of this hierarchy, placing it above the Statute itself.[46] It acts, in a way, as a constitution for the

---

43 A detailed discussion on the general sources of law applicable for the ICC and other international criminal tribunals can be found under Part One Chaper Three II.

44 Mahnoush H Arsanjani 'The Rome Statute of the International Criminal Court' (1999) 93 American Journal of International Law 22-43 at 29.

45 *The Prosecutor v Thomas Lubanga Dyilo* (Judgment on the Appeal of Mr. Thomas Lubanga Dyilo against the Decision on the Defense Challenge to the Jurisdiction of the Court pursuant to Article 19(2)(a) of the Statute of 3 October 2006) ICC-01/04-01/06-772 (14 December 2006) at para. 37.

46 Daniel Sheppard 'The International Criminal Court and "Internationally Recognized Human Rights": Understanding Article 21 (3) of the Rome Statute' (2010) 10 International Criminal Law Review 43-71 at 46; Gilbert Bitti 'Article 21 of the Statute of the ICC and the treatment of sources of law in the jurisprudence of the ICC' in Carsten Stahn and Göran Sluiter (eds) *The Emerging Practice of the International Criminal Court* (Brill The Hague 2008) 286-304, 293-4; of a different opinion are Gerhard Hafner and Christina Binder 'The Interpretation of Article 21 (3) ICC Statute, Opinion Reviewed' (2004) 9 Austrian Review of International and European Law 163-190, 173-177, who argue, inter alia, that Art 69(7) which states: 'Evidence obtained by means of a violation of this Statute or internationally recognized human rights shall not be admissible if [...]' indicates that internationally recognized human rights and the Statute are on equal footing. As the Statute does not provide an exhaustive list of applicable human rights nor does it exhaustively define the ones that are mentioned in the Statute, this argument is not plausible. The ICC itself seems to suggest a supremacy of internationally recognized human rights in the above-cited section of *The Prosecutor v Thomas Lubanga Dyilo (Judgment on the Appeal of Mr. Thomas Lubanga Dyilo against the Decision on the Defense Challenge to the Jurisdiction of the Court pursuant to Article 19(2)(a) of the Statute of 3 October 2006)* ICC-01/04-01/06-772 (14 December 2006) at para. 37.

court a norm on which all application of the sources of law have to be measured against.[47]

The phrasing of Art. 21 (3) is likely to stem from paraphrasing a similar one used before the ICTY which states that the ICTY Statute and its Rules of Procedure and Evidence were drafted with regard to and compliance of 'internationally recognized standards of fundamental human rights'[48] and itself referred to a section in the Secretary-General's Report on the Establishment of the ICTY in which the Secretary-General mentioned 'internationally recognized standards regarding the rights of the accused' which are 'in particular, contained in article 14 of the International Covenant on Civil and Political Rights'.[49] The origin of the terminology clarifies that the drafters of the statute thought of Art. 21 (3) Rome Statute as sort of a constitutional provision guaranteeing that trials before the ICC are conducted with regard to the rights of the accused and characterized by the leading principles of fairness, transparency and foreseeability. This was also explicitly mentioned in the last Draft Version of the Rome Statute where the drafters stated that:

> 'It was generally agreed that consistency with international human rights law would require that interpretation by the Court be consistent with the principle of nullum crimen sine lege. A view was also expressed that this should be explicitly stated in this article or be made clearer in article 21.'[50]

---

47 See also Daniel Sheppard 'The International Criminal Court and "Internationally Recognized Human Rights": Understanding Article 21 (3) of the Rome Statute' 10 (2010) International Criminal Law Review 43-71 at 46; Mahnoush H Arsanjani 'The Rome Statute of the Internatonal Criminal Court' 93 (1999) American Journal if International Law 22-42 at 29; Gilbert Bitti 'Article 21 of the Statute of the ICC and the treatment of sources of law in the jurisprudence of the ICC' in Carsten Stahn and Göran Sluiter (eds) The Emerging Practice of the International Criminal Court (Brill The Hague 2008) 286-304,300-2.

48 *Prosecutor v Tadić (Decision on the Prosecutors Motion Requesting Protective Measures for Victims and Witnesses)* IT-94-1 (10 August 1995) para. 25.

49 UNSC 'Report of the Secretary-General pursuant to Paragraph 2 of Security Council Resolution 808 (1993)' (3 May 1993) UN Doc S/25704 para 106.

50 Draft Art. 20 United Nations Diplomatic Conference of Plenipotentiaries on the Establishment of an International Criminal Court 'Report of the Preparatory Committee on the Establishment of an International Criminal Court: Addendum' (15-17 July 1998) A/Conf.183/2/Add.1 para. 63; in the draft article, what is now regulated under Article 21 was proposed to be Art. 20, while nullum crimen sine lege (now Article 22) was discussed as Article 21.

Hence, Art. 21 (3) Rome Statute requires the court to safeguard a fair trial in line with internationally recognized human rights.[51] It expands the list of fair trial rights already explicitly mentioned in the Statute and guarantees its adherence at every stage of the proceedings.[52] The ICC Appeals Chamber has discussed Art. 21 (3) Rome Statute in the context of a potential breach of the rights of the accused when it said [t]he Statute safeguards the rights of the accused [...] Such rights are entrenched in articles 55 and 67 of the Statute. More importantly, article 21 (3) of the Statute makes the interpretation as well as the application of the law applicable under the Statute subject to internationally recognised human rights. It requires the exercise of the jurisdiction of the Court in accordance with internationally recognized human rights norms.'[53]

2. What are 'internationally recognized human rights'?

It is less than clear what 'internationally recognized human rights' actually are. Comparing the phrasing with Art 7 (1) (h) of the Rome Statute, which speaks of 'grounds that are universally recognized as impermissible under international law' leaves room for the assumption that Art. 21 (3) requires something short of universal recognition.[54]

According to Art. 31 Vienna Convention on the Laws of Treaties,[55] Art. 21 (3) Rome Statute must be 'interpreted in good faith in accordance

---

51 See eg William A. Schabas *The International Criminal Court: A Commentary on the Rome Statute* (OUP Oxford 2010) 398-9; Joe Verhoeven 'Article 21 of the Rome Statute and the Ambiguities of Applicable Law' (2002) 33 Netherlands Yearbook of International Law 3-22, 14-15.

52 William A Schabas *The International Criminal Court: A Commentary on the Rome Statute* (OUP Oxford 2010) 398.

53 *Prosecutor v Thomas Lubanga Dyilo (Judgment on the Appeal of Mr. Thomas Lubanga Dyilo against the Decision on the Defense Challenge to the Jurisdiction of the Court pursuant to Article 19(2)(a) of the Statute of 3 October 2006)* ICC-01/04-01/06-772 (14 December 2006) para. 36.

54 George E Edwards 'International Human Rights Challenges to the New International Criminal Court: the Search and Seizure Right to Privacy' (2001) 26 Yale Journal of International Law 323-412 at 376-77.

55 Vienna Convention on the Law of Treaties (concluded 23 May 1969, entered into force 27 January 1980) 1155 UNTS 331; see also *Situation in the Democratic Republic of the Congo (Judgment on the Prosecutor's Application for Extraordinary Review of Pre-Trial Chamber I's 31 March 2006 Decision Denying Leave to Ap-*

with the ordinary meaning to be given to the terms of the treaty in their context and in the light of its object and purpose'. In any case, interpretation of the term 'internationally recognized human rights' should be carried out carefully and rather conservatively in line with the object and purpose of the Rome Statute which is ensuring common action in order to punish the 'most serious crimes of concern to the international community'.[56] The Rome Statute is not a human rights treaty in itself and the court it establishes is not a human rights court *per se*. The Preamble to the Rome Statute furthermore contains references to State sovereignty, territorial integrity and non-interference in internal affairs to emphasize the limits of the convention. Far-reaching inclusion of human rights concepts in different stages of becoming actual law and exceeding a conservative reading is not what the parties to the Rome Statue would have been ready to accept. A far-reaching human rights inclusion should therefore be rejected.

Furthermore, Art. 21 Rome Statute (just as Art. 38 ICJ Statute) is a secondary rule of international law, 'which provide for the formation of primary rules, those rules that state what has to be done and what cannot be done'[57]. The provision of Art. 21 (3) Rome Statute only guides the court in how its interpretation and application has to be conducted but it does not in itself define the applicable law for the court.[58]

What, then, does a more conservative approach on this question contain? The 1998 so-called Zutphen Draft of the Rome Statute referred, albeit in a different context, to the term 'internationally protected human rights'. In a footnote, it was made clear that this term was chosen to in-

---

peal) ICC-01/04-168 (13 July 2006) para. 33; *Prosecutor v Germain Katanga and Mathieu Ngudjolo Chui (Judgment on the appeal of Mr. Germain Katanga against the decision of Pre-Trial Chamber I entitled "Decision on the Defence Request Concerning Languages)* ICC-01/04-01/07-522 (27 May 2008) paras 38 and 39; *Prosecutor v Jean-Pierre Bemba Gombo (Judgment on the appeal of Mr Jean-Pierre Bemba Gombo against the decision of Trial Chamber III of 28 July 2010 entitled 'Decision on the review of the detention of Mr Jean-Pierre Bemba Gombo pursuant to Rule 118(2) of the Rules of Procedure and Evidence')* ICC-01/05-01/08-1019 (19 November 2010) para. 49.

56 See Preamble to the Rome Statute.

57 Noora Arajarvi 'Between Lex Lata and Lex Ferenda – Customary International (Criminal) law and the Principle of Legality ' (2010-11) 15 Tilburg Law Review 163-182 at 170.

58 Noora Arajarvi 'Between Lex Lata and Lex Ferenda – Customary International (Criminal) law and the Principle of Legality ' 15 Tilburg Law Review (2010-2011) 163-182 at 170.

clude non-treaty human rights guarantees, namely customary human rights law and that the term was meant to be broader than the term 'international law'.[59] The first part of this footnote is clear and has also been explicitly supported by jurisprudence of the court who stated that '[i]nternationally recognized may be regarded those human rights acknowledged by customary international law and international treaties and conventions'.[60]

The second part of the footnote is less susceptible to a clear interpretation, particularly because it is not further explained and has not been debated in any of the *travaux préparatoire*. It seems to suggest that 'internationally recognized human rights' seems to be a term more expansive than

59 Preparatory Committee on the Establishment of an International Criminal Court 'Report of the Inter-Sessional Meeting from 19 to 30 January 1998 in Zutphen, The Netherlands' (4 February 1998) UN Doc A/AC.249/1998/L.13at 47-50.

60 *The Prosecutor v Thomas Lubanga Dyilo* (Decision on the Prosecutor's "Application for Leave to Reply to 'Conclusions de la defense en reponse au memoire d'appeal du Procureur'" Separate Opinion of Judge Georghios M. Pikis) ICC-01/04-01/06-424 (12 September 2006) at para. 3; in 2004, Hafner/Binder examined in detail the various manifestations of *opinio iuris* for 'internationally recognized human rights'. For the case of international human rights treaties, they look at the number of ratification and the geographical distribution. After analysing the core human rights treaties (ICCPR, ICESCR, ICERD, CEDAW, CRC, CMW, CAT and their Optional Protocols) Hafner and Binder conclude that for all of these instruments apart from the CMW which only had 26 ratifications in 2004 (47 ratifications as of September 2013) and the second optional protocol to the ICCPR, which deals with the abolition of the death penalty (Second Optional Protocol to the International Covenant on Civil and Political Rights, aiming at the Abolition of the Death Penalty [adopted 15 December 1989, entered into force 11 July 1991] GAOR 44th Session Supp 49 vol 1, 207; 77 ratifications as of 2013), a *presumptio iuris* should exist as to their international recognition. Based on the numbers of ratifications they deemed sufficient for being 'widely ratified' and therefore recognized, this list now also includes the two optional Protocols to the Convention of the Rights of the Child on the Involvement of Children in Armed Conflict and on the sale of Children, Child Prostitution and Child Pornography ([25 May 2000] GAOR 54th Session Supp 49 vol 3, 6. As another one of the core human rights conventions triggering the *presumtio iuris*, the Convention on the Rights of Persons with Disabilities ([adopted 13 December 2006, entered into force 3 May 2008] 2515 UNTS 12) which, as of 2013, has been ratified by 134 States, could be mentioned; see Gerhard Hafner and Christina Binder 'The Interpretation of Article 21 (3) ICC Statute, Opinion Reviewed' (2004) 9 Austrian Review of International and European Law 163-190, 186-190.
152 and 164 ratifications respectively in 2013.).

merely customary international law.[61] The most likely interpretation in light of the object and purpose of the convention is that it referred to soft law relevant to the court, which the latter has to take into account and has to give due regard to, but by which it is not bound. [62] This would be first and foremost the jurisprudence of the treaty bodies interpreting internationally recognized human rights law, namely the major UN human rights conventions, as for example the ICCPR, interpreted by the Human Rights Committee ('HRC').[63] On the other hand, judgments of regional human rights courts have to be taken into account by the court to a greater extent than the treaty body decisions.[64] Even though the court itself is not party to any regional human rights treaty, the Member States to the Rome Statute are and, unlike the recommendations of the treaty bodies, the judgments of the regional human rights bodies are binding. For this reason, judgements of regional courts come under Art. 21 (1) (c) of the Rome Statute as part of the 'national laws that would normally exercise jurisdiction' the court takes recourse to when it seeks to distil general principles of law to apply and therefore also find their way into the canon of internationally recognized human rights to be consulted by the court in questions of fair trial.[65]

61 See also George E Edwards 'International Human Rights Challenges to the New International Criminal Court: the Search and Seizure Right to Privacy' (2001) 26 Yale Journal of International Law 323-412 at 381.

62 See also Daniel Sheppard 'The International Criminal Court and "Internationally Recognized Human Rights": Understanding Article 21(3) of the Rome Statute' (2010) 10 International Criminal Law Review 43-71, 69.

63 See also Daniel Sheppard 'The International Criminal Court and "Internationally Recognized Human Rights": Understanding Article 21(3) of the Rome Statute' (2010) 10 International Criminal Law Review 43-71, 69.

64 See also Daniel Sheppard 'The International Criminal Court and "Internationally Recognized Human Rights": Understanding Article 21(3) of the Rome Statute' (2010) 10 International Criminal Law Review 43-71, 69-70.

65 Daniel Sheppard 'The International Criminal Court and "Internationally Recognized Human Rights": Understanding Article 21(3) of the Rome Statute' (2010) 10 International Criminal Law Review 43-71, 69-70; Amal Alamuddin 'Collection of Evidence' in Karim A A Khan, Caroline Buisma and Christopher Gosnell (eds) *Principles of International Criminal Justice* (OUP Oxford 2010) 231-305 at 236.

Chapter Three: Human Rights Law and Substantive International Criminal Law

This chapter will explore the relationship between and the use of 'substantive' human rights law in the work of the material consideration of international criminal courts and tribunals. It will first scrutinize the similarities, the common development, but also the differences between the two fields of law. This is necessary to understand to what degree it is actually warranted for the courts and tribunals to refer to international human rights law before delving into the question to what degree the ad hoc tribunals and the ICC are entitled to refer to international criminal law in this context by their own secondary law.

I. Relationship ICL – Substantive HR:

> 'Crimes against humanity might usefully be viewed as an implementation of human rights norms within international criminal law. Just as human rights law addresses atrocities and other violations perpetrated by the State against its own population, crimes against humanity are focused on prosecuting the individuals who commit such violations'.[66]

International criminal law has been called a 'hybrid branch of law'[67]. It is a part of public international law that encompasses 'notions, principles and legal constructs'[68] from national criminal law as well as from both international humanitarian law and international human rights law.[69] International human rights law and international criminal law are obviously related as a violation of the one (e.g. the prohibition of slavery) often finds a mirror provision in the other (e.g. enslavement as a crime against humanity). Many crimes under international law do consist of mass violations of human rights. According to its Preamble and Art. 1 Rome Statute, the ICC is responsible for the prosecution of the most serious crimes of concern to the international community as a whole. This is an expression of a system of values and morals the international community as a whole seeks to pro-

---

66 William Schabas, Commentary on the Rome Statute, Article 7, p. 139.
67 Antonio Cassese *International Criminal Law* (Oxford University Press 2008) 7.
68 Antonio Cassese *International Criminal Law* (Oxford University Press 2008) 7.
69 Antonio Cassese *International Criminal Law* (Oxford University Press 2008) 4-10.

tect.[70] The codification of those values of the international community is, to a great extent, to be found in international human rights law.[71] Furthermore, the human rights movement and the focus of human rights institutions like the Inter-American Court of Human Rights (IACtHR) and the HRC on accountability of mass violations fertilized and spurred the development of legal concepts of international criminal law and are responsible for much of the political momentum that led to the ad hoc tribunals and later to the establishment of the ICC.[72]

At the same time, the two concepts are framed very differently in dogmatic legal terms. Human rights law formulates rights the individual has against the State.[73] International criminal law is a catalogue of prohibitions, obligations and criminal offences based on the principle of individual criminal responsibility[74]

---

70 Carsten Stahn and Sven-R. Eiffler 'Über das Verhältnis von Internationalem Menschenrechtsschutz und Völkerstrafrecht anhand des Statuts von Rom' (1999) 82(1) Kritische Vierteljahresschrift für Gesetzgebung und Rechtswissenschaft 253-277, 267.

71 Carsten Stahn and Sven-R. Eiffler 'Über das Verhältnis von Internationalem Menschenrechtsschutz und Völkerstrafrecht anhand des Statuts von Rom' (1999) 82(1) Kritische Vierteljahresschrift für Gesetzgebung und Rechtswissenschaft 253-277, 267.

72 William A Schabas *The International Criminal Court: A Commentary on the Rome Statute* (OUP Oxford 2010) 397.

73 However, the non-binding nature of many bodies which are accessible to individuals in order to individually claim their rights vis-à-vis States raises the question to what degree human rights can indeed be classified as rights of the individual; for this discussion see Jost Delbrück and Rüdiger Wolfrum *Völkerrecht* Volume I/2: *Der Staat und andere Völkerrechtssubjekte; Räume unter internationaler Verwaltung* (2nd edition De Gruyter Berlin 2002) with further references, in particular, to two of the most influencial scholars of modern public international law whose views differed substantively on the subject: whereas Hans Kelsen was of the opinion that human rights cannot be seen as rights of the individual if said individual cannot enforce the rights in national or international courts whose judgments are binding upon States (Hans Kelsen *Principles of International Law* [Rinehart and Company New York 1952] 143-4), Hersch Lauterpacht argued for the existence of human rights as individual rights even if the individual cannot enforce the rights directly (Hersch Lauterpacht *International Law and Human Rights* [FA Praeger London 1950] 27, 48, 61, 159-160).
(2nd edition De Gruyter Berlin 2002) 260-4.

74 See *Prosecutor v Kunarac (Judgment)* IT-96-23 (22 February 2001) para. 470; however, the extent to which State involvement is a prerequisite element of crimes against humanity has in recent years been controversially discussed, with many ar-

So how are the two disciplines related; what unites them what sets them apart?

There are obvious intersections: in the 1991 ILC Draft Code of Crimes against the Peace and Security of Mankind, the crimes now known as crimes against humanity were enlisted under the heading 'systematic or mass violations of human rights'.[75]

During the negotiation of the Rome Statute, there were repeated attempts to expand the jurisdiction of the court to so-called 'treaty crimes': crimes which were enshrined in international human rights treaties but the customary nature of which was not beyond doubt.[76] Examples of such 'treaty crimes' are, for instance, terrorism or drug trafficking. Ultimately, these crimes were not included as crimes punishable by the ICC. However, there are examples of such 'treaty crimes' to be found in the Rome Statute, albeit not listed as separate crimes, but under the heading of crimes against humanity or war crimes. The crimes of apartheid, forced disappearance (crimes against humanity) and intentional attacks on personnel in peacekeeping missions (war crimes) are punishable under the Rome Statute and had before only been explicitly punishable under human rights law conventions. This indicates flexibility and provides for a margin within which international criminal courts and tribunals can take recourse to international human rights law, may it be treaty law, custom or jurisprudence of international courts. Furthermore, it also indicates the interrelation between human rights law and international criminal law.

The extra-statutory conventions which the courts and tribunals use are made up first and foremost of the conventions directly related to the 'core

---

guing for a necessary involvement of State or at least State-like actors, see Claus Kress 'On the Outer Limits of Crimes against Humanity: The Concept of Organization within the Policy Requirement: Some Reflections on the March 2010 ICC *Kenya* Decision' (2010) 23 Leiden Journal of International Law 855–73; William A Schabas 'Prosecuting Dr Strangelove, Goldfinger, and the Joker at the International Criminal Court: Closing the Loopholes' (2010) 23 Leiden Journal of International Law 847–53; see also International Criminal Court 'Decision Pursuant to Article 15 of the Rome Statute on the Authorization of an Investigation into the Situation in the Republic of Kenya' ICC-01/09-19 (31 March 2010), Dissenting Opinion of Judge Hans-Peter 83–163.

75 UN ILC 'Draft Code of Crimes against the Peace and Security of Mankind' in 'Report of the International Law Commission on the Work of Its Forty-Third Session' (29 April – 19 July 1991) (1991) vol II part II UNYBILC 79.

76 See also Zimmermann in Trifferer 130f.

crimes' over which the ICC has jurisdiction, namely the Genocide Convention and the four Geneva Conventions and two Additional Protocols and their violation is often characterized by violations of human rights law at the same time as violations of international criminal law/international humanitarian law.[77] The case law of the ICTY and ICTR is replete with reference to jurisprudence of international judicial bodies applying international human rights law. However, there is no clear blueprint or structure in the reference to international human rights law in international criminal courts and tribunals. This is partly owed to the fact that there is no 'one-size-fits-all'-solution for the use of human rights law in international criminal law, as 'human rights' are in themselves a complex and fragmented concept in which the different rights are elaborated, enforceable and protected to varying degrees. These degrees could be classified according to the stages identified by Bassiouni, which are outlined in the following section. Furthermore, international criminal justice is developed in a decentralised manner by a variety of different practitioners (international courts and tribunals) and scholars whose conception of what 'international criminal law' is and what sources it derives from, vary according to the legal system they were educated in and their field of expertise. In-

77 Convention on the Prevention and Punishment of the Crime of Genocide (adopted 9 December 1948, entered into force 12 January 1951) 78 UNTS 277; Geneva Convention for the Amelioration of the Condition of the Wounded and Sick in Armed Forces in the Field (adopted 12 August 1949, entered into force 21 October 1950) 75 UNTS 31 (Geneva Convention I); Geneva Convention for the Amelioration of the Condition of Wounded, Sick and Shipwrecked Members of Armed Forces at Sea (adopted 12 August 1949, entered into force 21 October 1950) 75 UNTS 85 (Geneva Convention II); Geneva Convention relative to the Protection of Civilian Persons in Time of War (adopted 12 August 1949, entered into force 21 October 1950) 75 UNTS 287 (Geneva Convention IV); Geneva Convention relative to the Treatment of Prisoners of War (adopted 12 August 1949, entered into force 21 October 1950) 75 UNTS 135 (Geneva Convention III); Protocol Additional to the Geneva Conventions of 12 August 1949, and relating to the Protection of Victims of International Armed Conflicts (Protocol I) (adopted 8 June 1977, entered into force 7 December 1978) 1125 UNTS 3; Protocol Additional to the Geneva Conventions of 12 August 1949, and relating to the Protection of Victims of Non-International Armed Conflicts (Protocol II) (adopted 8 June 1977, entered into force 7 December 1978) 1125 UNTS 609. There are other conventions laying down the laws of war which are of relevance, for instance the 1907 Hague Convention, Convention respecting the Laws and Customs of War on Land and its Annex: Regulations concerning the Laws and Customs of War on Land (signed 18 October 1907, entered into force 26 January 1910) (1907) 205 CTS 277.

ternational (human) rights lawyers and scholars often arrive at different conclusions than their colleagues who are specialised in criminal law.

1. Hierarchy vs Horizontal Completion

One of the major theories on the interrelation between human rights and international criminal law has been developed by Cherif M. Bassiouni when he identified five stages of emergence and development of human rights.[78] First, he identifies the enunciative stage, '[t]he emergence and shaping of internationally perceived shared values through intellectual and social processes'[79]; second, the declarative stage, in which the shared values get pronounced as such at an international level. In the prescriptive stage, the values are proscribed in a normative binding form, for example in an international treaty. This stage is followed by the enforcement stage which is categorized by a quest for means of encoring the proscribed values. In the final and most elaborated stage, the criminalization stage, violations of these shared values are internationally punishable.[80] According to Bassiouni, there is a logical development of human rights from the shaping of shared values, the emergence of non-binding commitments towards them and the elaboration of specific normative prescriptions towards enforcement and finally a penalization of violations of these shared values.[81] For Bassiouni, 'international criminal proscriptions are the ulti-

78 MC Bassiouni 'The Proscribing Function of International Criminal Law in the Process of International Protection of Human Rights' (1982-83) 9 Yale J World Pub. Ord 193-216; see also, for preceding discussions on the interrelation oh human rights and international criminal law Robert K Woetzel 'International Criminal Law and Human Rights: The Sharp Edge of the Sword' (1968) 62 Proceedings of the American Society of International Law at Its Annual Meeting (1921-1969) 117-123.

79 MC Bassiouni 'The Proscribing Function of International Criminal Law in the Process of International Protection of Human Rights' (1982-83) 9 Yale J World Pub. Ord 193-216 at 195.

80 MC Bassiouni 'The Proscribing Function of International Criminal Law in the Process of International Protection of Human Rights' (1982-83) 9 Yale J World Pub. Ord 193-216.

81 MC Bassiouni 'The Proscribing Function of International Criminal Law in the Process of International Protection of Human Rights' (1982-83) 9 Yale J World Pub. Ord 193-216, 195.

ma ratio modality of enforcing internationally protected human rights'[82]. Similarly, Meron holds that criminalizing human rights norms through means of international criminal law enhances 'the bite of human rights law'[83] as it provides for additional enforcement mechanisms, adding to human rights law by providing measures against individual actors instead of States.[84]

This approach partly overlaps with the approach taken by the International Law Commission (ILC) when adapting its first Draft Articles of Crimes against the Peace and Security of Mankind in 1991.[85] The ILC's article entitled 'Systematic or mass violations of human rights' 'in substance covers the same field as article 5 of the Statute of the International Tribunal [for the Former Yugoslavia]' as the ILC states itself in 1994, meaning the substantive content of the draft article is the prohibition of crimes against humanity.[86] As a consequence, international criminal law and human rights law overlap on a lot of occasions and depend on each other in order to establish the given parameters in which the two disciplines shift, where they stand and in what direction they intend to develop further. Bassiouni's theory explains the relation between the two disciplines as to their emergence and common roots. But this model offers only limited value when it comes to the practical application of human rights law in international criminal law.

---

82 MC Bassiouni 'The Proscribing Function of International Criminal Law in the Process of International Protection of Human Rights' (1982-83) 9 Yale J World Pub. Ord 193-216, 196.

83 Theodor Meron 'Human Rights Marches into New Territory: The Enforcement of International Human Rights in International Criminal Tribunals' Fourth Marek Nowicki Memorial Lecture (28 November 2008) <http://web.ceu.hu/legal/pdf%20documents/Nowicki/Meron_Enforcement%20of%20HRwarsawnowicki13nov 08.pdf> (as last accessed on 10 June 2013; speech no longer accessible online 36).

84 Theodor Meron 'Human Rights Marches into New Territory: The Enforcement of International Human Rights in International Criminal Tribunals' Fourth Marek Nowicki Memorial Lecture (28 November 2008) <http://web.ceu.hu/legal/pdf%20documents/Nowicki/Meron_Enforcement%20of%20HRwarsawnowicki13nov 08.pdf> (as last accessed on 10 June 2013; speech no longer accessible online) 36.

85 UN ILC 'Draft Articles against the Peace and Security of Mankind' Yearbook of the International Law Commission [1991] vol II part II UNYBILC 79-107;.

86 UN ILC 'Report of the International Law Commission on the Work of Its Forty-Sixth Session' (2 May–22 July 1994) GAOR 49th Session Supp 10, 40 at 39; see also William Schabas, Commentary on the Rome Statute, Article 7, p. 141.

Carsten Stahn criticizes Bassiouni's analysis at a normative-legal level when it comes to the different application requirements for international criminal law and human rights law. He states that crimes under international law require an attack not of an individual, but of the international community as a whole and that they must therefore be seen in the context of a threat to international peace and security.[87]

Whereas it is undoubtedly true that international criminal law, from the outset, has been a means to counteract and punish crimes that 'endangered the international community or shocked the conscience of mankind'[88] and a reference to the peace and security of mankind is to be found in the preamble of the Rome Statute, it has never necessarily been the case that just because a crime under international law is shocking to the international community as a whole, it does also aleways constitute a threat to international peace and security. Specific instances of genocide or crimes against humanity, shocking as they might be, might not automatically threaten international peace and security.[89] Also, during recent years, observers witnessed a change of focus in international criminal law, which more and more deals with internal conflicts and situations and in which the threshold for crimes against humanity is dramatically lowered to the point where no state or state-like organization needs to be involved, which in turn tends to lower any threat to international peace and security.[90]

Still, it is undeniably true that international criminal law deals with crimes that are collective in nature, committed against a specific group of persons or population, rather than 'a limited and randomly selected num-

---

87 Carsten Stahn 'Internationaler Menschenrechtsschutz und Völkerstrafrecht' (1999) 3 Kritische Justiz 343-355, 351; Carsten Stahn and Sven-R. Eiffler 'Über das Verhältnis von Internationalem Menschenrechtsschutz und Völkerstrafrecht anhand des Statuts von Rom' (1999) 82(1) Kritische Vierteljahresschrift für Gesetzgebung und Rechtswissenschaft 253-277, 263.

88 United Nations War Crimes Commission *History of the United Nations War crimes Commission and the Development of the Laws of War* (HMSO London 1948) 179.

89 For example, the post-election violence in Kenya, is being dealt with before the ICC and during which the prosecution claims crimes against humanity have been committed, has never been subject to a Security Council Resolution, under Chapter VII or otherwise.

90 See International Criminal Court 'Decision Pursuant to Article 15 of the Rome Statute on the Authorization of an Investigation into the Situation in the Republic of Kenya' ICC-01/09-19 (31 March 2010).

ber of individuals'.[91] Nevertheless, the reason for their punishment, and what sets them apart from other crimes, is the mass violation of human rights, a violation that targets individuals systematically for a specific infringement of their human rights not because of their individual and personal characteristics but because they belong to a specific group as such. This does by no means contradict that the underlying offences, though not the scope of protection of these crimes, are human rights violations.

In addition, Bassiouni has been criticized, in particular, for his narrow view on international criminal proscriptions as the 'highest form' of human rights protection. Stahn claims that the relationship between the two disciplines is not a vertical but rather an horizontal one as the question whether or not the violation of a human right is punishable by means of criminal law does not create a hierarchy within international human rights law and does not make one set of human rights more meaningful and important than others.[92] According to Stahn, the reason why some human rights are protected by means of an international criminal threat of punishment is not that those rights are more important than others whose violation does not trigger criminal charges, but the reason is simply that these rights are more prone to infringement in the context of conflict.[93] He sees this further substantiated by the fact that the rights Bassiouni talks about are not protected in absolute terms but only in the context of armed conflict or when they are committed as part of a widespread or systematic attack.[94] Stahn's criticism here is only partly convincing. As the ICJ has held, human rights are applicable in times of peace as well as in times of armed conflict[95] and military occupation.[96] However, for all its talk about the indivisibility of human rights, the international system of human rights protection in itself introduces a hierarchy of human rights by identifying

91 *Prosecutor v Kunarac* (Appeal Judgment) IT-96-23 & IT-96-23/1-A (12 June 2002) para. 90.

92 Carsten Stahn ‚Internationaler Menschenrechtsschutz und Völkerstrafrecht' 3 *Kritische Justiz* (1999) 343-355, 354.

93 Carsten Stahn, Internationaler Menschenrechtsschutz und Völkerstrafrecht, at 354.

94 C. Stahn, Internationaler Menschenrechtsschutz und Völkerstrafrecht, at 351.

95 *Legality of the Threat or Use of Nuclear Weapons (Advisory Opinion)* [1996] ICJ Rep 226 para. 25.

96 *Legal Consequences of the Construction of a Wall in the Occupied Palestinian Territory (Advisory Opinion) [2004] ICJ Rep 136, paras 106-113; Armed Activities on the Territory of the Congo (Democratic Republic of the Congo v Uganda)* [2005] ICJ Rep 168 para 216.

some from which derogation is not possible even in times of 'public emergency' or 'war'.[97] Prime examples of emergencies that 'threaten the life of the nation'[98] are, amongst others, international as well as internal armed conflict and unrest.[99] Core minimum rights that are not eligible for derogation even in those times are, in all the instruments, the prohibition of torture, slavery and servitude, as well as *nullum crimen/nulla poene sine lege* and certain aspects of the right to life.[100] The ACHR and the ICCPR expand the prohibition of derogations to other rights such as the freedom of religion (ACHR and ICCPR), the rights of the child (ACHR) or the right to participate in government (ACHR). In addition, the HRC declared several elements of rights that are not listed in Art. 4 (2) factually non-derogable as well, given their status in general international law.[101] These include the right of persons deprived of their liberty to be treated with dignity,[102] the prohibition of genocide with explicit reference to Art. 27 ICCPR regulating the rights of minorities,[103] propaganda of war and hate speech[104] as well as deportation and forcible transfer of population. The latter is deemed non-derogable by the HRC with explicit reference to its status as a crime against humanity under the Rome Statute.[105] The core minimum rights, covered by all the conventions that include non-derogable provisions, as well as the majority of provisions deemed non- dero-

97 See Art. 4 (2) ICCPR, Art. 15 ECHR, Art. 27 ACHR (2); while the first speaks only of public emergency, the three latter instruments refers to both public emergency and war.

98 See Art. 4 (1) ICCPR, Art. 15 (1) ICCPR.

99 Jaime Oraá *Human Rights in States of Emergency in International Law* (Clarendon Press Oxford 1992) 30-31; see also UN Commission on Human Rights 'Study of the Right of Everyone to be Free from Arbitrary Arrest, Detention and Exile' (1962) UN Doc E/CN.4/826, 153.

100 See See eg Manfred Nowak U. N. Covenant on Civil and Political Rights: CCPR Commentary (N. P Engel Kehl 2005) 85.

101 UN HRC 'General Comment No 29: Derogations from Provisions of the Covenant during a State of Emergency (Art. 4)' (24 July 2001) GAOR 56th Session Supp 40 vol 1, 202; The HRC, in its General Comment, mostly followed the evaluations of the International Commission of Jurists in International Commission of Jurists *States of Emergency—Their Impact on Human Rights: A Comparative Study by the International Commission of Jurists* (International Commission of Jurists Geneva 1983).

102 Para. 13 (a).

103 Para. 13 (c).

104 Para. 13 (e).

105 Para. 13 (d).

gable by the HRC, mirror crimes under international law. It is in a situation of international or internal war, 'the greatest public emergency',[106] that crimes under international law are mostly committed. In these circumstances, international criminal law complements the provisions of international human rights law by providing penal sanctions in the case the most core rights are violated. Many of those are again mirrored in Common Article 3 of the 1949 Geneva Conventions, albeit modified to fit the subject-matter of the Geneva Conventions and its beneficiaries.[107] Other human rights, even if they are violated on a mass scale, will never trigger international legal responses. This is to say that whereas for some rights, international criminal law can indeed be seen as a complimentary set of instruments to be applied alongside human rights law on a horizontal level, for other rights, the relation is more of a vertical one. This is due to the hierarchy inherent in the international system of human rights protection to begin with.

The problem with Bassiouni's model in light of the subject of this book is rather that its simplicity, which makes it so appealing at first sight, presents a basic structural problem that renders the model to be of limited use in terms of practical application. This is exemplarily shown by the fact that the principle of *nullum crimen sine lege*, which is at length discussed under Part One Chapter Three III, is not mentioned.

2. Structural Differences vs Universality

The obvious overlap and the common roots of the two concepts has made human rights law a self-evident place to seek recourse when international criminal tribunals had to fill the gaps their respective statutes left when defining crimes under the tribunals' jurisdiction. The most ground-breaking jurisprudence in this respect, which is extremely telling when it comes to the relationship of human rights and international criminal law and its conception by practitioners is the ICTY judgement in the case against

---

106 UN Enable 'Human Rights in Time of Emergency' http://www.un.org/esa/socdev/enable/comp210.htm (31 October 2017).

107 Theo van Boven 'Distinguishing Criteria of Human Rights' in Karel Vasak and Philip Alston (eds) *The International Dimensions of Human Rights* (Greenwood Press Wetport 1982) 43.

Dragoljub Kunarac, in which the chamber delved into an in-depth analysis of the two concepts, their similarities and differences.[108]

The Chamber stated that because of the resemblance, in terms of goals, values and terminology between human rights and international criminal law, recourse to practices and instruments of human rights law is often taken by international criminal law in order to determine the content of customary international law with regards to a specific question of international criminal law.[109] The Trial Chamber also agreed with the chamber in *Furundžija* on its approach taken, the determination of the definition of torture under customary law, supplemented with specific elements which stem from the international criminal/international humanitarian law context in which the crimes under scrutiny of the ICTY were committed.[110] The court referred solely to 'international humanitarian law' in its argumentation, but it factually examined the definition of torture as a crime against humanity valid also outside of armed conflict. The court took account of the peculiarities of the conduct punishable under the ICTY Statute, which is limited to crimes committed in relation to an armed conflict, circumscribed as 'serious violations of international humanitarian law' by the UNGA resolution establishing the ICTY, but its conclusions are valid for the whole body of international criminal law.[111]

The ICTY, in *Kunarac*, bestowed great care in portraying the similarities and differences of the two regimes as well as the intersection in which the two meet. The court identified two crucial doctrinal points in which the human rights regime and the international criminal law regime differed fundamentally:

i. Firstly, the ICTY found the role of the State as an actor in international human rights law to fundamentally differ from the role of the State in international criminal law. In the human rights context, the ICTY found the State to be the 'ultimate guarantor' of the rights in questions, the entity which is bound to observe them and the one which will be accountable for violations and responsible for the halt of infringements.[112] Even though human rights can also have a horizontal

108 *Prosecutor v Kunarac (Judgment)* IT-96-23 (22 February 2001).
109 Prosecutor v Kunarac (Judgment) IT-96-23 (22 February 2001) para. 467.
110 Prosecutor v Kunarac (Judgment) IT-96-23 (22 February 2001) para. 468–69.
111 UNSC Res 808 (1993) (22 February 1993) SCOR 48th Year 28 para. 1; UNSC Res 827 (1993) (25 May 1993) SCOR 48th Year 29 para. 2.
112 Prosecutor v Kunarac (Judgment) IT-96-23 (22 February 2001) para. 470 (i).

effect on the relations between private actors, ultimately, it is that State that is under an obligation to protect its citizens or inhabitants against a violation of their rights by State as well as non-State agents. International criminal law, in contrast, is based on the principle of individual criminal responsibility and the role of the State as peripheral when it comes to accountability.[113] In order to illustrate that point, the ICTY cited two US-American decisions applying the Alien Tort Claims Act.[114] In *Filártiga v Peña-Irala,* the United States Court of Appeals held that torture perpetrated by a State official violated universally accepted customary human rights law.[115] 15 years later, the same court held in *Kadić v Karadžić*, that when it comes to acts (including torture) which could be qualified as genocide or war crimes, no State involvement was necessary in order to hold an individual accountable for said actions. [116]

With respect to the last argument brought forward by the Chamber, is has, however, to be observed that what leads to the actual accountability of a single individual under international criminal law, is, in the vast majority of cases and especially when it comes to genocide and crimes against humanity, his or her involvement in illegal conduct as part of a State organ or an organization affiliated with the State (or at least as part of a State-like entity exercising effective control over a specific territory). Even though non-State actors have in recent years become the centre of the international criminal law spotlight and have often been the focus of prosecutorial investigations and indictments before the ICC, this development has been criticized harshly by those who think that international criminal law has first and foremost been established to prosecute criminal behaviour of States, involving large segments of a State apparatus and resources, and not to help govern-

113 See further for the obligations of individuals in the context of international criminal law: Jost Delbrück and Rüdiger Wolfrum *Völkerrecht* Volume I/2: *Der Staat und andere Völkerrechtssubjekte; Räume unter internationaler Verwaltung* (2nd edition De Gruyter Berlin 2002) 265-6.

114 Alien Tort Claims Act (1789) 28 USC § 1350.

115 *Filártiga v Peña-Irala* United States Court of Appeals (2nd Cir 1980) 630 F 2d 876, 878–79.

116 *Kadić v Karadžić* United States Court of Appeals (2nd Cir 1995) 70 F 3d 232.

ments to dispose of insurgencies and rebel forces within their own country.[117]

In addition, some significant human rights provisions oblige States to make the violation of a certain human right a criminal offence based on individual criminal responsibility. This is, for example, the approach of Article 4 UN Convention against Torture and Other Cruel, Inhuman and Degrading Treatment or Punishment (CAT) according to which acts of torture, their attempt, complicity and participation shall be a criminal offence in any Member State. [118]

ii. The second structural differences lies, according to the view taken by the ICTY in *Kunarac*, in the functions of international criminal law as a penal regime in which the prosecutor on one side faces the individual defendant at the other side and of international human rights law in which the respondent is the State.[119]

For these reasons, the Trial Chamber concludes that international human rights law can only be referred to in international criminal law when taking into account the peculiarities which are inherent in this specific area of law.[120]

This can be countered with the HRC's observation that human rights standards contain an obligation to bring perpetrators of human rights violations to justice, thereby acknowledging that one area might trigger the other.[121]

---

117 Claus Kress 'On the Outer Limits of Crimes against Humanity: The Concept of Organization within the Policy Requirement: Some Reflections on the March 2010 ICC *Kenya* Decision' (2010) 23 Leiden Journal of International Law 855–73; William A Schabas 'Prosecuting Dr Strangelove, Goldfinger, and the Joker at the International Criminal Court: Closing the Loopholes' (2010) 23 Leiden Journal of International Law 847–53; see also International Criminal Court 'Decision Pursuant to Article 15 of the Rome Statute on the Authorization of an Investigation into the Situation in the Republic of Kenya' ICC-01/09-19 (31 March 2010), Dissenting Opinion of Judge Hans-Peter Kaul 83–163.

118 Convention against Torture and Other Cruel, Inhuman or Degrading Treatment or Punishment (adopted 10 December 1984, entered into force 26 June 1987) 1465 UNTS 112.

119 Prosecutor v Kunarac (Judgment) IT-96-23 (22 February 2001).para. 470 (ii).

120 *Prosecutor v Kunarac (Judgment)* IT-96-23 (22 February 2001) para. 471.

121 UN HRC 'General Comment No 31: The Nature of the General Legal Obligation Imposed on States Parties to the Covenant' (29 March 2004) GAOR 59th Session Supp 40 vol 1, 175.

A similar-sounding argument, which nonetheless follows a different logic, is brought forward by McIntyre. He states that the courts and tribunals are setting their own human rights standards in the context of courts dealing with crimes committed in times of armed conflict.[122] For him, the relevant question is not whether the court and tribunals adhere to international human rights standards but whether the standards they are setting themselves are deemed proper so that the court or tribunal can be said to comply with the rule of law.[123]

This point of view has, in turn, been described as dangerous by Sluiter. His arguments are twofold: firstly, he points to the universality of human rights as minimum standards, like the majority of the fair trial rights.[124] He does, however, admit that there are indeed rules that need to be adapted and re-interpreted in the context of international criminal courts and tribunals. Second, he claims that 'one notices the harmful tendency that this so-called re-interpretation of the human rights corpus in light of the unique character and circumstances of international criminal tribunals practically by definition results in reduced protection, and always favours the interests of prosecution and/or victims over those of the accused'.[125]

Though international criminal law and human rights law, as demonstrated above, have many things in common, they are, in some ways, exact opposites. Not only in the way elaborated on before the ICTY in *Kunarac,* but also in a dogmatic sense of emergence and applications of the two regimes a substantial structural difference exists. Human rights, as part of public international law, are subject to the gradual development and inter-

---

122 G McIntryre 'Defending Human Rights in the Area of International Humanitarian Law: Human Rights in the Jurisprudence of the ICTY' in Gideon Boas and William A Schabas (eds) *International Criminal Law Developments in the Case Law of the ICTY* (Brill Leiden 2003) at 194.

123 G McIntryre 'Defending Human Rights in the Area of International Humanitarian Law: Human Rights in the Jurisprudence of the ICTY' in Gideon Boas and William A Schabas (eds) *International Criminal Law Developments in the Case Law of the ICTY* (Brill Leiden 2003) at 194.

124 Göran Sluiter 'Human rights protection in the ICC pre-trial phase' in Carsten Stahn and Göran Sluiter (eds) *The Emerging Practice of the International Criminal Court* (Nijhoff Leiden 2009) 459-476, 461.

125 Göran Sluiter 'Human rights protection in the ICC pre-trial phase' in Carsten Stahn and Göran Sluiter (eds) *The Emerging Practice of the International Criminal Court* (Nijhoff Leiden 2009) 459-476, 461.

pretation of this area of law by way of custom and gradual codification.[126] They are also often formulated in a general way, which makes their interpretation by treaty bodies and courts a vital component of their implementation.[127] On the other hand, criminal law, albeit also often leaving lacunae in its subject-matter provisions that require interpretation by judges is by definition more static, because it operates in an environment in which the need to reach a verdict is limited by basic principles of criminal law of which *nullum crimen sine lege* is one of the most important.

II. Legal Basis for the Application of Extra-Statutory Substantive Law

Having established the close relationship between human rights law and international criminal law, their similarities and differences, and having concluded that, indeed, it can be, from a practical point of view, advisable or even necessary for an international criminal court or tribunal to seek guidance from the vast area of human rights law in specific cases, the question is: what is the basis on which the institutions are authorized to do so? The statutes of the respective international criminal courts and tribunals establish the crimes which are covered by their jurisdiction. However, these statutes are only applicable to the respective tribunals and do not represent universally valid codifications of international criminal law, which makes them not so much of a criminal code but rather a 'specification of the jurisdictional authority'[128] of the respective court of tribunal.[129] Neither is it correct to assume that these statutes do in all cases merely represent a written record of an already existing customary rule even though, it is well possible that some of the provisions laid down in the Rome Statute will be an orientation for other courts and tribunals and as such slowly turn to be customary international law.

---

126 See eg Hersch Lauterpacht 'Codification and Development of International Law' (1955) 49(1) American Journal of International Law 16-43.

127 See also Louise Doswald-Beck and Sylvain Vité 'International Humanitarian Law and Human Rights Law' (1993) 293 International Review of the Red Cross, available at <https://www.icrc.org/eng/resources/documents/misc/57jmrt.htm> (31 October 2017).

128 Antonio Cassese *International Criminal Law* (Oxford University Press 2008) 5.

129 Antonio Cassese *International Criminal Law* (Oxford University Press 2008) 14.

1. Ad Hoc Tribunals

Rather, international criminal law is based on a variety of sources, both written and unwritten ones. This is hard to consolidate with the traditional Romano-Germanic conception of criminal law as an entity that interprets and applies written legal provisions.[130] However, international criminal law, as a branch of public international law, is subject to the very same sources that apply to the rest of this field. As long as there is no exhaustive lists of crimes available for the respective tribunal (as it is the case at the Rome Stature for the ICC), the courts and tribunals therefore have to orientate themselves on the general sources of public international law.

A guideline for applicable sources and their hierarchy is enshrined in the famous Article 38 ICJ Statute, which reflects the sources of international law proper.[131] Article 38 designates that the ICJ shall apply

a. international conventions, whether general or particular, establishing rules expressly recognized by the contesting states;
b. international custom, as evidence of a general practice accepted as law;
c. the general principles of law recognized by civilized nations;
d. subject to the provisions of Article 59, judicial decisions and the teachings of the most highly qualified publicists of the various nations, as subsidiary means for the determination of rules of law.

Hence, the courts and tribunals can mostly draw upon primary sources (treaties and custom) as well as secondary sources (law-making processes envisaged by customary rules or treaty provisions) and finally general principles of law and international criminal law.[132]

The ICTR and the ICTY are, therefore, under a current pressure to justify their use of human rights law by reference to the state of customary international law in the area. As we will see in Chapter Two, they undertake this exercise applying varying degrees of effort and dogmatically sound methodology.

---

130 Antonio Cassese *International Criminal Law* (Oxford University Press 2008) 14.
131 Ian Brownlie *Principles of Public International Law* (6th ed OUP Oxford 2012) 5.
132 Antonio Cassese *International Criminal Law* (2nd edition OUP Oxford 2008) 14.

2. ICC

The law applicable for the ICC is, different from what is stipulated for the ad hoc tribunals, expressly stated in a provision which for large parts, mirrors Article 38 ICJ Statute but adapts it to the specific requirements of a criminal law regime. Article 21 Rome Statute is *lex specialis* to Article 38 ICJ Statute and the first codification of the sources of international criminal law[133]. Article 21(1) of the Rome Statute determines that the ICC shall apply

a) In the first place, this Statute, Elements of Crimes and its Rules of Procedure and Evidence;
(b) In the second place, where appropriate, applicable treaties and the principles and rules of international law, including the established principles of the international law of armed conflict;
(c) Failing that, general principles of law derived by the Court from national laws of legal systems of the world including, as appropriate, the national laws of States that would normally exercise jurisdiction over the crime, provided that those principles are not inconsistent with this Statute and with international law and internationally recognized norms and standards.

Article 21(2) and (3) clarify further:

2. The Court may apply principles and rules of law as interpreted in its previous decisions.
3. The application and interpretation of law pursuant to this article must be consistent with internationally recognized human rights, and be without any adverse distinction founded on grounds such as gender as defined in article 7, paragraph 3, age, race, colour, language, religion or belief, political or other opinion, national, ethnic or social origin, wealth, birth or other status.

Article 21 Rome Statute, unlike Article 38 ICJ Statute, provides a clear hierarchy between the sources of law. First and foremost, the ICC is to use

---

133 Margaret Mcauliffe deGuzman in: Otto Triffterer, Rome Statute, 2nd ed p 703; G Bitti 'Article 21 of the Statute of the ICC and the treatment of sources of law in the jurisprudence of the ICC' in Carsten Stahn and Göran Sluiter (eds) The Emerging Practice of the International Criminal Court (Koninkllijke Brill 2008) 285-304 at 286-7.

its statute and its Elements of Crime and Rules of Procedure and Evidence, all secondary sources may only be used if a gap exists in the Statute. Such was affirmed by the Appeals Chamber of the Court.[134]

The 'Elements of Crime' which, pursuant to Article 9 Rome Statute, assist the Court in the interpretation and application of the statutory rules on genocide, crimes against humanity and war crimes are a valuable, non-binding guideline for the court in defining the crimes under its jurisdiction. However, in order to capture the core definition of the crimes and what they contain, the courts and tribunals may often have to resort to documents other than the actual statutes related documents.

a. Art. 21 (3) Rome Statute

Article 21(3) Rome Statute explicitly mention that the application of the law according to Art. 21 must happen in accordance with internationally recognized human rights. Does this mean that the article gives the Court the authorization to look at human rights law for the definition of crimes under the statute? Rather, what the drafters of the Statute had in mind when drafting this provision were indeed procedural rights, namely the procedural rights of the accused.[135] This spirit of the provision becomes clear when one looks at a footnote that the article included in its Final Draft Version. It stated:

'It was generally agreed that consistency with international human rights law would require that interpretation by the Court be consistent with the principle of nullum crimen sine lege. A view was also expressed that this should be explicitly stated in this article or be made clearer in article 21.'[136]

---

134 *The Prosecutor v. Thomas Lubanga Dyilo* (Judgment on the Appeal of Mr. Thomas Lubanga Dyilo against the Decision on the Defense Challenge to the Jurisdiction of the Court pursuant to Article 19(2)(a) of the Statute of 3 October 2006) ICC-01/04-01/06-772 (14 December 2006) para. 34.

135 Margaret McAuliffe deGuzman 'Art. 21: Applicable law' in Otto Triffterer *Commentary on the Rome Statute of the International Criminal Court* (2nd edition Beck Munich 2008) 701-712, 711.

136 Draft Art. 20 United Nations Diplomatic Conference of Plenipotentiaries on the Establishment of an International Criminal Court 'Report of the Preparatory Committee on the Establishment of an International Criminal Court: Addendum' (15-17 July 1998) A/Conf.183/2/Add.1 para. 63; In the draft article, what is now

Hence, this provision entails the explicit right of the ICC to apply procedural customary international human rights law.[137] As such, it frees the ICC from engaging in discussions the ad hoc tribunals had to engage in regarding the legal authorization to apply procedural human rights standards.

However, the mere fact that the Rome Statute mentions human rights as an underlying constitutional principle against which the application and interpretation of the Rome Statute has to be measured does not mean that existing human rights norms can be turned into penal provisions under international law.

b. Art. 21 (1) (b) Rome Statute

According to Article 21 (1) (b) Rome Statute, the ICC can apply, 'where appropriate, applicable treaties and the principles and rules of international law, including the established principles of the international law of armed conflict'. The question arises what are 'applicable treaties' in the context of this provision. The ICTY took this to apply international conventions which bind the parties having jurisdiction in the case.[138] For the ICC, the same argument which has been used to dismiss the direct application of national laws is equally valid: in case of this approach, the ICC would apply different standards to different accused but for the same conduct.[139]

According to another, very restricted view, the 'applicable treaties' are merely the Geneva Conventions (and possibly the Genocide Convention) as they are incorporated in the definition of war crimes. [140]

---

regulated under Article 21 was proposed to be Art. 20, while *nullum crimen sine lege* (now Article 22) was discussed as Article 21.

137 See Part One Chapter Two above.

138 Margaret McAuliffe deGuzman 'Art. 21: Applicable law' in Otto Triffterer *Commentary on the Rome Statute of the International Criminal Court* (2nd edition Beck Munich 2008) 701-712, 706.

139 See also Margaret McAuliffe deGuzman 'Art. 21: Applicable law' in Otto Triffterer *Commentary on the Rome Statute of the International Criminal Court* (2nd edition Beck Munich 2008) 701-712, 704 in relation to the application of domestic law.

140 Margaret McAuliffe deGuzman 'Art. 21: Applicable law' in Otto Triffterer *Commentary on the Rome Statute of the International Criminal Court* (2nd edition Beck Munich 2008) 701-712, 704.

Art. 21 (1) (b) Rome Statute unproblematically applies to conventions which a) are part of customary international law and b) are punitive in nature (e.g. Genocide Convention or Geneva Convention and Protocols.) The problem of application of human rights treaties in the substantive context is less one in the case of treaties which provide for penal consequences in case of violation as for example the CAT. It is more problematic in the case of recently emerged concepts like gender-based rights and gender-based violence, concepts which are controversial amongst States and which, in their current state of evolution, consist of a multitude of binding as well as non-binding instruments with no punitive character.

Central to the understanding of the reference of international courts and tribunals to other areas of human rights is the concept of customary international law. A careful examination of whether or not a particular action is prohibited under customary international law is particularly important in the context of criminal law and the significance of the principle of legality.

The UN Secretary-General's report calling for the establishment of the ICTY explicitly states

[i]n the view of the Secretary-General, the application of the principle nullum crimen sine lege requires that the international tribunal should apply rules of international humanitarian law which are beyond any doubt part of customary law so that the problem of adherence of some but not all States to specific conventions does not arise. This would appear to be particularly important in the context of an international tribunal prosecuting persons responsible for serious violations of international humanitarian law.[141]

This report was later approved by the Security Council Resolution which established the ICTY.[142] 'According to the Secretary-General's Report as a whole (approved by the Security Council), international human rights law of crime and criminal procedure should generally apply in an international criminal tribunal'.[143]

But, whereas in a national legal criminal system, customary law is scarcely used in criminal trials, the international arena still depends to a

---

141 UNSC 'Report of the Secretary-General pursuant to Paragraph 2 of Security Council Resolution 808 (1993)' (3 May 1993) UN Doc S/25704 para. 34.

142 UNSC Res 827 (1993) (25 May 1993) SCOR 48th Year 29 para. 1.

143 Kenneth S Gallant 'International Criminal Courts and the Making of Public International Law: New Roles for International Organizations and Individuals' (2010) 43 The John Marshall Law Review 603–34, 609.

large degree on customary law to reflect the rapid developments within the international community, with which the development of new treaty law can only marginally keep up. In the words of Malcolm Shaw '[c]ustom within contemporary legal systems, particularly in the developed world, is relatively cumbersome and unimportant and often only of nostalgic value. In international law on the other hand it is a dynamic source of law in the light of the nature of the international system and its lack of centralised government organs'[144]

'Principles and rules of international law' in Art. 21 (1) (b) Rome Statute authorizes the court formally to apply the necessary customary law. This approach is shared amongst some of the most senior commentators and scholars in international criminal law.[145]

Schabas argues that the reference in Art. 21 (1) (b) Rome Statute to 'principles and rules of international law' suggests a resort to Art. 38 (1) (a)-(c) ICJ Statute and that Art. 21 (1) (b) encompasses all three sources of law enlisted in Art. 38(1) (a) – (c). He justifies this with reference to Art. 21 (1) (c) Rome Statute which, albeit including a reference to 'general principles of law' just as Art. 38 (1) (c) ICJ Statute follows a comparative criminal law approach which is not so much focussed on delineating the content of public international law as such but rather calls at the Court to look at national laws representing legal systems of the world (including the laws of States that would normally have jurisdiction over the case) to derive principles the court may apply.[146]

Art. 21 (1) (b) provides that the 'applicable treaties, and the principles and rules of international law' the court shall apply must only be applied as secondary rules and only 'where appropriate'. The court therefore has to find a reason for the application of Art. 21 (1) (b) or (c), an objective in

---

144 Malcolm N Shaw *International Law* (6 ed Cambridge University Press Cambridge 2008) 73.

145 Eg Alain Pellet who argues that 'In reality, there is little doubt that this provision [Art. 21(1)(b)] refers, exclusively, to customary international law, of which the "established principles of international armed conflict" clearly form an integral part' Alain Pellet 'Applicable Law' in Antonio Cassese, Paola Gaeta John RWD Jones (eds) *The Rome Statue of the International Criminal Court: A Commentary* vol 2 (OUP Oxford 2002) 1051-1084 at 1071 or William A. Schabas *The International Criminal Court: A Commentary on the Rome Statute* (OUP Oxford 2010) 391.

146 William A. Schabas *The International Criminal Court: A Commentary on the Rome Statute* (OUP Oxford 2010) 391.

the Statute or the Rules of Procedure and Evidence as the primary sources of law that those primary sources do not meet by themselves. Regarding the substantive parts of the Rome Statute, this follows logically from having jurisdiction over the crimes enlisted in Arts 6-9 pursuant to Art. 5 Rome Statute. Therefore the court also must have the incidental jurisdictionto decide how the crimes are defined and what they contain (*Kompetenz-Kompetenz*).[147] 'Incidental jurisdiction [...] covers the rules that the court can apply to settle a preliminary question whose resolution is necessary to decide on the principal question brought to the court. Of course, the final decision of the court is always based on the legal rules falling under its primary jurisdiction [...] the ''outside' rules [...] come into play as legal rules proper'.[148]

The ICC Chambers and the Office of the Prosecutor seem to agree in their understanding that the court is only allowed to apply substantive extra-statutory rules as long as they are customary international law.[149] In its first ever judgment, however, the court refers to customary international law only indirectly, citing the ICRC Study on Customary International Law in footnotes on the definition of a non-international armed conflict as one of several sources.[150] In her separate and dissenting opinion, Judge Odio-Benito referred to customary international law as one of several sources of law along with the Rome Statute and human rights treaties in general.[151]

147 Giulia Pinzauti 'The European Court of Human Rights' Incidental Application of International Criminal Law and Humanitarian Law- A Critical Discussion of *Kononov v. Latvia*' (2008) 6 Journal of International Criminal Justice 1043-1060, 1048-49 and explanations in fn 6.

148 Giulia Pinzauti 'The European Court of Human Rights' Incidental Application of International Criminal Law and Humanitarian Law- a Critical Discussion of Kononov v. Latvia' 6 (2008) Journal of International Criminal Justice 1048-49 1049.

149 See eg *Prosecutor v Thomas Lubanga Dyilo (Decision on the confirmation of charges)* ICC-01/04-01/803-tEN (29 January 2007) para 274; *Prosecutor v Thomas Lubanga Dyilo (Prosecution's Closing Brief)* ICC-01/04-01/06-2748-Red fn 78, paras 52, 53, 138, 150 (1 June 2011).

150 *Prosecutor v Thomas Lubanga Dyilo (Judgment)* ICC-01/04-01/06 (14 March 2012) fn 1646.

151 *Prosecutor v Thomas Lubanga Dyilo (Judgment. Separate and Dissenting Opinion of Judge Odio-Benito)* ICC-01/04-01/06 (14 March 2012) para 6.

c. Guidance and Interpretational Aid

'Interpretational aid'[152] or 'guidance'[153] are often-employed buzzwords in terms of a broad reference to human rights or humanitarian law. These vague terms tend to be invoked by court in tribunals when trying to avoid creating precedent by declaring a certain issue of human rights law binding law to be applied before their court. Referring to a legal source outside the respective Statute as 'guidance' or 'inspiration' seems to be an easy way out which contains the benefit of referring to a source of law to strengthen the legal weight and the persuasion of the argument while, at the same time, avoiding to set precedent for a future application of extra-statutory sources with all its complications. It is exactly for these reasons, however, that a use of these legally vague terms is problematic. The Statutes of the courts and tribunals are to be applied subject to the sources of public international law as listed in Art. 38 ICJ Statute or subject to the *lex specialis* of Art. 21 Rome Statute in case of the ICC. The judges would be entitled to use human rights law as guidance in order to determine whether or not a provision inside or outside the Statute, a legal concept or principle, is binding law according to one of the sources enlisted in either Art. 38 ICJ or Art. 21. Rome Statute. However, in order to do that the courts have to clearly label their exercise as interpretational aid towards clarifying the binding concept of a specific character under a specific provision of their sources. In the absence of that, invoking vague terms such 'inspiration' or 'guidance' means having the cake while eating it which, in terms of criminal law, is a dangerous exercise which can easily violate the rights of the defendant and should therefore be avoided.

---

152 *Prosecutor v Kunarac (Judgment)* IT-96-23 (22 February 2001) 482.

153 *Prosecutor v Blaškić (Judgment)* IT-95-14-T (3 March 2000) 329; *Prosecutor v Delić (Judgment)* IT-04-83-T (15 September 2008) footnote 153; *Prosecutor v Deronjić (Judgment)* IT-02-61-S (30 March 2004) para 159; *Prosecutor v Galić (Judgment)* IT-98-29-T (5 December 2003) footnote 87; *Prosecutor v Halilović (Judgment)* IT-01-48-T (16 November 2005) para 99; *Prosecutor v Haradinaj (Judgment)* IT-04-84-T (3 April 2008) para 107; *Prosecutor v Kordić (Appela Judgment)* IT-95-14/2-A (17 December 2004) para 69; *Prosecutor v Krajišnik (Judgment)* IT-00-39-T (27 September 2006) para. 705; *Prosecutor v Kupreškić (Judgment)* IT-95-16 (14 January 2000) paras 588, 590; *Prosecutor v Limaj (Judgment)* IT-03-66-T (30 November 2005) para 86; *Prosecutor v Tadić (Appeal Judgment)* IT-94-1-A (15 July 1999) para. 321; *Prosecutor v Delalić et al (Celebići Case Judgment)* IT-96-21-T (16 November 1998) para 432.

III. Application of Substantive Extra-Statutory Human Rights Law and the Principle of Nullum Crimen Sine Lege

1. The concept of nullum crimen sine lege?

The principles of *nullum crimen sine lege* (no crime without law) and *nulla poena sine lege* (no punishment without law) have been called the 'bulwark of the citizen against the state's omnipotence (...) the Criminal Code is the criminal's magna charta. It guarantees his or her right to be punished only in accordance with the requirements set out by the law and only within the limits laid down in the law'[154] for conduct that was 'unambiguously criminal at the time of its commission'.[155] There are four elements which together make up the *nullum crimen* principle in the national setting: the law must be written law; the crime must be defined with sufficient certainty; the law must not be applied retroactively; the crime must not be construed by way of analogy.[156] *Nullum crimen* and *nullla poena sine lege* are connected to the requirements of specificity, certainty, foreseeability and accessibility of criminal law.[157] The principles are the cornerstone of any punitive system which invokes legitimacy and basis on the rule of law. *Nullum crimen* and *nulla poena sine lege* touch upon one of the most fun-

154 Franz von Liszt ‚Die deterministischen Gegner der Zweckstrafe' (1893) 3 Zeitschrift für die gesamte Strafrechtswissenschaft 325-70 at 357 (translation by Antonio Cassese in *International Criminal Law* 2 ed Oxford University Press (2008) at 37).

155 Susan Lamb '*Nullum Crimen, Nulla Poena Sine Lege in International Criminal Law*' in Antonio Cassese, Paola Gaeta, John R. W. D. Jones (eds) The Rome Statute of the International Criminal Court: A Commentary Volume I Oxford University Press Oxford (2002) at 733.

156 See eg Susan Lamb '*Nullum Crimen, Nulla Poena Sine Lege in International Criminal Law*' in Antonio Cassese, Paola Gaeta, John R. W. D. Jones (eds) The Rome Statute of the International Criminal Court: A Commentary Volume I Oxford University Press Oxford (2002) at 734; *Prosecutor v. Vasiljević* (Judgment) IT-98-32-T (29 November 2002) para 193; see also Mohamed Shahabuddeen, 'Does the Principle of Legality Stand in the Way of Progressive Development of Law?' (2004) 2 Journal of International Criminal Justice 1007-1017, at 1008.

157 *Prosecutor v. Vasiljević (Judgment) IT-98-32-T (29 November 2002* para 193; see also Mohamed Shahabuddeen, 'Does the Principle of Legality Stand in the Way of Progressive Development of Law?' (2004) 2 Journal of International Criminal Justice 1007-1017, at 1008.

damental functions of criminal law, namely deterrence of crimes.[158] Any deterrent effect whatsoever as a prerequisite requires maximum foreseeability and legal certainty and regular enforcement of criminal law.[159]

2. Nullum Crimen Sine Lege in International Criminal Law

The application of the principle *nullum crimen sine lege* in international criminal law faces problems which are rooted in the peculiarities of international criminal law as a public international law regime applying criminal law.

In international criminal law in its current form, crimes are not defined in a specificity that would be required in national law. Many crimes are construed in a general manner and contain common place terms like 'inhumane acts'[160] or 'great suffering'[161] that lack the precision needed for the law to be applied without in-depth interpretation by the courts.[162] The international legal order, as opposed to national legal orders is merely loosely structured one with sovereign legislature[163] and the criteria of foreseeability and accessibility are therefore particularly difficult to measure and/or to fulfil.[164]

It has been claimed that the international legal order rests 'uncomfortably' besides *nullum crimen sine lege*.[165] Thedor Meron, in 1987, took the

---

158 See eg Andrew Ashworth *Principles of Criminal Law* (6th ed OUP Oxford 2009) 16-7.

159 See also Andrew Ashworth *Principles of Criminal Law* (6th ed OUP Oxford 2009) 16, 63-66.

160 See Art. 7 (1) (k) Rome Statute.

161 See Art. 8 (2)(a)(iii) Rome Statute.

162 See also A. Cassese International Criminal Law 2nd ed Oxford University Press (2008) at 41-2.

163 Margaret Mcauliffe deGuzman in: Triffterer, Rome Statute, 2nd ed p 703.

164 See also *Prosecutor v Vasiljevic (Judgment)* IT-98-32-T (29 November 2002) para. 193, Jonas Nilsson 'The Principle of Nullum Crimen Sine Lege' in Olaoluwa Olusanya *Rethinking International Criminal Law: The Substantive Part* (Europa Law Publishing Groningen 2007) 35-64, 62-63.

165 Susan Lamb '*Nullum Crimen, Nulla Poena Sine Lege in International Criminal Law*' in Antonio Cassese, Paola Gaeta, John R. W. D. Jones (eds) The Rome Statute of the International Criminal Court: A Commentary Volume I Oxford University Press Oxford (2002) at 746; see also Jonas Nilsson 'The Principle of Nullum Crimen Sine Lege' in Olaoluwa Olusanya *Rethinking International*

pragmatic stance that international criminal tribunals will 'continue to be guided by the degree of offensiveness of certain acts to human dignity'.[166] Yet, the offensive, debasing and criminal character of an act and, following from this, the foreseeability of the act as prohibited and enforced by criminal penalties is not always clear cut in the context of international criminal law. Whereas it is clear that the killing of a person in peacetime and in the absence of any grounds for justification such as self-defence, is a crime, the same conduct, in the context of an armed conflict, is not necessarily a punishable act and may in fact not be penalized. Apart from the fact that it therefore cannot be assumed that the penal nature of an act and its seriousness is always obvious in the context of mass crimes, there is another factor which makes *nullum crimen sine lege* in international law differ from its application in national law. International criminal law features crimes that do not necessarily have a counterpart of a similar manifestation in national law.[167] Others are based on acts which might have an equivalent in national criminal codes but these acts are extended by an additional element, which mirrors the context of the crime and the aggravated circumstances, which turns these actions into crimes affecting the international community as a whole.[168]

Hence, courts are needed to define the exact contents of these provisions gradually, applying the broad definitions to a multitude of different scenarios that might not even have been foreseen by their drafters on a case-by-case basis. Therefore, judicial analysis of statutory rules, treaties and customary law are a vital component of international criminal law, more so than in most national criminal courts.

Criminal Law: The Substantive Part (Europa Law Publishing Groningen 2007) 35-64 at 39.

166 Theodor Meron 'The Geneva Conventions as Customary Law' 1987 81(2) American Journal of International Law 348-370, 361.

167 A different opinion is voiced by Jonas Nilsson who argues that *nullum crimen sine lege* will hardly be a successful challenge in contemporary international criminal law precisely because of the seriousness of the crime and, as Nilsson claims, because 'these crimes, or crimes very similar to them, most likely existed in the domestic criminal law of the defendant' Jonas Nilsson 'The Principle of Nullum Crimen Sine Lege' in Olaoluwa Olusanya *Rethinking International Criminal Law: The Substantive Part* (Europa Law Publishing Groningen 2007) 35-64, 64.

168 Georg Dahm, Jost Delbrück and Rüdiger Wolfrum *Völkerrecht* Volume I/3: *Die Formen des völkerrechtlichen Handelns; Die inhaltliche Ordnung der internationalen Gemeinschaft* (2nd edition De Gruyter Berlin 2002), 1088.

Furthermore, the lack of a central authority or a court of higher instance complicates a stringent jurisprudence further and leads to the fact that any specification and interpretation of the general rules must remain decentralized and fragmentary.[169]

One of the consequences of this state of affairs is that judges, unlike in national legal systems, often have to take recourse to extra-statutory law, in particular to customary international law, in order to solve contemporary legal questions.[170] Because international criminal law is also a relatively recent discipline and as such cannot resort to *lex lata* as comprehensive and sophisticated as it might be the case in domestic systems,[171] it also cannot take recourse to a catalogue of well-defined and sufficiently large customary international law,[172] often, judgements in international criminal law 'appear instead to be largely *declaratory* of nascent and previously unexpressed customary principles'.[173]

This is the background before which the area of conflict between *nullum crimen sine lege* and the use of extra-statutory law arises. Public international law has always been vulnerable to criticism of being too vague, too open to interpretation, hardly law at all. The old criticism that 'the borderlines between interpretation of existing law and the making of new law are inevitably fluid'[174] are equally true for international criminal law in its contemporary work-in-progress-form.

---

169 Antonio Cassese *International Criminal Law* (Oxford University Press 2008) 42-3.

170 Regarding the importance of customary international law in a public legal order lacking a common legislative see Jost Delbrück and Rüdiger Wolfrum (eds) *Völkerrecht* Volume I/1: *Die Grundlagen; die Völkerrechtssubjekte* (2nd edition De Gruyter Berlin 1989), 55.

171 Noora Arajarvi 'Between Lex Lata and Lex Ferenda – Customary International (Criminal) Law and the Principle of Legality ' 15 Tilburg Law Review (2010-2011) 163-182 at 168.

172 Susan Lamb '*Nullum Crimen, Nulla Poena Sine Lege in International Criminal Law*' in Antonio Cassese, Paola Gaeta, John R. W. D. Jones (eds) The Rome Statute of the International Criminal Court: A Commentary Volume I Oxford University Press Oxford (2002) at 745.

173 Susan Lamb '*Nullum Crimen, Nulla Poena Sine Lege in International Criminal Law*' in Antonio Cassese, Paola Gaeta, John R. W. D. Jones (eds) The Rome Statute of the International Criminal Court: A Commentary Volume I Oxford University Press Oxford (2002) at 745.

174 Wolfgang Friedmann 'The North Sea Continental Shelf Cases – A Critique' (1970) 64 American Journal of International Law 229-240 at 235.

Acting under such preconditions, it seems particularly important to safeguard the rights of any accused by a strict interpretation of *nullum crimen sine lege.*

There is a dispute amongst scholars as to just how strictly *nullum crimen sine lege* should be applied in international criminal law.

The most extreme position is that the principle of *nullum crimen sine lege* is only applicable in domestic law.[175] This opinion is to be disregarded. Even though international criminal law is a branch of public international law and the sources relevant for public international law are therefore in principal applicable to international criminal law also, a mere reference to this does not relieve from a discussion of the principle problem that international law is a system of criminal law and ultimately will rule over the criminal punishment in form of deprivation of liberty of individuals. Hence, it requires principles guaranteeing a fair way of establishing guilt or innocence of this individual.

According to another straits of arguments, *nullum crimen sine lege* in international law is broader a. because of the nature of international law and b. because the protected interest is peace and security and the 'preservation of the world order',[176] tilting the balance to be struck between the competing interests in favour of the protection of peace and security. [177] In general, this is a variation of the discussion of substantive justice vs principle of legality, which in international criminal law prominently has been led at the time of the Nuremburg trial.[178] Supporters of the doctrine of substantive justice recognized supremacy of substantive justice to be met-

175 Wolff Heintschel von Heinegg 'Criminal International Law and Customary International Law' in Andreas Zimmermann (ed) *International Criminal Law and the Current Development of Public International Law* (Duncker and Humblot Berlin 2003) 27-46 at 28.

176 M Cherif Bassiouni *Crimes against Humanity in International Criminal Law (*2nd ed Kluwer Law International The Hague 1992) 144.

177 M Cherif Bassiouni *Crimes against Humanity in International Criminal Law* (2nd ed Kluwer Law International The Hague 1999) 144; see Bruce Broomhall 'Art 22: *Nullum crimen sine lege'* Otto Triffterer *Commentary on the Rome Statute of the International Criminal Court* (2nd edition Beck Munich 2008) 713-729, 718 fn 30 for Art. 22.

178 Most prominently Hans Kelsen 'Will the Judgment of the Nuremberg Tribunals Constitute a Precedent in International Law?' (1947) 1 International Law Quarterly 153-71, 165; Antonio Cassese 'Crimes against Humanity' in Antonio Cassese, Paola Gaeta John RWD Jones (eds) *The Rome Statue of the International Criminal Court: A Commentary* vol 1 (OUP Oxford 2002) 353-78, 354-5.

ed out over procedural questions regarding the formal prohibition of the conduct by law at the time the action was taken. [179] The doctrine of substantive justice, in contrast, concentrates on the prohibition of socially harmful conduct or conduct which is dangerous to society or, in the case of international criminal law, the international community and the preservation of its peace and security.[180] However, the major arguments behind the principle of *nullum crimen sine le*ge namely, legitimacy, deterrence rule of law, are not touched by these arguments, and they do require a narrow construction of *nullum crimen*. These principles and aims of criminal law are absolute and cannot be lightly given up, even in the context of mass crimes. Whereas 'threat to international peace and security' is in itself a wide term whose definition is contested and evolves over time, the right to a fair trial is absolute and not open to derogation.[181] A trial is either fair, or it is not. In any criminal trial, one of its most important components, *nullum crimen sine lege*, which is part of customary international law,[182] must be vigorously adhered to. This is even more crucial when keeping in mind that the undertaking of international criminal law was a controversial one from the beginning and has from the very start, been struggling with claims of violations of the principle of legality.[183] Whereas these claims might have had some truth to it in the era of Nuremberg[184], there is less need, in modern international courts and tribunals, with its in-

179 Claus Kreß 'Nulla poena nullum crimen sine lege' in Rüdiger Wolfrum (ed) *Max Planck Encyclopedia of Public International Law* 2nd ed (OUP 2012) vol VII 889-899 para 16.

180 Antonio Cassese *International Criminal Law* (2nd edition OUP Oxford 2008) 36.

181 See for example Art. 4 (2) ICCPR; Art. 15 (2) ECHR.

182 Susan Lamb '*Nullum Crimen, Nulla Poena Sine Lege in International Criminal Law*' in Antonio Cassese, Paola Gaeta, John R. W. D. Jones (eds) The Rome Statute of the International Criminal Court: A Commentary Volume I Oxford University Press Oxford (2002) at 734; Göran Sluiter 'Human Rights Protection in the ICC pre-trial phase' in Carsten Stahn and Göran Sluiter (eds) *The Emerging Practice of the International Criminal Court* (Nijhoff Leiden 2009) at 461.

183 See further Hans-Heinrich Jeschenk 'The General Principles of International Criminal Law Set out in Nuremberg, as Mirrored in the ICC Statute' (2004) Journal of International Criminal Justice 38-55, 40-42.

184 This is true, at the very least, when it comes to the prosecution for crimes against peace and crimes against humanity; See inter alia Claus Kreß ‚Nulla poena nullum crimen crimen sine lege‘ in Rüdiger Wolfrum (ed) Max Planck Encyclopedia of Public International Law Oxford University Press (2012) para 16; see also Antonio Cassese *International Criminal Law* (2nd edition OUP Oxford 2008) 38-39.

creasingly vast amount of case law, to open themselves to criticism because of a broad construction of the international crimes it has jurisdiction over.[185] This is particularly important when keeping in mind that since the Nuremberg Trials, basically all relevant universal and regional human rights treaties have included the principle *nullum crimen sine lege* as one of the basic components of the rule of law and a most fundamental human right.[186] This naturally had to have an effect on the conduct of international courts and tribunals set up by the international community and, again, shows the interconnectedness between international criminal law and human right law.[187] Criminal courts, due to their nature, and due to their power to infringe upon one of the individual's most basic human rights, the right to liberty of person,[188] are not the right forum to expedite the progressive development of international law. They can further such development by way of progressive interpretation of existing laws only to the extent a strict construction of the principle of *nullum crimen sine lege* allows it. In this sense, there approach has to be a 'conservative' one,[189] 'predictable and precise'.[190] A less stringent approach is also not necessary. International criminal law can evolve and new crimes can develop as the recently-included definition of aggression into the Rome Statute shows.[191] The successful definition of the crime of aggression, which had been deemed to be very unlikely before, shows that compromise and cooperation in the advancement of criminal law making is by all means possible in the international arena even given a strict application of *nullum crimen sine lege*.

185 See also Antonio Cassese *International Criminal Law* 2nd edition Oxford University Press (2008) at 40-1,see also Susan Lamb '*Nullum Crimen, Nulla Poena Sine Lege in International Criminal Law*' in Antonio Cassese, Paola Gaeta, John R W D Jones (eds) The Rome Statute of the International Criminal Court: A Commentary Volume I Oxford University Press Oxford (2002) at 740-1.

186 Antonio Cassese *International Criminal Law* 2nd edition Oxford University Press (2008) at 41.

187 Antonio Cassese International Criminal Law (2ed Oxford University Press 2008) at 40.

188 See Art. 8 ICCPR; Art. 3 UDHR, Srt. 5(1) ECHR, Art. 7(1) ACHR, Art. 6ACHRP.

189 Theodor Meron 'Revival of Customary Humanitarian Law' (2004) 99(4) American Journal of International Law 817-834, at 817.

190 Theodor Meron 'Revival of Customary Humanitarian Law' (2004) 99(4) American Journal of International Law 817-834, at 822.

191 Generally, the Rome Statute can be amended pursuant to its Articles 121 and 122.

This strict application does, however, have to be adapted to the realities of law making in international law, in particular, to the codification and progressive development of public international law through custom on one hand and to the young age of international criminal law as such. The scarceness of State practise in the classical sense in this area is an obstacle for the deduction of customary international law in the area. Susan Lam therefore claims that because of this scarceness, the jurisprudence of the ad hoc tribunals often seems to convey a *de lege ferenda* character.[192] Relying on the theory of modern positivism as suggested by Bruno Simma and Andreas Paulus that pays regard to the shifting position of States in international law and gives increased attention to alternative manifestations of State practise and *opinion juris*, a strict interpretation of *nullum crimen sine lege* is feasible without compromising the greater rationale behind international criminal justice.[193] This approach allows for a deduction of State practise and *opinio iuris* from an expanded range of actions by States and by international institutions. State's domestic legislations, but also their voting records, the acceptance of work of institutions like the International Law Commission or the ad hoc tribunals play a big part of the deduction of customary international law.[194]

3. How is this area of conflict solved in international criminal jurisprudence?

The *ad hoc* tribunals have elaborated on *nullum crimen sine lege* in a way that will be beneficial for the ICC in future proceedings. The ICTY was created with the explicit mission to only apply those legal norms which

---

192 Susan Lamb '*Nullum Crimen, Nulla Poena Sine Lege in International Criminal Law*' in Antonio Cassese, Paola Gaeta, John R. W. D. Jones (eds) The Rome Statute of the International Criminal Court: A Commentary Volume I Oxford University Press Oxford (2002) at 746.

193 Bruno Simma and Andreas L Paulus 'The Responsibility of Individuals for Human Rights Abuses in Internal Conflict: Toward a World Public Order of Human Dignity' (1999) 93 American Journal of International Law 302-315, 306-313.

194 Bruno Simma and Andreas L Paulus 'The Responsibility of Individuals for Human Rights Abuses in Internal Conflict: Toward a World Public Order of Human Dignity' (1999) 93 American Journal of International Law 302-315, 307.

were beyond doubt part of customary international law.[195] *Nullum crimen sine lege* therefore demanded of the chamber to prove, when prosecuting persons 'responsible for serious violations of international humanitarian law', that the crimes in question existed in customary international law.[196] Already in the early-on *Tadić* case, the tribunal set out four prerequisites for a crime to be an international crime under the court's jurisdiction: the infringement of a rule of international humanitarian law, the customary or treaty law character of the crime, the 'seriousness' of the violation of humanitarian law (the crimes must constitute a breach of important values), and the consequence of individual criminal responsibility set up by the rule in question.[197] In *Milutinović et al* the ICTY stated that certain behaviour had to be recognized as a crime 'qua custom at the time this crime was allegedly committed'.[198]

As the Trial Chamber in *Furudzija* has held, a conventional, non-statutory provision can have an extra-conventional effect 'to the extent that the definition at issue codifies, or contributes to developing or crystallizing customary international law'.[199] This is uncontroversial in the case of the ICTY which is only to apply customary international humanitarian law. The same is, however, equally true for any other criminal court or tribunal. Extra-statutory law can only be applied if it derived in accordance to the

---

195 UNSC 'Report of the Secretary-General pursuant to Paragraph 2 of Security Council Resolution 808 (1993)' (3 May 1993) UN Doc S/25704 para. 34.

196 Report of the Secretary-General Pursuant to Paragraph 2 of Security Council Resolution 808 (1993)' UN Doc S/25704 at para. 29.

197 Tadić Interlocutory Appeal, para. 94; Bruno Simma and Andreas L Paulus 'The Responsibility of Individuals for Human Rights Abuses in Internal Conflict: Toward a World Public Order of Human Dignity' (1999) 93 American Journal of International Law 302-315 at 311; for an analysis of the realities of judicial law-making in the early stages of the ICTY but arguing that the controversial Tadić Appeal Decision was an the result of unique, exceptional circumstances see Tamás Hoffmann 'The Gentle Humanizer of Humanitarian Law – Antonio Cassese and the Creation of the Customary Law of Non-International Armed Conflict' in Carsten Stahn and Larissa van den Herik (eds) Future Perspectives on International Criminal Justice (Asser Press Leiden 2010). 58-80.

198 *Prosecutor v Milutinović et al (Decision on Dragoljub Ojdanic's Motion Challenging Jurisdiction–Joint Criminal Enterprise)* IT-99-37-AR72 (21 May 2003) para. 9.

199 *Prosecutor v Furundžija (Judgment)* IT-95-17 (10 December 1998) para. 160; more on the ad hoc tribunal's interpretation of the principle of nullum crimen sine lege see Gerhard Werle and Florian Jeßberger *Principles of International Criminal Law* (3rd ed OUP Oxford 2014) 40.

rules of law-making found in the respective statutes (if any) or under Art. 38 ICJ Statute and is customary in nature (see above under Part One Chapter Two and Part One Chapter Three II.). As Art. 38 ICJ Statute is applicable as the indicator of sources for the *ad hoc* tribunals and Art. 38 ICJ Statute mirrors Art. 21 Rome Statute in the listed sources, nothing indicates that the sources of substantive law at the ICC should differ from those of the *ad hoc* tribunals, in particular, because the ICTY has also engaged in identifying general principles of law through comparative analysis in its jurisprudence.[200] It is absolutely necessary in order to safeguard a fair trial and the observance of the principle of legality. In order to apply an extra-statutory legal provision or use an interpretation by a court or treaty body affiliated with a legal instrument other than the statute of the respective court or tribunal, the responsible trial chamber needs to prove whether the provision it seeks to apply is indeed part of customary international law. This can at times be a difficult and controversial undertaking. The court and tribunals need to carefully examine provisions with regard to their status in customary international law. They then need to examine whether the provision in question can be applied within the regime of international criminal law, which is different, in nature and purpose, from human rights law.

On the other hand, the *ad hoc* tribunals as well as the ICC repeatedly clarified that *nullum crimen sine lege* does not prevent them from 'interpreting and clarifying elements of a particular crime'.[201] The ICTY also relied heavily on the jurisprudence of the ECtHR in order to conclude that *nullum crimen sine lege* does also not preclude 'the progressive development of the law by the court'.[202]

---

200 *Prosecutor v Erdemović (Appeal Judgment, Joint Separate Opinion of Judge Mc Donald and Judge Vohrah)* IT-96-22-A (7 October 1997) para 40.

201 *Prosecutor v. Vasiljević (Judgment)* IT-98-32-T (29 November 2002) para. 196; see also *Prosecutor v Aleksovski (Appeal Judgment)* IT-95-14/1 (24 March 2000) paras126-17; *Prosecutor v Delalić et al (Celebići Case Appeal Judgement)* IT-96-21-A (20 February 2001) para 173; see also *Prosecutor v Imanishimwe* et al *(Appeal Judgment)* ICTR-99-46-A (7 July 2006) para 127.

202 *Prosecutor v Milutinović et al (Decision on Dragoljub Ojdanic's Motion Challenging Jurisdiction–Joint Criminal Enterprise)* IT-99-37-AR72 (21 May 2003) para 38, referring to *Kokkinakis v Greece (Judgment)* (ECtHR) Series A No 260 A paras 36 and 40; *EK v Turkey (Judgment)* appl 28496/95 <http://hudoc.echr.coe.int/sites/eng/pages/search.aspx?i=001-64586> (31 October 2017) para 52; *SW v*

The jurisprudence of the ECtHR is non-binding to any international criminal court or tribunal as such. But when interpreting the principle of *nullum crimen sine lege* as a part of customary international law, the ECtHR offers the most sophisticated canon of jurisprudential analysis of this principle and, as such, can be consulted by international courts and tribunals. This has been recognized by the ICTR when it stated '[r]egional human rights treaties, such as the European Convention of Human Rights (ECHR)[203] and the American Convention on Human Rights (ACHR)[204] and the jurisprudence developed thereunder, are persuasive authority which may be of assistance in applying and interpreting the Tribunal's applicable law. Thus, they are not binding of their own accord on the tribunal. They are however, authoritative, as evidence of international custom.'[205]

According to the ICTY Appeals Chamber, *nullum crimen sine lege* only prohibits the court 'from creating new law or from or from interpreting existing law beyond the reasonable limits of acceptable clarification.'[206]

Being able to rely on customary law (which is applicable given the structural differences of international criminal law discussed in Part One Chapter Three I. 2. above) in accordance to Art. 38 ICJ Statute or Art. 21 Rome Statute already provides the courts and tribunal with a substantial degree of flexibility that mirror the realities of international law but do not provide persons with a degree of legal certainties they might be able to rely on in national jurisdictions. The relatively young age of international criminal law and the fragmentation of its jurisprudence increase the given vagueness. This reality has to be accepted. Any further lowering of the standard of *nullum crimen sine lege* on account of the peculiarities of international criminal law is not compatible with international human rights

---

United Kingdom (Judgment) (ECtHR) Series A No 335 B paras 35-36; *CR v United Kingdom (Judgment)* (ECtHR) Series A No 335 C para 34.

203 COE 'Convention for the Protection of Human Rights and Fundamental Freedoms' (signed 4 November 1950, entered into force 3 September 1953) 213 UNTS 221.

204 American Convention on Human Rights (signed 22 November 1969, entered into force 18 July 1978) 1144 UNTS 123 (Pact of San José).

205 *Barayagwiza v Prosecutor (Decision)* ICTR-97-19-A (3 November 1999) at para. 40.

206 *Prosecutor v Milutinović et al (Decision on Dragoljub Ojdanic's Motion Challenging Jurisdiction–Joint Criminal Enterprise)* IT-99-37-AR72 (21 May 2003) para. 38.

law and jeopardises one of the most fundamental achievements the international community subscribed to: fair proceedings leading to transparent and comprehensible outcomes based on the rule of law. Furthermore, the vaguer the applicable law is, the more restrictive should the interpretation and of the provision be conducted.[207] For this reason, the attempt of the ICTY Chamber in *Vasiljević* to water down the e principle of *nullum crimen sine lege* in international criminal law are to be rejected.[208] The Trial Chamber in this case argued that the standards of accessibility and foreseeability have to be adapted to the 'specificity of customary international law'.[209]

As Nilsson rightly argues, the specificity of customary international law primarily lies in its character as non-written law as well as in the lack of a centralized authority involved in its creation.[210] Yet, for non-written law, the ECtHR has affirmed the application of *nullum crimen sine lege* in principal without restrictions. [211]

As guaranteeing fair proceedings is an essential safeguard shielding individuals from the excess of authorities, this standard cannot be lightly given up.[212] The compromises that have to be made regarding some degree of adjustment in international criminal law in this respect are due to the nature of public international law as such and the sources from which it derives. Compromises can, however, not be made with reference to the nature of the crime in questions or any potential threat to peace and security they might constitute.

---

207 *Kokkinakis v Greece (Judgment)* (ECtHR) Series A No 260 A paras 7-9.

208 *Prosecutor v Vasiljević* (Judgment) IT-98-32-T (29 November 2002) para 193; see also *Prosecutor v Hadžihasanović et al (Decision on Joint Challenge to Jurisdiction)* IT-01-47-PT (12 November 2002) para. 62.

209 *Prosecutor v Vasiljević* (Judgment) IT-98-32-T (29 November 2002) para 193.

210 Jonas Nilsson 'The Principle of Nullum Crimen Sine Lege' in Olaoluwa Olusanya *Rethinking International Criminal Law: The Substantive Part* (Europa Law Publishing Groningen 2007) 62.

211 Eg *Sunday Times v United Kingdom* (ECtHR) Series A No 30 para 47.

212 See further Jonas Nilsson 'The Principle of Nullum Crimen Sine Lege' in Olaoluwa Olusanya *Rethinking International Criminal Law: The Substantive Part* (Europa Law Publishing Groningen 2007) 62-63.

Chapter Four: Concluding Remarks

What is at stake when it comes to the extra-statutory application of legal provisions in substantive criminal law is nothing less than the principle of *nuella poena sine lege*. International criminal law offers a unique area of conflict in this respect because it combines criminal law, the formulation of which, in national systems, is mainly in the hand of the legislative branch, with public international law, which evolves through the way States act and the gradual acceptance of these acts and the underlying motivations for these acts as customs and principals of law.[213]

This book argues in favour of a narrowly constructed application of extra-statutory human rights law. As we have seen, international criminal law and international human rights law share many similarities. Structural and dogmatic differences, which could call for precaution when invoking human rights law in substantive international criminal law do in fact exist, but they are fewer in number than sometimes argued and are often subject to discussion and resolution.

It is argued here that the true danger in applying human rights law in substantive international criminal law lies not in the conceptional differences of the two, but in the potential violation of the principle of *nullum crimen sine lege* by way of recourse to extra-statutory law. Because of this danger, the organs of the ICC, foreseen as the main institution for the practical application of international criminal law in the future, need to be in agreement about the legal basis of their application of extra-statutory substantive law and to what degree of application the court is authorized by it. Here, it is argued that Art. 21(3) Rome Statute is a provision which guarantees the rights of the accused person, but cannot be invoked for applying extra-statutory substantive law. In this case, Art. 21 (1) (b) Rome Statute is the more appropriate source of law. Therefore, a narrow construction of the statutes of the *ad hoc* tribunals and the ICC is advised and concludes that extra-statutory substantive international criminal law can only be applied as part of customary international law (general principles of law play less of a role in the substantive part of international criminal justice). Recourse to vague terms like 'interpretational guidance' should be avoided for the sake of legal clarity and fairness of criminal proceedings. For the same reasons, voices which see the role of *nullum crimen sine lege* in in-

---

213 Margaret McAuliffe deGuzman in: Triffterer, Rome Statute, 2nd ed p 704.

ternational criminal law less prominent than in national legal systems are rejected.

As these parameters of the recourse to international human rights law are defined, the next part of the book will deal with the actual application of human rights law by the *ad hoc* tribunals as well as the ICC. It will be examined to what degree the doctrinal framework set out by general international law as well as the respective statutes is adhered to, to what degree the courts and tribunals actually use international human rights law in their substantive considerations and how this use is categorized and justified.

Part Two: How are Different Areas of Human Rights Law Referred to in International Criminal Jurisprudence?

Part Two of this book deals with three different areas of human rights and their use in international criminal law by way of example: the prohibition of torture, the protection of minorities and women's rights/gender issues. These three areas were chosen because they are, in themselves, elaborated to differing degrees in human rights law and they are understood and used to different degrees in international criminal law. This helps to highlight the spectrum of the use of human rights law in international criminal law. This approach makes it possible to explore, by way of comparison, under which circumstances judges are willing to refer to human rights law and to draw conclusions regarding the prerequisites necessary in order to facilitate such use. It also serves to examine whether human rights law is more likely to be referenced in areas where human rights law and the protected rights it contains overlap with what is likely to be prohibited under national criminal legal systems.

The limitations to these three areas of human rights law does by no means suggest that those are the only areas in which international criminal law benefits from human rights law. Other areas of international human rights law which have a relevance to international criminal law and in which international criminal law might to some degree depend on the findings and developments of human rights law included, but are, inter alia, the rights of children (see the prohibition of the enlistment and use of children under the age of 15 under Art. 38 Convention on the Rights of the Child[214] as well as the classification of such action as a war crime under Art. 8 (2) (b) (xxvi) Rome Statute), the issue of hate speech (see first and foremost the case against *Ferdinand Nahimana and others* before the ICTR[215]), the prohibition of slavery which can be a crime against humanity under Art. 7 (1) (c) and (g) Rome Statute, and the prohibition of arbitrary

---

214 Convention on the Rights of the Child (adopted 20 November 1989, entered into force 2 September 1990) 1577 UNTS 3.

215 *Prosecutor v Nahimana (Judgment)* ICTR-99-52-T (3 December 2003).

deprivation of liberty, prohibited in various human rights instruments as well as in Art. 7 (1) (e) Rome Statute.[216]

Chapter One: Prohibition of Torture and 'Other Inhumane Acts'

I. Where was the Prohibition of Torture Referred to at Ad Hoc Tribunals?

One of the areas of human rights law, which have had a clear impact on international criminal law is the prohibition of torture under human rights law. The ICTY and the ICTR have repeatedly resorted to the provisions established under human rights law to protect the individual from torture and other cruel, inhuman or degrading treatment or punishment. The focus of the courts' and tribunals' attention is usually put on the CAT.

1. The Specific Elements in the Definition of Torture as a Crime against Humanity

The tribunals referred to the definition of torture in the CAT in order to identify how torture is defined under customary international law. The crime of torture as a war crime or a crime against humanity is not defined in their respective statutes (Art. 5 (f) ICTY Statute[217] and Art. 3 (f) ICTR Statute[218]), and as the *ad hoc* tribunals, unlike the ICC, have not adopted 'elements of crimes' in order to assist the interpretation and application of the law, the judges often had and still have to consult sources outside their statutes in order to look for definitions for specific crimes.

---

216 See also Theodor Meron 'Human Rights Marches into New Territory: The Enforcement of International Human Rights in International Criminal Tribunals' Fourth Marek Nowicki Memorial Lecture (28 November 2008) <http://web.ceu.hu/legal/pdf%20documents/Nowicki/Meron_Enforcement%20of%20HRwarsawnowicki13nov 08.pdf> (as last accessed on 10 June 2013; speech no longer accessible online); *Prosecutor v Krnojelac (Judgment)* IT-97-25 (15 March 2002) paras 110–114.

217 UNSC 'Statute of the International Criminal Tribunal for the Former Yugoslavia' UNSC Res 827 (1993) (25 May 1993) SCOR 48th Year 29.

218 UNSC 'Statute of the International Tribunal for Rwanda' UNSC Res 955 (1994) (8 November 1994) SCOR 49th Year 13.

In the following, the strategies of the ICTY and the ICTR in regard to the definition of torture will be outlined.

The references of the *ad hoc* tribunals to human rights conventions with regards to the definition of torture as a crime under international law are, however, partly contradictory and do not establish a clear picture of the definition of torture in international customary law. Common to the tribunals' analysis is the starting point of their argumentation, which is Art. 1 (1) CAT. Art. 1 (1) CAT reads follows

> '[f]or the purposes of this Convention, torture means any act by which severe pain or suffering, whether physical or mental, is intentionally inflicted on a person for such purposes as obtaining from him or a third person information or a confession, punishing him for an act he or a third person has committed or is suspected of having committed, or intimidating or coercing him or a third person, or for any reason based on discrimination of any kind, when such pain or suffering is inflicted by or at the instigation of or with the consent or acquiescence of a public official or other person acting in an official capacity. It does not include pain or suffering arising only from, inherent in or incidental to lawful sanctions'.

a. Akayesu

The first judgement of the ICTR, the *Akayesu* judgement, used the CAT's definition without any modification and therefore held that the definition of torture pursuant to Art. 1 CAT was congruent to the definition of torture as a crime against humanity, without giving any reasons for its findings.[219] This approach has been repeated by other chambers of the ICTR in later cases.[220]

---

219 *Prosecutor v Akayesu (Judgment)* ICTR-96-4-T (2 September 1998) para. 681.

220 Eg *Prosecutor v Musema (Judgment)* ICTR-96-13-T (27 January 2000) para. 285; the *Musema* Judgment even adopted the second sentence of Art. 1 (1) CAT ('It does not include pain or suffering arising only from, inherent in or incidental to lawful sanctions'.) as being part of the definition of torture under international criminal law, without undergirding its assumption with any reasoning.

b. Delalić and others (Čelebići)

The ICTY, on the other hand, established different approaches regarding the evaluation of torture under customary international law. The need for using human rights for guidance in interpretation is especially obvious when it comes to the ICTY. As the first international criminal tribunal since the end of World War II, the ICTY was primarily faced with defining the crimes under its jurisdiction within the boundaries of *nullum crimen sine lege*. In *Delalić and others*, the Court held, in a first step, that the prohibition of torture is recognized as being part of customary international law and *ius cogens*.[221] Then, in a second step, the court turned to the definition of the prohibited phenomenon and how torture can be defined under customary international law. The court held that the definition of torture contained in the CAT 'includes' the definitions contained in both the United Nations Declaration on the Protection of All Persons from Being Subjected to Torture and Other Cruel, Inhuman or Degrading Treatment or Punishment ('Torture Declaration')[222], which was used as a basis for the CAT and the Inter-American Convention to Prevent and Punish Torture [223] and 'thus reflects a consensus which the Trial Chamber considered to be representative of customary international law'.[224] The court also pointed to the number of ratification of the CAT (109 as of 1998) as an indication for its status as customary international law.[225]

After the court concluded that the CAT definition is representative of customary international law, the Trial Chamber considered, in a third step 'in more depth the requisite level of severity of pain or suffering, the exis-

---

221 *Prosecutor v Delalić et al (Judgment)* IT-96-21 (16 November 1998) para. 454; regarding the prohibition of torture being part of *ius cogens*, see also UN Commission on Human Rights 'Torture and other Cruel, Inhuman or Degrading Treatment or Punishment: Report by the Special Rapporteur, Mr. P. Kooijmans, appointed Pursuant to Commission on Human Rights resolution 1985/33' (19 February 1986) UN Doc E/CN.4/1986/15 para. 3.

222 UNGA Res 3452 (XXX) 'Declaration on the Protection of All Persons from Being Subjected to Torture and Other Cruel, Inhuman or Degrading Treatment or Punishment' (9 December 1975) 30th Session Supp 34, 91.

223 Inter-American Convention to Prevent and Punish Torture (done 9 December 1985, entered into force 28 February 1987) (1986) 25 ILM 519.

224 *Prosecutor v Delalić et al (Judgment)* IT-96-21 (16 November 1998) para. 459.

225 *Prosecutor v Delalić et al (Judgment)* IT-96-21 (16 November 1998) para. 453.

tence of a prohibited purpose, and the extent of the official involvement that are required in order for the offence of torture to be proven'.[226]

For this undertaking, the court turned to the jurisprudence of the HRC, the European Court of Human Rights ('ECtHR') and the European Commission of Human Rights ('ECommHR'), all of which do not apply the CAT, but other, at times conflicting definitions. In particular, the judgments in the *Greek Case*[227] and the *Ireland v United Kingdom Case*[228] to which the Trial Chamber refers, were rendered before the CAT was even adopted.

Even though the Trial Chamber mentioned the ECtHR's reference to Art. 1 (2) Torture Declaration in the *Ireland v United Kingdom Case*[229] which reads '[t]orture constitutes an aggravated and deliberate form of cruel, inhuman or degrading treatment or punishment' the Trial Chamber omitted to mention that this was an opinion which the ECommHR did not share. The definition of torture applied by the ECommHR differs significantly from the one applied by the ECtHR. In the *Greek Case*, the ECommHR held that what distinguishes inhuman treatment from torture was that the latter required the infliction of severe pain or suffering for a prohibited purpose.[230] The Commission held that

> '[t]he word "torture" is often used to describe inhuman treatment, which has a purpose, such as the obtaining of information or confessions, or the infliction of punishment, and is generally an aggravated form of inhuman treatment'.[231]

The Commission argued that what distinguished torture from inhuman treatment or punishment is not the intensity of the pain and suffering, but rather that the severe pain and suffering is inflicted for a prohibited pur-

---

226 *Prosecutor v Delalić et al (Judgment)* IT-96-21 (16 November 1998) para. 460.

227 *Greek Case* (ECommHR App Nos 3321/67 [*Denmark v Greece*]; 3322/67 [*Norway v Greece*]; 3323 [*Sweden v Greece*]; 3344/67 [*Netherlands v Greece*]) (1969) 12 YECommHR.

228 *Ireland v United Kingdom* (ECtHR) Series A No 25; *Ireland v United Kingdom* (ECommHR App 5310/71) (1976) Series B No 23-I.

229 *Ireland v United Kingdom* (ECtHR) Series A No 25 para. 167.

230 *Greek Case* (ECommHR App Nos 3321/67 [*Denmark v Greece*]; 3322/67 [*Norway v Greece*]; 3323 [*Sweden v Greece*]; 3344/67 [*Netherlands v Greece*]) (1969) 12 YECommHR 168.

231 *Greek Case* (ECommHR App Nos 3321/67 [*Denmark v Greece*]; 3322/67 [*Norway v Greece*]; 3323 [*Sweden v Greece*]; 3344/67 [*Netherlands v Greece*]) (1969) 12 YECommHR 168, 186.

pose.[232] This approach also prevailed amongst the drafters of the CAT, in which no mention of torture being an aggravated form of cruel inhuman or degrading treatment or punishment was made.

The ECtHR, on the other hand, has taken a different approach, which does not focus on the purpose of the conduct, but rather on the intensity of the pain and suffering inflicted. In its famous Northern Ireland Case, it held that

> 'the five techniques [interrogation techniques used by British security forces against suspect terrorists […] as applied in combination, undoubtedly amounted to inhuman and degrading treatment, although their object was the extraction of confessions, the naming of others and/or information and although they were used systematically, they did not occasion suffering of the particular intensity and cruelty implied by the word torture as so understood'[233].

The Trial Chamber seems to elide contradictions and chooses the dogmatically flawed path of declaring the CAT definition of torture to be customary international law and subsequently using inherently contradictory definitions taken from other instruments and regional courts and treaty bodies cumulatively in order to fill in the gaps left open by the CAT definition. Furthermore, the court fails to explain how jurisprudence interpreting a regional convention which was not applicable on the territory on which the events before the court took place should be indicative of a pre-defined norm to be followed by the actors at the time.[234] Regional jurisprudence

---

232 See more in detail under Part Two Chapter One I. 1. F. below.

233 *Ireland v United Kingdom* (ECtHR) Series A No 25 para. 167.

234 This paradox is becoming even more obvious in the case of the ICC. As of 2017, all but of of the situations under investigation y the ICC is concerned with are within African States. However, the jurisprudence of the ECtHR and the IACtHR is developed to a much greater extent than that of the African Court on Human and Peoples' Rights. Therefore, if the ICC refers to human rights jurisprudence, it basically always refers to regional jurisprudence developed on another continent. Sheppard writes: '[T]he court [the ICC] tends to simply adopt reasons from the human rights courts that they find compelling. The Court may be entitled to do so, but in the context of locating quasi-constitutional norms, the Court should take care to explain on what basis it adopts the reasons of the European court interpreting a European convention as supportive of a paramount principle applicable to a set of cases that have arisen exclusively from Africa'; see Daniel Sheppard 'The International Criminal Court and "Internationally Recognized Human Rights": Understanding Article 21(3) of the Rome Statute' (2010) 10 International Criminal Law Review 43-71, 54.

could, of course, be an indication of customary international law in a specific area, but the court makes no such assumption, but simply quotes regional case law to support the argumentation the ICTY choose to follow.

The acts before the ICTY did without doubt lead to severe mental or physical pain or suffering on part of the victims. They included beatings with various objects including baseball bats, shovels, metal chains, wooden implements;[235] burnings with various objects including hot pincers and heated knifes[236]; suffocation[237] as well as forcible sexual vaginal and anal intercourse.[238]

However, by demanding cumulatively that the pain or suffering in question needed to be 'aggravated' in comparison to inhuman or degrading treatment or punishment, and additionally for the aggravated pain or suffering to be inflicted for a prohibited purpose, the Trial Chamber unreasonably raised the requirements for torture both under human rights and international criminal law.

Additionally, the Trial Chamber does not scrutinize whether international criminal law actually requires torture to be inflicted by a State official. The court merely affirms that this is the case, adding, without any further examination that

'[i]n the context of international humanitarian law, this requirement must be interpreted to include officials of non-State parties to a conflict, in order for the prohibition to retain significance in situations of internal armed conflicts or international conflicts involving some non-State entities'.[239]

Thereby, it adds another requirement that has not been held to be a constituent element of torture under international criminal and humanitarian law by other chambers.[240]

---

235 *Prosecutor v Delalić et al (Celebići Indictment)* IT-96-21 (19 March 1996) paras 23 and 26–28.

236 *Prosecutor v Delalić et al (Celebići Indictment)* IT-96-21 (19 March 1996) paras 23 and 26–28.

237 *Prosecutor v Delalić et al (Celebići Indictment)* IT-96-21 (19 March 1996) paras 23 and 26.

238 *Prosecutor v Delalić et al (Celebići Indictment)* IT-96-21 (19 March 1996) paras 24–25.

239 *Prosecutor v Delalić et al (Judgment)* IT-96-21 (16 November 1998) para. 473.

240 See eg *Prosecutor v Kunarac (Judgment)* IT-96-23 (22 February 2001) paras 488–96.

Moreover, the court took recourse to human rights when deciding the question whether rape can be considered torture, a question which the court answers in the affirmative[241]. Additionally, the ICTY looked into the jurisprudence of the ECtHR, the ECommHR and the HRC again, mainly relying on the same points of arguments as in the torture discussion, when it defined inhuman treatment punishable as a grave breach of the Geneva Conventions under Art. 2 (c) ICTY Statute.[242]

c. Furundžija

A different Trial Chamber more openly criticized the lack of doctrinal precision and reasoning taken in *Akayesu*. In *Furundžija* the Trial Chamber pointed out that the definition given in Art. 1 CAT was explicitly limited to the 'purposes of this Convention'. The ICTY stated, however, that an extra-conventional effect may 'be produced to the extent that the definition at issue codifies, or contributes to developing or crystallising customary international law'.[243] The Court continued by scrutinizing whether the definition in the CAT can be said to reflect customary international law. The Court first stated that the definition given in the CAT, while being explicitly limited to the CAT, could be understood in a broader manner because it outlined 'all the necessary elements implicit in international rules on the matter'.[244] Here, the court did not consider whether the 'international rules on the matter' were the same ones, with the same reference points, pursuing the same goals, in both human rights and international criminal law. Given the differences in terms of goals and purposes in the different fields of law, it is questionable whether 'the matter' of torture can even be seen as congruent in both human rights and international criminal law. Surely, it would have been helpful to the dogmatic credibili-

241 *Prosecutor v Delalić et al (Celebići Indictment)* IT-96-21 (19 March 1996) paras 475-497; See Part Two Chapter Three I. 2. below.

242 See paras. 534–42.

243 *Prosecutor v Furundžija (Judgment)* IT-95-17 (10 December 1998) para. 160; see also Fausto Pocar 'International Criminal Tribunals and Serious Violations of International Humanitarian Law against Civilians and Prisoners of War' in Manoj Kumar Sinha (ed) International Criminal Law and Human Rights (Manak Delhi 2010) 1-26, 8-9.

244 *Prosecutor v Furundžija (Judgment)* IT-95-17 (10 December 1998) para 160.

ty of the court to discuss at least whether the rules governing torture are understood to be the same in both fields of law.

Then the Trial Chamber examined other relevant documents on the subject, namely the Torture Declaration. The fact that the Torture Declaration was adopted within the UNGA by consensus and therefore no country did object to it was referred to by the ICTY as an indication of the support of the definition by all UN Member States.[245] However, even though the definitions in the Torture Declaration and the CAT are similar, they are not identical. Art. 1 (1) CAT contains much broader requirements of the involvement of an official than the Torture Declaration.[246] Furthermore, the CAT lists additional prohibited purposes for the infliction of severe pain of suffering which cannot be found in the Torture Declaration, namely coercion and discrimination of any kind'. Art. 1 (2) Torture Declaration does, moreover, explicitly state that '[t]orture constitutes an aggravated and deliberate form of cruel, inhuman or degrading treatment or punishment', a sentence which was omitted under the CAT. Hence it cannot be said that the global consensus that was achieved with the adoption of the Torture Declaration does necessarily also consist with regard to the CAT.[247] A few countries have in fact issued reservations or 'declarations of understanding' regarding the definition of torture in the CAT,[248] to which a couple of other countries objected.[249]

---

245 *Prosecutor v Furundžija (Judgment)* IT-95-17 (10 December 1998) para. 160.

246 Art. 1 CAT: 'inflicted by or at the instigation of or with the consent or acquiescence of a public official or other person acting in an official capacity'; Art. 1 (1) Torture Declaration: 'intentionally inflicted by or at the instigation of a public official'.

247 See also UN Commission on Human Rights 'Torture and other Cruel, Inhuman or Degrading Treatment or Punishment: Report by the Special Rapporteur, Mr. P. Kooijmans, appointed Pursuant to Commission on Human Rights resolution 1985/33' (19 February 1986) UN Doc E/CN.4/1986/15 para. 31.

248 Botswana and Qatar made reservations regarding the definition of torture; the USA has issued broad 'understandings' which in fact amount to reservations; see <https://treaties.un.org/Pages/ViewDetails.aspx?src=treaty&mtdsg_no=iv-9&chapter=4&lang=en> (31 October 2017); see also Manfred Nowak and Elisabeth McArthur *The United Nations Convention against Torture: A Commentary* (OUP Oxford 2008) 50–51.

249 See the objections of Denmark, Norway and Sweden to the reservation of Botswana; of Finland, France, Germany, Luxembourg, the Netherlands Norway, Spain and Sweden to the reservation of Qatar; and of the Netherlands and Sweden to the understandings of the USA; <https://treaties.un.org/Pages/ViewDetails.aspx?src=treaty&mtdsg_no=iv-9&chapter=4&lang=en> (31 October 2017).

The Court further pointed to a substantially similar definition of torture used in the Inter-American Convention to Prevent and Punish Torture and emphasizes that the CAT's definition is used by the Special Rapporteur on torture other cruel, inhuman or degrading treatment or punishment[250], the ECtHR[251], the ECommHR[252] and the HRC[253].

This is, again a flawed analysis, because not two of these institutions or instruments use exactly the same definition and characterize the exact same actions as torture.

The ICTY in *Furundžija* concludes that the main elements of the definition of Art. 1 CAT are part of customary law, but notes that there are some specific elements which pertain to torture in the context of international criminal law, more specifically in the context of armed conflicts which are not necessarily spelled out in the CAT.[254] The court emphasized that the 'general spirit of international humanitarian law',[255] whose primary purpose is the safeguarding of human dignity, requires one of the possible reasons of torture to be the humiliation of the victim. The court does, however, also mention that the purpose of humiliation is close to one that is explicitly enshrined in the CAT, namely the purpose of intimidation of the victim.[256] In fact, the Inter-American Commission on Human Rights mentions humiliation as the one of the impermissible purposes for the infliction for severe pain and suffering in connection to charges of torture be-

---

250 See UN Commission for Human Rights 'Torture and other Cruel, Inhuman or Degrading Treatment or Punishment: Report by the Special Rapporteur, Mr. P. Kooijmans, appointed Pursuant to Commission on Human Rights resolution 1985/33' (19 February 1986) UN Doc E/CN.4/1986/15. The Special Rapporteur, in this first report, does however, not solely depend on the definition of the CAT and the Torture Declaration. He uses the definition of both instruments, but substantiates this definition by use of jurisprudence of human rights bodies like the HRC, the ECtHR and the European Commission of Human Rights; see paras 30–39.

251 *Ireland v United Kingdom* (ECtHR) Series A No 25 para. 167.

252 *Greek Case* (ECommHR App Nos 3321/67 [*Denmark v Greece*]; 3322/67 [*Norway v Greece*]; 3323 [*Sweden v Greece*]; 3344/67 [*Netherlands v Greece*]) (1969) 12 YECommHR 168.

253 UN HRC 'General Comment No 20: Replaces General Comment 7 concerning Prohibition of Torture and Cruel Treatment or Punishment (Art. 7)' (3 April 1992) GAOR 47th Session Supp 40, 193.

254 *Prosecutor v Furundžija (Judgment)* IT-95-17 (10 December 1998) paras 161–62.

255 *Prosecutor v Furundžija (Judgment)* IT-95-17 (10 December 1998) para 162.

256 Further see Chad G Marzen 'The Furundzija Judgment and its Continued Vitality in International Law' (2010) 43 Creighton Law Review 505–27, particularly 517.

fore the commission.[257] It stated that 'rape is considered to be a method of psychological torture because its objective, in many cases, is not just to humiliate the victim but also her family or community'.[258] This is, however, not mentioned by the ICTY.

Furthermore, it is not evident how the 'general spirit of humanitarian law' requires humiliation to be recognized as a prohibited purpose in the context of torture whereas human rights law would not require such recognition. Torture constitutes 'the most brutal attack on human dignity and personality'[259] and bears great resemblance to slavery as both crimes are characterized by an imbalance of power and complete powerlessness on part of the victim. This core aspect of the phenomenon of torture does not differ in situations of armed conflict, unrest or official peace. It is this imbalance of power that makes the vulnerable party prone to human rights abuses such as torture. It is hard to see therefore how the 'spirit of humanitarian law' should, in the context of torture, demand for an additional purpose to be included in the list of prohibited purposes different from the ones established in human rights law.

The court further emphasizes that 'at least one of the persons involved in the torture process must be a public official or must at any rate act in a non-private capacity, e.g. as a *de facto* organ of a State or any other authority-wielding entity'.[260] The chamber fails to further specify the term 'authority-wielding entity', which cannot be found in any international convention dealing with torture. It does not specify whether it let go of the official' requirement as a whole or whether it includes into the term 'authority-wielding entities' only State-like authorities. In case of the latter, the court could have backed up its reasoning with the help of the CAT. Even though this is not as clearly pronounced in the CAT, the CAT does,

---

257 *Fernando and Raquel Mejia v Peru* Case 10.970 IACommHR Report No 5/96 (1 March 1996); a couple of years later, the Committee against Torture also explicitly listed humiliation as belonging to the prohibited purposes under Arrest. 1 CAT, see UN Committee against Torture 'Communication No 262/2005, *VL v Switzerland* (20 November 2006) UN Committee against Torture 'Report of the Committee against Torture 37th session (6-24 November 2006) 38th session (30 April-18 May 2007)' GAOR 62nd session Supp 44, 207 para 8.10.

258 *Fernando and Raquel Mejia v Peru* Case 10.970 IACommHR Report No 5/96 (1 March 1996) para. 3; see further under See Part Two Chapter Three I. 2. below.

259 Manfred Nowak and Elisabeth McArthur *The United Nations Convention against Torture: A Commentary* (OUP Oxford 2008) 76.

260 *Prosecutor v Furundžija (Judgment)* IT-95-17 (10 December 1998) para. 162.

however, include the term 'other person acting in official capacity', which leaves room for the inclusion of 'de facto authorities', private actors whose authority is comparable with that of State actors.[261]

As for the forms of torture, the ICTY refers to human rights law in order to conclude that rape can constitute a form of torture. In particular, the ICTY referred to jurisprudence of the ECtHR[262] and the IACtHR[263].

d. Kvočka

In *Kvočka*, the Trial Chamber started its legal findings on torture by stating that '[t]orture has been defined by the Tribunal jurisprudence as severe mental or physical suffering deliberately inflicted upon a person for a prohibited purpose, such as to obtain information or to discriminate against the victim'.[264]

In the *Kvočka* Judgment, the ICTY determined the required severity for torture as an offence under Art. 3 ICTY Statute (Violations of the Laws and Customs of War) and Art. 5 ICTY Statute (Crimes against Humanity),

---

261 Manfred Nowak and Elisabeth McArthur *The United Nations Convention against Torture: A Commentary* (OUP Oxford 2008) 77–79.

262 *Aydin v Turkey* (ECtHR) Reports 1997-VI <http://hudoc.echr.coe.int/eng?i=001-58371> (31 October 2017); *Aksoy v Turkey* (ECtHR) Reports 1996-VI 2260.

263 *Fernando and Raquel Mejia v Peru* Case 10.970 IACommHR Report No 5/96 (1 March 1996; The treaty body of the CAT itself, the Committee against Torture, has later held that rape, when inflicted for one of the purposes mentioned in the convention, can constitute a form of torture (see UN Committee against Torture 'Communication No 262/2005, *VL v Switzerland*' [20 November 2006] UN Doc CAT/C/37/D/262/2005).

264 *Prosecutor v Kvočka (Judgment)* IT-98-30 (2 November 2001) para. 137.

with reference to the HRC[265], the ECommHR[266] the ECtHR[267], international legal scholars as well as a Report by the UN Special Rapporteur on

265 *Ibid.* para. 146, referring to UN HRC 'Consideration of Reports Submitted by States Parties under Article 40 of the Covenant: Israel' (28 July 1998) GAOR 53rd Session Supp 40 vol 1, 45: 'The Committee notes also the admission by the State party delegation that the methods of handcuffing, hooding, shaking and sleep deprivation have been and continue to be used as interrogation techniques, either alone or in combination. The Committee is of the view that the guidelines can give rise to abuse and that the use of these methods constitutes a violation of article 7 of the Covenant in any circumstances' (at para. 19), see also UN HRC 'Communications No 623/1995, 624/1995, 626/1995 and 627/1995, *Domukovsky et al. v. Georgia*' (6 April 1998), UN Docs CCPR/C/62/D/623, 624, 626 & 627/1995, para. 18.6; UN HRC 'Communication No. 124/82, *Muteba v Zaire*' (25 March 1983) UN Doc CCPR/C/OP/2 at 158; UN HRC Communication 194/85, *Miango Muiyo v Zaire*' (27 October 1987) UN Doc CCPR/C/OP/2 at 219; UN HRC 'Communication 366/89, *Kanana v. Zaire*' (2 November 1993) UN Doc CCPR/C/49/D/366/1989; UN HRC 'Communication No. 11/1977, *Grille Motta v Uruguay*' (29 July 1980) UN Doc Supp. No. 40 (A/35/40) at 132; UN HRC 'Communication No. 52/1979, *Lopez Burgos v Uruguay*' (29 July 1981) UN Doc CCPR/C/OP/1 at 88; UN HRC 'Communication No 63/1979, *Sendic v Uruguay*' (28 October 1981) UN Doc No Supp. No. 40 (A/37/40) at 114 (1982); UN HRC 'Communication No. 74/1980, *Angel Estrella v Uruguay*' (29 March 1983) UN Doc Supp. No. 40 (A/37/40) at 114 (1982); UN HRC 'Communication No. 147/83, *Arzuaga Gilboa v Uruguay*' (1 November 1985) UN Doc CCPR/C/OP/2 at 176; UN HRC Communication No 159/1983, *Cariboni v Uruguay*' (27 October 1987) UN Doc Supp. No. 40 (A/43/40) at 184; UN HRC 'Communication 162/1983, *Berterretche Acosta v Uruguay*' (25 October 1988) UN Doc Supp. No. 40 (A/44/40) at 183; UN HRC 'Communication No 161/1983, *Herrera Rubio v Colombia*' (2 November 1987) UN Doc CCPR/C/OP/2 at 192; UN HRC 'Communication No 176/1984, *Lafuente Peñarrieta et al v Bolivia*' (2 November 1987) UN Doc CCPR/C/OP/2 at 201.

266 *Prosecutor v Kvočka (Judgment)* IT-98-30 (2 November 2001) paras 142-4, referring to *Ireland v United Kingdom* (ECtHR) Series A No 25; the acts in question in the case at hand where the so-called 'five techniques' applied by members of the Royal Ulster Constabulary against alleged terrorist by the Irish Republican Army. The 'techniques' were wall-standing, hooding, subjection to noise, deprivation of sleep and deprivation of food and drink (see para. 96). The ECommHR concluded, however, that the cumulative use of this technique did not amount to torture but to inhuman treatment (see para. 167).

267 *Prosecutor v Kvočka (Judgment)* IT-98-30 (2 November 2001) para. 150, referring to *Aksoy v Turkey* (ECtHR) Reports 1996-VI, 2260.

Torture[268], and accordingly compiled a list of several acts which are per se severe enough to *per se* constitute torture and of those which can constitute torture depending on the circumstances.[269] The Chamber stated that it is not possible to lay out a precise threshold for the severity of suffering but that it depends on objective as well as subjective criteria. Regarding objective factors, the Chamber concluded that '[b]eating, sexual violence, prolonged denial of sleep, food, hygiene, and medical assistance, as well as threats to torture, rape, or kill relatives were among the acts most commonly mentioned as those likely to constitute torture. Mutilation of body parts would be an example of acts *per se* constituting torture'.[270] It also outlined a catalogue of helpful subjective factors which can be drawn, namely, 'physical or mental effect of the treatment upon the particular victim and, in some cases, factors such as the victim's age, sex, or state of health'.[271] In its definition of inhuman treatment, the court refers to a decision of the ECtHR which found that a long-lasting effect was not required for a mistreatment to fall within the ambit of Art. 3 ECHR.[272] Furthermore, the ICTY refers to the HRC's and the ECtHR's evaluation of inappropriate conditions of detention as inhuman and/or degrading treatment.[273]

---

268 *Prosecutor v Kvočka (Judgment)* IT-98-30 (2 November 2001) para. 144, referring to UN Commission on Human Rights Special Rapporteur Sir Nigel Rodley 'Question of torture and other cruel, inhuman or degrading treatment or punishment' (3 July 2001) UN Doc A/56/156.

269 *Prosecutor v Kvočka (Judgment)* IT-98-30 (2 November 2001), para. 142–51.

270 *Prosecutor v Kvočka (Judgment)* IT-98-30 (2 November 2001), para. 144.

271 *Prosecutor v Kvočka (Judgment)* IT-98-30 (2 November 2001), para. 143.

272 *Prosecutor v Kvočka (Judgment)* IT-98-30 (2 November 2001), para. 159; *Costello-Roberts v United Kingdom* (ECtHR) Series A No 247 C.

273 *Prosecutor v Kvočka (Judgment)* IT-98-30 (2 November 2001), para. 169; UN HRC 'Communication No 188/84, *Portorreal v Dominican Republic*' (5 November 1987) UN Doc Supp No 40 (A/43/40) at 207; UN HRC 'Communication No 775/97, *Brown v Jamaica*' (23 March 1999) UN Doc CCPR/C/65/D/775/1997; UN HRC 'Communication No. 74/1980, *Angel Estrella v Uruguay*' UN Doc Supp. No. 40 (A/37/40) at 114 (1982); *Denmark, Norway and Sweden v Greece* (ECommHR App 4448/70) (1970) 13 YECommHR 108; *Denmark, Norway, Sweden and the Netherlands v Greece* (ECommHR App 3321-3323/67 and 3344/67) (1968) 11 YECommHR 690; *Cyprus v Turkey* (ECommHR App 8007/77) (1979) 13 DR 85.

e. Krnojelac

In Krnojelac, the Court had, for yet another time, to deal with the question of the purposes for which the infliction of pain or suffering has to be inflicted to amount to torture. Here, the respective Trial Chamber does not follow the chambers in *Furundžija* and *Kvocka.* In contrast, it explicitly dismisses the argumentation followed in those two cases regarding humiliation as a potential purpose for torture. The Chamber invoked the principle of legality in order to argue that the purpose to humiliate the victim

'is not expressly mentioned in any of the principal international instruments prohibiting torture. Nor is there a clear jurisprudential disposition towards its recognition as an illegitimate purpose. There may be a tendency, particularly in the field of human rights, towards the enlargement of the list of prohibited purposes, but the Trial Chamber must apply customary international humanitarian law as it finds it to have been *at the time when the crimes charged were alleged to have been committed.* In light of the principle of legality, the proposition that "the primary purpose of humanitarian law is to safeguard human dignity" is not sufficient to permit the court to introduce, as part of the *mens rea,* a new and additional prohibited purpose, which would in effect enlarge the scope of the criminal prohibition against torture beyond what it was at the time relevant to the indictment under consideration'.[274]

The Trial Chamber does not, however, discuss or mention that the list in Art. 1 CAT and in other instruments is merely meant to be indicative and is not an exclusive catalogue.

f. Kunarac and others

The most sophisticated approach of an international criminal tribunal regarding the interrelation of the prohibition of torture under the international human rights regime and under international criminal law can be found in yet another case before the ICTY, the *Kunarac* judgement.[275] The arguments put forward by the court in order to carve out the similarities and

---

274 *Prosecutor v Krnojelac (Judgment)* IT-97-25 (15 March 2002) para. 186.

275 *Prosecutor v Kunarac (Judgment)* IT-96-23 (22 February 2001) paras 465–97; for the Trial Chamber's findings on torture see also Fausto Pocar 'International Criminal Tribunals and Serious Violations of International Humanitarian Law

systemic differences between human rights and international criminal law have been examined (and partially refuted) in Part One Chapter Three I. 2.

The Trial Chamber, after reaffirming the similarities of international criminal law and international human rights law in terms of goals, values and terminology, the Trial Chamber goes on to disentangle the two subjects and to look at their dogmatic differences. Even though the arguments brought forward can partially be refuted, the caution called for by the court because of the different dogmatic roots and considerations underlying the two areas of law is important. To what degree these dogmatic differences play out in practice has to be determined on a case-to-case-basis. This is necessary because, as examined above, human rights in themselves are such a heterogeneous conglomerate and the violations of specific rights is punishable by means of criminal law to very differing degrees. This is why the Court in *Kunarac*, after outlining the differences of the two subject, and concluding that international human rights law can only be transposed to international criminal law when taking into account the peculiarities which are inherent in this specific area of law[276] carefully examines each element of a potential definition of torture in light of the jurisdiction of the court as a violation of the laws and customs of war as well as a crime against humanity.

The Trial Chamber in *Kunarac* then turned to examine the specific extra-conventional effect of the definition in Article 1 CAT. It noted that the specific limitation in Art. 1 and the statement in Art. 2 (1) according to which this article is 'without prejudice to any international instrument or national legislation which does or may contain provisions of wider application'—thereby entitling individuals to a broader protection then enshrined in the CAT in the case broader definitions in other international conventions or national laws are applicable to the benefit of an individual —have to be kept in mind when applying the CAT definition in the context of international criminal law.

Subsequently, the Court consulted the relevant instruments in the context which, apart from the ones already mentioned above, also include provisions which prohibit torture, cruel, inhuman or degrading treatment, but do themselves not provide a definition. These instruments are Art. 5 Uni-

---

against Civilians and Prisoners of War' in Manoj Kumar Sinha (ed) *International Criminal Law and Human Rights* (Manak Delhi 2010) 1-26, 9-11.

276 *Prosecutor v Kunarac (Judgment)* IT-96-23 (22 February 2001) para. 471.

versal Declaration of Human Rights[277], Art. 3 ECHR, as well as Art. 7 ICCPR. The ICTY looks at the jurisprudence of the ECtHR and the ECommHR and the HRC to find out how torture is defined in the European human rights context. As explained above, however[278], the definitions used by the ECtHR and the Commission differ significantly.

What the court does is that it looks at both the ECtHR and the Commission's understandings of the concept of torture cumulatively and extracts the basic preconditions for torture that they both use.[279] This can, however, not be correct as the understanding of torture by the ECommHR and the ECtHR do not complement each other. Both institutions used definitions of torture which can lead them to draw different conclusions as to whether or not a specific action amounts to torture, like in the *Northern Ireland* Case, in which the techniques in question were qualified as torture by the ECommHR,[280] but as inhuman and degrading treatment by the ECtHR.[281].

The intention of the CAT drafters is more coherent with the approach taken by the Commission than with the one taken by the ECtHR. The decisive criteria for torture (distinguishing it from cruel, inhuman or degrading treatment) 'is not the intensity of the pain or suffering inflicted but the purpose of the conduct, the intention of the perpetrator and the powerlessness of the victim.'[282]

---

277 UNGA Res 217 A (III) 'Universal Declaration of Human Rights' (10 December 1948) GAOR 3rd Session Part I Resolutions 71.

278 See under Part Two Chapter One I 1. b above.

279 *Prosecutor v Kunarac (Judgment)* IT-96-23 (22 February 2001) para. 478.

280 *Ireland v United Kingdom* (ECommHR App 5310/71) (1976) Series B No 23-I, 410; However, even if the Commission in its reasoning points to the 'systematic application of the techniques for the purpose of inducing a person to give information' its main point of argumentation lays in the combined application of the five techniques 'which prevent the use of the senses ' and which 'directly affects the personality physically and mentally. The will to resist or to give in cannot, under such conditions, be formed with any degree of independence' (*Ireland v United Kingdom* (ECommHR App 5310/71) (1976) Series B No 23-I, 410). The Commission concludes that [a]lthough the five techniques —also called 'disorientation' or 'sensory deprivation techniques'—might not necessarily cause any severe after-effects the Commission sees in them a modern system of torture falling into the same category as those systems which have been applied in previous times as a means of obtaining information and confessions'(ibid).

281 *Ireland v United Kingdom* (ECtHR) Series A No 25 para. 168.

282 Manfred Nowak and Elisabeth McArthur *The United Nations Convention against Torture: A Commentary* (OUP Oxford 2008) 558; see also UN Committee against

The *Kunarac* Chamber compares the different definitions and their interpretation by the various courts and treaty bodies and concludes that the definition of the CAT does not reflect customary international law. It aims at an inter-State level, means to be applied to the responsibilities of States and does, furthermore, not prevent other, broader definitions in regional or national human rights instruments, which provide individuals with a more thorough protection.[283] This is a valid conclusion. Apart from the arguable differences in the role of the State that the trial chamber identified, there seems to be not sufficient quantity of State practice and *opinio iuris* to conclude that the CAT definition of torture has prevailed to a degree that it is to be considered part of customary international law. The trial chamber would have nevertheless benefitted from a more thorough examination of the contradictions within regional human rights regimes as the analysis of the differing approaches taken by the ECommHR and the ECtHR show.

The trial chamber concludes that even though its definition does not constitute customary international law, the CAT can nonetheless be used by international criminal courts and tribunals as guidance and 'interpretational aid'. It goes on to examine which parts of the CAT definition of torture can indeed be seen as customary international law 'from the specific viewpoint of international criminal law relating to armed conflicts'.[284] In this, it delves into analysis deeper than many other Chambers that rather use references to 'inspiration' or 'interpretational aid' as an excuse to pick and choose. The Trial Chamber identifies in that way three elements which are non-contentious and have become part of customary international law, namely the intentional (a) infliction of severe mental or physi-

---

Torture Special Rapporteur M Nowak 'Civil and Political Rights, Including the Questions of Torture and Detention: Torture and other Cruel, Inhuman or Degrading Treatment: Report of the Special Rapporteur on the Question of Torture (23 December 2005) UN Doc E/CN.4/2006/6.

283 Kunarac para. 482; the findings of the Kunarac Chamber in this respect were upheld on appeal and have been used as elements of crimes of some sorts by many other ICTY Chambers which cited them as the requirements of torture as a crime against humanity before the ICTY; see *Prosecutor v Kunarac (Appeal Judgment)* IT-96-23 & IT-96-23/1-A (12 June 2002 paras 142-148; see also eg *Prosecutor v Haradinaj* (Judgment) IT-04-84-T (3 April 2008) para. 127; *Prosecutor v Mićo Stanišić (Judgment)* IT-08-91-T (27 March 2013) para 47.

284 *Kunarac*, para. 488; see also *Prosecutor v Furundžija (Judgment)* IT-95-17 (10 December 1998) para. 162.

cal suffering (b) for a specific purpose (c).[285] Three other elements were, according to the Trial Chamber, still controversial. Those were the list of purposes with which the pain and suffering must be inflicted in order to come under the realm of torture; the question whether or not the act in question has to be committed in relation to an armed conflict; and finally whether the act has to be inflicted by or at the instigation of or with the consent or acquiescence of a public official or other person acting in an official capacity.[286] The Trial Chamber affirmed that the purposes listed in the CAT have become part of customary law, but left open whether any other purposes have been recognized as such, thereby not following the jurisprudence of the Chamber in *Furundžija*, which had assumed humiliation of the victim to be one of the possible purposes for the conduction of torture.[287] Though all crimes over which the ICTY has jurisdiction have to have a nexus to an armed conflict, the court held that crimes against humanity under the ICTY Statute require a lesser degree of connection to the armed conflict than war crimes whose commission have to be 'closely related' to the hostilities.[288]

Regarding the third, the 'public official element', the trial chamber sees this as a result of the nature of the CAT as a human rights convention and the resulting direction of States as obligated parties or respondents.[289] For the purposes of the ICTY, however, 'the involvement of the State does not modify or limit the guilt of the responsibility of the individual who carried out the crimes in question'.[290] The Chamber outlines the difference between provisions which trigger State responsibility and provisions which provide for individual criminal responsibility, claiming that 'human rights norms are almost exclusively of the first sort.' On that basis, the Trial Chamber holds the presence of a State official or other authority is not necessary for the act to be regarded as torture under international humanitarian law, or for the personal culpability of the perpetrator.

285 *Kunarac* para. 483.
286 *Prosecutor v Kunarac (Judgment)* IT-96-23 (22 February 2001) para 484.
287 *Prosecutor v Furundžija (Judgment)* IT-95-17 (10 December 1998) para. 162.
288 *Prosecutor v Kunarac (Judgment)* IT-96-23 (22 February 2001) para. 487.
289 *Prosecutor v Kunarac (Judgment)* IT-96-23 (22 February 2001) paras 488-96.
290 *Prosecutor v Kunarac (Judgment)* IT-96-23 (22 February 2001) para 493.

However, human rights provisions dealing with torture do also oblige the State to sanction of acts of torture.[291] This puts them in contrast to many other human rights which are mostly formulated as rights the individual has against the State rather than prohibitions whose violation results in criminal liability. Pursuant to Art. 4 (1) CAT, for example,

> '[e]ach State Party shall ensure that all acts of torture are offences under its criminal law'. Furthermore, State Parties are obliged to make torture, as well as the attempt to commit torture and the complicity in torture, punishable by 'appropriate penalties'.[292]

The Committee against Torture even goes as far as, in its contemporary jurisprudence, granting victims of torture a subjective right to have perpetrators of torture punished by appropriate penalties.[293] These considerations make the Trial Chambers' conclusion regarding the difference in nature of international human rights and international criminal law less convincing. Instead of concentrating on the perceived difference of the provisions prohibiting torture in human rights and international criminal law, the Trial Chamber could have easily found support for its position that torture does not necessarily require the involvement of a State official. The ICCPR, for

---

291 See explicitly on the CAT *Questions on the Obligation to Prosecutoe or Extradite (Belgium v Senegal)* [2012] ICJ Rep 422 CAT para 95: 'prosecution is an international obligation under the Convention, the violation of which is a wrongful act engaging the responsibility of the State'.

292 Art. 4 (2) CAT.

293 UN Committee against Torture 'Decision 212/2002, *Guridi v Spain*' (24 May 2005) UN Doc CAT/C/34/D/212/2002 para 6.7: 'With regard to the alleged violation of article 4, the Committee recalls its previous jurisprudence to the effect that one of the purposes of the Convention is to avoid allowing persons who have committed acts of torture to escape unpunished. The Committee also recalls that article 4 sets out a duty for States parties to impose appropriate penalties against those held responsible for committing acts of torture, taking into account the grave nature of those acts. The Committee considers that, in the circumstances of the present case, the imposition of lighter penalties and the granting of pardons to the civil guards are incompatible with the duty to impose appropriate punishment. The Committee further notes that the civil guards were not subject to disciplinary proceedings while criminal proceedings were in progress, though the seriousness of the charges against them merited a disciplinary investigation. Consequently, the Committee considers that there has been a violation of article 4, paragraph 2, of the Convention.' With the same reasoning, a violation of Art. 4 (1) CAT would trigger a subjective right to a victim of torture under the CAT; see Manfred Nowak and Elisabeth McArthur *The United Nations Convention against Torture: A Commentary* (OUP Oxford 2008) 250–52.

example, does not contain any State official requirement. The HRC stated in its General Comment No. 20:

'It is the duty of the State party to afford everyone protection through legislative and other measures as may be necessary against the acts prohibited by article 7, whether inflicted by people acting in their official capacity, outside their official capacity or in a private capacity.[294]'

The CAT, by including the term 'other person acting in an official capacity' does also not restrict torture per definition to State officials. The phrasing opens the definition up to de facto authorities like rebel, guerrilla and insurgent groups.[295]

Hence the court in *Kunarac* contradicted the chamber in *Delalić* leading to the paradoxical result that within one and the same tribunal, torture as a crime under international law is punishable pursuant to different requirements: according to one Chamber, the perpetrator has to be a State official or acting with the consent or acquiescence of one, for another chamber, this requirement is not part of the definition of torture under international criminal law.

Nevertheless, the *Kunarac* approach is more convincing than the trial chamber's approach in *Delalic. Delalic* uses the ECtHR/ECommHR jurisprudence not for the definition of torture itself, but in order to fill the gap which the definition that the court deems to constitute customary international law, leaves open. *Kunarac*, on the other hand, uses other jurisprudence already on the level of the definition itself, in order to find out whether the CAT definition constitutes customary international law.

The Kunarac approach is methodologically more convincing as it examines the definitions used in other jurisdictions already in order to determine if the CAT definition is customary law. This makes sense, as the definitions of other instruments and the jurisprudence based on these can point to the existence (or the absence) of State practice and *opinio iuris*. In contrast it is not convincing to first claim that a certain definition is part of customary international law and to then subsequently use the jurisprudence of completely different bodies governed by a distinct treaty, in order to fill the holes that this definition leaves.

294 UN HRC 'General Comment No 20: Replaces General Comment 7 concerning Prohibition of Torture and Cruel Treatment or Punishment (Art. 7)' (3 April 1992) GAOR 47th Session Supp 40, 193 para. 2.

295 Manfred Nowak and Elisabeth McArthur *The United Nations Convention against Torture: A Commentary* (OUP Oxford 2008) 78–79.

Nevertheless, it is evidentially worrisome that the lack of a common dogmatic approach and a streamlined interpretation of the specific elements of the crimes over which the ICTY has jurisdiction lead to such an unequal application of the law.

g. Brđanin

In the aftermath of the *Kunarac* judgment, *Brđanin* employed the progressive nature of customary international law as an argument.[296] Having been convicted of the aiding and abetting of torture, *Brđanin*'s defense council argued on appeal that the definition of torture under customary international law had changed since the *Kurnarac* and *Furundžija* judgments and the threshold of pain to qualify as torture now had to be significantly higher. In defense of his arguments, he cited the so-called Bybee Memorandum of the Bush Administration according to which '[p]hysical pain amounting to torture must be equivalent in intensity to the pain accompanying serious physical injury such as organ failure, impairment of bodily function, or even death'.[297] This is an interesting invoking of instant custom by way of reference to legal memoranda of a single State. In its own argumentation, the Appeals Chamber emphasized the consistent reliance of the ICTY on the definition of the torture convention and rejected the notion that a change in custom can be the automatic consequence of the State practice of only one State 'no matter how powerful or influential'.[298] It also dismissed the argument by reference to the drafting history of the CAT that showed that the drafters of the CAT sought to distinguish 'severe pain and suffering' from 'extreme pain and suffering' which requires a higher threshold and argues that ECtHR and other institutions, have endorsed the definition of the CAT. Whereas these are convincing arguments from a human rights point of view, the Appeal Chamber does not explain why the same arguments should be valid in the context of international criminal

296 *Prosecutor v Brđanin (Appeal Judgment)* ICTY-99-36-A (3 April 2007) paras 244-252.

297 US Department of Justice, Office of Legal Counsel 'Memorandum for Alberto R. Gonzales, Counsel to the President Re: Standard of Conduct for Interrogation under 18 U.S.C. §§ 2340-2340A' (1 August 2002) https://www.aclu.org (31 October 2017) 1.

298 *Prosecutor v Brđanin (Appeal Judgment)* ICTY-99-36-A (3 April 2007) para. 247.

law and the fact that a definition has been repeatedly employed by authorities in international human rights law should have automatic effect on the development of a crime under international criminal law. Here, it would have been more convincing if the court left it at referring to the limited number of parties which endorsed that definition and not mixed human rights law and international criminal law at random and in a dogmatically unsound manner.

2. The Definition of 'Other Inhumane Acts'

Pursuant to Art 5 (i) ICTY Statute and Art 3 (i) ICTR Statute, 'other inhuman acts' are punishable as crimes against humanity. Art. 7 (1) (k) Rome Statute contains a qualifying clause describing as punishable '[o]ther inhumane acts of a similar character intentionally causing great suffering, or serious injury to body or to mental or physical health'. The blueprint for this kind of vague catchall provision can be traced back to the Nuremberg Charter, which listed 'murder, extermination, enslavement, deportation, and other inhumane acts committed against any civilian population, before and during the war' under crimes against humanity.[299]

Determining the exact content of 'inhumane acts' can be more laborious than the definition of many other crimes under international law as the term is particularly vague and the definition of the adjective 'inhumane' involves a value judgment to a greater degree than it may be the case in many other crimes.

299 The Nuremburg Charter further mentioned persecution of on racial, political or religious grounds as a crime against humanity, albeit only in execution of or connection to any other crime under the jurisdiction of the Tribunal; Charter of the [Nuremberg] International Military Tribunal (8 August 1945) 82 UNTS 284; Inhumane acts were also listed in Art. 2 (1) (c) Control Council Law No10 ('Punishment of Persons Guilty of War Crimes, Crimes against Peace and against Humanity' [done 20 December 1945] [1946] 3 Official Gazette of the Control Council for Germany 50), Art. 5 (c) Charter of the International Military Tribunal for the Far East [19 January 1946] 4 Bevans 20) and Prinicple VI (c) Principles of International Law Recognized in the Charter of the Nuremberg Tribunal and the Judgment of the Tribunal UNILC 'Report on Principles of the Nuremberg Tribunal' (29 July 1950) GAOR 5th session Supp 12, 11 (Nuremberg Principles); see further Machtheld Boot, Rodney Dixon and Christopher K Hall 'Article 7: Crimes against Humanity' in Otto Triffterer *Commentary on the Rome Statute of the International Criminal Court* (2nd edition Beck Munich 2008) 159-273, 230.

The qualification contained in Art. 7 (1) (k) Rome Statute as well as the Elements of Crime of 'other inhumane acts' clarify that the inhumane acts have to be of a similar character to the other crimes against humanity listed, meaning they must reach a similar degree of seriousness. This is the result of a line of jurisprudence that already started with *Tadić* which stated that 'other inhumane acts", must consist of acts inflicted upon a human being and must be of a serious nature.'[300] The *Tadić* Chamber also cited the ILC Draft Code of Crimes against the Peace and Security of Mankind, which contains a similar reference to the required gravity of the acts, as well as a second requirement, namely the that acts 'the act must in fact cause injury to a human being in terms of physical or mental integrity, health or human dignity.'[301]

In the *Kupreskic* judgment, the Court delved deeper into defining what sort of acts were to be considered inhuman. In doing so, it takes recourse to human rights law. The Court examines the UDHR as well as the two covenants and concludes that there is a set of acts which are prohibited in these instruments which can be characterised as inhumane acts and prosecuted as crimes against humanity in the case the chapeau requirements are fulfilled.[302] Examples that the Court mentions are 'serious forms of cruel or degrading treatment of persons belonging to a particular ethnic, religious, political or racial group, or serious widespread or systematic manifestations of cruel or humiliating or degrading treatment with a discriminatory or persecutory intent' or forcible transfer of civilians.[303] There are several problems with this approach: first, the Court does not clarify what the category of inhume treatments adds in the case, for example, of degrading of persons belonging to a specific ethnic group with persecutorial intent. Why are those acts not simply prosecuted as persecution? Second,

---

300 *Prosecutor v Tadić (Opinion and Judgment)* IT-94-1 (7 May 1997) para 728; see also Stakic,in which counts of inhumane acts as crimes against humanity were dismissed as the chamber was not convinced that the acts in question had reached the necessary gravity: *Prosecutor v Stakić (Judgment)* IT-97-24-T (31 July 2003) para 723.

301 UN ILC 'Draft Code of Crimes against the Peace and Security of Mankind' (1996) GAOR 51st Session Supp 10, 9, 103; *Prosecutor v Tadić (Opinion and Judgment)* IT-94-1 (7 May 1997) para 729.

302 *Prosecutor v Kupreškić (Trial Chamber Judgment)* IT-95-16 (14 January 2000) para 566.

303 *Prosecutor v Kupreškić (Trial Chamber Judgment)* IT-95-16 (14 January 2000) para 566.

when seeking to define what inhumane acts in fact are, the court applies formulas, like 'cruel and degrading treatment' which are just as vague and in need of interpretation as 'inhumane acts' is. The Court ignores there that there is an elaborate discourse, at the ICTY and beyond, on how to fill, for example 'cruel and degrading treatment' with meaning and narrow it down to specific acts. Third, the court mentions the UDHR, the ICCPR and the ICESCR, but then, when enlisting the acts which, in its opinion, constitute other inhumane acts, takes as examples the ICCPR, the CAT, the ECHR and the IACHR or from rules of humanitarian law. It also makes no mention why the prohibitions enshrined in these instruments should be applicable at all to the ICTY. As such, it gives the impression that the Court merely uses these instruments as buzzwords rather than engaging with them on a dogmatic level in order to deduce the meaning of the term 'inhumane treatment'. Lastly and intertwined with the earlier remark, the court uses no dogmatically coherent methodology to fill the term 'inhumane acts' with meaning. The Court states that cruel and degrading treatment is prohibited by certain instruments and that a certain act constitutes cruel and degrading treatment, albeit without referencing back to any of the instruments mentioned. As such, the Court pays lip service to human rights law and basically uses it as a backup for its preconceived notion that a certain action, which ought to be punishable fits under vague formula by substituting it with a different vague formula. As with torture, in the case of inhumane acts, human rights law is referenced in an incoherent way which fails to take into account the need for justification as to why it is applicable in the first place.

II. Where Could the Prohibition of Torture Have Been Referred to?

When it comes to torture, the problem lies in how it was referenced and the incoherence in the determination of customary international law. This lack of a coherent, common dogmatic approach can lead to practical inequality in the application of the law as seen in the cases of *Delalić* and *Kunarac*, where the respective chambers came to different conclusions regarding the State official requirement in the definition of torture.[304] Un-

304 *Prosecutor v Delalić et al (Judgment)* IT-96-21 (16 November 1998) para. 473 and *Prosecutor v Kunarac (Judgment)* IT-96-23 (22 February 2001) paras 488–96; see Part Two Chapter One 1 b. and f. above.

derlying the prohibition of torture is the CAT, a high-profile, 'robust'and widely ratified convention.[305] The prohibition torture is a part of *ius cogens*, and as such, emanates authority like not many other concepts in international human rights, which are, at times, dominated by vague terms, soft law or reluctant ratification practice. Furthermore, the system of the prohibition of torture in itself is coherent, particularly compared to other areas of human rights law. Where is the Link?

1. State Obligations Regarding the Prohibition of Torture under Human Rights Law

a) CAT

The CAT is the primary international instrument prohibiting torture and other cruel, inhuman or degrading treatment or punishment. It was adopted in 1984 and contains the most often quoted and referred to definition of torture. According to Art. 1 (1) CAT

> '[f]or the purposes of this Convention, torture means any act by which severe pain or suffering, whether physical or mental, is intentionally inflicted on a person for such purposes as obtaining from him or a third person information or a confession, punishing him for an act he or a third person has committed or is suspected of having committed, or intimidating or coercing him or a third person, or for any reason based on discrimination of any kind, when such pain or suffering is inflicted by or at the instigation of or with the consent or acquiescence of a public official or other person acting in an official capacity. It does not include pain or suffering arising only from, inherent in or incidental to lawful sanctions'.

Apart from providing for a comprehensive definition, from an international criminal law perspective, the CAT provides a number of relevant provisions. Arts 5–7 provides for universal jurisdiction in cases of torture.[306]

---

305 The CAT has 162 parties as of November 2017.

306 This means that the value protected by the CAT was seen by its drafters as so important that no connection in terms of territory, offer or victim is needed in order to prosecute the violation of said value. This places a double obligation on the States bound by the CAT: they have to make the violation of the prohibition of torture a crime enforceable in their national courts and effectively prosecute offenders when they have the possibility to do so; see further eg Rüdiger Wolfrum 'The Decentralized Prosecution of International Offences Through National

Art. 5 (2) incorporates the principle of *aut dedere aut iudicare* into the CAT framework. Additionally, Art. 17 CAT establishes, its treaty body, the Committee against Torture, which receives and reviews individual communications as well as State reports. Its definition of torture in Article 1 is a standard-setting tool for interpreting other instruments that do not contain a definition and, as demonstrated above,[307] it us frequently consulted to determine the customary definition of torture.[308]

The General Comments of Committee against Torture are not particularly helpful for international courts and Tribunals. Apart from the fact that it has only issued three general comments between 1998 and 2017, these deal with issues that do not concern international criminal law, like *non-refoulment* and the right to redress and rehabilitation for victims. Only General Comment No 1 on the implementation of Article 2 CAT, which sets out the absolute and non-derogable prohibition of torture could have been useful, albeit it was only published in 2008, when much of the problems surrounding the definition and the character of the prohibition of torture were already solved by the tribunals, at least to a degree that they simply relied on each other's previous decisions.[309]

b) Universal Declaration of Human Rights

The Universal Declaration prohibits torture under Art. 5, albeit without defining what torture or cruel, inhuman and degrading treatment or punishment is. Interestingly, the Universal Declaration does not assume that torture, at the same time, always constitutes cruel, inhuman or degrading treatment or punishment, as it mentions the two in the alternative.

Courts' in Yoram Dinstein and Mala Tabory *War Crimes in International Law* (Martinus Nijhoff The Hague 1996) 233-249, 235-36.

307 See Part Two Chapter One I above.

308 Sandesh Sivakumaran 'Torture in International Human Rights and International Humanitarian Law: The Actor and the *Ad hoc* Tribunals' (2005) 18 Leiden Journal of International Law 541-556, 543.

309 UN Committee against Torture 'General Comment No 2: Implementation of Article 2 by States Parties' (24 January 2008) UN Doc CAT/C/GC/2.

c) International Covenant on Civil and Political Rights

The prohibition of torture is enshrined in Art. 7 ICCPR. It reads as follows:

> [n]o one shall be subjected to torture or to cruel, inhuman or degrading treatment or punishment. In particular, no one shall be subjected without his free consent to medical or scientific experimentation.

As such, Article 7 ICCPR does not contain its own definition of what torture is. It has, however, been clarified by the ICCPR's treaty body, the HRC, that torture requires an act that intentionally inflicts severe physical or mental pain or suffering to fulfill a certain purpose, such as extortion of information or confessions, as punishment, intimidation or discrimination of a person.[310] If any of the elements are missing, the action can still be characterized as cruel, inhuman or degrading treatment.[311] Unlike under the CAT, torture under the ICCPR can also be inflicted on a horizontal level.[312] According to Art. 4 (2) ICCPR, no derogation from this provision is possible during a state of emergency. In its General Comment No 20, the HRC stated that prolonged solitary confinement can amount to a violation of Art. 7 ICCPR.[313] It has also held that longer periods of *incommunicado* detention amount to cruel and inhuman treatment; more than three years of incommunicado detention can be classified as torture.[314] As a universal

310 Manfred Nowak U. N. Covenant on Civil and Political Rights: CCPR Commentary (N P Engel Kehl 2005); see also Manfred Nowak and Elisabeth McArthur The United Nations Convention against Torture: A Commentary (OUP Oxford 2008) 39-41.

311 Manfred Nowak U. N. Covenant on Civil and Political Rights: CCPR Commentary (N P Engel Kehl 2005), 161, 163.

312 Manfred Nowak U. N. Covenant on Civil and Political Rights: CCPR Commentary (N P Engel Kehl 2005) 161.

313 UN HRC 'General Comment No 20: Replaces General Comment 7 concerning Prohibition of Torture and Cruel Treatment or Punishment (Art. 7)' (3 April 1992) GAOR 47th Session Supp 40, 193 para. 6; see also UN HRC Communication 'No 577/1994 *Polaly Campos v Peru*' (6 November 1997) UN Doc CCPR/C/61/D/577/1994 para 9.

314 See eg UN HRC 'Communication No 1780/2008, *Aouabdia v. Algeria*' (22 March 2011) UN Doc CCPR/C/101/D/1780/2008; UN HRC 'Communication No 1640/2007, *El Abani v The Libyan Arab Jamahiriya*' (26 July 2010) UN Doc CCPR/C/99/D/1640/2007; UN HRC 'Communication No 1588/2007, *Benaziza v. Algeria* (26 July 2010) UN Doc CCPR/C/99/D/1588/2007; UN HRC 'Communication No 1295/2004, *El Awani v. The Libyan Arab Jamahiriya*, (11 July 2007)

and not merely a regional instrument, referring to the ICCPR and, in particular, the sophisticated 'jurisprudence' of its HRC can be immensely useful for the ICC in order to raise the legal weight of the judgment and the credibility of the court as a global and not merely a 'Western' or European institution.

d) Other Instruments Prohibiting Torture

The ECHR prohibits torture pursuant to Article 3. It states '[n]o one shall be subjected to torture or to inhuman or degrading treatment or punishment'. Article 15 (2) ECHR, at the same time, emphasizes the importance of the prohibition of torture by proclaiming it one of the absolute, non-derogable rights. The Inter-American Convention follows the pattern of the ICCPR and the ECHR by providing for the prohibition of torture in Article 5 (2) (without defining acts of torture) while, in Art 27 (2) IACHR declaring that a derogation from the prohibition is not possible. Article 5 ACHPR combines the prohibition of torture with the prohibition of slavery and puts these two in systemic relation with the dignity of person. Article 5 ACHPR reads '[e]very individual shall have the right to the respect of the dignity inherent in a human being and to the recognition of his legal status. All forms of exploitation and degradation of man particularly slavery, slave trade, torture, cruel, inhuman or degrading punishment and treatment shall be prohibited.' Other regional thematic convention solely dedicated to the prohibition of torture are the European Convention for the Prevention of Torture and Inhuman or Degrading Treatment or Punishment[315] and the Inter-American Convention to Prevent and Punish Torture, which contains a substantially similar definition of torture.[316] The European Convention for the Prevention of Torture and Inhuman or Degrading Treatment or Punishment focuses on the prevention of torture by establishing a European Commission for the Prevention which, similar to the UN

CCPR/C/90/D/1295/2004, para. 6.5; communication No. 1422/2005; UN HRC 'Communication No. 458/1991, *Womah Mukong v Cameroon*' (21 July 1994) UN Doc. CCPR/C/51/D/458/1991, para. 9.4.

315 COE 'European Convention for the Prevention of Torture and Inhuman or Degrading Treatment or Punishment' (done 26 November 1987, entered into force 1 February 1989) 1561 UNTS 363.

316 Inter-American Convention to Prevent and Punish Torture (done 9 December 1985, entered into force 28 February 1987) (1986) 25 ILM 519.

Committee against Torture, also monitors the treatment of incarcerated persons. In contrast, the Inter-American Convention to Prevent and Punish Torture goes further than that and again affirms the status of the prohibition of torture as an absolute prohibition under the penalty of law.

Hence, it is obvious that there are a number of instruments of international human rights law international Courts and Tribunals can draw from when adjudicating torture

2. The Prohibition of Torture under International Criminal Law

Acts of torture can be subsumed under different crimes under international law, and can constitute genocide, crimes against humanity and war crimes. All crimes will be discussed as laid out in the Rome Statute as the prime instrument governing the permanent ICC of the future. In case of differing definitions in any of the *ad hoc* or the hybrid courts, these differences will be pointed out.

a) Genocide

(1) Causing serious bodily or mental harm (Art. 6 (b) Rome Statute)

Under the definition of genocide in the Genocide Convention, which has been taken on by the statutes of the *ad hoc* tribunals as well as the Rome Statute, and are reflective of customary international law,[317] there are several modalities under which actions constituting torture under human rights law can also be prosecuted as genocide. Art. 6 (b) Rome Statute (Art. II (b) Genocide Convention) states that genocide can be committed by 'causing serious bodily or mental harm to members of the group' as long as the *mens rea*, the intent to destroy, in whole or in part, a national, ethnical, racial or religious group, is given. The wording 'serious bodily or mental harm' reminds of Art. 1 (1) CAT which refers to 'severe pain or suffering, whether physical or mental'. Footnote 3 to the respective element in the ICC's Elements of Crimes (Element 1 of Art. 6 (b) Rome

317 *Application of the Convention on the Prevention and Punishment of the Crime of Genocide (Bosnia and Herzegovina v Serbia and Montenegro) (Merits)* ([2007] ICJ Rep 43 para. 161.

Statute) expressively states 'this conduct [the perpetrator caused serious bodily or mental harm to one or more persons] may include, but is not restricted to, acts of torture, rape, sexual violence or inhuman or degrading treatment'.[318]

The only difference in the two definitions is 'serious harm.' It could, interpreted literally, refer to a permanent damage in comparison to 'pain or suffering'. However, two arguments can be brought forward against such an assumption. First, the ICTR has clarified in its jurisprudence that '[c]ausing serious bodily or mental harm to members of the group does not necessarily mean that the harm is permanent and irremediable'.[319] And second the definition of the word 'harm' in the English language merely refers to '[e]vil (physical or otherwise) as done to or suffered by some person or thing; hurt, injury, damage, mischief'.[320] Genocidal intent, hence the intent to destroy, in whole or in part, a national, ethnical, racial or religious group' is not a purpose of torture *per se*. However, the intent to destroy a group requires a discriminatory intent, which is prohibited under Art. 1 (1) CAT. Furthermore, the prohibited intent does not have to be the only purpose for which the severe pain or suffering is inflicted. The perpetrator can have other motivations apart from the ones listed in the CAT. Hence torture inflicted with genocidal intent constitutes genocide.[321] The relation between genocide by inflicting serious bodily or mental harm and torture is also underlined in the first report on torture by the UN Special Rapporteur.[322] The same is true for cruel, inhuman or degrading treatment or punishment which is committed fulfilling the *mens rea* of genocide. As cruel, inhuman or degrading treatment or punishment can be defined as

---

318 Elements of Crimes (adopted and entered into force 9 September 2002) Doc ICC-ASP/1/3 (Pt. II-B), footnote 3.

319 *Prosecutor v Akayesu (Judgment)* ICTR-96-4-T (2 September 1998).para. 502; see also *Prosecutor v Kayishema and others (Judgment)* ICTR-95-1-T (21 May 1999) para. 108; *Prosecutor v Rutaganda (Judgment)* ICTR-96-3-T (6 December 1999) para. 51; *Prosecutor v Gacumbitsi (Judgment)* ICTR-01-64-T (17 June 2004) para. 291.

320 Oxford English Dictionary www.oed.com/view/th/class/83601 (31 October 2017).

321 So eg *Prosecutor v Stakić (Judgment)* IT-97-24-T (31 July 2003) para. 516; *Application of the Convention on the Prevention and Punishment of the Crime of Genocide (Bosnia and Herzegovina v Serbia and Montenegro) (Merits)* ([2007] ICJ Rep 43 paras 291-297; 319.

322 UN Commission on Human Rights 'Torture and other Cruel, Inhuman or Degrading Treatment or Punishment: Report by the Special Rapporteur, Mr. P. Kooij-

'the infliction of severe pain or suffering, whether physical or mental, by or at the instigation of or consent or acquiescence of a public official or another person acting in an official capacity. Such conduct can be both intentional or negligent, with or without a particular purpose', [323]

For the crime of genocide, universal jurisdiction is recognized, even if not explicitly provided for in the Genocide Convention.[324]

(2) Deliberately inflicting on the group conditions of life calculated to bring about its physical destruction in whole or in part (Art. 6 (c) Rome Statute)

The prime example for this modality of genocide is deportation.[325] However, there are other actions which fulfil the *actus rea* of 'deliberately inflicting on the group conditions of life calculated to bring about its physical destruction in whole or in part'. These might be, for example 'placing a group of people on a subsistence diet, reducing required medical services'.[326] These are techniques which, according to the ECommHR and the ECtHR can amount to torture, or at least constitute cruel, inhuman or degrading treatment, even more so if they are used simultaneously (see e.g. the *Ireland v United Kingdom* cases).[327] Generally, the denial of a person's basic needs can constitute torture when the required 'severe' thresh-

---

mans, appointed Pursuant to Commission on Human Rights resolution 1985/33' (19 February 1986) UN Doc E/CN.4/1986/15.
E/CN.4/1986/15 para. 26.

323 Manfred Nowak and Elisabeth McArthur *The United Nations Convention against Torture: A Commentary* (OUP Oxford 2008) 558.

324 Universal jurisdiction has also been recognized for crimes against humanity and war crimes, see Rüdiger Wolfrum 'Prosecution of International Crimes by International and National Criminal Courts: Concurring Jurisdiction' Studi di Diritto Internazionale in Onore di Gaetano Arangio-Ruiz vol 3 (Editoriale scientifica Naples 2004) 2199-2209, 2200.

325 UN ILC 'Report of the International Law Commission on the Work of Its Forty-Eighth Session' vol II part II UNYBILC 46.

326 William A Schabas 'Article 6: Genocide' in O Triffterer *Commentary on the Rome Statute of the International Criminal Court* (2nd edition Beck Munich 2008) 143-157, 153.

327 See also UN Department of Economic and Social Affairs 'Study on the right of everyone to be free from arbitrary arrest, detention and exile' (1965) UN Doc E/CN.4/826/Rev. 1.see already in 1965 (even though this interpretation was attributed to the 'broad' definition.).

old is reached.[328] The ICJ has also included encirclement, shelling and starvation as examples of ways to deliberately inflict conditions of life calculated to bring about a group's physical destruction in whole or in part and ruled that these actions constitute genocide when they are accompanied with the necessary genocidal intent.[329]

(3) Imposing measures intended to prevent births within the group (Art. 6 (d) Rome Statute)

This modality of committing genocide covers acts such as '[forced] sterilization, compulsory abortion, segregation of the sexes and obstacles to marriage'.[330]

The Special Rapporteur on Torture has repeatedly mentioned sterilization conducted without informed consent and compulsory abortions within his mandate[331] and suggested that countries should review their anti-torture legislation in relation to these actions.[332]

---

328 J Herman Burgers and Hans Danelius *The United Nations Convention against Torture: A Handbook on the Convention against Torture and Other Cruel, Inhuman or Degrading Treatment or Punishment* (Nijhoff Dordrecht 1988) 118.

329 *Application of the Convention on the Prevention and Punishment of the Crime of Genocide (Bosnia and Herzegovina v Serbia and Montenegro) (Merits)* ([2007] ICJ Rep 43 paras 323-328.

330 William A Schabas 'Article 6' in Otto Triffterer *Commentary on the Rome Statute of the International Criminal Court* (2nd edition Beck Munich 2008) 1143-157, 53, with reference to the travaux préparatoires of Art. II para. d Genocide Convention.

331 Eg UN Committee against Torture 'Consideration of Reports Submitted by States Parties under Article 19 of the Convention: Conclusions and Recommendations of the Committee against Torture: China (12 December 2008) UN Doc CAT/C/CHN/CO/4 para. 29.

332 See eg UNGA 'Interim report of the Special Rapporteur on torture and other cruel, inhuman or degrading treatment or punishment' (22 July 2008) UN Doc A/63/175 paras 40–41.

b) Crimes against Humanity

(1) Torture (Art. 7 (1) (f) Rome Statute)

Torture has been recognized as a war crime since the 19th century.[333] Additionally, it was mentioned at the report of the Commission of the Responsibility of the Authors of the War and the Enforcement of Penalties as an example of a violation of the 'laws against humanity', albeit under the heading 'violations of the laws and customs of war'.[334] The Allied Control Council Law No 10 explicitly mentioned torture as a crime against humanity.[335] As the prohibition of torture is commonly held to be a part of *ius cogens*,[336] it is also uncontroversial under international criminal law, particularly as a crime against humanity and a war crime. What remains in dispute, as shown above, is rather the definition of the term torture for the purposes of the two crimes.[337]

In contrast to the ICTY and the ICTR Statutes, the Rome Statute provides for a definition of torture as a crime against humanity under Art. 7 (2) (e). It reads

> '"torture" means the intentional infliction of severe pain and suffering, whether physical or mental, upon a person in custody or under the control of the accused; except that torture shall not include pain of suffering arising from, inherent in or incidental to, lawful sanctions'.

This differs in various respects from the definition of torture under human rights law. The most conspicuous difference is that the Rome Statute does not refer to a purpose to be pursued with the infliction of pain and suffering.[338] This is explicitly stated in the Elements of Crimes for torture as a

---

333 See Part Two Chapter One III. 2 c) below.

334 Commission of the Responsibility of the Authors of the War and the Enforcement of Penalties 'Report Presented to the Preliminary Peace Conference' (March 1919) (1920) 14 AJIL 95–154, 113.

335 Control Council Law No 10 'Punishment of Persons Guilty of War Crimes, Crimes against Peace and against Humanity' (done 20 December 1945) (1946) 3 Official Gazette of the Control Council for Germany 50.

336 See, with further references, Malcolm N Shaw *International Law* (6th edition CUP Cambridge 2008) 326.

337 See Part Two Chapter One I. 1.

338 Machtheld Boot, Rodney Dixon and Christopher K Hall 'Article 7: Crimes against Humanity' in Otto Triffterer Commentary on the Rome Statute of the International Criminal Court (2nd edition Beck Munich 2008) 159-273, 254-5-.

crime against humanity. The respective footnote reads '[i]t is understood that no specific purpose need be proved for this crime'.[339] This could mean an extension of the acts to be qualified as torture. However, the emphasis of no 'specific' purpose being necessary could, in a logical *argumentum e contrario*, also be interpreted in a way that Art. 7 Rome Statute requires some sort of purpose and indeed the footnote is said to have been introduced as such as the result of a political compromise.[340] The Elements of Crimes also clarify that the question whether the pain or suffering reached the threshold of 'severe' pain of suffering is to be determined objectively and, hence, does not depend on the value-judgment of the accused. The Elements of Crimes clarify that '[w]ith respect to mental elements associated with elements involving value judgment, such as those using the terms "inhumane" or "severe", it is not necessary that the perpetrator personally completed a particular value judgment, unless otherwise indicated'.[341] Therefore, 'knowledge', which generally constitutes a necessary part of the mental element required for criminal liability under Art. 30 (1) Rome Statute, is not required when it comes to torture. It is enough that an accuse person indented to inflict severe pain or suffering.[342] The waiving of the requirement of knowledge is also a result of the criteria established by the ICTY jurisprudence which has been discussed above, in particular *Kunarac* and *Furundžija*.[343]

As such, the Rome Statute stands in explicit contradiction to the way intent was understood by the US Department of Justice during the Bush Administration. In their memorandum of 1 August 2002, Assistant Attorney General Jay S. Bybee and Deputy Assistant Attorney General John Yoo interpret the US reservation to the CAT according to which an act must 'specifically intended to inflict severe physical or mental pain or suf-

339 Elements of Crimes (adopted and entered into force 9 September 2002) Doc ICC-ASP/1/3 (Pt. II-B) Footnote 14.

340 Machtheld Boot, Rodney Dixon and Christopher K Hall 'Article 7: Crimes against Humanity' in Otto Triffterer Commentary on the Rome Statute of the International Criminal Court (2nd edition Beck Munich 2008) 159-273, 255.

341 Elements of Crimes (adopted and entered into force 9 September 2002) Doc ICC-ASP/1/3 (Pt. II-B) General Introduction para. 4.

342 See Machtheld Boot, Rodney Dixon and Christopher K Hall in 'Article 7: Crimes against Humanity' in Otto Triffterer *Commentary on the Rome Statute of the International Criminal Court* (2nd edition Beck Munich 2008) 159-273, 252.

343 *Prosecutor v Kunarac (Judgment)* IT-96-23 (22 February 2001) para. 483; *Prosecutor v Furundžija (Appeal Judgment)* IT-95-17/1-A (21 July 2000) para. 111.

fering' in order to commit torture, to mean that the infliction of severe pain 'must be the defendant's precise objective.'[344]

Furthermore, there is no requirement of the pain of suffering being inflicted by a State official. However, and this is also in contrast to the ICTY jurisprudence which denied the requirement of an involvement of a State official for charges of torture as a war crime, Art. 7 Rome Statute does already include in its chapeau element the requirement that the attack against any civilian population has to be conducted 'in furtherance of a State or organizational policy' (Art. 7 (2) (a) Rome Statute). This provides for a rather high threshold for cases of crimes against humanity in general, and does also apply in cases of torture as a crime against humanity.

The requirement 'upon a person in custody or under the control of the accused' is also not explicitly included in the CAT definition of torture. However, it is clear from both the drafting history of the CAT and the Torture Declaration and the jurisprudence of the human rights treaty bodies, that one of the characterizing elements of torture is the helplessness of the victim and, necessarily, the control that the perpetrator has over the victim. Therefore, this element does not add a new requirement to the definition of torture.

(2) Rape, sexual slavery, enforced prostitution, forced pregnancy, enforced sterilization, or any other form of sexual violence of comparable gravity (Art. 7 (1) (g) Rome Statute)

These modalities of crimes against humanity are discussed in detail in Chapter Three below.

(3) Enforced disappearance of persons (Art. 7 (1) (i) Rome Statute)

Forced disappearance, which had been associated in particular with dictatorial regimes in Latin America in the 1970s and 1980s, has been addressed as a human rights problem separate from the prohibition of arbi-

---

344 US Department of Justice, Office of Legal Counsel 'Memorandum for Alberto R. Gonzales, Counsel to the President Re: Standard of Conduct for Interrogation under 18 U.S.C. §§ 2340-2340A' (1 August 2002) https://www.aclu.org (last accessed 1 Ocotober 2015) 3.

trary arrest by a number of international instruments and treaty bodies/courts. The UNGA, in 1992, adopted the Declaration on the Protection of All Persons from Forced Disappearance in 1992.[345] Two years later, the Organization of American States adopted a regional convention addressing forced disappearance.[346] Finally, in 2006, the UNGA adopted the International Convention on the Protection of All Persons from Forced Disappearance ('Forced Disappearance Convention').[347]

According to Art. 2 Forced Disappearance Convention, forced disappearance means

> 'the arrest, detention, abduction or any other form of deprivation of liberty by agents of the State or by persons or groups of persons acting with the authorization, support or acquiescence of the State, followed by a refusal to acknowledge the deprivation of liberty or by concealment of the fate or whereabouts of the disappeared person, which place such a person outside the protection of the law'.

The definition used in the Rome Statute is slightly different, but nevertheless contains all the elements set out in the Forced Disappearance Convention.

Like torture, forced disappearance is hence characterized by the helplessness of the victim and the complete control which the perpetrator exercises over the victim. Particular to cases of forced disappearance is that the State will not even acknowledge its responsibility for the person's arrest or his or her detention. This does naturally increase the risk of ill-treatment during detention, as, at the same time, the risk of the State being held accountable for ill-treatment decreases.

However, not only does forced disappearance and *incommunicado* detention increase the risk of torture, it can amount to torture itself. Already in 1981, the *Institut des droits de l'homme Du Barreau de Paris* issued a draft declaration in which it stated that forced disappearance undermines the 'physical, psychological and moral integrity or security of any per-

345 UNGA Res 47/133 'Declaration on the Protection of All Persons from Enforced Disappearance' (18 December 1992) GAOR 47th Session Supp 49 vol 1, 207.

346 Inter-American Convention on Forced Disappearance of Persons (done 9 June 1994, entered into force 28 March 1996) (1994) 33 ILM 1529.

347 International Convention for the Protection of All Persons from Enforced Disappearance (adopted 20 December 2006, entered into force 23 December 2010) GAOR 61st Session Supp 49 vol 1, 408.

son'.[348] In 1983, the UN Working Group on Enforced and Involuntary Disappearances stated in its report that '[t]he very fact of being detained as a disappeared person, isolated from one's family for a long period is certainly a violation of the right to humane conditions of detention and has been represented to the Group as torture'.[349] The HRC has mentioned *incommunicado* detention in its General Comment No 20 concerning prohibition of torture and cruel treatment or punishment and urged State Parties to enforce provisions against this sort of detention, to hold detainees only in official places of detention and to keep a register with the place and the person responsible for detention publicly accessible to relatives and friends of a detained person.[350] If this is not the case, *incommunicado* detention can be qualified as cruel and inhuman treatment or even even as torture.

The HRC has furthermore held in an individual communication that the applicant 'by being subjected to prolonged incommunicado detention [for more than three years] in an unknown location, is the victim of torture and cruel and inhuman treatment'.[351] In other cases, the HRC has accepted claims regarding violations of Art. 7 in forced disappearance cases, albeit those claims were not based on forced disappearance alone, but were supported by claims of further ill-treatment during detention.[352] The IACtHR

---

348 *Le Refus de L'oubli: La Politique de Disparation Forcée de Personne*s (Editions Berger-Levrault Paris 1981) 313 (translation by the author.).

349 UN Commission on Human Rights 'Question of the Human Rights of All Persons Subject to any Form of Detention or Imprisonment: Question of Enforced or Involuntary Disappearances: Report of the Working Group on Enforced or Involuntary Disappearances' (21 January 1983) UN Doc E/CN.4/1983/14 para. 131.

350 UN HRC 'General Comment No 20: Replaces General Comment 7 concerning Prohibition of Torture and Cruel Treatment or Punishment (Art. 7)' (3 April 1992) GAOR 47th Session Supp 40, 193, para. 11; UN Commission on Human Rights 'Torture or other cruel, inhuman or degrading treatment or punishment' Res 2003/32 (2003) UN Doc E/CN.4/RES/2003/32 para. 14.

351 UN HRC 'Communication No 440/1990, *El-Megreisi v Libyan Arab Jamahiriya* (23 March 1994) UN Doc CCPR/C/50/D/440/1990 para. 5.4; UN HRC 'Communication No 540/1993, *Laureano Atachahua v Peru*' (26 March 1996) GAOR 51st Session Supp 40, vol 2, 42 para. 8.5.

352 eg UN HRC 'Communication No. 449/1991, *Mojica v Dominican Republic*' (5 July 1994) UN Doc CCPR/C/51/D/449/1991 para. 5.7; UN HRC 'Communication No. 458/1991, *Womah Mukong v Cameroon'* (21 July 1994) U.N. Doc. CCPR/C/51/D/458/1991 para. 9.4; UN HRC 'Communication No. 428/1990, *Bozize v Central African Republic*' (7 April 1994) UN Doc CCPR/C/50/D/

has also considered prolonged isolation and communication to be a violation of Art. 5 IACHR.[353]

Additionally, the ECtHR and the ECommHR have found violations of Art 3 ECHR regarding the relatives of 'disappeared' persons in Turkey[354] and the HRC has held that the pain and suffering experienced by a disappeared persons' family amounts to a violation of Art. 7 ICCPR.[355]

(5) Other inhumane acts of a similar character intentionally causing great suffering, or serious injury to body or to mental or physical health (Art. 7 (1) (k) Rome Statute)

The 1996 ILC Draft Code of Crimes against the Peace and Security of Mankind contains a differently framed wording of this catch-all provision, namely 'other inhuman acts which severely damage physical or mental integrity, health or human dignity, such as mutilation and severe bodily harm'.[356] Even though this addition was not included into the Rome Statute, it already shows that actions that fall under Art. 7 (1) (k) Rome Statute can also be actions which are in the proximity of torture.

It will be interesting to see what sorts of actions the ICC will subsume under this provision, as many of the acts which have been held by the *ad hoc* tribunals to constitute 'other inhumane acts', like for example enforced prostitution or other sexual violence, are explicitly listed in the Rome Statute as separate crimes. One of the possible acts which have been held to constitute both torture and inhumane acts already during the Nuremberg Medical Trial are biological, medical and scientific experi-

---

428/1990 para. 5.2; UN HRC 'Communication No. 950/2000, *Sarma v Sri Lanka*' (6 July 2003) UN Doc CCPR/C/78/D/950/2000 para. 9.5.

353 *Velasquez Rodriguez v Honduras (Judgment)* IACtHR Series C No 4 (29 July 1988) para. 156.

354 Eg *Cyprus v Turkey* (ECtHR) Reports 2001-IV 1 para. 157; *Kurt v Turkey* (ECtHR) Reports 1998-III 1152 paras 130–43.

355 UN HRC 'Communication No. 950/2000, *Sarma v Sri Lanka*' UN Doc CCPR/C/78/D/950/2000.para. 9.5.

356 Art. 18 (k) UN ILC 'Draft Code of Crimes against the Peace and Security of Mankind' (1996) GAOR 51st Session Supp 10, 9.

ments.[357] In the context of war crimes, biological, medical and scientific experiments are expressly punishable under Art. 8 (2) (a) (II) Rome Statute.

c) War Crimes

Within the context of war crimes, there are several provisions of the Rome Statute which prohibit torture under certain circumstances. As an in-depth analysis of the connections would go beyond the scope of this book, they are listed for the sake of completeness without further explanation.

(1) Grave breaches of the Geneva Conventions

- Torture or inhuman treatment, including biological experiments (Art. 8 (2) (a) (II) Rome Statute
- (1.2) Wilfully causing great suffering (Art. 8 (2) (a) (iii) Rome Statute

(2) Other serious violations of the laws and customs applicable in international armed conflict

- Subjecting persons who are in the power of an adverse party to physical mutilation or to medical or scientific experiments of any kind which are neither justified by the medical, dental or hospital treatment of the person concerned nor carried out in his or her interest, and which cause death to or seriously endanger the health of such person or persons (Art. 8 (2) (b) (x) Rome Statute)
- Committing outrages upon personal dignity, in particular humiliating and degrading treatment (Art. 8 (2) (b) (xxi) Rome Statue)
- Committing rape, sexual slavery, enforced prostitution, forced pregnancy, as defined in article 7, paragraph 2 (f), enforced sterilization, or any other form of sexual violence also constituting a grave breach of the Geneva Conventions (Art. 8 (2) (b) (xxii) Rome Statute)

---

357 See *Trials of War Criminals Before the Nuremberg Military Tribunals Under Control Council Law No 10* (US Government Printing Office Washington DC 1952) vol I 16, vol II 182.

- Intentionally using starvation of civilians as a method of warfare by depriving them of objects indispensable to their survival, including wilfully impeding relief supplies as provided for under the Geneva Conventions (Art. 8 (2) (b) (xxiii) Rome Statute)

(3) In the case of an armed conflict not of an international character, serious violations of article 3 common to the four Geneva Conventions

- Violence to life and person, in particular murder of all kinds, mutilation, cruel treatment and torture (Art. 8 (2) (c) (i) Rome Statute)
- Committing outrages upon personal dignity, in particular humiliating and degrading treatment (Art. 8 (2) (c) (ii) Rome Statute)

(4) Other serious violations of the laws and customs applicable in armed conflicts not of an international character, within the established framework of international law

- Committing rape, sexual slavery, enforced prostitution, forced pregnancy, as defined in article 7, paragraph 2 (f), enforced sterilization, and any other form of sexual violence also constituting a serious violation of article 3 common to the four Geneva Conventions (Art. 8 (2) (e) (vi) Rome Statute)
- Subjecting persons who are in the power of another party to the conflict to physical mutilation or to medical or scientific experiments of any kind which are neither justified by the medical, dental or hospital treatment of the person concerned nor carried out in his or her interest, and which cause death to or seriously endanger the health of such person or persons (Art. 8 (2) (e) (xi) Rome Statute)

IV. Concluding Remarks

In conclusion, it is clear that the *ad hoc* tribunals needed guidance on how to define torture and that the definition of the CAT was the most obvious place from which to seek said guidance. It is also clear that the tribunals were sympathetic towards the CAT definition and inclined to use it.

The reason for that is, at least partly, the well-established nature of the prohibition of torture in international law. It is is a well-known component of national, regional and international protection of the individual. The CAT is a high-profile convention with a high number of ratification. The prohibition torture is a part of *ius cogens*, and as such, it emanates authority and it is easily accessible. It is also mirrored by a prohibition of torture that can be found in many national legal systems.

However, one cannot fully agree with Judge Pocar's statement that 'over multiple judgments and with concerted deliberate effort, the ICTY has contributed significant value to international criminal jurisprudence through honing in on a concrete definition of torture under international humanitarian law'.[358] In the case of torture, one can observe frequent use in absence of a coherent methodology for said use. For one, the definitions applied by the different Trial and Appeals Chambers were not always congruent and, at times, were contradictory and mutually exclusive. And second, the dogmatic approaches applied, the extent to which international legal dogma was applied at all, varied so much between the different chambers that the overall record of the tribunals when it comes to a dogmatically convincing definition of torture for the purpose of international criminal and international humanitarian law can be labelled mixed at best.

Chapter Two: Minority Rights Law[359]

I. What is a Minority in the Context of Crimes under International Law?

The definition of the term 'minority' and the rights attached to minority status are often portrayed to be controversial.[360]

358 Fausto Pocar 'International Criminal Tribunals and Serious Violations of International Humanitarian Law against Civilians and Prisoners of War' in Manoj Kumar Sinha (ed) *International Criminal Law and Human Rights* (Manak Delhi 2010) 1-26, 12.

359 Chapter Two of this thesis is partly based and draws from on the author's master thesis entitled ‚A Race between Education and Catastophe? The Role of Minority Issues in the Prevention of Crimes under International Law' (Lund University 2006), available at http://lup.lub.lu.se/luur/download?func=downloadFile&recordOId=1555279&fileOId=1563606 (31 October 2017).

360 For the overview of minority rights in an historic context see Jost Delbrück and Rüdiger Wolfrum *Völkerrecht* Volume I/2: *Der Staat und andere Völker-*

The definition which is most often used and referred to traces back to a study by Francesco Capotorti, then Special Rapporteur of the Sub-Commission on Prevention of Discrimination and Protection of Minorities. According to Capotorti, a minority is defined as:

> A group numerically inferior to the rest of the population of a State, in a non-dominant position, whose members-being nationals of the State-possess ethnic, religious or linguistic characteristics differing from those of the rest of the population and show, if only implicitly, a sense of solidarity, directed towards preserving their culture, traditions, religion or language.[361]

In recent years, it has, however, been more and more disputed whether members of a minority need to be citizens of the State in which they invoke their rights as members of a minority group, especially because modern globalized societies with influx of migrants might require to grant minority protection also to non-citizens.[362] One argument in favour of the expansion of minority definition to so-called 'new minorities' is that otherwise it would be much easier for governments to exclude groups by simply denying them citizenship. Historically, and in particular under the League of Nations, the term 'minority' has been understood as applying only to citizens.[363] However, HRC stated that Art 27 ICCPR is applicable not only to State citizens, but also to aliens constituting a minority within

---

rechtssubjekte; Räume unter internationaler Verwaltung (2nd edition De Gruyter Berlin 2002) 271-3.

361 UN Commission on Human Rights Special Rapporteur of the Sub-Commission on Prevention of Discrimination and Protection of Minorities, Francesco Capotorti 'Study on the Rights of Persons belonging to ethnic, religious and linguistic minorities' (1979) UN Doc E/CN.4/Sub.2/384/Rev. 1 para 568; see also a detailed critical discussion of the elements of Capotorti's definition in Jost Delbrück and Rüdiger Wolfrum *Völkerrecht* Volume I/2: *Der Staat und andere Völkerrechtssubjekte; Räume unter internationaler Verwaltung* (2nd edition De Gruyter Berlin 2002), 276-281.

362 Manfred Nowak *U. N. Covenant on Civil and Political Rights: CCPR Commentary* (N. P Engel Kehl 2005) 647; see also Rüdiger Wolfrum '"New Minorities" as a Result of Migration' in Caterine Brölmann, Rene Lefeber and Marjoleine Zieck *Peoples and Minorities in International Law* (Nijhoff Dordrecht 1993) 153–166; Jost Delbrück and Rüdiger Wolfrum *Völkerrecht* Volume I/2: *Der Staat und andere Völkerrechtssubjekte; Räume unter internationaler Verwaltung* (2nd edition De Gruyter Berlin 2002) 278-9.

363 Manfred Nowak *U. N. Covenant on Civil and Political Rights: CCPR Commentary* (N. P Engel Kehl 2005) 645.

the meaning of the Covenant.[364] Art 27 itself does not hint at the exclusion of foreigners from its protection, as it only speaks of 'persons,' not 'citizens.' However, mostly due to political realities, it might not be realistic or sustainable to grant or demand instant minority protection to actual cases of recent arrivals in a country.[365]

No matter which definition is the most appropriate when it comes to granting individuals minority rights in the strict sense, "[t]he existence of [minority] communities is a question of fact; it is not a question of law."[366] In the context of international criminal law, the protection of a group does not depend on its nationality, but rather on its vulnerability and need for protection. In this sense, even though minority rights law as obvious links to the provisions of international human rights law safeguarding equality and non-discrimination, the instruments of minority protection go beyond that as they have in common the assumption that formal equality and the prohibition of discrimination are not enough to address ethnic or religious differences on a legal level.[367] The 1948 Convention on the Prevention and Punishment of the Crime of Genocide (hereinafter: the Genocide Convention) refers to the destruction of a national, ethnical, racial or religious group as such, and does not ask for any additional formal requirements. Clearly, it would be an absurdity to distinguish between nationals and non-nationals: the prohibition transcends the category.[368] The same must be true for the other crimes under international law examined here, namely crimes against humanity and war crimes.

---

364 UN HRC 'General Comment No 15: The Positions of Aliens under the Covenant' (9 April 1986) GAOR 41st Session Supp 40, 117 para 7; UN HRC 'General Comment No 23: The Rights of Minorities (Art. 27)' (8 April 1994) GAOR 49th Session Supp 40 vol 1, 106 para 5.1.

365 Gudmundur Alfredsson 'Minorities, Indigenous and Tribal Peoples: Definition of Terms as a Matter of International Law' in Nazila Ghanea and Alexandra Xanthaki (eds) *Minorities, Peoples and Self-Determination, Essays in Honour of Patrick Thornberry* (Nijhoff Leiden 2005) 167.

366 *Greco-Bulgarian Communities* (Advisory Opinion) PCIJ Series B No 17 22.

367 Stefan Oeter 'Der Schutz nationaler Minderheiten im Völkerrecht' in Rüdiger Wolfrum (ed) *Gleichheit und Nichtdiskriminierung im nationalen und internationalen Menschenrechtsschutz* (Springer Berlin 2003) 187-214, 197-8.

368 Patrick Thornberry *International Law and the Rights of Minorities* (Clarendon Press Oxford 1991) 8.

II. Where Has Minority Rights Law Been Referred to?

In *Tadić*, the ICTY Trial Chamber discussed the take of the ILC Draft Code on the relationship between 'the crime of "persecution on political, racial, religious or ethnic grounds" and that of "institutionalized discrimination on racial, ethnic, or religious grounds involving the violation of fundamental human rights and freedoms and resulting in seriously disadvantaging a part of the population"'.[369] It clarifies that '[i]t is the violation of the right to equality in some serious fashion that infringes on the enjoyment of a basic or fundamental right that constitutes persecution, although the discrimination must be on one of the listed grounds to constitute persecution under the Statute'.[370] This statement in its early-on case could have served as a gateway for minority rights to be incorporated into the tribunals 'analyses. Unfortunately, this has not been the case, and minority rights are scarcely referred to in both the ICTY's and the ICTR's decisions.

The *Krstić* Case is one of the rare examples were an *ad hoc* tribunal explicitly refers to instruments available under minority rights law in order to establish the groups protected by the prohibition of genocide. It was the first judgment in which the ICTY held that the events that happened in Srebrenica constituted genocide. [371] The decision was later upheld on appeal[372] and in the *Bosnian Genocide Case* of the ICJ.[373] In order to establish the state of customary international law on genocide at the time of the events in Srebrenica took place, the ICTY refers to the Genocide Convention, the Rome Statute and the ICTR case law, as well as to the Report of the International Law Commission (ILC) on the Draft Code of Crimes against Peace and Security of Mankind[374] and the two reports of the Sub-

---

369 *Prosecutor v Tadić (Opinion and Judgment)* IT-94-1 (7 May 1997) para 697; UN ILC 'Draft Code of Crimes against the Peace and Security of Mankind' (1996) GAOR 51st Session Supp 10, 9, 98.

370 *Prosecutor v Tadić (Opinion and Judgment)* IT-94-1 (7 May 1997) para. 697.

371 *Prosecutor v Krstić (Judgment)* IT-98-33-T (2 August 2001) paras 539-599.

372 *Prosecutor v Krstić (Appeal Judgment)* IT-98-33-A (19 April 2004).

373 *Application of the Convention on the Prevention and Punishment of the Crime of Genocide (Bosnia and Herzegovina v Serbia and Montenegro) (Merits)* ([2007] ICJ Rep 43 paras 231-376.

374 UN ILC 'Commentary on the ILC Draft Code of Crimes against the Peace and Security of Mankind' GAOR 51st Session Supp 10, 9, in particular 106-114.

Commission on Prevention of Discrimination and Protection of Minorities of the UN Commission on Human Rights.[375]

First, the trial chamber establishes the *actus rea* of genocide, i.e. murder and serious bodily and mental harm had occurred. Then, the chamber turns to whether the *mens rea* existed in the actors, establishing whether they had the intent to destroy, in whole or in part, a national, ethnic, racial or religious group. In order to define groups protected by the Genocide Convention, the court refers to minority rights law by establishing that the preparatory work conducted on the Convention and the work of the international bodies in relation to the protection of minorities "partially overlap and are on occasion synonymous".[376] The Chamber states that even though the European human rights instruments use the term 'national minorities' while universal documents more commonly refer to 'ethnic, religious or linguistic minorities,' the two expressions appear to embrace the same goals.[377] Furthermore, it establishes that

"[t]he preparatory work of the Convention shows that setting out such a list was designed more to describe a single phenomenon, roughly corresponding to what was recognised, before the second world war, as "national minorities", rather than to refer to several distinct prototypes of human groups. To attempt to differentiate each of the named groups on the basis of scientifically objective criteria would thus be inconsistent with the object and purpose of the Convention."[378]

The chamber further holds that Bosnian Muslims are a protected group under the Genocide Convention and that such a group cannot be limited to the Bosnian Muslim population in a specific geographical area.[379] However, the court acknowledges that the destruction may target only a part of the geographically limited part of the larger group because the perpetrators

---

375 UN Commission of Human Rights Special Rapporteur of the Sub-Commission on Prevention of Discrimination and Protection of Minorities, Nicodème Ruhashyankiko 'Study on the Question of the Prevention and Punishment of the Crime of Genocide' (4 July 1978) UN Doc E/CN. 4/Sub. 2/ 416; UN Commission of Human Rights Special Rapporteur of the Sub-Commission on Prevention of Discrimination and Protection of Minorities, Benjamin Whitaker, 'Revised and Updated Report on the Question of the Prevention and Punishment of the Crime of Genocide' (2 July 1985) E/CN.4/Sub. 2/1985/6.

376 *Prosecutor v Krstić (Judgment)* IT-98-33-T (2 August 2001) para. 555.

377 *Prosecutor v Krstić (Judgment)* IT-98-33-T (2 August 2001) para. 555.

378 *Prosecutor v Krstić (Judgment)* IT-98-33-T (2 August 2001) para. 556.

379 *Prosecutor v Krstić (Judgment)* IT-98-33-T (2 August 2001) paras 559-60.

regard the intended destruction as sufficient to annihilate the group as a distinct entity in the respective geographic area.[380]

Furthermore, the court points out that genocide, as opposed to persecution as a crime against humanity, does require the intent to physically destroy a group and not merely eradicate its culture and identity as a distinct social entity.[381] It is however acknowledged by the tribunal that a physical or biological attack on a protected group is often accompanied by simultaneous attacks on cultural or religious property and symbols and the intent to deliberately destroy a minority's identity can therefore serve as evidence for the intent to physically destroy the group.[382]

The *Krstić* Judgment is exceptional in several ways: apart from the explicit reference to minority rights law in order to establish protected groups under international criminal law, the court touches on the concept of group identity and the eradication thereof in the context of both persecution and genocide. The notion that the attack of a minority group's identity can serve as evidence of intent to physically eliminate them shows the connection between the neglect of minority rights and the outbreak of violence against minorities. It also demonstrates how much a broad understanding of both concepts can positively affect the development of each of the two branches of international law.

III. Where Could Minority Right Law Have Been Referred to?

Minority rights law, like the international courts and tribunals in the areas of genocide or persecution as a crime against humanity, intensively concern themselves with the individual-group dichotomy.[383] The need for us-

380 *Prosecutor v Krstić (Judgment)* IT-98-33-T (2 August 2001) para 590.

381 *Prosecutor v Krstić (Judgment)* IT-98-33-T (2 August 2001) para 574-575.

382 *Prosecutor v Krstić (Judgment)* IT-98-33-T (2 August 2001) para 580.

383 See for the historic development of this dichotomy: UN Commission on Human Rights Special Rapporteur of the Sub-Commission on Prevention of Discrimination and Protection of Minorities, Francesco Capotorti 'Study on the Rights of Persons belonging to ethnic, religious and linguistic minorities' (1979) UN Doc E/CN.4/Sub.2/384/Rev. 1; Manfred Nowak *U. N. Covenant on Civil and Political Rights: CCPR Commentary* (N P Engel Kehl 2005) 652-657; UN HRC 'General Comment No 23: The Rights of Minorities (Art. 27)' (8 April 1994) GAOR 49th Session Supp 40 vol 1, 106; Carsten Stahn 'Internationaler Menschenrechtsschutz und Völkerstrafrecht' (1999) 3 Kritische Justiz 345; for decisions of the

ing minority rights for guidance in interpretation is especially obvious when it comes to the ICTY. From the time of its establishment, the tribunal's assignment was to punish large-scale violations of international humanitarian law in the territory of the former Yugoslavia.[384] As the first international criminal tribunal since the end of World War II, the ICTY had to face a variety of problems regarding the doctrine of *nullum crimen sine lege*.

1. The Categorization of Groups Falling under the Ambit of Protected Groups Within the Definition of Genocide

In the first judgement of the ICTR, the *Akayesu* judgment, no such reference to minority rights law is made. This is all the more surprising when keeping in mind that genocide was the core crime the ICTR was establish to deal with and the first couple of judgments still had to counter the predication that a genocide had not taken place at all.[385] For this, the *Akayesu* judgment delves into the colonial history of Rwanda and explains how the categories of Hutu and Tutsi were exploited by the German and Belgian colonial powers and what before were fluid denominations attributed to individuals and referring to lineage and social class became stable categories attributed to groups.[386]At the same time, persons also increasingly referred to themselves belonging to a stable group called Tutsi, as a result of the racial and racist considerations introduced by the colonial powers and based on, inter alia, physical appearance that set the taller, 'Tutsi' with fairer, more 'European' features apart from the majority population.[387] Here, the court clarified that, according to the *travaux préparatoires* of the Genocide Convention, the convention seeks to protect any stable and per-

---

Human Rights Committee see eg UN HRC 'Communication No 167/1984, *Ominayak, Chief of the Lubicon Lake Band v Canada*' (26 March 1990) GAOR 45th Session Supp 40 vol 2, 1; UN HRC 'Communication No 197/1985, *Kitok v Sweden*' (27 July 1988) GAOR 43rd Session Supp 40, 221; UN HRC 'Communication No 511/1992, *Länsman v Finland*' (26 October 1994) GAOR 50th Session Supp 40 vol 2, 66.

384 United Nations Security Council Resolution 808, Article 1; United Nations Security Council Resolution 827, Article2 UN Doc. S/RES/827, 25 May 1993.

385 *Prosecutor v Akayesu (Judgment)* ICTR-96-4-A (1 June 2001) paras 112-129;.

386 *Prosecutor v Akayesu (Judgment)* ICTR-96-4-A (1 June 2001) paras 78-84.

387 *Prosecutor v Akayesu (Judgment)* ICTR-96-4-A (1 June 2001) para 83.

manent group.[388] However, the court could have gained much from arguing with the help of minority rights law and how ethnic minorities are defined there. As, for example, the term 'ethnic minority', introduced by the Sub-Commission on Prevention of Discrimination and Protection of Minorities in the 1950s, does not only encompass what had been known as 'racial' minorities but also contained cultural as well as historical elements, the narrative of the coming into existence of the Tutsi as a distinct ethnical group in light of colonial history would have strengthen the argument.[389] Furthermore, other criteria such as subjective acceptance of membership or family ties of the person could have been employed as evidence of the Tutsi as an ethnic group in line with international law.[390] The same goes for other ICTR judgments whose subjective approach focused on the perpetrators: Tutsi were an ethnic group because the perpetrators believed them to be one.[391] Even though the ICTR and referring to it, later the ICTY hold that the determination of the protected group has to be done on a case-by-case basis using objecting and subjective criteria, no reference to human rights law is made.[392]

---

388 *Prosecutor v Akayesu (Judgment)* ICTR-96-4-A (1 June 2001) paras 511, 316; see also *Prosecutor v Musema (Judgment)* ICTR-96-13-T (27 January 2000) para. 162; See also *Prosecutor v Rutaganda (Judgment)* ICTR-96-3-T (6 December 1999) para. 57.

389 Manfred Nowak *U. N. Covenant on Civil and Political Rights: CCPR Commentary* (N P Engel Kehl 2005) 649.

390 Manfred Nowak *U. N. Covenant on Civil and Political Rights: CCPR Commentary* (N P Engel Kehl 2005) 653; see also *Prosecutor v Akayesu (Judgment)* ICTR-96-4-A (1 June 2001) paras 170-172 where the court included a large quote of an expert witnesson how persons came to view themselves as a Tutsi ethnic group but no mention of international alw on this subject is made; see also *Prosecutor v Brđanin (Judgment)* IT-99-36-T (1 September 2004) para. 683.

391 *Prosecutor v Kayishema (Judgment)* ICTR-95-1-T (21 May 1999) para 98; see also *Prosecutor v Semanza (Judgment)* ICTR-97-20-T (15 May 2003) para 317; *Prosecutor v Kajelijeli (Judgment)* ICTR-98-44A-T (1 December 2003) para 811; see also *Prosecutor v Brđanin (Judgment)* IT-99-36-T (1 September 2004) para. 683; in judgments where the affiliation to a group was based on the perception of the perpetrators, no mention was made of minority rights law, see also see also *Prosecutor v Brđanin (Judgment)* IT-99-36-T (1 September 2004) para. 683.

392 See *Prosecutor v Semanza (Judgment)* ICTR-97-20-T (15 May 2003) para 317; *Prosecutor v Kajelijeli (Judgment)* ICTR-98-44A-T (1 December 2003) para 811; *Prosecutor v Brđanin* (Judgment) IT-99-36-T (1 September 2004) para 684; *Prosecutor v Blagojević (Judgment)* IT-02-60-A (9 May 2007) para 667.

2. The Definition of Persecution

Whereas tribunals were able to take recourse to prior definitions in the case of torture, in one way or another, no prior definition was available for persecution as a crime against humanity. Even though persecution on political, racial or religious grounds was listed as a crime against humanity in Article 6 (c) of the Nuremberg Charter, it was not clearly defined in international criminal law or in the world's major criminal justice systems.[393] It was also not defined in any statute or treaty prior to the adoption of the Rome Statute in 1998.[394] The respective trial chamber in *Tadić* could therefore not draw guidance from international criminal law instruments when establishing the content of the crime of persecution. It found that the commission of the crime must involve discrimination on racial, religious or political grounds that is intended to infringe an individual's basic or fundamental human rights.[395] At least when it comes to discrimination on racial or religious grounds, the prohibition of such forms of discrimination is set out clearly by the international instruments governing the rights of minorities. Furthermore, discrimination on these grounds with the intent to infringe an individual's fundamental human rights is, both generally and specifically in the context of the former Yugoslavia, a violation of the rights of minorities. Generally, the concept of persecution is very similar to that of gross and systematic violations of human rights. [396] Additionally, persecution is the link between crimes against humanity and genocide 'in that acts that might begin as persecution of a minority group may lead, in the most extreme manifestation, to a plan for the intentional destruction of the group.[397] As such, at a lowest common denominator, they protect the same groups (even though persecution under the Rome Statute provides a wider range of protection in terms of groups than genocide), so that find-

---

393 *Prosecutor v Tadić (Opinion and Judgment)* IT-94-1 (7 May 1997) para. 694.

394 Machtheld Boot *Genocide, Crimes Against Humanity, War Crimes-Nullum Crimen Sine Lege and the Subject Matter Jurisdiction of the International Criminal Court* (Intersenita Antwerp 2002) 284-5.

395 *Ibid.* 285 *Prosecutor v Tadić (Opinion and Judgment)* IT-94-1 (7 May 1997) paras. 695-697; 712-713.

396 William A Schabas *The International Criminal Court: A Commentary on the Rome Statute* (OUP Oxford 2010) 175.

397 William A Schabas *The International Criminal Court: A Commentary on the Rome Statute* (OUP Oxford 2010) 175.

ings valid for the protected groups in the crime of genocide could also have served the court with regards to persecution.

However, the Chambers dealing with the definition of persecution as a crime against humanity did not take recourse to any of the instruments or cases dealing with minority rights law. In the *Kupreškić* Case, the Chamber emphasised that in order to define the crime of persecution, it cannot relate to the definition of persecution under human rights or refugee law, as the court deemed this a violation of the principle of legality.[398] The Chamber concentrates on the definition of persecution set out in refugee law and concludes that it is based more on the perception and fear of being prosecuted than on factual and legal findings.

Despite this fact, the tribunal does not mention the instruments of minority protection that are closely connected to the concepts of persecution and non-discrimination and that could have been helpful for guidance in this matter.

Neither do other Trial Chamber which was faced with the need to define persecution and the intensity of the denial of rights necessary for an act to fall under the ambit of persecution. In particular, an instrument like the ICCPR, ratified by 169 States, and the products of its treaty body would have had considerable authority.[399] In *Kvocka* (and later in *Krnojelac*), the Chambers, when faced with having to decide the threshold of persecution stated 'jointly or severally, the acts alleged in the Amended Indictment must amount to persecution'.[400] But that did not mean that each discriminatory act alleged must individually be regarded as a violation of international law.'[401] While it is certainly true that persecution can be established in cumulating many individual acts that, taken by themselves, do not reach the necessary threshold (as the *Kvocka* Chamber es-

398 *Prosecutor v Kupreškić (Trial Chamber Judgment)* IT-95-16 (14 January 2000) para. 589.

399 Status of ratifications as of November 2017.

400 *Prosecutor v Kvočka (Judgment)* IT-98-30 (2 November 2001) 186; see also *Prosecutor v Krnojelac (Judgment)* IT-97-25 (15 March 2002) para 434; see also Theodor Meron 'Human Rights Marches into New Territory: The Enforcement of International Human Rights in International Criminal Tribunals' Fourth Marek Nowicki Memorial Lecture (28 November 2008) <http://web.ceu.hu/legal/pdf%20documents/Nowicki/Meron_Enforcement%20of%20HRwarsawnowicki13nov08.pdf> (as last accessed on 10 June 2013; speech no longer accessible online) 29.

401 *Prosecutor v Kvočka (Judgment)* IT-98-30 (2 November 2001) 186; see also *Prosecutor v Krnojelac (Judgment)* IT-97-25 (15 March 2002) para 434.

tablishes referring to trials dealing with the persecution of European Jews before and during World War II), the Chamber overlooks that many of the acts it examines (e.g. acts of murder, rape, torture, humiliation and physical abuse) are in fact violations of minority rights law and therefore violations of international law.[402] It is unfortunate that the ICTY, established to contribute to peace and reconciliation in a conflict that centred largely on minority issues, missed the opportunity to show the interdependence between the crime of persecution and the protection of minorities.

3. The Definition of a Stigmatised Group within the Crime of Persecution

The ICTY fails to take recourse to minority rights law when defining a group subjected to persecution. In Kvocka, it characterizes genocide as 'an extreme and most inhuman form of persecution'[403] thereby acknowledging the systemic similarities between the two crimes, which, in turn, are closely related to the protection of minorities.[404] The respective Chambers of the ICTY have repetitively used the criterion of stigmatisation instead. In *Prosecutor v Dragan Nikolić*, for example, the Court refers to discriminatory measures directed solely towards the Muslim population like the requirement of *laissez-passers*, the restriction of accounts towards person of Muslim faith, the requirement to hand in weapons, summary arrests, detention, torture and massive transfer of civilians that incorporated a greater policy of ethnic cleansing.[405]

Even though the Court uses terms and principles of minority rights law, it does so without directly referring to the law, its instruments, and the scholarly work and findings. With this, the decisions lose legal weight and the court misses out on an opportunity to make use of an area of law closely interlinked with international criminal law. In *Jesilić*, for example, the court uses the term 'national, ethnical and racial groups' to established

402 Manfred Nowak *U. N. Covenant on Civil and Political Rights: CCPR Commentary* (N. P Engel Kehl 2005) 662-663.

403 *Prosecutor v Kvočka (Judgment)* IT-98-30 (2 November 2001) 636.

404 This approach has also been cited by the ICJ in *Application of the Convention on the Prevention and Punishment of the Crime of Genocide (Bosnia and Herzegovina v Serbia and Montenegro) (Merits)* [2007] ICJ Rep 43 para 188.

405 *Prosecutor v Nikolić (Review of Indictment Pursuant to Rule 61of the Rules of Procedure and Evidence)* ICTY IT-94-2-R61 (20 October 1995) ('the *Nikolic* Decision'), para. 27.

persecuted groups; however, this does not coincide with the use of the respective minority rights instruments or scholarly works in this area to give more weight to their interpretation. [406] Although it is obvious that the concepts used by the Court are crucial i.e. the identification by others and the self-identification within the group, these conceptions are also considered in minority rights law and a discussion of these concepts would have increased the authority of the delivered judgment.

IV. Where is the Link?

1. State Obligations regarding the Protection of Minorities from Crimes under International Law

Minorities have always been a particularly vulnerable group and from the conception of the concept on, minority rights have been more closely linked to violent conflict then other categories of human rights.[407] However, minority rights have been seen by some to be a cause and not a cure for conflict. Particularly, at the time the UDHR was drafted, after World War II, minority rights law was looked upon with scepticism due to the misuse of the concept by Nazi Germany and the fact that various instruments conceived by the League of Nations could not protect them.[408] Minority rights have been portrayed as divisive, as they categorize groups of people and convey different rights to them according to their ethnic, religious, national or racial background.[409] Many hoped that the new emphasis on human rights would resolve the problems associated with minority

---

406 *Prosecutor v Jelisić (Judgement)* ICTY-IT-95-10 (14 December 1999) para. 70 et. seq.

407 Minority Rights Group International 'Briefing: Why a minority rights approach to conflict? The case of Southern Sudan' (2008) <http://www.academia.edu/3622460/Why_a_minority_rights_approach_to_conflict_The_case_of_Southern_Sudan> (31 October 2017) 2.

408 Lyal S Sunga 'International Criminal Law: Protection of Minorities' in Zelim A Skurbaty (ed) *Beyond a One-Dimensional State: An Emerging Right to Autonomy?* (Nijhoff Leiden 2005) 255-275, 256.

409 Minority Rights Group International 'Briefing: Why a minority rights approach to conflict? The case of Southern Sudan' (2008) <http://www.academia.edu/3622460/Why_a_minority_rights_approach_to_conflict_The_case_of_Southern_Sudan> (31 October 2017) 2.

rights by guaranteeing basic civil and political rights regardless of group membership.[410] The end of the Cold War and the decline of authoritarianism, which led to the outbreak of many previously suppressed internal (ethnic) conflicts made the international community rethink their stance on minority protection.[411] Ignoring real grievances along ethnic lines seemed to not be the solution anymore.[412] Hence, several universal and regional instruments for the protection of minorities were adopted in the early nineties that seem to focus on the resolution of intra-state conflict and the maintenance of peace and security.[413]

However, even before that, the international community thought to protect the existence of minorities on several occasions in both universal and regional human rights and international law instruments. This section will focus on the most crucial instruments of under general human right law from which an obligation to protect minorities from crimes under international law can nevertheless be inferred.

Even though international provisions for the protection of minorities could be found long before the evolvement of modern international human rights law[414], the International Bill of Human Rights, consisting of the

---

410 Will Kymlicka *Multicultural Citizenship: A Liberal Theory on Minority Rights* (OUP Oxford 1996) 2-3.

411 Helen Quane 'Rights in Conflict? The Rationale and Implications of using Human Rights in Conflict Prevention Strategies' (2007) 47 Virginia. Journal of International Law 463-523, 498.

412 Minority Rights Group International 'Briefing: Why a minority rights approach to conflict? The case of Southern Sudan' (2008) <http://www.academia.edu/3622460/Why_a_minority_rights_approach_to_conflict_The_case_of_Southern_Sudan> (31 October 2017) 2.

413 Helen Quane 'Rights in Conflict? The Rationale and Implications of using Human Rights in Conflict Prevention Strategies' (2007) 47 Virginia. Journal of International Law 463-523, 498.

414 E.g. in the religious treaties of peace treaties of Augsburg (Abschied des Augsburger Reichstages [Augsburger Friede] [25 September 1555] in K Zeumer (ed) *Quellensammlung zum Staats-, Verwaltungs- und Völkerrecht* vol 2.1 *Quellensammlung zur Geschichte der Deutschen Reichsverfassung in Mittelalter und Neuzeit* [2nd edn Siebeck Mohr Tübingen 1913] 341) and Westphalia (Treaty of Peace between the Holy Roman Empire and Sweden and the Treaty of Peace between France and the Holy Roman Empire [signed and entered into force 24 October 1648] [1648–49] 1 CTS 198, 319 [these two treaties form the Westphalian Peace Treaty]) and the Peace Treaties following World War I.; System of Minority Protection set up by the League of Nations; Manfred Nowak *U. N. Covenant on Civil and Political Rights: CCPR Commentary* (N. P Engel Kehl 2005) 480.

UDHR, the ICCPR and the IESCR, only specifically mentions minorities in Article 27 ICCPR.

All major human rights treaties are in their substantive part preceded by general non-discrimination clauses. Art. 2 Universal Declaration of Human Rights in so far served as a blueprint for all major international and regional human rights conventions.[415]

Art. 2 UDHR reads 'Everyone is entitled to all the rights and freedoms set forth in this Declaration, without distinction of any kind, such as race, colour, sex, language, religion, political or other opinion, national or social origin, property, birth or other status.' The same is repeated, in substance, in Arts. 2 (1) ICCPR, Art. 2 (2) ICESCR, Art. 2 (1) CRC and Art. 2 ACHPR coining the reference to a 'common Art. 2 of international human rights instruments on the prohibition of discrimination'.[416] The same approach can be found in Art. 1 ACHR and Art. 14 ECHR. Apart from Art. 14 ECHR, none of the provisions deal with the status of a national minority explicitly in the context of non-discrimination. All of them do, however, include a protection against discrimination on a similar basis as the Genocide Convention, namely on the grounds of race, religion, national origin.[417]

a) Charter of the United Nations

The Charter of the United Nations ('UN Charter') does not deal with minorities explicitly. Amongst the purposes of the UN's foundation are the maintenance of international peace and security, the development of

415 Rüdiger Wolfrum 'The Prohibition of Discrimination in International Human Rights Treaties: The Development from an Accessory Norm to an Independent One' in Dirk Hanschel and Others *Mensch und Recht: Festschrift für Eibe Riedel* (Duncker und Humblot Berlin 2013) 2009-2019, 2012.

416 Rüdiger Wolfrum 'The Prohibition of Discrimination in International Human Rights Treaties: The Development from an Accessory Norm to an Independent One' in Dirk Hanschel and Others *Mensch und Recht: Festschrift für Eibe Riedel* (Duncker und Humblot Berlin 2013) 2009-2019, 2012.

417 Though ethnicity is not covered in the range of protection, the reference to 'race' partially covers the same groups. A reference to 'ethnicity' does, however, include a wider range of groups than the controversial 'race' as, on top of biologically or physically recognisable attributes, it also covers cultural and historical elements; see; Manfred Nowak *U. N. Covenant on Civil and Political Rights: CCPR Commentary* (N. P Engel Kehl 2005) 649.

friendly relations amongst nations and the promotion and protection of human rights.[418] The main governing principles on which the United Nations are based are the principle of State sovereignty (Article 2 (1) UN Charter) and the prohibition of the use of force, stipulated in Article 2 (4) UN Charter. Article 55 UN Charter expresses the aim of promoting "universal respect for, and observance of human rights and fundamental freedoms for all without distinction as to race, sex, language or religion." The Member States pledge themselves to take joint and separate actions to achieve the aims set out in Article 55.[419] This is the framework in which minority protection within the United Nations takes place.

Regarding the protection of minorities against crimes which are committed against them outside of a State's own boundaries, the prohibition of the use of force outlaws the threat or use of force against the territorial integrity of other states. Force is only permitted in well-defined exceptions, namely for the purpose of self-defence under Article 51 and when the Security Council decided to take action pursuant to Articles 39 and 42, as acknowledged by the Responsibilty to Protect according to which the Security Council is prepared to take collective action, including under Chapter VII UN Charter, to protect populations from genocide, war crimes, ethnic cleansing and crimes against humanity.[420] There has been much discussion and controversy about a third exception, humanitarian intervention, but it cannot be said to have crystallised into an exception to Article 2 (4) under international law.[421] It has been argued that as a consequence of the Responsibility to Protect, in some extreme cases of mass violence against a population, the international community has an obligation to intervene and

---

418 Article 1(1), 1(2) and 1(3) Charter of the United Nations (adopted 26 June 1945, entered into force 24 October 1945) 1 UNTS 16.

419 Article 56 Charter of the United Nations (adopted 26 June 1945, entered into force 24 October 1945) 1 UNTS 16.

420 UNGA Res 60/1 '2005 World Summit Outcome' (16 September 2005) GAOR 60th Session Supp 49 vol 1, 3 para. 139; see also Anne Peters 'Article 24' in Bruno Simma, Daniel Khan and others *The Charter of the United Nations: A Commentary* (3rd ed OUP Oxford 2012) 761-786, 766-767 see Part Two Chapter Two IV. 1 e) below.

421 See Christine Gray 'The use of force and the international legal order' in Malcolm D Evans (ed) *International Law* (3rd ed OUP Oxford 2010) 621-623.

that in these cases, the use of veto power on part of a member of the Security Council should be considered illegal or invalid.[422]

Things are much less clear when it comes to the treatment of populations by their own State. Even though the UN Charter sets out some standards in the field of human rights, for example on non-discrimination in Articles 1 and 55 regarding self-determination or in chapters XI-XIII, it does not contain a bill of rights. The initial proposal of several States to include a declaration of rights analogous to national constitutions was dropped under pressure of the major powers and the issue was essentially postponed.[423] For this reason, one has to look further into the instruments adopted under the auspices of the United Nations and within other international and regional organisations to see the extent to which minorities are protected within the state they are living.

b) International Covenant on Civil and Political Rights

Article 27 ICCPR reads:

'In those States in which ethnic, religious or linguistic minorities exist, persons belonging to such minorities shall not be denied the right, in community with other members of their group, to enjoy their own culture, to profess and practise their own religion, or to use their own language'.

The formulation 'persons belonging to such minorities' emphasises that Article 27 sets out an individual right and not a group right, even though it is the collective enjoyment of the right that is protected.[424] Article 27 is the only provision in the ICCPR that is formulated in a negative way, which shows that the first State obligation towards minorities is to refrain

---

422 Anne Peters 'Humanity as the A and Ω of Sovereignty' (2009) 20 EJIL 513-544, 536-540.

423 William A.Schabas *Preventing Genocide and Mass Killing: The Challenge for the United Nations* (Minority Rights Group International London 2006) https://eprints.mdx.ac.uk/7840/1/MRGGenocideReport.pdf (31 October 2017) 7.

424 UN Commission on Human Rights Special Rapporteur of the Sub-Commission on Prevention of Discrimination and Protection of Minorities, Francesco Capotorti 'Study on the Rights of Persons belonging to ethnic, religious and linguistic minorities' (1979) UN Doc E/CN.4/Sub.2/384/Rev. 1, 35; Manfred Nowak *U. N. Covenant on Civil and Political Rights: CCPR Commentary* (N. P Engel Kehl 2005) 655-657.

from interference and to practice tolerance.[425] Particularly prohibited are all measures directed against or threatening the existence of ethnic, linguistic or religious minorities.[426] In this respect, General Comment No. 29 of the HRC is of particular importance as it states that:

"...the international protection of the rights of persons belonging to minorities includes elements that must be respected in all circumstances. This is reflected in the prohibition of genocide under international law, the inclusion of a non-discrimination clause in Article 4 itself (paragraph 1), as well as in the non-derogable nature of Article 18."[427]

However, the obligation set out in Article 27 goes beyond the mere prohibition of discrimination of minorities. Instead, it contains an element of a right to *de facto* equality, to positive protection against discrimination.[428] It can require legislative, judicial or administrative- measures to be taken in order to guarantee the rights set out in Article 27, a fact that has been made clear by the HRC in its General Comment No 23.[429] This means that State at least have an obligation to prosecute acts that qualify as genocide.[430]

Another provision that can be invoked in the protection of minorities is Article 20 (2) ICCPR. According to this provision, States have an obligation to protect minorities against national, racial or religious hatred that constitutes incitement to discrimination, hostility or violence.

---

425 Manfred Nowak *U. N. Covenant on Civil and Political Rights: CCPR Commentary* (N. P Engel Kehl 2005) 657-658.

426 Manfred Nowak *U. N. Covenant on Civil and Political Rights: CCPR Commentary* (N. P Engel Kehl 2005) 662.

427 UN HRC 'General Comment No 29: Derogations from Provisions of the Covenant during a State of Emergency (Art. 4)' (24 July 2001) GAOR 56th Session Supp 40 vol 1, 202..

428 Manfred Nowak *U. N. Covenant on Civil and Political Rights: CCPR Commentary* (N. P Engel Kehl 2005) 500; critical as to the practical significance of Art. 27 ICCPR and the reluctance of the HRC to interpret Article 27 in a wider and more progressive manner: Stefan Oeter 'Der Schutz nationaler Minderheiten im Völkerrecht' in Rüdiger Wolfrum (ed) Gleichheit und Nichtdiskriminierung im nationalen und internationalen Menschenrechtsschutz (Springer Berlin 2003) 187-214, 196.

429 UN HRC 'General Comment No 15: The Positions of Aliens under the Covenant' (9 April 1986) GAOR 41st Session Supp 40, 117 para 6.1.

430 Peter Finell *Accountability under Human Rights Law and International criminal law against Minority Groups Committed by Non-State Actors* (Åbo Akademi Institute for Human Rights, Åbo/Turku May 2002) 20.

In order to preclude genocidal policies to be executed through legally binding court judgements, Article 6 (2) ICCPR stipulates that death sentences must not contravene the Genocide Convention and that in any killing which constitutes genocide, the State Party is not allowed to derogate from its obligations under the Genocide Convention (Article 6 (3)).[431]

c) United Nations Declaration on the Rights of Persons belonging to National or Ethnic, Religious and Linguistic Minorities

On 18 December 1992, the United Nations General Assembly adopted the United Nations Declaration on the Rights of Persons belonging to National or Ethnic, Religious and Linguistic Minorities (UNDM)[432], which, although not legally binding, has been regarded as an important step forward in the internationalisation of minority rights.[433] It can be applied to render States politically accountable for how they treat their minorities.[434] The Declaration was 'inspired by' Article 27 ICCPR.[435] It builds up on, specifies and adds to the rights enshrined in the ICCPR and in the other two documents that together make up the International Bill of Human Rights.[436] The rights contained are set out as rights of individuals, whereas

431 See also Carsten Stahn 'Internationaler Menschenrechtsschutz und Völkerstrafrecht' (1999) 3 Kritische Justiz 343-355at 346.

432 UNGA Res 47/135 'Declaration on the Rights of Persons Belonging to National or Ethnic, Religious and Linguistic Minorities' (18 December 1992) GAOR 47th Session Supp 49 vol 1, 210.

433 Patrick Thornberry, 'The UN Declaration on the Rights of Persons Belonging to National or Ethnic, Religious and Linguistic Minorities: Background, Analysis, Observations, and an Update' in Alan Phillips/Allan Rosas (eds) *Universal Minority Rights* (Åbo Akademi University Institute for Human Rights/Minority Rights Group International Turku/Åbo and London 1995) 13-76, 14.

434 Helen Quane 'Rights in Conflict? The Rationale and Implications of using Human Rights in Conflict Prevention Strategies' (2007) 47 Virginia. Journal of International Law 463-523 501.

435 UN ECOSOC 'Commentary of the Working Group on Minorities to the United Nations Declaration on the Rights of Persons Belonging to National or Ethnic, Religious and Linguistic Minorities' (4 April 2005) UN Doc E/CN.4/Sub.2/AC. 5/2005/2 para. 3.

436 UN ECOSOC 'Commentary of the Working Group on Minorities to the United Nations Declaration on the Rights of Persons Belonging to National or Ethnic, Religious and Linguistic Minorities' (4 April 2005) UN Doc E/CN.4/Sub.2/AC. 5/2005/2 para. 4.

duties of the State are in part formulated as duties towards minorities as a group, which means that even though only individuals can claim the rights, the State cannot fully implement them without ensuring adequate conditions for the existence and identity of the group as a whole.[437]

In terms of minority protection from crimes under international law, the preamble of the UNMD is of particular importance. The preamble sets out the principle goals and purposes that the declaration is meant to achieve and can, in accordance with Article 31 (2) Vienna Convention on the Law of Treaties, be drawn upon to establish the meaning of the operative provisions.[438] Preambles have been used in treaty interpretation by the ICJ '(i) in order to elucidate the meaning of clauses the purpose of which otherwise would be doubtful' and '(ii) to indicate the judicial 'climate' in which the operative clause should be read, whether for instance liberally or restrictively, broadly or strictly'.[439] In the case of the UNMD, the preamble refers to, amongst other things, the promotion of the principles set out in, *inter alia*, the Genocide Convention.

The preamble also acknowledges that the promotion and protection of the rights of persons belonging to a minority contributes to the political and social stability of the countries in which they live.[440] Furthermore, they acknowledge that strengthening minorities' positions by providing them with the rights set out in the operative articles is a way not merely to improve their individual well-being or that of the group they belong to, but is a way to contribute to the stability of the whole state or region. The

437 UN ECOSOC 'Commentary of the Working Group on Minorities to the United Nations Declaration on the Rights of Persons Belonging to National or Ethnic, Religious and Linguistic Minorities' (4 April 2005) UN Doc E/CN.4/Sub.2/AC. 5/2005/2 para. 14.

438 Vienna Convention on the Law of Treaties (concluded 23 May 1969, entered into force 27 January 1980) 1155 UNTS 331.

439 Gerald G Fitzmaurice 'The Law and Procedure of the International Court of Justice: Treaty Interpretation and Certain Other Treaty Points' (1951) 28 *British Yearbook of International Law* 28 1-28, at 25; Sir Gerald G Fitzmaurice 'The Law and Procedure of the International Court of Justice 1951-4: Treaty Interpretation and Other Treaty Points' (1957) 33 *British Yearbook of International Law* 203-38, at 227; see *Asylum Case (Colombia/Peru) (Judgement)* [1950] ICJ Rep 266, 282; *Rights of Nationals of the United States of America in Morocco (France v United States of America)* [1952] ICJ Rep 176, 196.

440 '[...]Considering that the promotion and protection of the rights of persons belonging to national or ethnic, religious and linguistic minorities contribute to the political and social stability of States in which they live'.

preamble also emphasises again the close relationship between the prohibition of genocide and the protection of minorities.[441] This relationship is also addressed in the operative part of the Declaration, namely in Article 1(1), which starts: 'States shall protect the existence ... of minorities'. From this article, a basic right to be protected from genocide is inferred; although the right to existence is not expressly mentioned in the Genocide Convention itself, the key General Assembly resolution on which the Convention is based states that genocide is 'a denial of the right of existence of entire human groups'.[442] The Commentary of the working group on minorities to the Declaration explicitly mentions the prohibition of the elimination of minorities within the context of Article 1.[443] The Working Group also states that not only the physical destruction of minority group is covered by the requirement of protection in Article 1(1). States must also protect minorities from attempts to deliberately weaken them (e.g. by forced transfer of population).[444] Additionally, the

Independent Expert on Minorities, created by a Human Rights Commission's resolution focuses on the link between minorities and conflict as a key element and promotes the Declaration on the Rights and Duties of Persons Belonging to National or Ethnic, Religious and Linguistic Minorities. [445]

441 William A. Schabas *Preventing Genocide and Mass Killing: The Challenge for the United Nations* (Minority Rights Group International London 2006) <https://eprints.mdx.ac.uk/7840/1/MRGGenocideReport.pdf> (31 October 2017) 456.

442 UNGA Res 96 (I) 'The Crime of Genocide' (11 December 1946) GAOR 1st Session Part II Resolutions 188; Thornberry in Alan Phillips/Allan Rosas (eds) *Universal Minority Rights* (Åbo Akademi University Institute for Human Rights/ Minority Rights Group International Turku/Åbo and London 1995) 40.

443 UN ECOSOC 'Commentary of the Working Group on Minorities to the United Nations Declaration on the Rights of Persons Belonging to National or Ethnic, Religious and Linguistic Minorities' (4 April 2005) UN Doc E/CN.4/Sub.2/AC. 5/2005/2 paras 21 and 24.

444 UN ECOSOC 'Commentary of the Working Group on Minorities to the United Nations Declaration on the Rights of Persons Belonging to National or Ethnic, Religious and Linguistic Minorities' (4 April 2005) UN Doc E/CN.4/Sub.2/AC. 5/2005/2 para. 24.

445 Commission on Human Rights, Resolution 2005/79 'Rights of persons belonging to national or ethnic, religious and linguistic minorities' (21 April 2005) E/CN. 4/2005/L.10/Add.14,.

d) Responsibility to Protect

The 'Responsibility to Protect' is part of the Outcome Document adopted at the United Nations summit in September 2005 by representatives of the United Nations member States, mostly heads of States or governments. It accepts that:

'[E]ach state has the responsibility to protect its populations from genocide, war crimes, ethnic cleansing and crimes against humanity. This responsibility entails the prevention of such crimes, including their incitement, through appropriate and necessary measures'.[446]

The document also affirms that the international community has the responsibility to use diplomatic, humanitarian and other peaceful means under Chapter VI and VII of the UN Charter to protect populations against these crimes and show willingness to take collective action, in a timely and decisive manner, through the Security Council, in accordance with Chapter VII, if peaceful means are inadequate. [447] It further acknowledges that the promotion and protection of minority rights contributes to the social and political stability.[448] The 'Responsibility to Protect' was later reaffirmed by the Security Council.[449] In 2009, the UN Secretary-General issued a report reaffirming the 'Responsibility to Protect' and outlining a three-pillar approach in which the first pillar focuses on the States' primaty responsibility in protecting its own populations, the second pillar deals with international assistance and capacity-building in this area and in the third pillar, timely and decisive action by the international community is described as an obligation in cases States fail to fulfil their protection obligations.[450]

Even though the outcome document does not mention minorities explicitly, acknowledging the responsibility of States to protect their own populations from crimes under international law is a step forward in the protection of minorities. The kinds of scenarios that trigger the responsi-

446 UNGA Res 60/1 '2005 World Summit Outcome' (16 September 2005) GAOR 60th Session Supp 49 vol 1, 3 para. 138.

447 UNGA Res 60/1 '2005 World Summit Outcome' (16 September 2005) GAOR 60th Session Supp 49 vol 1, 3 para. 139.

448 UNGA Res 60/1 '2005 World Summit Outcome' (16 September 2005) GAOR 60th Session Supp 49 vol 1, 3 para. 130.

449 UNSC Res 1674 (2006) (28 April 2006) UN Doc S/Res/1674.

450 UNGA 'Implementing the responsibility to protect: Report by the Secretary-General' (19 January 2009) UN Doc A/63/677.

bility to protect are those situations in which minorities are the most likely victims. Worthy of mention in this context is also the appointment of a Special Advisor on the Prevention of Genocide by the UN Secretary-General based on a Security Council Resolution.[451] The mandate of the Special Advisor does not only refer to genocide but also to mass murders and other large-scale human rights violations such as ethnic cleansing.[452]

e) International Convention on the Elimination of All Forms of Racial Discrimination

The International Convention on the Elimination of All Forms of Racial Discrimination (ICERD)[453] is concerned with discrimination based on affiliation to a specific racial group.

Article 1 ICERD defines racial discrimination as 'any distinction, exclusion, restriction or preference based on race, colour, descent, or national or ethnic origin'. As such, the ICERD emanates from a broad list of criteria which must not be used for unequal treatment and can circumvent a definition of and limitation to the controversial term 'race.'[454] In the context of Article 1 ICERD, Minorities are the natural victims of racial discrimination in most States and have been frequently discussed within the General Recommendations issued by the Committee on the Elimination of Racial Discrimination and the reporting procedure under the Convention.[455] The notions of (racial) discrimination and minority protection have

---

451 UNSC Res 1366 (2001) (30 August 2001) SCOR [1 January 2001–31 July 2002] 283.

452 Asbjörn Eide and Rianne Letschert, 'Institutional Developments in the United Nations and at the Regional Level' (2007) 14(2) International Journal on Minority and Group Rights 299-332 at 305.

453 International Convention on the Elimination of all Forms of Racial Discrimination (opened for signature 7 March 1966, entered into force 4 January 1969) 660 UNTS 195.

454 Rüdiger Wolfrum 'Das Verbot der Diskriminierung aufgrund von Rasse, Herkunft, Sprache oder Hautfarbe im Völkerrecht' in Rüdiger Wolfrum (eds) *Gleichheit und Nichtdiskriminierung im nationalen und internationalen Menschenrechtsschutz* (Springer Berlin 2003) 215-231, 221-2.

455 Patrick Thornberry *International Law and the Rights of Minorities* (Clarendon Press Oxford 1991) 272; see eg. UN Committee on the Elimination of Racial Discrimination 'General Recommendation XXVII on Discrimination against Roma' (16 August 2000) GAOR 55th Session Supp 18, 154; UN Committee on the

been regarded as twin concepts that both make up the principle of equality. [456]

This is also the approach of the CERD Committee, the ICERD's treaty body which recognized ethnic cleansing as a violation of ICERD and ethnic discrimination as a first step to future ethnic cleansing[457]

f) Council of Europe Framework Convention for the Protection of National Minorities

The Council of Europe's Framework Convention for the Protection of National Minorities ('Framework Convention')[458] was agreed on after the Heads of States and Government of the Council of Europe Member States adopted the Vienna Declaration in 1993. There, they expressed 'awareness that the protection of national minorities is an essential element of stability and democratic security in our continent' and resolved to enter 'into political and legal commitments relating to the protection of national minorities in Europe and to instruct the Committee of Ministers to elaborate appropriate international legal instruments'.[459] It is the first binding international instrument which focuses only on the protection of national minori-

---

Elimination of Racial Discrimination 'Conclusions and recommendations of the Committee on the Elimination of Racial Discrimination on Romania' (2001) UN Doc CERD/C/304/Add.85 paras 10-11, 14-15; UN Committee on the Elimination of Racial Discrimination 'Conclusions and recommendations of the Committee on the Elimination of Racial Discrimination on Azerbaijan' (2005) UN Doc CERD/C/AZE/CO/4 para 14.

456 Warwick A McKean *Equality and Discrimination in International Law* (Clarendon Oxford 1983) p 159.

457 UN Committee on the Elimination of Racial Discrimination 'Annual Report' (20 September 1995) GAOR 50th Session Supp 18 para. 219; see also David S Weissbrodt 'The Approach of the Committee on the Elimination of Racial Discrimination to Interpreting and applying International Humanitarian Law' (2010) 19 Minnesota Journal of International Law 327–62, 345.

458 COE 'Framework Convention for the Protection of National Minorities' (opened for signature 1 February 1995, entered into force 1 February 1998) 2151 UNTS 243.

459 COE 'Vienna Declaration of the Heads of State and Government of the Member States of the Council of Europe on the Reform of the Control Mechanism of the ECHR, on National Minorities, and on a Plan of Action against Racism' (9 October 1993) (1993) 14 HRLJ 373–76.

ties.[460] The Framework Convention aims at addressing 'unstable minority-majority relations that have a clear potential to destabilize peace and security in Europe'.[461]

The preamble of the Framework Convention mentions the protection of the existence of national minorities as one of the aims treaty. It refers to the upheavals in European history, which have shown that the protection of national minorities is essential to the stability, democratic security and peace in Europe. The preamble reflects the concern of the Council of Europe and its Member States about the risk to the existence of national minorities and is inspired by Article 1 (1) United Nations Declaration on the Rights of Persons belonging to National or Ethnic, Religious and Linguistic Minorities.[462]

g) Other Instruments Relevant to the Protection of Minorities from Crimes under International Law

At the international level, further provisions concerning the rights of minorities can be found in Article 30 of the Convention on the Rights of the Child[463] and Article 5 (c) United Nations Educational, Scientific and Cultural Organization (UNESCO) Convention against Discrimination in Education.[464]. Art 7(2) of the UN Declaration on the Rights of Indigenous Peoples explicitly spells out that indigenous peoples 'shall not be subjected to any act of genocide or any other act of violence, including forcibly removing children of the group to another group'.[465]

---

460 UN 'Pamphlet No 8 of the UN Guide for Minorities' available at http://www.ohchr.org/Documents/Publications/GuideMinorities8en.pdf (31 October 2017) 2.

461 Rainer Hofmann 'The Framework Convention for the Protection of National Minorities: An Introduction' in Marc Weller (ed) *The Rights of Minorities: A Commentary on the European Framework Convention for the Protection of National Minorities* (OUP Oxford 2005) 1-24, 6.

462 Council of Europe 'Explanatory Report of the Council of Europe on the Framework Convention for the Protection of National Minorities' (1995) H (95) 10, para. 24.

463 Convention on the Rights of the Child (adopted 20 November 1989, entered into force 2 September 1990) 1577 UNTS 3.

464 Convention against Discrimination in Education (adopted 14 December 1960, entered into force 22 May 1962) 429 UNTS 93.

465 UNGA Res 61/295 'United Nations Declaration on the Rights of Indigenous Peoples' (13 September 2007) GAOR 61st Session Supp 49 vol 3, 15.

On the regional level, Article 14 Convention for the Protection of Human Rights and Fundamental Freedoms (or European Convention on Human Rights, ECHR) contains a provision regarding minorities.[466] Protocol 12 ECHR is also of importance to the protection of minorities as it deals with the prohibition of discrimination.[467] Within the context of the OSCE, the appointment of a High Commissioner on National Minorities[468] and the adoption of the Copenhagen Document that emphasises the importance of the protection of national minorities to 'justice, stability and peace in the participating States'[469] and introduces far-reaching provisions regarding their rights.[470]

The African Charter on Human and People's Rights (ACHPR) does not mention minorities explicitly, although it contains a prohibition of discrimination.[471] In 1994, the Heads of States and Governments of the African Union's (AU) predecessor, the Organization of African Unity (OAU), passed the Declaration on a Code of Conduct for Inter-African Relations in which they called for the protection of ethnic, cultural, linguistic and religious identity of minorities. [472]

The American Convention on Human Rights and the American Declaration on the Rights and Duties of Man also lack an explicit mentioning of

466 COE 'Convention for the Protection of Human Rights and Fundamental Freedoms' (signed 4 November 1950, entered into force 3 September 1953) 213 UNTS 221.

467 COE 'Protocol No 12 to the Convention for the Protection of Human Rights and Fundamental Freedoms' (signed 4 November 2000, entered into force 1 April 2005) CETS No 177.

468 Created at the CSCE Summit on 9-10 July 1992 in Helsinki; CSCE 'Helsinki Summit Document: The Challenges of Change' (10 July 1992) (1992) 31 ILM 1385.

469 CSCE 'Document of the Copenhagen Meeting of the Conference on the Human Dimension of the CSCE' (29 June 1990) (1990) 29 ILM 1305 para. 30.

470 CSCE 'Document of the Copenhagen Meeting of the Conference on the Human Dimension of the CSCE' (29 June 1990) (1990) 29 ILM 1305 para. 30-39; Johannes Binder *The Human Dimension of the OSCE: From Recommendation to Implementation* (Verlag Österreich Vienna 2001) 38.

471 Art. 2 African Charter on Human and Peoples' Rights (adopted 27 June 1981, entered into force 21 October 1986) 1520 UNTS 217 (Banjul Charter).

472 Article 4 Organization of African Unity, Assembly of Heads of State and Government 'Declaration on a Code of Conduct for Inter-African Relations' Thirtieth Ordinary Session, Tunis, Tunisia, 13-15 June 1994 available at <https://www1.umn.edu/humanrts/africa/INTAFN.htm> (31 October 2017).

minorities. [473] Nevertheless, they contain several provisions that are of particular importance to minorities, most importantly the principle of non-discrimination and the right to culture as stipulated in Article XIII of the American Declaration.

2. Protection of Minorities under International Criminal Law

The following chapter examines different international crimes according to the minority issue inherent in them. Minorities have always been especially vulnerable to the violation of their rights, from small-scale interference with their rights to culture, religion, language to mass violence against them. The commission of crimes under international law directed against minorities is the ultimate violation of their rights. Even though there is little mention in the texts of international criminal law of 'rights', as the law aims for the condemnation or 'criminalisation' of acts, the context of the criminal prohibition makes it clear that the reason why a particular conduct is regarded as criminal is precisely because it violates a fundamental right.[474]

All the crimes examined in the following are crimes as laid out in the Rome Statute. If necessary, the differences between the crimes as set out by the Charters of the Nuremberg and Tokyo Tribunals[475] and the Statutes of the ICTY and the ICTR are explained. The examined crimes have been selected because of their special interconnection with minority protection and the violation of minority rights. This does not in any way infer that the crimes examined are the only crimes that minorities are particularly vulnerable to.

a) Genocide (Art. 6 Rome Statute)

> *'The fact of genocide is as old as humanity. To this day, there has been no society protected by its structure from committing that crime. Every case of*

473 American Declaration of the Rights and Duties of Man (10 December 1948) (1949) 43 AJIL Supp 133.

474 Patrick Thornberry *International Law and the Rights of Minorities* (Clarendon Press Oxford 1991) 58.

475 Charter of the International Military Tribunal for the Far East (19 January 1946) 4 Bevans 20.

> *genocide is a product of history and bears the stamp of the society which has given birth to it'.*[476]

The Genocide Convention can be seen as the first of the post-World War II general conventions which has any bearing on minority protection and is listed by the United Nations secretariat as the one of the international instruments which provide special protective measures for ethnical, religious, or linguistic groups. [477]

The Genocide Convention is based on General Assembly Resolution 96 (I) of 1946, which was adopted in the aftermath of World War II and was clearly influenced by the genocide committed by Germany against national minorities within its own territory and the occupied, allied or annexed territories.[478]

When the Genocide Convention was adopted in 1948, the deliberate intent of its drafters was to derive the scope of criteria from the 'already well-recognized concept in international law then known as "national mi-

---

476 Jean-Paul Sartre 'On Genocide' in Richard A Falk, Gabriel Kolko and Robert Jay (eds) *Crimes of War* (Random House New York 1971) 534.

477 Convention on the Prevention and Punishment of the Crime of Genocide (adopted 9 December 1948, entered into force 12 January 1951) 78 UNTS 277.

478 UNGA Res 96 (I) 'The Crime of Genocide' (11 December 1946) GAOR 1st Session Part II Resolutions 188; see also comment by John Maktos Chairman UN Ad Hoc Committee on Genocide 'Summary Records of the Fifth Meeting' (8 April 1948) UN Doc E/AC.25/SR.5; in the statute of the Nuremberg International Military Tribunal, crimes that which would now be labelled genocide were prosecuted under the heading of crimes against humanity. However, in the drafting of the IMT Statute, the term genocide was already discussed and the concept of the term as a violation of the rights of minorities was clearly spelled out. Justice Robert Jackson, at the beginning of the London Conference in 1945, compiled a 'Planning Memorandum' explaining the evidence to be brought before the Tribunal. In this memorandum, Jackson mentioned '[g]enocide or destruction of racial minoritiesand subjugated populations by such means and methods as (1) underfeeding; (2) sterilization and castration; (3) depriving them of clothing, shelter, fuel, sanitation, medical care; (4) deporting them for forced labour; (5) working them in inhumane conditions' see United States Representative to the International Conference on Military Trials Robert H Jackson 'Planning Memorandum' (US Government Printing Office Washington 1949) 6; see also HG van der Wilt, J Vervliet and others (eds): *The Genocide Convention: The Legacy of 60 Years* (Martinus Nijhoff Leiden 2012) 5-6.

norities,'"[479] This interpretation was confirmed by the International Criminal Tribunal for the former Yugoslavia (ICTY) in its *Krstić* judgment where the court said:

National, ethnical racial or religious groups are not clearly defined in the [Genocide] Convention or elsewhere. In contrast, the preparatory work on the Convention and the work conducted by international bodies in relation to the protection of minorities show that the concepts of protected groups and national minorities partly overlap and are on occasion synonymous. (…). The preparatory work of the Convention shows that setting out such a list [of protected groups] was designed more to describe a single phenomenon, roughly corresponding to what were recognized, before the second world war, was 'national minorities', rather than to refer to several distinct prototypes of human groups.

The requirement of permanence of a group affiliation which cannot or only with difficulties be changed or challenged by the members of the group themselves, finds it reflection in the term 'minorities': even though there is no generally accepted definition of the term, it is generally required that it contains, besides a subjective element and an individual sense of belonging to a group, certain objective criteria which differ from the rest of the population and are usually permanent and stable.[480]

Furthermore, the Genocide Convention and Article 6 of the Rome Statute protect 'national, ethnical, racial or religious' groups. Similarly, Article 27 ICCPR refers to 'ethnic, religious or linguistic minorities'.[481] This already shows a high degree of overlap between the concept of a minority under international human rights law and the groups protected by the prohibition of genocide, especially when considering that 'ethnic' in Article 27 ICCPR is open to a broad interpretation and therefore covers, *inter alia*, what is referred to as racial and national minorities.[482] Even if

479 William A Schabas 'Developments relating to Minorities in the Law of Genocide' in Kristin Henrard and Robert Dunbar *Synergies in Minority Protection: European and International Law Perspectives* (CUP Cambridge 2008) 192.

480 UN Commission on Human Rights Special Rapporteur of the Sub-Commission on Prevention of Discrimination and Protection of Minorities, Francesco Capotorti 'Study on the Rights of Persons belonging to ethnic, religious and linguistic minorities' (1979) UN Doc E/CN.4/Sub.2/384/Rev. 1. 28.

481 International Covenant on Civil and Political Rights (adopted 19 December 1966, entered into force 23 March 1976) 999 UNTS 171.

482 Manfred Nowak U. N. Covenant on Civil and Political Rights: CCPR Commentary (N P Engel Kehl 2005) 492.

the two protected groups/right holders are not completely synonymous, the clear link between minorities and genocide has also been confirmed by the HRC, which in its Article 29 stated that 'the international protection of the rights of persons belonging to minorities includes elements that must be respected in all circumstances. This is reflected in the prohibition of genocide under international law…'.[483]

Even though the individual is clearly a victim of genocidal measures, the perpetration of the act extends beyond its actual commission. The murder of a particular individual, for example, must therefore be committed for the realization of an ulterior motive, namely the specific intent to destroy, in whole or in part, a national ethnical, racial or religious group.[484] This group element does again bring the prohibition of genocide into the clear vicinity of the system of minority protection, which has been struggling since its beginnings with the individual vs collective dichotomy and has been described as a bundle of 'individual rights, but with a group reference'.[485] Resolution 96 (I) United Nations General Assembly already emphasized the group element inherent in the crime of genocide by stating that 'genocide is a denial of the right of existence of entire human groups, as homicide is the denial of the right to live of individual human beings'. The Genocide Convention as well as the Rome Statute protect against the commission of acts by both State officials and private persons.[486]

In conclusion, the fact that the Genocide Convention itself does not apply the term 'minorities' can simply be seen as an acknowledgment of the

---

483 UN HRC 'General Comment No 29: Derogations from Provisions of the Covenant during a State of Emergency (Art. 4)' (24 July 2001) GAOR 56th Session Supp 40 vol 1, 202; see also Rüdiger Wolfrum 'Das Verbot der Diskriminierung aufgrund von Rasse, Herkunft, Sprache oder Hautfarbe im Völkerrecht' in Rüdiger Wolfrum (eds) *Gleichheit und Nichtdiskriminierung im nationalen und internationalen Menschenrechtsschutz* (Springer Berlin 2003) 215-231, 218, where the Genocide Convention is listed das the first international convention dealing with a specific aspect of racial discrimination.

484 See eg *Prosecutor v Akayesu (Judgment) ICTR-96-4-T (2 September 1998)* para. 522.

485 Jost Delbrück and Rüdiger Wolfrum *Völkerrecht* Volume I/2: *Der Staat und andere Völkerrechtssubjekte; Räume unter internationaler Verwaltung* (2nd edition De Gruyter Berlin 2002) 279, translation by the author.

486 Art. Convention on the Prevention and Punishment of the Crime of Genocide (adopted 9 December 1948, entered into force 12 January 1951) 78 UNTS 277; Art. 25 (1) Rome Statute of the International Criminal Court (adopted 17 July 1998, entered into force 1 July 2002) 2187 UNTS 90.

fact that a numerical inferiority is not legally necessary in order to gain the protection of the Genocide Convention. This does, however, not challenge the fact, which had also been acknowledged by the drafters of the convention, that minorities are 'genocide's most frequent targets'[487] and 'natural victims'[488] of genocidal measures and therefore the prime beneficiaries of the Genocide Convention and Article 6 of the Rome Statute which protect minorities against physical destruction.

b) Crimes against Humanity/Persecution

The gap in minority protection with regards to the criminal prosecution of acts directed against minorities which fall short of genocide was, on a global level, partly remedied only with the adoption of the Rome Statute. The concept of crimes against humanity had before been inserted into the Statutes of the Nuremberg International Military Tribunal and the Military Tribunal of the Far East[489]. The insertion of crimes against humanity into the Statute of the Nuremberg Tribunal was done in an attempt to cover the crimes committed by Germany against its own minorities. [490]

(1) Important Developments in Terms of Minority Protection

In the context of minority protection, the development from the international military tribunals after World War II to the *ad hoc* tribunals established in the 1990s and finally to the Rome Statute and the ICC brought two major developments which ought to be highlighted: first the disappearance of the link between the crime and an armed conflict as a requirement; and second, the expansion of international jurisdiction to both State and non-State actors.

487 UN Secretary-General 'Address to the Commission on Human Rights' (7 April 2004) <http://www.un.org/press/en/2004/sgsm9245.doc.htm> (31 October 2017).

488 Patrick Thornberry *International Law and the Rights of Minorities* (Clarendon Press Oxford 1991) 59.

489 Charter of the International Military Tribunal for the Far East (19 January 1946) 4 Bevans 20.

490 Lyal S Sunga 'International Criminal Law: Protection of Minorities' in Zelim A Skurbaty (ed) Beyond a One-Dimensional State: An Emerging Right to Autonomy? (Nijhoff Leiden 2005) 255-275, 270.

(1.1) Crimes against Humanity and Armed Conflict

Control Council Law No. 10,[491] issued by the Control Council for Germany on 20 December 1945, omitted the restriction of crimes against humanity to acts connected to war from the definition of such crimes. However, this does not mean that crimes against humanity as defined in the Nuremberg Charter can be considered the cornerstone of a system of international criminal law equally applicable in times of war and peace, protecting the human rights of inhabitants of all countries, 'of any civilian population',[492] against anybody, including their own states and governments. According to its preamble, Council Law No. 10 was enacted to give effect to the Nuremberg Charter, which was mentioned in Article I as an integral part of Council Law No. 10.[493] This link was thought to give the definition of crimes against humanity in Control Council Law No. 10 the same connotation as in the Nuremberg Charter.[494] Therefore, even though the Nuremberg Trials were an important contribution to minority protection and the evolution of international criminal law, crimes against humanity as interpreted in Nuremberg aimed to ensure that inhumane acts in violation of general principles of the law committed in connection with war should be punished. Crimes against humanity were treated as 'accompanying' or 'accessory' crimes to either crimes against peace or war crimes.[495]

Article 5 ICTY Statute explicitly links the concept of crimes against humanity to the existence of an armed conflict of an international or national character, whereas according to Article 3 of the ICTR Statute, the crime must be committed on national, political, ethnic, racial or political

491 Control Council Law No 10 'Punishment of Persons Guilty of War Crimes, Crimes against Peace and against Humanity' (done 20 December 1945) (1946) 3 Official Gazette of the Control Council for Germany 50.

492 Egon Schwelb 'Crimes against Humanity' (1946) 23 British Yearbook of International Law 178-226, 206.

493 Egon Schwelb 'Crimes against Humanity' (1946) 23 British Yearbook of International Law 178-226, 218.

494 Patrick Thornberry *International Law and the Rights of Minorities* (Clarendon Press Oxford 1991) 89; Egon Schwelb 'Crimes against Humanity' (1946) 23 British Yearbook of International Law 178-226 217-8.

495 Egon Schwelb 'Crimes against Humanity' (1946) 23 British Yearbook of International Law 178-226, 206; Kriangsak Kittichaisaree *International Criminal Law* (OUP Oxford 2001) 87.

grounds, linking crimes against humanity more closely to the protection of minorities. This additional requirement of discriminatory intent in each of the enumerated crimes is omitted in the Rome Statute. This does not, however, mean that the relevance towards minority issues has been neglected at the Rome Conference. On the contrary, the delegations felt the need to avoid an onerous and unnecessary burden for the prosecution while at the same time not excluding other forms of crimes against humanity that can be committed without a discriminatory motive.[496] Nevertheless, with the notion that not *all* crimes against humanity require a discriminatory motive, the drafters of the Rome Statute also acknowledged that the (vast) majority of these crimes are indeed committed out of a discriminatory intent.

Article 7 (1) (h) Rome Statute dismisses any link of the concept of crimes against humanity to an armed conflict. The majority of delegations believed that such a limitation would have rendered crimes against humanity largely redundant, as they would have been subsumed in most cases within the definition of war crimes.[497] This is of capital importance to minority protection as many attacks on minorities are committed in situations where the intensity of violence falls short of the definition of an armed conflict,[498] particularly in cases of crimes perpetrated against minorities by their own governments. [499]

Despite this major contribution to the protection of minority groups, one has to keep in mind that the threshold for crimes against humanity is still a very high one. The acts listed in Article 7 must be 'committed as part of a widespread or systematic attack directed against any civilian population, with knowledge of the attack.' Therefore, even though the omission of a nexus between the commission of crimes against humanity and an armed conflict is a big step forward in the prevention of crime perpetrated against minorities, numerous organized crimes perpetrated against

---

496 Darryl Robinson 'Defining "Crimes against Humanity" at the Rome Conference' (1999) 93 American Journal of International Law 43-57, 46-47.

497 Darryl Robinson Defining "Crimes against Humanity" at the Rome Conference' (1999) 93 American Journal of International Law 43-57, 46-47.

498 Lyal S Sunga 'International Criminal Law: Protection of Minorities' in Zelim A Skurbaty (ed) *Beyond a One-Dimensional State: An Emerging Right to Autonomy?* (Nijhoff Leiden 2005) 255-275, 271.

499 Darryl Robinson Defining "Crimes against Humanity" at the Rome Conference' (1999) 93 American Journal of International Law 43-57, 46.

minorities still fall short of the high requirements necessary for labelling a crime an international 'crime against humanity'.

(1.2) Crimes Against Humanity and Non-State Actors

According to Article 7 Rome Statute, crimes against humanity can be committed by both State and non-State actors. Similarly, both the ICTY and the ICTR held that their jurisdiction covers action by non-State actors as well as actions committed by State actors.[500] On the one hand, it obviously seems to be an improvement of their situation if they are protected from crimes committed by both State and private actors. On the other hand, it is to be feared that governments use the ICC to get rid of insurgents and rebel forces while at the same time drawing attention away from their own human rights violations.[501] As the ICC was established to deal with such (State) actors that typically go unpunished as opposed to non-State actors, which, once the State can catch them, are exposed to its full force, this is a worrying development.[502] It needs to be kept in mind when following the ICC's investigations that they so far mostly concentrate on cases transferred by co-operative governments concerning rebel forces and members of previous governments.[503] Yet it is still also worth noting that a State which refers a situation to the ICC cannot pick and choose which actors the court is going to focus on. This means that, at least theoretically, there is a possibility that the Prosecutor of the ICC will in fact expand his investigations to cover State as well as non-State actors, a fact that the former Prosecutor, Luis Moreno Ocampo, repeatedly emphasized.[504] Keeping

---

500 *Prosecutor v Tadić (Opinion and Judgment)* IT-94-1 (7 May 1997). para. 654; *Prosecutor v Kayishema (Judgment)* ICTR-95-1-T (21 May 1999) para. 126.

501 William A. Schabas *Preventing Genocide and Mass Killing: The Challenge for the United Nations* (Minority Rights Group International London 2006) <https://eprints.mdx.ac.uk/7840/1/MRGGenocideReport.pdf> (31 October 2017) 24.

502 William A. Schabas *Preventing Genocide and Mass Killing: The Challenge for the United Nations* (Minority Rights Group International London 2006) https://eprints.mdx.ac.uk/7840/1/MRGGenocideReport.pdf >2 (31 October 2017) 24.

503 Situations in the Democratic Republic of the Congo, Mali, Uganda, and the Central African Republic.

504 Eg in an interview with the Coalition for the International Criminal Court http://www.iccnow.org/?mod=newsdetail&news=1841 (last retrieved October 2015).

in mind the ICTR's experience, however, which was faced with Rwandan refusals to co-operate once it mentioned the possibility of investigating atrocities committed by the Rwandan Patriotic Front (now: Rwandan Patriotic Army) backed by present Rwandan government, such a development seems to be unlikely.

Nonetheless, some of the most prominent cases, before the ICC, the situation in Darfur and Libya, which were referred to the ICC by the Security Council and the situation in Kenya, which was initiated by the Prosecutor using his *proprio motu* powers, are an exception to this pattern. Furthermore, the ICC is keeping situations in further countries under preliminary examination (e.g. Afghanistan, Colombia, Iraq/UK, Nigeria and Ukraine), including a variety of both State and non-State actors. [505] Therefore, it is still to be seen whether the ICC will continue to focus its efforts on the prosecution of non-State actors, a development that would be regrettable.

(2) Specific Crimes and Their inherent Minority Element

(2.1) Murder/Extermination

Murder as listed in Article 7 (a) Rome Statute and extermination (Article 7 (b)) cover the widespread or systematic targeting of a minority group that falls short of the definition of genocide.[506] What distinguishes murder from extermination is that extermination requires an element of mass destruction that is not imperative for murder.[507]

505 See https://www.icc-cpi.int/pages/preliminary-examinations.aspx?ln=en (31 October 2017).

506 Lyal S Sunga 'International Criminal Law: Protection of Minorities' in Zelim A Skurbaty (ed) *Beyond a One-Dimensional State: An Emerging Right to Autonomy?* (Nijhoff Leiden 2005) 255-275.

507 *Prosecutor v Akayesu (Judgment)* ICTR-96-4-T (2 September 1998) para 591.

(2.2) Deportation or Forcible Transfer of Population

The crimes of deportation and forcible transfer of population were often used in the past by ultra-nationalist governments in their attempts to ethnically cleanse the territory of its minority population.[508]

Deportation or forcible transfer of populations is defined under Article 7 (2) (d) as 'forced displacement of the persons concerned by expulsion or other coercive acts from an area in which they are lawfully present, without grounds permitted under international law'. Article 7 (d) Rome Statute, as opposed to Article 5 (d) ICTY Statute and Article 3 (d) ICTR Statute, refers to 'forcible transfer of population' as an alternative offence. 'Deportation' is defined as the forced removal of people from one country to another, whereas 'forcible transfer of population' means the compulsory movement of people from one area to another within the same state.[509] This reflects the experiences in conflicts such as the former Yugoslavia, where the victims were transferred within the territory of Yugoslavia as a part of a greater policy of 'ethnic cleansing.'[510]

(2.3) Rape, Sexual Slavery, Enforced Prostitution, Forced Pregnancy, Enforced Sterilisation, or any other Form of Sexual Violence of Comparable Gravity

In comparison to the ICTY and the ICTR Statute, Article 7 (g) Rome Statute takes a much wider approach on sexual violence. Whereas Articles 5 (g) ICTY Statute and 3 (g) ICTR Statute mention only rape, the drafters of the Rome Statute seemed to have learned from past experiences, especially of the two *ad hoc* tribunals, which for a long time tended to marginalise sexual violence. It acknowledges that sexual violence as a crime against humanity can be committed through various actions. Sexual

---

508 E.g the deportation of more than 1 million Armenians by Turkish authorities between 1915 and 1917, *see* Adam Jones *Genocide* (Routledge London 2006) 107.

509 M Cherif Bassiouni *Crimes against Humanity in International Criminal Law* (2nd ed Kluwer Law International The Hague 1999) 301.

510 Even though there is no formal legal definition of the term 'ethnic cleansing', it is often conducted through means of forcible transfer, deportation or persecution and was labelled a form of genocide by the UN General Assembly in UNGA Res 47/121 'The Situation in Bosnia and Herzegovina' (7 April 1993) GAOR 47th Session Supp 49 vol 1, 44.

violence is often used as a means to demoralise minority populations by committing acts on individuals that are said to affect the 'honour' of the group as a whole. Furthermore, this form of violence can be used in the context of ethnic violence to destroy minorities by forcing their female members to give birth to babies that are considered to belong to a different ethnic group in order to 'pollute and water down the blood line',[511] which can constitute an act of genocide.[512] However, it should be noted that the way international criminal and international humanitarian law has dealt with sexual violence against women, concentrating on concepts of honour of the community rather than the physical harm caused to an individual, has been heavily criticised by feminist scholars (see also under Part Two Chapter Three).[513] In this respect, the Rome Statute with its expansion of the perception of sexual violence as a crime against humanity beyond rape is a positive development in the protection of women's physical individual integrity.

(2.4) Persecution as a Crime against Humanity with a Particularly Prominent Minority Element

The crime of persecution is a criminal offence which minorities are particularly prone to. The crime as defined in the Rome Statute covers a broad range of actions. Article 7 (1) (h) Rome Statute contains persecution 'against any identifiable group or collectivity on political, racial, national, ethnic, cultural, religious, gender (…) or other grounds that are universally recognized as impermissible under international law' as a crime against humanity. Furthermore, in Article 7 (2) (g) Rome Statute the term is defined to mean 'the intentional and severe deprivation of fundamental rights contrary to international law by reasons of the identity of the group or collectivity.' The Rome Statute is the first international criminal instru-

---

511 Amy E Ray, 'The Shame of it: Gender-Based Terrorism in the Former Yugoslavia and the Failure of International Human Rights Law to Comprehend the Injuries' (1997) 46 *American University Law Review* 793-840, 805-6.

512 *Prosecutor v Akayesu (Judgment)* ICTR-96-4-T (2 September 1998) para 688.

513 Eg Judith Gardam and Hilary Charlesworth 'Protection of Women in Armed Conflicts' (2000) 22(1) *Human Rights Quarterly* 148-166, 159.

ment defining persecution.[514] However, its definition derives in part from the jurisprudence of the ICTY, which dealt with large-scale persecutions of minorities during the conflicts that followed the dissolution of Yugoslavia. According to the ICTY, whose judgments can shed light on the interpretation of Articles 7 (1) (h) and (2) (g) Rome Statute, 'it is the violation of the right to equality in some serious fashion that infringes on the enjoyment of a basic or fundamental right that constitutes persecution (...) on one of the listed grounds to constitute persecution under the Statute',[515] 'the gross and blatant denial, on discriminatory grounds, of a fundamental right, laid down in international customary or treaty law, reaching the same level of gravity as the other acts prohibited in Article 5 [ICTY Statute]'.[516] The *Tadic* definition roots in the descriptive explanations of the 1991 Draft Code of Crimes against the Peace and Security of Mankind which states that persecution is aimed at subjecting 'individuals or groups of individuals to a life in which enjoyment of in which enjoyment of some of their basic rights is repeatedly or constantly denied.'[517] The commentary to the 1996 Draft Code of Crimes stated that the common denominator of persecution was the denial of the human rights and fundamental freedoms to which every individual is entitled without distinction as recognized in the Charter of the United Nations (Articles 1 and 55) and the International Covenant on Civil and Political Rights (Article 2)'[518]

The notion of persecution as such contains a group element, and includes the targeting of individuals because of their group membership as well as targeting the group as such.[519] Persecution as a crime against humanity encompasses acts from killing to limitations on the type of profes-

---

514 Machtheld Boot, Rodney Dixon and Christopher K Hall 'Article 7: Crimes against Humanity' in Otto Triffterer Commentary on the Rome Statute of the International Criminal Court (2nd edition Beck Munich 2008) 159-273, 256.

515 *Prosecutor v Tadić (Opinion and Judgment)* IT-94-1 (7 May 1997) para. 697.

516 *Prosecutor v Kupreškić (Trial Chamber Judgment)* IT-95-16 (14 January 2000) para. 621.

517 UN ILC 'Draft Code of Crimes against the Peace and Security of Mankind' (1991) vol II part II UNYBILC 79, 104.

518 UN ILC 'Draft Code of Crimes against the Peace and Security of Mankind' (1996) GAOR 51st Session Supp 10, 9.

519 See Machtheld Boot, Rodney Dixon and Christopher K Hall 'Article 7: Crimes against Humanity' in Otto Triffterer Commentary on the Rome Statute of the International Criminal Court (2nd edition Beck Munich 2008) 159-273, 217.

sions open to targeted groups[520] and acts of physical, economic or judicial nature in violation of an individual's right to equal enjoyment of basic rights.[521] As such, the prohibition of persecution in international criminal law supplements the general principles of equality and non-discrimination in international human rights law in a common effort to protect minorities in heterogeneous societies. Generally, the acts prohibited can be grouped into 'serious bodily harm and mental harm, infringements upon freedom and attacks against property'[522] and therefore cover a wide range of threats against minorities.

The acts must be carried out with the intent of depriving the victim of the political, social or economic rights enjoyed by members of the wider society for reason of his or her membership in a particular protected group[523]. One recent development of particular importance to minority protection is the categorizing of systematic hate speech against minorities as persecution by the ICTR[524]. The deprivation of rights which are a result of the act of persecution include fundamental rights from which no derogation is permitted. However, the list of acts enlisted in the Rome Statute shows that also acts from which States are generally allowed to derogate can constitute persecution.[525]

As examined, a large variety of acts committed against minorities can be subsumed under the heading of 'persecution'. Generally, what is commonly referred to as 'cultural genocide' is indeed mostly covered by the notion of persecution. The legal concept of crimes against humanity thus constitutes a useful tool capable of covering many of forms of attacks against minorities, including on their cultural heritage.

520 *Prosecutor v Tadić (Opinion and Judgment)* IT-94-1 (7 May 1997) para. 704.

521 *Prosecutor v Tadić (Opinion and Judgment)* IT-94-1 (7 May 1997) para. 710.

522 Machtheld Boot, Rodney Dixon and Christopher K Hall 'Article 7: Crimes against Humanity' in Otto Triffterer Commentary on the Rome Statute of the International Criminal Court (2nd edition Beck Munich 2008) 159-273, 258.

523 *Prosecutor v Kupreškić (Trial Chamber Judgment)* IT-95-16 (14 January 2000) para. 634.

524 *Prosecutor v Nahimana (Judgment)* ICTR-99-52-T (3 December 2003).para. 1072.

525 Machtheld Boot, Rodney Dixon and Christopher K Hall 'Article 7: Crimes against Humanity' in Otto Triffterer Commentary on the Rome Statute of the International Criminal Court (2nd edition Beck Munich 2008) 159-273, 263.

(2.5) Enforced Disappearance of Persons

The delegations at the Rome Conference agreed that enforced disappearance, which was previously identified as a crime against humanity only in international instruments[526] but not in the statutes of any of the international tribunals, was an inhumane act similar to the other acts in character and gravity, which warranted specific acknowledgement.[527] It is punishable pursuant to Article 7 (1) (i) Rome Statute. The practice of enforced disappearance has been employed by governments on many occasions to rid the country of political opponents and to silence dissidents over such issues as greater autonomy for minority groups.[528]

(2.5) The Crime of Apartheid

In general terms, apartheid refers to the racial segregation and discrimination policies enacted by a government against a part of its own people.[529] Historically, the term evolved from the segregation policies institutionalized by the government of South Africa from the late 1940s until 1994. It has been a punishable crime against humanity since 1976, when the United Nations Apartheid Convention entered into force.[530]

Article 7 (1) (j) Rome Statute chooses a broader approach than the one taken by the Apartheid Convention. Whereas the latter states that Apartheid includes “similar policies and practices of racial segregation

---

526 UNGA Res 47/133 ‘Declaration on the Protection of All Persons from Enforced Disappearance’ (18 December 1992) GAOR 47th Session Supp 49 vol 1, 207; Inter-American Convention on Forced Disappearance of Persons (done 9 June 1994, entered into force 28 March 1996) (1994) 33 ILM 1529; UN ILC ‘Draft Code of Crimes against the Peace and Security of Mankind’ (1996) GAOR 51st Session Supp 10, 9.

527 Darryl Robinson Defining ”Crimes against Humanity” at the Rome Conference’ (1999) 93 American Journal of International Law 43-57, 55.

528 Lyal Sunga ‘International Criminal Law: Protection of Minorities’ Zelim A Skurbaty (ed) *Beyond a One-Dimensional State: An Emerging Right to Autonomy?* (Nijhoff Leiden 2005) 255-275, 272.

529 Claire de Than and Edwin Shorts *International Criminal Law and Human Rights* (Sweet &Maxwell London 2003) 110.

530 International Convention on the Suppression and Punishment of the Crime of Apartheid (adopted 30 November 1973, entered into force 18 July 1976) 1015 UNTS 243.

and discrimination as practised in southern Africa" (Article II), the Rome Statute does not contain that phrase and instead, in Article 7 (2) (h), defines apartheid as:

> 'inhumane acts of a character similar to those referred to in paragraph 1, committed in the context of an institutionalized regime of systematic oppression and domination by one racial group over any other racial group or groups and committed with the intention of maintaining that regime'.

This expands the scope of application of that prohibition and eliminates the connection to the South African apartheid system that was unique in the sense that it was a minority which oppressed the majority. The fact that in many cases a minority group is suppressed can be inferred from the commentary by the working group on minorities to the UNDM Minorities in which apartheid is expressively mentioned as a way to exclude minorities from society.[531]

c) 'Ethnic Cleansing' in International Criminal Law

Targeting of minorities is often associated with the term 'ethnic cleansing'. However, ethnic cleansing is not a technical term used or defined in the Rome Statute or any of the statutes of international courts or tribunals. Nevertheless, it is an often-used term, in the media as well as in the international arena, especially during the conflicts following the dissolution of the former Yugoslavia[532]. Ethnic cleansing 'was used initially as a euphemistic expression to describe a variety of practices undertaken with the objective of expelling or inducing the departure of persons who did not belong to a particular group from a defined area'.[533] The UN General Assembly has expressly linked 'ethnic cleansing' to minority protection and

---

531 UN ECOSOC 'Commentary of the Working Group on Minorities to the United Nations Declaration on the Rights of Persons Belonging to National or Ethnic, Religious and Linguistic Minorities' (4 April 2005) UN Doc E/CN.4/Sub.2/AC. 5/2005/2 para 25.

532 Eg in UNGA Res 60/1 '2005 World Summit Outcome' (16 September 2005) GAOR 60th Session Supp 49 vol 1, 3 paras 138-140, in which the responsibility of a State to protect 'its populations from genocide, war crimes, ethnic cleansing and crimes against humanity' was set out.

533 William J Fenrick 'The crime against humanity of persecution in the jurisprudence of the ICTY' (2001) 32 Netherlands Yearbook of International Law 81-96, 89.

racial discrimination in its resolution 48/91 on 'Ethnic Cleansing and Racial Discrimination'[534].

The ICJ in the case of the *Application of the Convention on the Prevention and Punishment of the Crime of Genocide (Bosnia and Herzegovina* v. *Serbia and Montenegro)* defined ethnic cleansing as 'rendering an area ethnically homogenous by using force or intimidation to remove persons of given groups from the area'[535]. Ethnic cleansing often comes hand in hand with other gross violations of human rights, as it may be conducted, *inter alia*, by means of forcible transfer, deportation murder or rape. Therefore, the legal categorization of the term is highly controversial and the additional value that the term brings compared to the use of already acknowledged legal terms is disputed. Nevertheless, the term has often been referred to by the ICTY, also in indictments, and has been linked to crimes against humanity in general[536] and also, more particular, to the crime of persecution[537].

But not only crimes against humanity, also genocide has been associated with the term 'ethnic cleansing'.[538] However, compared to the acts covered in the Genocide Convention, 'ethnic cleansing' seems to pursue a different goal, namely the expulsion of an ethnic minority and its culture from a given area as opposed to the extinction of that minority. One frequent component of 'ethnic cleansing', namely forcible population transfer, was, like the destruction of a minorities' cultural life, deliberately ex-

---

534 UNGA Res 48/91 'Third Decade to Combat Racism and Racial Discrimination' (20 December 1993) GAOR 48th Supp 49 193.

535 *Application of the Convention on the Prevention and Punishment of the Crime of Genocide (Bosnia and Herzegovina v Serbia and Montenegro) (Merits)* ([2007] ICJ Rep 43 para 190; see also UNSC 'First Interim Report of the Commission of Experts established pursuant to Paragraph 2 of UNSC Resolution 780 (1992) (9 February 1993) UN Doc S/25274 (1993) para. 55 and M Cherif Bassiouni and Peter Manikas *The Law of the International Criminal Tribunal for the Former Yugoslavia* (Transnational Publishers Irvington-on-Hudson 1996) 608.

536 *Prosecutor v Kupreškić* (Trial Chamber Judgment) IT-95-16 (14 January 2000) para. 606.

537 *Prosecutor v Sikirica et al* (Judgement on Defence Motions to Acquit) IT-95-8-T (3 September 2001) para. 90.

538 See UNGA Res 47/121 'The situation in Bosnia and Herzegovina' (18 December 1992) GAOR 47th Session Supp 49, 44 and the UN Commission on Human Rights Special Rapporteur Bacre Waly Ndiaye 'Report of the Special Rapporteur of the Commission on Human Rights on extrajudicial, summary or arbitrary executions (6 October 1996) UN Doc A/51/457, para. 69.

cluded from the Genocide Convention. This is true at least if it is not paired with a genocidal intent and done in circumstances 'calculated to bring about its [the group's] physical destruction in whole or in part'.

Additionally, already the Nuremberg Charter grouped the acts committed in crimes of the 'murder type' and crimes of the 'persecution type'[539], which suggests that the crime of persecution is not typically committed through the killing of individuals (even though it may well lead to it), but through their systematic discrimination in public life. This categorization of crimes by the Nuremberg Trials has later been upheld by the International Law Commission and the ICTY.[540] Looking at the above-mentioned definition of ethnic cleansing by the ICTY, ethnic cleansing seems not to fall under the 'murder type' of crimes against humanity (which at Nuremberg also covered what is now know legally known as genocide) as envisages by the Nuremberg Trial. Therefore, an equation of ethnic cleansing with genocide seems to be inaccurate.

In conclusion, 'ethnic cleansing' seems to be, at least partly, subsumed by the above-discussed crime of persecution (Article 7 (1) (h) Rome Statute) and the more specific means by which an area is rendered 'ethnically homogenous' are mostly punishable as crimes against humanities by themselves (see e.g. murder and extermination as enshrined in Article 7 (1) (a) and (b) Rome Statute or the prohibition of deportation or forcible transfer of population in Article 7 (1) (d) Rome Statute).

---

539 See *Prosecutor v Tadić (Opinion and Judgment)* IT-94-1 (7 May 1997) para. 694.

540 UNILC 'Principles of International Law recognized in the Charter of the Nürnberg Tribunal and in the Judgment of the Tribunal, with commentaries' 'in (1950) vol II UNYBILC 375-378, para. 120; *Prosecutor v Tadić (Opinion and Judgment)* IT-94-1 (7 May 1997) paras 651 and 694.

d) War Crimes (Art. 8 Rome Statute)

The law of war as set out in its fundamental instruments, the 1907 Hague Regulations[541], the 1949 Geneva Conventions[542] and their 1977 Protocols,[543] does not refer to minorities as such, but provides specific protection to especially vulnerable groups in conflicts, like civilians or prisoners of war. Therefore, in this context, minorities are only protected as victims of a conflict, even though they are indirectly shielded by the underlying principles of the law of war, impartiality and non-discrimination.[544] Furthermore, the principle of non-discrimination is also enshrined in many articles within the Geneva Conventions, for example Article 3 common to all four Geneva Conventions.[545]

The most essential problem in terms of minority protection and war crimes is deciding in which situations a certain act constitutes a war crime. Traditionally, the instruments governing the law of war, with the exception

541 1907 Hague Regulations Respecting the Laws and Customs of War on Land, 18 October 1907, annexed to the Convention respecting the Laws and Customs of War on Land (signed 18 October 1907, entered into force 26 January 1910) (1907) 205 CTS 277.

542 Geneva Convention for the Amelioration of the Condition of the Wounded and Sick in Armed Forces in the Field (adopted 12 August 1949, entered into force 21 October 1950) 75 UNTS 31 (Geneva Convention I); Geneva Convention for the Amelioration of the Condition of Wounded, Sick and Shipwrecked Members of Armed Forces at Sea (adopted 12 August 1949, entered into force 21 October 1950) 75 UNTS 85 (Geneva Convention II); Geneva Convention relative to the Treatment of Prisoners of War (adopted 12 August 1949, entered into force 21 October 1950) 75 UNTS 135 (Geneva Convention III); Geneva Convention relative to the Protection of Civilian Persons in Time of War (adopted 12 August 1949, entered into force 21 October 1950) 75 UNTS 287 (Geneva Convention IV).

543 Protocol Additional to the Geneva Conventions of 12 August 1949, and relating to the Protection of Victims of International Armed Conflicts (Protocol I) (adopted 8 June 1977, entered into force 7 December 1978) 1125 UNTS 3; Protocol Additional to the Geneva Conventions of 12 August 1949, and relating to the Protection of Victims of Non-International Armed Conflicts (Protocol II) (adopted 8 June 1977, entered into force 7 December 1978) 1125 UNTS 609.

544 Peter Finell *Accountability under Human Rights Law and International criminal law against Minority Groups Committed by Non-State Actors* (Åbo Akademi Institute for Human Rights, Åbo/Turku May 2002) 44.

545 *Peter Finell Accountability under Human Rights Law and International criminal law against Minority Groups Committed by Non-State Actors (Åbo Akademi Institute for Human Rights, Åbo/Turku May 2002).*

of Article 3 common to the four Geneva Conventions, deal with international armed conflicts fought between one state and another. Consequently, war crimes as enshrined in the Nuremberg and Tokyo Charters related to crimes committed during international armed conflicts. However, after World War II, the international community has perceived a shift from international, conventional wars, to internal guerrilla style conflicts and civil wars between non-state actors and states. [546] Since 1945, more than 250 internal conflicts and abuses of repressive regimes resulted in an estimated 86 million casualties.[547]

As a result, most of the crimes under international law that have been committed within the context of a conflict occurred within an internal, not an international armed conflict. This is particularly true for crimes committed against minorities because they are, as previously discussed, particularly vulnerable against attacks from their own governments and the governments of the countries they live in respectively. In the situation of the former Yugoslavia, crimes were committed as part of an internal or internationalized armed conflict. For this reason, the ICTY Statute covers war crimes both as grave breaches of the Geneva Conventions relating to international armed conflicts (Article 2) and 'violations of the laws and customs of war' (Article 3) which has been held to cover any serious violation other than grave breaches irrespective if it occurs within an international or an internal armed conflict.[548]

Out of these experiences, many delegations at the Rome Conference, supported by a wide range of NGOs, insisted that the ICC should have jurisdiction not only over crimes committed in inter-state wars but also over those atrocities that occurred within the context of an internal armed conflict.[549] This view ultimately prevailed and accordingly Article 8 (2) Rome

---

546 *See* e.g. Lotta Harbom and Peter Wallensteen *Patterns of Major Conflicts 1997-2008- Stockholm International Peace Research Institute Yearbook 2007: Armaments, Disarmaments and International Security* (OUP Oxford 2007).

547 M Cherif Bassiouni, 'Accountability for Violations of International Humanitarian Law and Other Serious Violations of Human Rights' in M Cherif Bassiouni (ed) *Post-Conflict Justice* (Transnational Publishers Ardsley New York 2002) 6.

548 Kriangsak Kittichaisaree *International Criminal Law* (OUP Oxford 2001) 132-3; *Prosecutor v Tadić (Decision on the Defence Motion for Interlocutory Appeal on Jurisdiction) IT-94-1-AR72 (2 October 1995)* paras. 86-94.

549 Sunga in Zelim A Skurbaty (ed) *Beyond a One-Dimensional State: An Emerging Right to Autonomy?* (Nijhoff Leiden 2005) 255-275, 273.

Statute distinguishes among four categories of war crimes:[550] Concerning international armed conflicts, Article 8 (2) Rome Statute defines war crimes as grave breaches of the Geneva Conventions of 1949 (Article 8 (2) (a) Rome Statute) and secondly, 'other serious violations of the laws and customs applicable in international armed conflict, within the established framework of international law' (Article 8 (2) (b) Rome Statute). As for non-international armed conflicts, Article 8 (2) defines war crimes as serious violations of Article 3 common to the four Geneva Conventions (Article 8 (2) (c)) and secondly, 'other serious violations of the laws and customs applicable in armed conflicts not of an international armed character, within the established framework of international law' (Article 8 (2) (d))[551]. The minority aspects in most of the war crime containing such an aspect have already been discussed, in a different form, under the heading of crimes against humanity. The issues discussed there are just as valid for war crimes, albeit taking account of the specific prerequisite for armed conflict for each of the provisions. Therefore, the provisions with a minority aspect will be simply listed here for the sake of completeness.

(1) International Armed Conflicts

Provisions especially relevant to the protection of minorities in international armed conflicts include*, inter alia*,:

(1.1) Article 8 (2) (a) Rome Statute: Grave Breaches of the Fourth Geneva Convention Protecting Civilian Persons in Times of War:

The prohibition of wilful killing (Article 8 (2) (a) (i)) Rome Statute;

- The prohibition of torture or inhuman treatment, including biological experiments (Article 8 (2) (a) (ii)) Rome Statute;
- The prohibition of wilfully causing great suffering, or serious injury to body and health (Article 8 (2) (a) (iii)) Rome Statute;

550 Sunga in Zelim A Skurbaty (ed) *Beyond a One-Dimensional State: An Emerging Right to Autonomy?* (Nijhoff Leiden 2005) 255-275, 273.
551 Sunga in Zelim A Skurbaty (ed) *Beyond a One-Dimensional State: An Emerging Right to Autonomy?* (Nijhoff Leiden 2005) 255-275, 273.

- The prohibition of unlawful deportation or transfer or unlawful confinement (Article 8 (2) (a) (vii)) Rome Statute.

(1.2) Article 8 (2) (b) Rome Statute: Other serious violations of the Laws and Customs Applicable in International Armed Conflict, within the Established Framework of International Law:

- The prohibition of attacks against the civilian population (Article 8 (2) (b) (i)) Rome Statute;
- The prohibition of deportation or forcible transfer (Article 8 (2) (b)(viii)) Rome Statute;
- The prohibition of attack of religious, charitable, scientific, cultural objects (Article 8 (2) (b) (xi)) Rome Statute;
- The prohibition of sexual violence (Article 8 (2) (b) (xxii)) Rome Statute.

(2) Non- International Armed Conflicts

When it comes to internal conflicts, the most crucial provisions on terms of minority protections are:

(2.1) Article 8 (2) (c) Rome Statute: Serious Violations of Article 3 Common to the four Geneva Conventions of 12 August 1949

The prohibition of violence to life and person, in particular murder of all kinds, mutilation, cruel treatment and torture (Article 8 (2) (c) (i) Rome Statute);
The prohibition of outrages on human dignity, in particular humiliating and degrading treatment (Article 8 (2) (c) (ii)) Rome Statute;

(2.2) Article 8 (2) (e) Rome Statute : Other Serious Violations of the Laws and Customs Applicable in Armed Conflicts not of an International Character, within the Established Framework of International Law:

- The prohibition of intentionally directing attacks against the civilian population as such or against individual civilians not taking direct part in hostilities (Article 8 (2) (e) (i) Rome Statute);
- The prohibition of intentionally directing attacks against buildings dedicated to religion, education, art, science or charitable purposes, historic monuments, hospitals and places where the sick and wounded are collected, provided they are not military objectives (Article 8 (2) (e) (iv) Rome Statute);
- The prohibition of rape, sexual slavery, enforced prostitution, forced pregnancy, as defined in Article 7 (2) (f) Rome Statute, enforced sterilisation and any other form of sexual violence also constituting a serious violation of Article 3 common to the four Geneva Conventions (Article 8 (2) (e) (vi) Rome Statute);
- The prohibition of ordering the displacement of the civilian population for reasons related to the conflict, unless the security of the civilians involved or imperative military reasons so demand (Article 8 (2) (e) (viii) Rome Statute).

V. Concluding Remarks

As one can see from the above analysis, recourse to minority right is scarcer than, for example, reference to torture under human rights law. There are several reasons for this, which are to be found both in the system of minority rights law as a concept of human rights as well as in the crimes which contain an element of minority protection. As a first reason, minority rights law are much less established than the prohibition of torture is. The instruments governing it contain few concrete provisions, the content of rights are actually granted to minorities is often contested and the legal nature of many of these rights is controversial on a national level as well as internationally. While minorities are protected through provisions in major international and regional conventions, the rights are frequently misunderstood, looked upon with suspicion by many States for reasons that rooted in history or practical policy, which is mirrored by reservations issued to Article 27 ICCPR.[552] This makes minority rights less accessible and too abstract, in particular for judges who do not have a background in public international law. Secondly, those crimes under international law which contain an element of minority protection, like genocide or persecution, do often have no or no well-established counterpart in national criminal codes. Therefore many instances in which recourse to minority rights would have made the judgments more convincing or would have facilitated the Chamber's arguments remained idle.

Chapter Three: Women's Rights/The Prohibition of Gender-Based Violence

The concept of gender-based crimes has experienced a rapid development in international criminal law within the last decade. They went from being an overlooked, side-lined issue linked to family honour to one of the most discussed and researched areas in international criminal law today. Gender-based crimes also triggered prosecutorial creativity in dealing with those crimes under a variety of other concepts (e.g. rape as torture, genocide, outrages against personal dignity, enslavement, sexual slavery or persecution). The degree to which sexual crimes are prioritized and properly included in indictment does, however, vary considerably between the respective tribunals and seems, to a large degree depend on the persistence and experience of investigators in that field.[553] The developments of gender-based crimes are also mirrored in the general development of the human rights of women in international human rights law and of the understanding and conceptualisation of violence against women and gender-related violence in particular. Like gender-based crimes under international

552 See the Declarations of France, Turkey Declarations and Reservations of the States Parties to the International Covenant on Civil and Political Rights https://treaties.un.org/Pages/ViewDetails.aspx?src=TREATY&mtdsg_no=IV-4&chapter=4&lang=en (31 October 2017).

553 See further Alison Cole 'International criminal law and sexual violence: an overview' in Clare McGlynn and Vanessa Munro *Rethinking Rape Law: International and Comparative Perspectives* (Routledge Abingdon 2010) 47-60 and Doris Buss 'Learning our lesions: The Rwanda Tribunal record on prosecuting rape' in Clare McGlynn and Vanessa Munro *Rethinking Rape Law: International and Comparative Perspectives* (Routledge Abingdon 2010) 61-75.

criminal law, violence against women has for a long time not been seen as an issue relevant to human rights law and its instruments.

According to feminist theory of international law, the reason for this is that the human rights system and international criminal and humanitarian law, are build, like all other legal systems, primarily by men, privileges their experiences and consequently protects humans from violations which predominantly men are likely to suffer from.[554] International humanitarian law has long been in the line of criticism of feminist international legal scholars as a legal system which either relegates women to the status of victims, or accords them legitimacy only in their role as child-bearers.[555] As a consequence of that, international human rights law protects first and foremost violations within the 'public' sphere, violations committed by the State or its agents. Persons who typically suffer from these sorts of violations are active in the public sphere. Women, in contrast, are often confined to the private sphere. Therefore, international human rights law as it was conceived after World War II does often not meet the realities of their existence and therefore also does not protect them. Violations women traditionally suffer from are committed within this private sphere, often by private persons. However, the conceptualisation of human rights law as horizontal rights which put obligations solely on States and, ultimately, makes the State the only responsible for violations.[556] The actions of non-

554 Hilary Charlesworth, Christine Chinkin and Shelley Wright 'Feminist approaches to international law' (1991) 85(4) *American Journal of International Law* 613-645, 625-634; Helen Durham and Katie O'Byrne ‚The dialogue of difference: gender perspectives on international humanitarian law' 92 (2010) International Review of the Red Cross 31–52, 34.

555 Helen Durham and Katie O'Byrne ‚The dialogue of difference: gender perspectives on international humanitarian law' 92 (2010) International Review of the Red Cross 31–52, 34; Gardam and Jarvis point out that of 42 provisions in the Geneva Conventions and the related Protocols which specifically deal with women, almost half of them address them in their capacities as mothers, while the other predominant theme of specific protection of women, with regards to sexual violence, is centred on notions of modesty and chastity: Judith Gardam and Michelle J Jarvis Women *Armed Conflict and International Law* (Kluwer Law International The Hague 2001) 96-7; a modern understanding of sexual violence places an emphasis rather on the violation of the victim's 'physical and moral integrity', see eg *Prosecutor v Češić* (Sentencing Judgment) IT-95-10/1-S (11 March 2004) para. 53.

556 See eg Robert McCorquodale 'Non-state actors and international human rights law' in Sarah Joseph and Adam McBeth (eds) *Research Handbook on International Human Rights Law* (Elgar Cheltenham 2010) 97-114, 100, 101.

State actors can only lead to 'State responsibility in cases of human rights violations in exceptional circumstances[557]. Within these exceptions, the due diligence standard of State responsibility is particularly momentous for recognizing violence against women as violations in the context of human rights law.[558] That way an act which is 'not directly imputable to a State'[559] because it was, for example committed by a private person, can nevertheless trigger the responsibility of a State 'not because of the act itself, but because of the lack of due diligence to prevent the violation'.[560] This concept opened the door for a more creative use of human rights law in order to protect women from systematic violence, usually committed by private persons, in times of peace, and, simultaneously, makes human rights law in this area an obvious source to be consulted by practitioners of international criminal law dealing with issues of gender-related violence.

International human rights documents increasingly mention armed conflict and mass atrocities as situations where women's human rights are endangered and use concepts developed by international criminal or humanitarian law in areas of violence against women. Non-binding human rights documents such as reports by special rapporteurs or by the UN Secretary-General have pointed to a certain violation of women's physical and/or psychological integrity during an armed conflict as 'crimes of a very serious nature with a wide range of severe effects on the victim'[561]. Hence, there is a relatively high degree of reference to international criminal and humanitarian law permeating human rights documents and discourse in the area of sexual violence. This trend might be fuelled as modern international criminal courts and tribunals increasingly gain experience with judging sexual violence. At the ICTY, as of September 2016, 78 individu-

557 UN ILC 'Draft Articles on Responsibility of States for Internationally Wrongful Acts' (2001) GAOR 56th Session Supp 10, 43.

558 See further Alice Edwards 'Everyday rape: International human rights law and violence against women in peacetime' in Clare McGlynn and Vanessa Munro *Rethinking Rape Law: International and Comparative Perspectives* (Routledge Abingdon 2010) 92-108, 102-104.

559 *Velásquez Rodríguez v Honduras (Judgment)* IACtHR Series C No 4 (29 July 1988) para 172.

560 *Velásquez Rodríguez v Honduras (Judgment)* IACtHR Series C No 4 (29 July 1988) para 172.

561 UNSC 'Annex II: Final Report of the United Nations Commission of Experts established Pursuant to Security Council Resolution 780 (1992)' (27 May 1994) UN Doc S/1994/674.

als (48% of the accused) had sexual violence charges included in their indictment.[562] However, only 32 of the accused have been convicted for acts of sexual violence.[563] The prosecution of the ICC was heavily criticised for not bringing charges of sexual violence against *Thomas Lubanga Dyilo*, instead focussing solely of charges of enlisting and conscripting child soldiers.[564] With the case against *Germain Katanga*, the ICC had a case which focused on sexual crimes. In March 2014, Katanga was convicted of crimes against humanity and war crimes but he was acquitted of all modalities related to sexual crimes (rape and sexual slavery) as the court held that even though it found beyond reasonable doubt that the crimes had been committed, Katanga's responsibility had not been adequately proved.[565] However, the majority of cases active before the ICC now include charges of sexual violence and in those in which sexual violence is not included, the prosecutor often explicitly stated that sexual violence continues to be investigated.[566]

---

562 ICTY 'Crimes of Sexual Violence: In Numbers' http://www.icty.org/sid/10586 (31 October 2017).

563 ICTY 'Crimes of Sexual Violence: In Numbers' http://www.icty.org/sid/10586 (31 October 2017).

564 See *Prosecutor v Thomas Lubanga Dyilo (Decision on the confirmation of charges)* ICC-01/04-01/803-tEN (29 January 2007); Brigid Inder 'Reflection: Gender Issues and Child Soldiers – The Case of Thomas Lubanga Dyilo' The Lubanga Trial at the International Criminal Court (31 August 2011) http://www.lubangatrial.org/2011/08/31/reflection-gender-issues-and-child-soldiers-the-case-of-prosecutor-v-thomas-lubanga-dyilo-2/ (31 October 2017).

565 http://www.icc-cpi.int/en_menus/icc/press%20and%20media/press%20releases/Pages/pr986.aspx (31 October 2017).

566 This is for example the case in the situation in Libya brought before the ICC by the UN Security Council. Even though the charges are limited to murder and persecution as crimes against humanity (and sexual violence could also be included under the heading of persecution), the Prosecutor explicitly and repeatedly stated that sexual violence is one focus of the continuous investigations, see eg International Criminal Court The Office of the Prosecutor 'Statement to the United Nations Security Council on the situation in Libya, pursuant to UNSCR 1970 (2011)' (2 November 2011) <http://www.iccnow.org/documents/StatementICCProsecutorLibyaReporttoUNSC021113.pdf> (31 October 2017) paras 14-17, 22. Currently, the majority of cases before the ICC include charges of sexual violence.

I. Where Were Women's Human Rights Referred to?

1. Sexual Assault as Persecution

Reference to human rights law in international criminal jurisprudence is scarcer. However, there are instances in which human rights law is referenced, albeit often in a general and incomplete matter which does not examine human rights law thoroughly and often gives the impression that a reference to human rights law is somewhat expected and the 'human rights box' has to be ticked before judges can turn to comparative law in this area. This, for example, happened with 'enforced prostitution and painful circumcision.'[567] Those offences are mentioned by the ICTY in *Milutinovic* as possible examples of sexual assault other than rape. The ICTY was faced with the problem of determining whether the court has jurisdiction over 'sexual assault' and whether it can qualify as persecution, as this is not clear from looking at the ICTY Statute. The tribunal therefore looked at several other documents, for example its Rules of Procedure and Evidence[568], which contain specific rules for dealing with victims of sexual assault, a fact from which the Chamber defers a will of drafters to prosecute and punish such acts.[569] Furthermore, the tribunal examined its own case law.[570] First and foremost, however, the tribunal consulted 'other authorities' in the area of human rights law, such as the Final Report by the Commission of Experts cited above and the Report of the Secretary-General, which mentioned 'widespread and systematic rape and other sexual assault' as crimes against humanity over which the ICTY should have jurisdiction.[571]

Nevertheless, the Chamber did not resort to 'hard law' like CEDAW. It concluded that '[t]he term "sexual assault" is not explicitly used in any international human rights treaty. The Convention on the Elimination of All

567 UNSC 'Annex II: Final Report of the United Nations Commission of Experts established Pursuant to Security Council Resolution 780 (1992)' (27 May 1994) UN Doc S/1994/674.

568 UN International Criminal Tribunal for the Former Yugoslavia 'Rules of Procedure and Evidence' (as amended 10 December 2009) IT/32/Rev. 44.

569 *Prosecutor v Milutinovic* (Judgment) IT-05-87-T (26 February 2009) para. 185.

570 Particularly at *Prosecutor v Furundžija (Judgment)* IT-95-17 (10 December 1998) and *Prosecutor v Stakić (Judgment)* IT-97-24-T (31 July 2003).

571 UNSC 'Report of the Secretary-General Pursuant to Paragraph 2 of Security Council Resolution 808 (1993)' (3 May 1993) Un Doc S/25704.

Forms of Discrimination Against Women does not mention sexual assault, although it makes reference to the prohibition on "exploitation of prostitution"'. The same is stated by the Trial Chamber in *Furundžija*, where it held that '[n]o international human rights instrument specifically prohibits rape or other serious sexual assault'[572]. In both cases, the Chambers then resort to human rights provisions safeguarding physical integrity. In *Furundžija*, the ICTY Trial Chamber refers to the prohibition of cruel, inhuman or degrading treatment in Art. 7 ICCPR, Art. 5 Banjul Charter and Art. 5 Inter-American Convention on Human Rights. Furthermore, reference is made to Art. 4 Banjul Charter which prohibits violations of the right to integrity of a person and the jurisprudence of the ECommHR (*Cyprus v Turkey*[573]) and the ECtHR (*Aydin v Turkey*[574]) which deals with rape committed by State officials, acts that the Court and the Commission classified as a violation of Art. 3 of the ECHR. In *Milutinovic*, the Chamber holds that '[t]he right not to be sexually assaulted has (…) been subsumed under more general fundamental rights relating to physical integrity'[575] The Chamber is here referring to the above-quoted explanation in *Furundžija* and does not give its own explanations on the matter.

While it remains true that the 'sexual assault' is not explicitly used in any human rights treaty, the Chamber fails to look at the interpretation of the Convention on the Elimination of All Forms of Discrimination against Women (CEDAW) by its treaty body, the Commission on the Elimination of All Forms of Discrimination against Women.[576] How and to what extent the jurisprudence and the general recommendations of this quasi-judicial body could have been of help to the ICTY is examined below (under Part Two Chapter Three).

572 *Prosecutor v Furundžija (Judgment)* IT-95-17 (10 December 1998) para. 170.

573 *Cyprus v Turkey* (EComHR App 6780/74 and 6950/75) 4 EHRR 482.

574 *Aydin v Turkey* (ECtHR) Reports 1997-VI <http://hudoc.echr.coe.int/eng?i=001-58371> (31 October 2017); the case of *Aydin v Turkey* is referred to by several other Chambers as well, for example in *Prosecutor v Kvočka (Judgment)* IT-98-30 (2 November 2001), para. 145.

575 *Prosecutor v Milutinovic* (Judgment) IT-05-87-T (26 February 2009) para. 188.

576 Convention on the Elimination of All Forms of Discrimination against Women (adopted 18 December 1979, entered into force 3 September 1981) 1249 UNTS 13.

2. Rape as Torture

In the first case at the ICTR, *Prosecutor v Akayesu*, the court argues that 'rape is a form of aggression and that the central elements of the crime of rape cannot be captured in a mechanical description of objects and body parts'[577]. This mirrors, as the chamber explicitly mentions, an approach central to the CAT, which 'does not catalogue specific acts in its definition of torture, focusing rather on the conceptual framework of state-sanctioned violence'.[578] The Chamber furthermore compares rape to torture in terms of the purposes the acts serve and the violation of personal dignity, leading to the conclusion that rape indeed constitutes torture 'when inflicted by or at the instigation of or with the consent or acquiescence of a public official or other person acting in an official capacity'.[579]

In *Prosecutor v Delalić et al (Celebići Case)*, the ICTY was faced with the need to determine whether rape could be considered torture in violation of the Geneva Conventions. [580] After examining the provisions under humanitarian law, which prohibit rape and other forms of sexual assault and after concentrating on the definition of rape, the chamber discussed the jurisprudence of international judicial bodies on the issue of rape as torture. Reference was made by the court to the Inter-American Commission on Human Rights in the *Fernando and Raquel Mejia v Peru* Case[581] and the ECtHR in *Aydin v Turkey*[582]. The Trial Chamber uses these two cases to determine the constituent elements of torture and also to outline the difference between torture on the one hand and inhuman or degrading treatment on the other. In *Aydin v Turkey*, the ECtHR held that the difference between torture and inhuman or degrading treatment was 'to allow the special stigma of "torture" to attach only to deliberate inhuman treat-

577 *Prosecutor v Akayesu (Judgment)* ICTR-96-4-T (2 September 1998) paras 596, 687.

578 *Prosecutor v Akayesu (Judgment)* ICTR-96-4-T (2 September 1998) para 687.

579 *Prosecutor v Akayesu (Judgment)* ICTR-96-4-T (2 September 1998) para 597-.

580 *Prosecutor v Delalić et al (Celebići Case Judgment)* IT-96-21 (16 November 1998).

581 *Fernando and Raquel Mejia v Peru* Case 10.970 IACommHR Report No 5/96 (1 March 1996); see *Prosecutor v Delalić et al (Celebići Case Judgment)* IT-96-21 (16 November 1998) paras 481-486.

582 *Aydin v Turkey* (ECtHR) Reports 1997-VI <http://hudoc.echr.coe.int/eng?i=001-58371> (31 October 2017); see *Prosecutor v Delalić et al (Celebići Case Judgment)* IT-96-21 (16 November 1998) paras 487-489.

ment causing very serious and cruel suffering'.[583] The ECtHR, as well as the responsible ICTY Trial Chamber in *Celebići*, concludes that rape does involve such a severe level of suffering that the crime can be categorized as torture. To this end, the ICTY Chamber also refers to a similar oral statement by the Special Rapporteur on Torture[584] and a statement by the Commission of Experts outlining the physical and psychological suffering experienced by victims of rape.[585] Finally, the ICTY examined whether any of the prohibited purposes necessary for the act to be classified as torture are given. To this end, the Chamber considered the prohibited purpose of discrimination and pointed to the report of the Special Rapporteur on Contemporary Forms of Slavery, Systematic Rape, Sexual Slavery and Slavery-like Practices during Armed Conflict and, albeit indirectly, also to the work of the CEDAW Committee. In its Report on 'Contemporary forms of Slavery: Systematic Rape, Sexual Slavery and Slavery-like Practices during Armed Conflict' the Special Rapporteur cites the CEDAW Committee saying that 'violence directed against a woman because she is a woman, including "acts that inflict physical, mental or sexual harm or suffering", represents a form of discrimination that seriously inhibits the ability of women to enjoy human rights and freedoms'.[586] The ICTY fails to clarify that the CEDAW Committee sees gender-based vio-

583 *Aydin v Turkey* (ECtHR) Reports 1997-VI <http://hudoc.echr.coe.int/eng?i=001-58371> (31 October 2017) para. 82; see also *Ireland v United Kingdom* (ECtHR) Series A No 25, para. 167.

584 *Prosecutor v Delalić et al (Celebići Case Judgment)* IT-96-21-T (16 November 1998) para 491, referring to the oral introduction of the Special Rapporteur on Torture, Mr P Kooijmans, to his 1992 report to the Commission on Human Rights according to which rape or other forms of sexual assault against women in detention were a particularly ignominious violation of the inherent dignity and the right to physical integrity of the human being, they accordingly constituted an act of torture' UN Doc E/CNA/1992/SR.21 para.35. See UN Commission on Human Rights 'Question of the human rights of all persons subjected to any form of detention or imprisonment, in particular: torture and other cruel, inhuman or degrading treatment or punishment: Report of the Special Rapporteur, Mr. Nigel S. Rodley' (12 January 1995) UN Doc E/CNA/1995/34.

585 *Prosecutor v Delalić et al (Celebići Case Judgment)* IT-96-21-T (16 November 1998) para 492, referring to UNSC 'Final Report of the Commission of Experts Established Pursuant to Security Council Resolution 935 (1994): Annex IX' (9 December 1994) UN Doc S/1994/1405, Section D.

586 UN Commission on Human Rights 'Systematic rape, sexual slavery and slave-like practices during armed conflict: Final report submitted by Ms. Gay J. McDougall, Special Rapporteur' (22 June 1998) UN Doc E/CN.4/Sub.2/1998/13,

lence explicitly in the context of State parties obligations and defines discriminatory and therefore illegal gender-based violence broadly, not only as violence committed against a woman because she is a woman, but also violence which affects women disproportionally[587] as discrimination prohibited by CEDAW. Here, the court fails to acknowledge that discrimination, which it has earlier identified as one possible of the necessary prohibited purposes in torture, manifests itself in the mass occurrence of violence against women. States can be in breach of CEDAW in this case, either when they do not live up to the due diligence standard of prevention and punishment of violent acts against women or if the perpetrators are State agents. These findings of the CEDAW Committee are directly relevant to many cases of sexual violence under international law and open an entry point for prosecutorial innovations. By cutting the CEDAW Committee's definition in half and taking the definition of gender-based violence that arguably has the higher threshold and is harder to prove (violence is committed against a woman because she is a woman) the court limited the application area of the definition in cases of crime requiring discrimination like persecution or torture. The reason why the ICTY chose to only employ part of the CEDAW Commission's definition could be that the Court thought itself on safer ground in terms of the customary nature of the definition when using the more narrow part of the definition. However, the approach to place all violence against women in the context of discrimination has been established years before the *Celebići* judgement and supported by a variety of institutions and UN agencies. In 1993, the UNGA adopted the Declaration on the Elimination of Violence against Women ('DEVW'), which acknowledges in its preamble that

'violence against women is a manifestation of historically unequal power relations between men and women, which have led to domination over and discrimination against women by men and to the prevention of the full advancement of women, and that violence against women is one of the

para. 55; see also UN Committee on the Elimination of Discrimination against Women 'General Recommendation No 19: Violence against Women' (30 January 1992) GAOR 47th Session Supp 38, 1, para. 6.

587 UN Committee on the Elimination of Discrimination against Women 'General Recommendation No 19: Violence against Women' (30 January 1992) GAOR 47th Session Supp 38, 1, para. 6.

crucial social mechanisms by which women are forced into a subordinate position compared with men'.[588]

Article 1 DEVW states

> '[f]or the purposes of this Declaration, the term "violence against women" means any act of gender-based violence that results in, or is likely to result in, physical, sexual or psychological harm or suffering to women, including threats of such acts, coercion or arbitrary deprivation of liberty, whether occurring in public or in private life.'

These provisions seem to suggest that the terms violence against women and gender-based violence are used basically used as synonyms, even though the CEDAW Committee uses gender-based violence both in a broader and in a narrower sense than violence against women.[589] It is broader than the term violence against women because the former also encompasses violence in which gender is not the 'main or sole determinant' of the violence committed.[590] It is also narrower than the term gender-based violence as violence against women obviously excludes any violence committed against men or intersex persons in which gender is the decisive factor.[591] However, the DEVW states that both terms refer to actions rooted in systematic oppression and discrimination. As the ICTY case at hand concerns the rape of women, the events fall under the application area of both terms, even if they are not congruent. Furthermore, the approach of the CEDAW Committee was endorsed by the Special Rappor-

588 UNGA Res 48/104 'Declaration on the Elimination of Violence against Women' (20 December 1993) GAOR 48th Session Supp 49 vol 1, 217.

589 See also Alice Edwards *Violence against Women under International Human Rights Law* (CUP Cambridge 2011) at 20, where she states that, even though the two terms are used interchangeably in international law, international human rights instruments tend to prefer the term 'violence against women' while the 'jurisprudence, guidelines and policy statements of the broader UN' favor 'gender-based violence'.

590 Alice Edwards 'Everyday rape: International human rights law and violence against women in peacetime' in Clare McGlynn and Vanessa Munro *Rethinking Rape Law: International and Comparative Perspectives* (Routledge Abingdon 2010) 92-108, 97-98.

591 Alice Edwards 'Everyday rape: International human rights law and violence against women in peacetime' in Clare McGlynn and Vanessa Munro *Rethinking Rape Law: International and Comparative Perspectives* (Routledge Abingdon 2010) 92-108, 98.

teur on Violence against Women from her first report of 1994 on.[592] The decision of the court to limit the definition to the first part is even less conceivable as it is accompanied with no further analysis in the findings. The court merely states that two women were raped because they were women, without further analysis to back up this statement.[593] Furthermore, the court lets slip the opportunity to link back to the fundamental treaty in the area of gender-related violence and discrimination against women and to strengthen its argumentation by reiterating the fact that rape, particularly when committed by State officials, can constitute a breach of CEDAW.

The court could also have referred to the elaborate description of the scope of the DEVWD in Article 2 and the modalities in which violence against women can be committed.[594]

Finally, the Court cites, without further analysis, the Special Rapporteur's report: '[i]n many cases the discrimination prong of the definition of torture in the Torture Convention provides an additional basis for prosecuting rape and sexual violence as torture'.[595] As explained, the court takes 'discrimination' to be an additional purpose which is pursued by the

592 UN Commission on Human Rights' Special Rapporteur Radhika Coomaraswamy 'Preliminary report submitted by the Special Rapporteur on violence against women, its causes and consequences in accordance with Commission on Human Rights resolution 1994/45' (22 November 1994) E/CN.4/1995/42 para. 29; see also UN ECOSOC Res 1996/12 (23 July 1997) UN Doc E/RES/1996/12 and UN Commission on Human Rights Special Rapporteur Radhika Coomaraswamy 'Report of the Special Rapporteur on violence against women, its causes and consequences, submitted in accordance with Commission on Human Rights resolution 2002/52, Addendum 1: International, regional and national developments in the area of violence against women 1994-2003' (27 February 2003) UN Doc E/CN. 4/2003/75/Add.1 paras 5, 56; several Special Rapporteurs have repeatedly also used a variation of the phrase 'violence and other forms of discrimination against women' see eg UN Commission on Human Rights Special Rapporteur Yakin Ertürk 'Integration of the human rights of women and the gender perspective: Violence against Women; The due diligence standard as a tool for the elimination of violence against women: Report of the Special Rapporteur on Violence against Women, its causes and consequences' (20 January 2006) E/CN.4/2006/61 para. 97; UNGA 'Advancement of women: Note by the Secretary-General' (1 August 2011) UN Doc A/66/215 para 13.

593 See *Prosecutor v Delalić et al (Celebići Case Judgment)* IT-96-21-T (16 November 1998) paras 941 and 963.

594 See Part Two Chapter Three III e below.

595 *Prosecutor v Delalić et al (Celebići Case Judgment)* IT-96-21-T (16 November 1998) para 493; UN Commission on Human Rights 'Systematic rape, sexual

intentional inflicting of severe mental or physical pain or suffering. This is in line with Art. 1 (1) CAT. The court strengthens its argument by referring to the CEDAW Committee. Its reasoning is sexual violence constitutes discrimination which is one of the purposes with which the severe mental and physical harm must be inflicted in order to constitute torture. The equation of gender-based violence with discrimination is one of the cornerstones of the modern human rights jurisprudence on gender issues. The CEDAW Committee issues two General Recommendations (No 12 and No 19) which state that CEDAW obliges Member States to protect women from violence and that '[g]ender-based violence is a form of discrimination that seriously inhibits women's ability to enjoy rights and freedoms on a basis of equality with men'[596] thereby bringing violence against women under the ambit of CEDAW.

In its findings and after the analysis of the human rights provisions discussed, the Trial Chamber enumerates four constituent elements of torture:

> (i) There must be an act or omission that causes severe pain or suffering, whether mental or physical,
>
> (ii) which is inflicted intentionally,
>
> (iii) and for such purposes as obtaining information or a confession from the victim, or a third person, punishing the victim for an act he or she or a third person has committed or is suspected of having committed, intimidating or coercing the victim or a third person, or for any reason based on discrimination of any kind,

(iv) and such act or omission being committed by, or at the instigation of, or with the consent or acquiescence of, an official or other person acting in an official capacity. [597]

The most remarkable conclusions which the Court draws after having resulted the jurisprudence and other documents of human rights law, are that a. the court takes into account not only the physical but also the psychological suffering that rape causes and also states that b. 'it is difficult to

---

slavery and slave-like practices during armed conflict: Final report submitted by Ms. Gay J. McDougall, Special Rapporteur' (22 June 1998) UN Doc E/CN.4/Sub.2/1998/13, para. 55.

596 UN Committee on the Elimination of Discrimination against Women 'General Recommendation No 19: Violence against Women' (30 January 1992) GAOR 47th Session Supp 38, 1 para 1.

597 Unlike this definition and art. 1 CAT, Art. 7 (1) (f) Rome Statute does not require any 'specific' purpose, see Part Two III 2. (b) (2) above.

envisage circumstances in which rape, by, or at the instigation of a public official, or with the consent or acquiescence of an official, could be considered as occurring for a purpose that does not, in some way, involve punishment, coercion, discrimination or intimidation. In the view of this Trial Chamber this is inherent in situations of armed conflict'.[598] The Trial Chamber therefore concludes that whenever the aforementioned criteria are fulfilled, rape constitutes torture. This approach has been followed by several other Trial and Appeals Chambers, which refer to the *Celebići* -approach and usually, in a footnote, also to the Trial Chamber's reference to 'reports and decisions of organs of the UN and regional bodies'.[599]

II. Where Could Women's Human Rights Have Been Referred to?

1. Genocide

The case of *Jean-Paul Akayesu* at the ICTR was the first time an international criminal tribunal held that rape, under certain circumstances, can amount to genocide.[600] The initial indictment to the case, which was submitted by the Prosecutor on 13 February 1996 and confirmed on 16 February 1996, did not contain any acts of sexual violence.[601] It was only during the proceedings when the judges started asking questions to a witness who had mentioned that her daughter had been raped during the genocide, that the prosecutor investigated those crimes and the indictment was subsequently amended in June 1997.[602] The Court heard many more accounts of rapes and other forms of sexual violence and based on them held Akayesu responsible for rape as genocide, as the court found that the rapes were committed solely against Tutsi women and with the intent of destroying

598 *Prosecutor v Delalić et al (Celebići Case Judgment)* IT-96-21-T (16 November 1998) para 495.

599 See *Prosecutor v Kunarac et al (Appeal Judgment)* IT-96-23 & IT-96-23/1-A (12 June 2002) para. 151 (fn 206); *Prosecutor v Brđanin* (Judgment) IT-99-36-T (1 September 2004) para. 485 (fn 1265);.

600 *Prosecutor v Akayesu (Judgment)* ICTR-96-4-T (2 September 1998).

601 *Prosecutor v Akayesu (Amended Indictment)* ICTR-96-4-I (June 1997) para. 6.

602 See for example the account by one of the Judges to the case: Navanethem Pillay 'Protection of the Health of Women through International Criminal Law: Can International Criminal Law contribute to Efforts to Improve the Health of Women?' (2008) 22 Emory International Law Review 15–28, 17–18.

the Tutsi group as a whole.[603] The Chamber affirmed that rape and sexual violence 'constitute genocide in the same way as any other act as long as they were committed with the specific intent to destroy, in whole or in part, a particular group, targeted as such'.[604] The judges further stated that '[t]hese rapes resulted in physical and psychological destruction of Tutsi women, their families and their communities. Sexual violence was an integral part of the process of destruction, specifically targeting Tutsi women and specifically contributing to their destruction and to the destruction of the Tutsi group as a whole'.[605] However, the *Akayesu* judgement does not cite any other international criminal law or human rights law documents or instruments supporting its finding that rape and/or sexual violence can constitute genocide, even though such (soft law) documents can be found in the realm of international human rights law. The classification of rape as genocide did not start during the *Akayesu* proceedings. The foundation is obviously to be found in the Genocide Convention. The key element for actions to be characterized as genocide is the genocidal special intent.

The notion of rape as genocide had come up in human rights documents years earlier; it was, for instance, mentioned in para. 145 (d) Beijing Platform for Action of the Fourth World Conference on Women in 1995, which called upon governments to '[r]eaffirm that rape in the conduct of armed conflict constitutes a war crime and under certain circumstances it constitutes a crime against humanity and an act of genocide as defined in the Convention on the Prevention and Punishment of the Crime of Genocide'.[606] Furthermore, the Platform for Action pushed for investigations of those acts and prosecution of those responsible.

Another document which points to the relation between rape and genocide is the Final Report of the Special Rapporteur on systematic rape, sexual slavery and slavery-like practices during armed conflict of June 1998 which affirms the importance of the correct legal classification of acts of sexual violence and slavery as 'international crimes of slavery, crimes

---

603 *Prosecutor v Akayesu (Judgment)* ICTR-96-4-A (1 June 2001) paras 706, 724, 731–34.

604 *Prosecutor v Akayesu (Judgment)* ICTR-96-4-A (1 June 2001) paras 731.

605 Ibid.

606 Fourth World Conference on Women 'Beijing Declaration and Platform for Action' in 'Report' (17 October 1995) UN Doc A/CONF.177/20, 4.

against humanity, genocide, grave breaches of the Geneva Conventions, war crimes or torture'[607]

Referring to these soft law documents as indicators of customary international law would have at the same time strengthened and facilitated the courts arguments. The developments in *Akayesu* led to more indictments and/or convictions for rape as genocide in the ICTR and ICTY. Even though the link between rape and genocide is not explicitly drawn in the Rome Statute itself (by way of including sexual violence of one of the acts through which genocide can be committed), the ICC's Elements of Crime contain a footnote to Element No 1 to Art. 6 (a) dealing with genocide committed by causing serious bodily or mental harm. The footnote states that '[t]his conduct may include, but is not necessarily restricted to, acts of torture, rape, sexual violence or inhuman or degrading treatment'.[608]

2. Definition of Rape

Prior to the establishment of the ICTR and the ICTY, there was no commonly accepted definition of rape in international law. As *Akayesu*, the first case before the ICTR, as mentioned above,[609] included charges of rape, the tribunal was forced to define the term. In order to do so, the ICTR considered the definitions found in 'certain national jurisdictions'[610] without specifying which jurisdictions it was referring to and arrived at the conclusion that those jurisdictions defined rape as 'non-consensual intercourse', while some included acts ' which involve the insertion of objects and/or the use of bodily orifices not considered to be intrinsically sexual'.[611] The Court went on comparing rape to torture under international human rights law and stated

> '[t]he Chamber considers that rape is a form of aggression and that the central elements of the crime of rape cannot be captured in a mechanical description

---

607 UN Commission on Human Rights 'Systematic rape, sexual slavery and slave-like practices during armed conflict: Final report submitted by Ms. Gay J. McDougall, Special Rapporteur' (22 June 1998) UN Doc E/CN.4/Sub.2/1998/13, para. 8; see also para. 34.

608 Elements of Crimes (adopted and entered into force 9 September 2002) Doc ICC-ASP/1/3 (Pt. II-B), footnote 3.

609 See Part Two Chapter Three I. 2. above.

610 *Prosecutor v Akayesu (Judgment)* ICTR-96-4-T (2 September 1998) para. 596.

611 *Prosecutor v Akayesu (Judgment)* ICTR-96-4-T (2 September 1998) para. 596.

> of objects and body parts. The Convention against Torture and Other Cruel, Inhuman and Degrading Treatment or Punishment does not catalogue specific acts in its definition of torture, focusing rather on the conceptual frame work of state sanctioned violence. This approach is more useful in international law. Like torture, rape is used for such purposes as intimidation, degradation, humiliation, discrimination, punishment, control or destruction of a person. Like torture, rape is a violation of personal dignity, and rape in fact constitutes torture when inflicted by or at the instigation of or with the consent or acquiescence of a public official or other person acting in an official capacity. [612]

The Chamber did not, however, look at any instruments available regarding women's rights. It goes on defining rape as 'a physical invasion of a sexual nature, committed on a person under circumstances which are coercive'. Additionally, the ICTR holds sexual violence, which it states includes rape, to be 'any act of a sexual nature which is committed on a person under circumstances which are coercive'.[613] This definition of rape which is used is a very wide one and does leads to new ambiguities, for example when it comes to the question what an 'invasion' consists of.

The approach taken by the ICTR in *Akayesu* was nevertheless subsequently confirmed by the ICTY in *Delalić.* [614] There, the chamber dealt solely with charges of rape as torture as a crime against humanity and not with accusations of genocide. The court did not include any own reasoning of the definition of rape, but simply cited the one used in *Akayesu* and stated that it saw no reason to depart from that approach. [615] The court then went on to examine the state of international jurisprudence of judicial and quasi-judicial bodies on the issue of rape as torture. In particular, the tribunal considered the jurisprudence of the Inter-American Commission on Human Rights and the ECtHR on the matter.

In *Furundžija* the ICTY held that due to the principle of specificity and the principle of *nullum crimen sine lege*, in order to define the elements of rape in international law, one had to resort to a comparison of the different national jurisdictions and analyse what elements they see as a prerequisite for establishing rape. The court in *Furundžija* deemed that necessary be-

612 *Prosecutor v Akayesu (Judgment)* ICTR-96-4-T (2 September 1998) para 597; see also para 687.

613 *Prosecutor v Akayesu (Judgment)* ICTR-96-4-A (1 June 2001), para. 598.

614 *Prosecutor v Delalić et al (Celebići Case Judgment)* IT-96-21 (16 November 1998).

615 *Prosecutor v Delalić et al (Celebići Case Judgment)* IT-96-21 (16 November 1998) 478–79.

cause it held that 'no elements other than those emphasized may be drawn from international treaty or customary law, nor is resort to general principles of international criminal law or to general principles of international law of any avail. As the chamber held that, even though rape and sexual assault is expressly prohibited under international humanitarian law and courts and tribunals have convicted accordingly,[616] no human rights instrument specifically prohibited rape and sexual assault, the Trial Chamber therefore considered that, to arrive at an accurate definition of rape (...) it is necessary to look for principles of criminal law common to the major legal systems of the world. These principles may be derived, with all due caution, from national laws'.[617] The Chamber did, however, acknowledge an implicit protection from rape and sexual assault by provisions protecting physical integrity, which the chamber saw as 'undeniably part of customary law'.[618] As such, human rights provisions, concepts and discourse indirectly found their way into the definition of rape used in *Furundžija*.[619] It also goes to show that judges often feel the need to demonstrate that norms developed under international criminal law or international humanitarian law conform with human rights law and how international criminal law, through shaping the customary law in this area, might also contribute to furthering a definition of rape under human rights law.[620]

---

616 *Prosecutor v Furundžija (Judgment)* IT-95-17 (10 December 1998), para 168.

617 *Prosecutor v Furundžija (Judgment)* IT-95-17 (10 December 1998), paras 168-171, 177.

618 *Prosecutor v Furundžija (Judgment)* IT-95-17 (10 December 1998), para 170; that sexual violence in armed conflict violates a number of basic human rights had been stated in the Vienna Declaration and Programme of Action of 1993: 'Violations of the human rights of women in situations of armed conflict are violations of the fundamental principles of international human rights and humanitarian law. All violations of this kind, including in particular murder, systematic rape, sexual slavery, and forced pregnancy, require a particularly effective response'; UN World Conference on Human Rights 'Vienna Declaration and Programme of Action' (25 June 1993) UN Doc A/CONF.157/23 para 38.

619 Theodor Meron 'Human Rights Marches into New Territory: The Enforcement of International Human Rights in International Criminal Tribunals' Fourth Marek Nowicki Memorial Lecture (28 November 2008) <http://web.ceu.hu/legal/pdf%2 0documents/Nowicki/Meron_Enforcement%20of%20HRwarsawnowicki13nov 0 8.pdf> (as last accessed on 10 June 2013; speech no longer accessible online) 23.

620 Theodor Meron 'Human Rights Marches into New Territory: The Enforcement of International Human Rights in International Criminal Tribunals' Fourth Marek Nowicki Memorial Lecture (28 November 2008) <http://web.ceu.hu/legal/pdf%2

The *Furundžija* Trial Chamber's definition of rape, deducted from general principles of criminal law common to the major legal stems of the world was the following. The objective elements of rape were 1. a. the sexual penetration, however slight, of the vagina or anus of the victim by the penis of the perpetrator or any other object used by the perpetrator; or b. of the mouth of the victim by the penis of the perpetrator; 2. by coercion or force or threat of force against the victim or a third person.[621]

In *Kunarac*, a comparison of different national jurisdictions was undertaken in order to determine the scope and the limits of consent with the result that one of the elements of rape were not established. The Trial Chamber in *Kunarac* had to engage in such a comparison because the definitions which had been developed earlier by the ICTR in *Akayesu* and the ICTY in *Furundžija* were too unspecific for the former and too narrow when it comes to the latter for the case in question. The Chamber was of the opinion that in the specific case in question, a narrow definition of consent as applied in *Furundžija* would neglect other factors which 'would render an act of sexual penetration *non-consensual or non-voluntary* on the part of the victim'[622]

In *Furundžija,* the Trial Chamber took recourse to rather unorthodox arguments in order to affirm its jurisdiction over sexual violence. For instance, it stated that forced oral penetration constituted rape even though the Chamber held that there might not be sufficient State Practice to substantiate this claim under customary international law. The reason for this, according to the Trial Chamber, was that in the context of an armed conflict, the conduct in question was aggravated into aggravated sexual assault.[623] Therefore, the Chamber held that no violation of *nullum crimen sine lege* occurred. In this, the Court very much acted as a lawmaker driving a creative, yet risky line of argument without sufficient backing from legal doctrine. The Court cannot argue that State practice of *some* States

0documents/Nowicki/Meron_Enforcement%20of%20HRwarsawnowicki13nov 08.pdf > (as last accessed on 10 June 2013; speech no longer accessible online) 23-4.

621 *Prosecutor v Furundžija (Judgment)* IT-95-17 (10 December 1998) para. 185.

622 *Prosecutor v Kunarac* (Judgment) IT-96-23-T & IT-96-23/1-T (22 February 2001) para. 438.

623 Prosecutor v Furundžija (Judgment) IT-95-17 (10 December 1998) para 184; Mia Swart 'Judicial Lawmaking at the ad hoc Tribunals: The Creative Use of the Sources of International Law and "Adventurous Interpretation"' (2010) 70 ZaöRV 459-486, 467-8.

(but not enough) categorize forced oral intercourse as rape and that the context of the of an armed conflict somehow helps to bridge this gap by making any prohibited act somehow more grave so that therefore the act falls into the court's subject-matter jurisdiction.

Here, referring to human rights instruments regarding violence against women would have greatly facilitated the court's argumentation. As we will see below, even though violence against women is not specifically dealt with in any of the major human rights treaties, General Recommendation No 19 of the CEDAW Committee brought gender-based violence within the ambit of CEDA. Gender based violence is defined as 'violence that is directed against a woman because she is a woman or that affects women disproportionally. It includes physical, mental or sexual harm or suffering, threats of such acts, coercion and other deprivations of liberty'.[624] As such, the General Recommendation transformed CEDAW 'from an anti-discrimination treaty into a gender-based violence treaty'.[625] Using this argumentation, the court would have been on more solid doctrinal ground as the CEDAW Committee provides authoritative interpretation of the CEDAW.

The legal nature and relevance of the general recommendations (or 'General Comments' as they are called in some of the treaty bodies) is disputed. Some commentators see them as authoritative interpretations, [626] while others ascribe them mere advisory character and regard it as apt if they are merely taken into consideration or even deny them any legal weight altogether.[627] It seems hard to argue that the General Recommendations/Comments, can be more than non-binding soft law. Already the

---

624 UN Committee on the Elimination of Discrimination against Women 'General Recommendation No 19: Violence against Women' (30 January 1992) GAOR 47th Session Supp 38, 1,.

625 Alice Edwards ‚Violence against Women as Sex Discrimination: Judging the Jurisprudence of the United Nations Human Rights Treaty Bodies' (2008) 18 Texas Journal of Women and the Law 1–54.

626 See eg Manfred Nowak *U. N. Covenant on Civil and Political Rights: CCPR Commentary* (N P Engel Kehl 2005) 49; Nowak does, however, emphasis that the General Comments (of the HRC) cannot be more that non-binding interpretations; nevertheless, the HRC–and this argumentation can be conferred to the other treaty bodies as well–has, in his opinion, the authority to interpret the ICCR and he underlines the 'authoritative and universal character of these interpretations'.

627 See Philip Alston 'The Historical Origins of the Concept of "General Comments" in Human Rights Law' in Laurence Boisson de Chazournes and Vera Gowlland-

terms 'recommendations' or 'comments' point to their non-binding character. The text of CEDAW itself does not contain anything to the way that the CEDAW Committee should be invested with judicial authority the States Parties explicitly subordinated to.

Nevertheless, the General Comments of the CEDAW Committee constitute a valuable, even an indispensable source of interpretation of CEDAW (as the General Recommendations/Comments of the other committees do for their respective treaties). This is because all human rights treaties are by necessity formulated in a very broad manner that leaves a lot of room for interpretation. As already Cesare Beccaria has pointed out (quoted by Philip Alston), '"rights" and "obligations" are, in some respects at least "abbreviated symbols of the rational argument" rather than ideas themselves'.[628] This vagueness of terms leads to insecurity on the side of the rights-holders and provide those who are obliged to guarantee and protect the rights with an opportunity to manipulate them and deprive them of their content. This is where General Recommendations by the experts sitting in the treaty bodies comes in. The development, at the international arena, of jurisprudence, which elaborates on and clarifies the normative content and the obligations and implications deriving from a specific treaty provision, decreases the possibilities for Member States to interpret their obligations in a way which would essentially deprive them of their purpose. Even though the General Recommendations are not binding in a strict legal sense, they constitute a powerful tool as the interpretation by the 'guardian of the convention', a Committee made up of independent experts from all over the world whose recommendations on a specific issue are of great weight and cannot easily be disregarded by national courts and State officials. This is even more so because, until now, all the General Recommendations of the Committee have been adopted by consen-

Debbas *The International Legal System in Quest of Equity and Universality: Liber Amicorum Georges Abi-Saab* (Nijhoff The Hague 2001) 763-776, 764.

628 Philip Alston 'The Historical Origins of the Concept of " General Comments" in Human Rights Law' in Laurence Boisson de Chazournes and Vera Gowlland-Debbas *The International Legal System in Quest of Equity and Universality: Liber Amicorum Georges Abi-Saab* (Nijhoff The Hague 2001) 763-776, 767; Cesare *Beccaria On Crime and Punishment and Other Writings* (Cambridge University Press 1995) 12.

sus,[629] (even though this is no requirement stipulated in the Rules of Procedure of the CEDAW Committee).[630] Hence, one cannot look at CEDAW isolated from the consideration of its interpretation and clarification by the CEDAW Committee. If the ICTY looks at CEDAW in order to establish the extent to which sexual assault constitutes the denial of fundamental rights, it should also consider the limits and fields of application assigned to the convention by its treaty body.

The CEDAW Committee deals with violence against women on a structural level, as 'group-based harm, a practice of social inequality carried out on an individual level'.[631] Gender-based violence is seen as systematic and endemic and in this respect, the legal and sociological language used is very similar to the mass-scale crimes international criminal law is dealing with. In this respect, international criminal law has a lot to gain from the jurisprudence and the General Recommendations of the CEDAW Committee as well as other treaty bodies when it comes to gender-based crimes prosecuted on an international level. The discourse of the CEDAW and the CESCR on the one side and the international criminal courts and tribunals are similar. As we will see, many more opportunities to put endemic violence against women within the context of discrimination and therefore persecution could have been realized had the Chambers referred to the available instruments and discussions.

629 Email correspondence with two members of the CEDAW Committee, Professor Ruth Halperi-Kaddari (16 September 2010) and Professor Niklas Bruun (17 September 2010).

630 Rule 31 of the Rules of Procedure of the CEDAW Committee stipulates: '1. The Committee shall endeavour to reach its decisions by consensus. 2. If and when all efforts to reach consensus have been exhausted, decisions of the Committee shall be taken by a simple majority of the members present and voting' UN Committee on the Elimination of Discrimination against Women 'Rules of Procedure of the Committee on the Elimination of Discrimination against Women' (2001) UN Doc A/56/38 Annex I.

631 See Alice Edwards ,Violence against Women as Sex Discrimination: Judging the Jurisprudence of the United Nations Human Rights Treaty Bodies' (2008) 18 Texas Journal of Women and the Law 1–54,25.

3. Persecution

As mentioned above, the *Milutinovic* judgment was the first judgment in which the court had to explore the issue of sexual assault as persecution. As the ICTY Statute did not provide for persecution on gender grounds to be charged, the Court, even though it does not explicitly state so in the judgment, discusses persecution on political, racial and religious grounds by rape and sexual assault of 'Kosovo Albanians, in particular women by forces of the Federal Republic of Yugoslavia and Serbia.[632] 'In the judgment, the responsible ICTY Chamber states that '[t]he term "sexual assault" is not explicitly used in any international human rights treaty. The Convention on the Elimination of All Forms of Discrimination Against Women does not mention sexual assault, although it makes reference to the prohibition on "exploitation of prostitution"'. While this remains a true statement, the Court overlooked that 'sexual assault', like rape, has indeed been characterized as one of the modes of violence against women, which is outlawed by CEDAW. In General Recommendation 19 of 1992, the CEDAW Committee stated that '[t]he Convention in article 1 defines discrimination against women. The definition of discrimination includes gender-based violence, that is, violence that is directed against a woman because she is a woman or that affects women disproportionately. It includes acts that inflict physical, mental or sexual harm or suffering, threats of such acts, coercion and other deprivations of liberty. Gender-based violence may breach specific provisions of the Convention, regardless of whether those provisions expressly mention violence'. [633] The committee explicitly refers to the correlation between sexual assault and armed conflict in emphasizing that '[w]ars, armed conflicts and the occupation of territories often lead to increased prostitution, trafficking in women and sexual assault of women, which require specific protective and punitive measures.'[634] Furthermore, the CEDAW Committee urges States Parties to

---

632 *Prosecutor v Milutinović* (Judgment) IT-05-87-T (26 February 2009) para 183; generally on rape and sexual assault as persecution see paras 183-203.

633 UN Committee on the Elimination of Discrimination against Women 'General Recommendation No 19: Violence against Women' (30 January 1992) GAOR 47th Session Supp 38, 1, para. 6.

634 UN Committee on the Elimination of Discrimination against Women 'General Recommendation No 19: Violence against Women' (30 January 1992) GAOR 47th Session Supp 38, 1, para. 16.

'ensure that laws against family violence and abuse, rape, sexual assault and other gender-based violence give adequate protection to all women, and respect their integrity and dignity'.[635] The committee additionally states that gender-based violence, (which includes sexual assault), 'which impairs or nullifies the enjoyment by women of human rights and fundamental freedoms under general international law or under human rights conventions, is discrimination within the meaning of article 1 of the Convention'.[636] One of the rights mentioned by the committee, the enjoyment of which is impaired or nullified by gender-based violence is '[t]he right to equal protection according to humanitarian norms in time of international or internal armed conflict'.[637]

Instead of or in supplement to the Court's arguments regarding sexual assault constitution torture and therefore a denial of a fundamental human right, the Court could have also referred directly to sexual assault as a form of gender-based violence constituting discrimination prohibited under Art. 1 CEDAW. The analysis conducted by the CEDAW Committee in its General Recommendation would in this respect have been of great value to the judges.

In *Milutinovic*, the Trial Chamber also dealt with the question whether the term 'sexual assault' encompasses acts, which can also include rape or whether it only refers to acts, which fall short of the definition of rape. Even though the court finally and rightly decides that 'sexual assault' can include, but is not limited to, rape, the Chamber disregarded human rights documents that substantiate this position. The Committee on the Rights of the Child, for instance, stated in its General Comment No. 3 that '[v]iolence, including rape and other forms of sexual abuse, can occur in the family or foster setting or be perpetrated by those with specific responsibilities towards children'.[638]

---

635 UN Committee on the Elimination of Discrimination against Women 'General Recommendation No 19: Violence against Women' (30 January 1992) GAOR 47th Session Supp 38, 1, para. 24 (b).

636 UN Committee on the Elimination of Discrimination against Women 'General Recommendation No 19: Violence against Women' (30 January 1992) GAOR 47th Session Supp 38, 1, para. 7.

637 UN Committee on the Elimination of Discrimination against Women 'General Recommendation No 19: Violence against Women' (30 January 1992) GAOR 47th Session Supp 38, 1, para. 7 (c).

638 UN Committee on the Rights of the Child General Comment No. 3 (2003) (17 March 2003) UN Doc CRC/GC/2003/3 para. 34.

Not only equality was seen as a foundational principle of the CEDAW, the CEDAW Committee argued that the prohibition of gender-related violence should be one as well.[639] This approach was affirmed by the Committee on Economic, Social and Cultural Rights, which states in its General Comment No 16 :

'[g]ender based violence is a form of discrimination that inhibits the ability to enjoy rights and freedoms, including economic, social and cultural rights, on a basis of equality. States parties must take appropriate measures to eliminate violence against men and women and act with due diligence to prevent, investigate, mediate, punish and redress acts of violence against them by private actors'.[640]

It was also repeated by the Secretary General in its 2006 report of violence against women where he stated that

'Evidence gathered by researchers of the pervasive nature and multiple forms of violence against women, together with advocacy campaigns, led to the recognition that violence against women was global, systemic and rooted in power imbalances and structural inequality between men and women. The identification of the link between violence against women and discrimination was key'.[641]

The Committee on Economic, Social and Cultural Rights also repetitively discussed violence against women as a matter of inequality between

---

639 Alice Edwards ,Violence against Women as Sex Discrimination: Judging the Jurisprudence of the United Nations Human Rights Treaty Bodies' (2008) 18 Texas Journal of Women and the Law 1–54, 23.

640 UN Committee on Economic, Social and Cultural Rights 'General Comment No 16: The Equal Right of Men and Women to the Enjoyment of all Economic, Social and Cultural Rights (Art. 3 of the Covenant)' (11 August 2005) ESCOR [2006] Supp 2, 116, para. 27.

641 UNGA 'In-Depth Study on All Forms of Violence against Women: Report of the Secretary-General' (6 July 2006) UN Doc A/61/122/Add.1, para. 30; see also the very first sentence of the executive summary of the publication version 'Violence against women is a form of discrimination and a violation of human rights. (…)The scope and extent of violence against women are a reflection of the degree and persistence of discrimination that women continue to face', UNGA 'In-Depth Study on All Forms of Violence against Women: Report of the Secretary-General' (Publication Version) (6 July 2006) http://www.un.org/womenwatch/daw/vaw/publications/English%20Study.pdf (31 October 2017) i and further UNGA 'Intensification of efforts to eliminate all forms of violence against women Report of the Secretary-General' (4 August 2008) UN Doc A/63/214 para. 6.

men and women within its jurisprudence on many occasions.[642] The approach of the HRC on the matter is less clear. In its General Comment No 28 entitled 'Equality of Rights between Man and Women', the HRC stated that the 'full effect' of Art. 3 ICCPR is impaired 'whenever any person is denied the full and equal enjoyment of any right'.[643] The HRC mentions, *inter alia*, rape, domestic violence and abduction as actions which impair the full and equal enjoyment of human rights for women. But it does not explicitly mention that gender-based violence constitutes sex discrimination. In its jurisprudence, however, the HRC also often discusses violence against women as infringements of certain rights within the ICCPR in relation to inequality.[644] The Committee on the Elimination of Racial Discrimination had issued a General Recommendation in which it affirmed that racial discrimination can effect men and women differently and that, *inter alia*, sexual violence against members of a certain ethnic group or coerced sterilization of indigenous women, constitutes discrimination banned under ICERD.[645]

This will however still leave the problem of defining what discrimination in relation to persecution is. In terms of criminal law there is also the dilemma that if one categorizes sexual violence as discrimination, the perpetrator must also have fulfilled the *mens rea* of discrimination and not only that of rape or other forms of sexual violence.[646] Another point arguing for caution when charging or deciding discrimination focused counts is that possibly the language of torture as a violation of physical integrity and basic human dignity is stronger than the language of discrimination. In human rights law, however, where torture, sexual violence and discrim-

642 See Alice Edwards ‚Violence against Women as Sex Discrimination: Judging the Jurisprudence of the United Nations Human Rights Treaty Bodies' (2008) 18 Texas Journal of Women and the Law 1–54, 24.

643 UN HRC 'General Comment No 28: Equality of Rights between Men and Women (Art. 3)' (29 March 2000) GAOR 55th Session Supp 40 vol 1, 133.

644 See Alice Edwards ‚Violence against Women as Sex Discrimination: Judging the Jurisprudence of the United Nations Human Rights Treaty Bodies' (2008) 18 Texas Journal of Women and the Law 1–54, 25.

645 UN Committee on the Elimination of Racial Discrimination 'General Recommendation XXV on Gender-Related Dimensions of Racial Discrimination' (20 March 2000) GAOR 55th Session Supp 18, 152, para. 2.

646 See partly See Alice Edwards ‚Violence against Women as Sex Discrimination: Judging the Jurisprudence of the United Nations Human Rights Treaty Bodies' (2008) 18 Texas Journal of Women and the Law 1–54, 27; see *Prosecutor v Kunarac (Judgment)* IT-96-23 (22 February 2001) para. 816.

ination can fall under the heading of crimes against humanity, war crimes or even genocide, it seems less of a danger that the respective crimes carry markedly different levels of perceived wrongness with them.

Even though these arguments can lead to the prosecution deciding against using discrimination-based charges, such a decision can only made on a case by case basis and the judges as well as the prosecution should possess the knowledge necessary to use this argumentation if it fits the facts of the case.

III. Where is the Link?

In 2000, the UN Security Council adopted Resolution 1325 on women and security, which highlighted the role of women in conflict and peace building.[647] Together with UNSC Resolution 1820, in which the Security Council stated that States, in tomes of conflict, have an obligations to protect their population against sexual violence as part of their responsibility to 'protect and ensure the human rights of their citizens',[648] this resolution explicitly stressed the relevance of CEDAW the obligations of States not only in peace time but also during conflict.[649] At the same time, CEDAW outlines concrete actions and obligations necessary to achieve the commitments of Resolutions 1325 and 1820 one of which is the protection of women and girls from gender-based violence.[650] Resolutions 1325 and 1820 highlight the interrelation between CEDAW as a human rights instrument with commitments to protect women in conflict and punish perpetrators of gender-based violence. On the other hand, the Resolutions demonstrate the vagueness with which this interrelation is often hinted at, characterized by the insecurity regarding how CEDAW and other human rights instruments tie in with these commitments. This approach is symptomatic for bodies dealing with the mass commission of sexual crime in the context of conflict: reference to human rights law is somewhat expect-

---

647 UNSC Res 1325 (2000) (31 October 2000) SCOR 55th Year 177.

648 UNSC Res 1820 (2008) (19 June 2008) SCOR [1 August 2007–31 July 2008] 154.

649 UNIFEM 'CEDAW and Security Council Resolution 1325: A Quick Guide' <https://www.un.org/ruleoflaw/blog/document/cedaw-and-security-council-resolution-1325-a-quick-guide/> (31 October 2017) 4.

650 *Ibid.*

ed and so lip service is paid to human rights, while an insecurity on the content, the authorities to be consulted and the general usefulness of human rights law to the area of gender-based crimes can be detected.

In the following, human rights instruments are analysed concerning their gender-based crime content and intersections are pointed out where reference would foster gender-based crime cases. In turn, crimes under international criminal and humanitarian law are scrutinized regarding their potential for being used to punish gender-based crimes.

1. State Obligations regarding Violence against Women

The concept of special human rights for women is a relatively recent phenomenon, which has long been neglected on the agenda of universal human rights. This neglect has a variety of reasons. First, the legal inequality of men and women has for a long time been completely accepted in domestic legal systems and has not even been questioned by those striving to implement a system of universal human rights protection. Second, even the ones who were sympathetic to legal equality for both sexes at the time of the drafting of the Universal Bill of Rights meant to achieve this purpose by creating the Universal Declaration of Human Rights and (as envisaged in the early stages of drafting the Covenants) a legally binding document mirroring the Declaration, which would encompass fundamental rights of all of humankind independent of sex. At the time of drafting the Universal Bill of Rights, the approach that prevailed opted simply for including equality and non-discrimination clauses into the respective instruments. The UDHR, for example, reaffirms the belief 'in the equal rights for men and women' in its preamble. Art. 2 UDHR contains a non-discrimination clause, which also prohibits discrimination on the ground of sex. Finally, Art. 16 UDHR enshrines equal rights for both sexes regarding marriage. Several provisions regarding non-discrimination and equality can also be found in the ICCPR and the ICESCR. However, these provisions are very general and focus on treating all people 'equal' by seeking to guarantee, through the implementation of non-discrimination, that human rights are accessible for all persons alike. Such a 'fits all' approach to human rights has in the years that followed been held as disregarding the special needs, specific situation and vulnerabilities of individuals belonging to particularly disenfranchised groups such as minorities, disabled people, children or women. Subsequently, a strand in the field of human rights prevailed which recognized the importance of legally acknowledging the different needs of different groups, partly also advocating special measures in order to achieve true equality and the full enjoyment of human rights by these groups. In the field of protection of women's human rights, these instruments include the Convention on the Political Rights of Women,[651] the Convention on Consent to Marriage, Minimum Age for Marriage and Registration of Marriages[652] as well as several treaties by the International Labour Organisation on aspects of women and work.[653]

In recent years, the approach of creating 'special protection schemes' for particular groups has been criticised by scholars and activists within these groups as contributing to side-lining these groups in major discussions and disregarding them in fields and conventions in which they are not explicitly mentioned. Particularly with regards to women's rights, some scholars have suggested that 'the price of the creation of separate institutional mechanisms and special measures dealing with women within the UN system has typically been the creation of a "women's ghetto", given less power, fewer resources and a lower priority than "mainstream" human rights bodies'.[654] As much as there is some truth to the argument that it is easier to disregard special groups in 'mainstream' discussions with reference to a special protection regime which is dealing with a certain group and as much as the question should be allowed which groups 'deserve' a special protection regime and whether the reason why such a regime is established for one group but not for another can be legitimately raised, it can be doubted whether the complete absence of special protection regimes and the fostering of those groups' rights through more generally applicable measures would be a promising approach. It is more likely that women's concern would have continued to, as Chinkin and

---

651 Convention on the Political Rights of Women (adopted 20 December 1952, entered into force 7 July 1954) 193 UNTS 135.

652 Convention on Consent to Marriage, Minimum Age for Marriage and Registration of Marriages (adopted 7 November 1962, entered into force 9 December 1964) 521 UNTS 231 (Marriage Convention).

653 See also Hilary Charlesworth 'Inside/Outside: women and the International Human Rights System' in Aristotle Constantinides and Nikos Zaikos *The Diversity of International Law: Essays in Honour of Professor Kalliopi K Koufa* (Nijhoff Leiden 2009), 382–98, 386.

654 Hilary Charlesworth and Christine Chinkin *The Boundaries of International Law: A Feminist Analysis* (Manchester University Press Manchester 2000) 219.

Charlesworth put it, 'to be submerged by what are regarded more "global issues"'.[655]

a. International Covenant on Civil and Political Rights

The ICCPR contains several provisions with respect to women's rights which can be of relevance in the context of international criminal law.

First, the ICCPR contains a number of provisions, which prohibit discrimination on the basis of sex. Art. 2 (1) ICCPR provides that

> ' [e]ach State Party to the present Covenant undertakes to respect and to ensure to all individuals within its territory and subject to its jurisdiction the rights recognized in the present Covenant, without distinction of any kind, such as race, colour, sex, language, religion, political or other opinion, national or social origin, property, birth or other status'.

Article 3 is solely dedicated to the equal enjoyment of civil and political rights by both men and women and reads '[t]he States Parties to the present Covenant undertake to ensure the equal right of men and women to the enjoyment of all civil and political rights set forth in the present Covenant'. The HRC also has issued a specific General Comment on Art. 3 ICCPR (General Comment No. 28),[656] in which it enlists State obligations regarding several articles in the ICCPR in light of the obligation to equality enshrined in Art. 3 ICCPR. Several of these obligations are relevant in the context of international criminal law. The HRC does, for example, discuss issues like rape, female genital mutilation and forced abortion and sterilization in the context of torture and cruel, inhuman or degrading treatment or punishment und Art. 7 (and also under Art. 24 ICCPR dealing with the rights of the child).[657] It also explicitly acknowledges that women are particularly vulnerable in armed conflict and requests States Parties to

655 Hilary Charlesworth and Christine Chinkin *The Boundaries of International Law: A Feminist Analysis* (Manchester University Press Manchester 2000) 219.

656 UN HRC 'General Comment No 28: Equality of Rights between Men and Women (Art. 3)' (29 March 2000) GAOR 55th Session Supp 40 vol 1, 133.

657 UN HRC 'General Comment No 28: Equality of Rights between Men and Women (Art. 3)' (29 March 2000) GAOR 55th Session Supp 40 vol 1, 133 para 11.

inform the HRC about measures taken in these situations 'to protect women from rape, abduction and other forms of gender based violence'.[658]

Furthermore, the HRC requires information on national laws outlawing these actions, on preventive measures and on legal remedies for victims; rape cases are also mentioned in para. 20 as an example of the violation of the right to privacy by taking into account a woman's sexual life when determining her scope of legal protection. [659] The Committee also states that parties are under an obligation to inform the HRC about measures taken 'to eliminate trafficking of women and children, within the country or across borders, and forced prostitution' under Art. 8 ICCPR which deals with the prohibition of slavery. Furthermore, the Committee addresses several issues, which could be relevant in the case of establishing persecution on gender grounds. For instance, the HRC asks States to provide information on clothing requirements for women in public (at para. 13), marital or parental powers over women (at para. 16), whether the right to fair trial and access to courts under Art. 14 ICCPR can fully be exercised by women, (at. Para 18), the degree to which women can enjoy the right to be recognized as persons before the law (at para. 19).

Art. 4 ICCPR, which deals with the possibility of derogation from certain rights in times of emergency states that

> in time of public emergency which threatens the life of the nation and the existence of which is officially proclaimed, the States Parties to the present Covenant may take measures derogating from their obligations under the present Covenant to the extent strictly required by the exigencies of the situation, provided that such measures are not inconsistent with their other obligations under international law and do not involve discrimination solely on the ground of race, colour, sex, language, religion or social origin.

A state of emergency can, for example, be proclaimed in case of internal disturbances, civil unrest or an armed conflict of an international or non-international character. This means that some of the scenarios which call for a public emergency coincide with the situations in which was violations of human rights law and crimes under international law are extraordinarily often committed.

---

658 UN HRC 'General Comment No 28: Equality of Rights between Men and Women (Art. 3)' (29 March 2000) GAOR 55th Session Supp 40 vol 1, 133, para. 8.

659 UN HRC 'General Comment No 28: Equality of Rights between Men and Women (Art. 3)' (29 March 2000) GAOR 55th Session Supp 40 vol 1, 133, para 20.

Finally, Art. 24 ICCPR deals with the rights of the child and again prohibits any discrimination on the basis of gender. It states ' [e]very child shall have, without any discrimination as to race, colour, sex, language, religion, national or social origin, property or birth, the right to such measures of protection as are required by his status as a minor, on the part of his family, society and the State.' According to General Comment No. 18 of the HRC, 'discrimination' as understood by the ICCPR is similarly construed as the same term in CEDAW or the ICERD.[660]

Art. 23 ICCPR deals with the right to found a family. Art. 23 (2) states that man and women of marriageable age shall have a right to marry. Art. 23 (3) ICCPR makes clear that '[n]o marriage shall be entered into without the free and full consent of the intending spouses'. This provision is the direct human rights equivalent to the prohibition of forced marriage. Forced marriage as a crime against humanity has been recognised by the Special Court for Sierra Leone as a crime against humanity and has been subsumed under 'other inhumane acts' (Art. 2 (i) Statute of the Special Court for Sierra Leone[661]). The Rome Statute can charge 'forced marriage' either as an inhumane act (Art. 7 (1) (k) Rome Statute) or as the Special Rapporteur of the Working Group on Contemporary Forms of Slavery as enslavement (Art. 7 (1) (c) Rome Statute) or, more precisely, sexual slavery (Art. 7 (1) (g) Rome Statute).[662]

Even though the HRC discusses many of these issues in terms of structural discrimination of women in its General Comment 28, the HRC has generally been hesitant to employ discrimination terminology and to address issues of prevalent harmful ideologies and structural causes for the

660 UN HRC 'General Comment No 18: Non-Discrimination' (9 November 1989) GAOR 45th Session Supp 40 vol 1, 173, para. 7.

661 Statute of the Special Court for Sierra Leone (concluded 16 January 2002; entered into force 12 April 2002) 2178 UNTS 145.

662 UN Commission on Human Rights 'Systematic rape, sexual slavery and slave-like practices during armed conflict: Final report submitted by Ms. Gay J. McDougall, Special Rapporteur' (22 June 1998) UN Doc E/CN.4/Sub.2/1998/13 para. 8: 'In addition, this report emphasizes that practices such as (...)forced, temporary "marriages" to soldiers; and other practices involving the treatment of women as chattel, are both in fact and in law forms of slavery and, as such, violations of the peremptory norm prohibiting slavery'.

violation of women's human rights.[663] Rather, the HRC Committee's focus, when addressing States Parties obligations generally or in Concluding Observations, has been on measures of criminal law, on 'the investigation, prosecution and punishment of these crimes'.[664] In this, the HRC can again draw from a more refined system of criminal law and international criminal law and humanitarian law. This approach certainly offers more hands-on practical advice to States Parties and also more concrete ways of addressing problems which makes it easier and more likely for States Parties to adhere to the HRC's evaluations. On the other hand, the HRC misses out on opportunities for contributing an own approached focussed on a more long-term resolution in the field of women's human rights. As van Leeuwen put it 'the Committee only requests state parties to address the symptom of the disease, the manifestation of physical violence, but not the disease itself: gender inequality.'[665]

b. International Covenant on Economic, Social and Cultural Rights

The realm of the ICESCR is, at first glance, further removed from international criminal law than the ICCPR, which protects, *inter alia*, the right to life and physical integrity, rights which are often primarily at stake in situations in situations of armed conflict and mass turmoil. At second glance, however, the ICESCR enshrines the claim of certain rights which are crucial to the full participation and enjoyment of everyday life on a non-discriminatory basis. Art. 2 (2) ICESCR set out that the rights in the Covenant will be exercised without discrimination to race, colour, sex, language, religion, political or other opinion, national or social origin, property, birth or other status.[666] Art. 3 ICESCR mirrors Art. 3 ICCPR in

---

663 Fleur van Leeuwen *Women's Rights are Human Rights: The Practice of the United Nations Human Rights Committee and the Committee on Economic, Social and Cultural Rights* (Intersentia Antwerp 2010) 143.

664 Fleur van Leeuwen *Women's Rights are Human Rights: The Practice of the United Nations Human Rights Committee and the Committee on Economic, Social and Cultural Rights* (Intersentia Antwerp 2010) 143.

665 Fleur van Leeuwen *Women's Rights are Human Rights: The Practice of the United Nations Human Rights Committee and the Committee on Economic, Social and Cultural Rights* (Intersentia Antwerp 2010) 143.

666 International Covenant on Economic, Social and Cultural Rights (adopted 16 December 1966, entered into force 3 January 1976) 993 UNTS 3.

that it states that the parties to the ICESCR 'undertake to ensure the equal right of men and women to the enjoyment of all economic, social and cultural rights set forth in the present Covenant.' The Committee on Economic, Social and Cultural Rights (CESCR) clarified in General Comment No 16 that Arts 2, Arts 3 and 2 (2) ICESCR (and Arts 2(1) and 3 ICCPR) are not stand-alone provisions and, unlike Art 26 ICCPR, have to be read in conjunctions with the specific rights set out in the Covenants.[667]

Furthermore, in Art. 7 ICESCR, which outlines the right of everyone to the enjoyment of just and favourable conditions of work, Art. 7 (a) (i) obliges States parties to guarantee '[f]air wages and equal remuneration for work of equal value without distinction of any kind, in particular women being guaranteed conditions of work not inferior to those enjoyed by men, with equal pay for equal work'. A grave violation of this right to guarantee the right to work to both sexes equally and not to disregard women when it comes to the conditions of work and its remuneration, could subsequently be an indication for persecution on gender grounds. A flagrant example, in which a grave violation of the right to work was one of many evidence of gender-based persecution, was the issuing and the subsequent enforcement of edicts prohibiting all but a few women to work outside home under the Taliban regime.[668]

What has been said above for the HRC[669] is also true when it comes to interpretation of the ICESCR by its treaty body, the Committee on Economic, Social and Cultural Rights (CESCR). The Committee prefers to not concern itself so much with the structural routes of inequality, but rather calls for measures of criminal law to be applied in order to punish and redress violence against women. For example in its General Comment No 16 on the equal right of men and women to the enjoyment of all economic, social and cultural rights, the CESCR states '[g]ender based violence is a form of discrimination that inhibits the ability to enjoy rights and freedoms, including economic, social and cultural rights, on a basis of equali-

---

667 UN Committee on Economic, Social and Cultural Rights 'General Comment No 16: The Equal Right of Men and Women to the Enjoyment of all Economic, Social and Cultural Rights (Art. 3 of the Covenant)' (11 August 2005) ESCOR [2006] Supp 2, 116, para. 2.

668 Widney Brown and Laura Grenfell 'The International Crime of Gender-Based Persecution and the Taliban' (2003) 4 Melbourne Journal of International Law 347–75, 350, 365–66.

669 See Part Two Chapter Three 1 a above.

ty. States parties must take appropriate measures to eliminate violence against men and women and act with due diligence to prevent, investigate, mediate, punish and redress acts of violence against them by private actors'[670]

Generally, the CESCR, more so than its counterpart, the HRC, outlines, in its General Comments Nos 3 and 20, the nature of State obligations towards the fulfilment of the rights enshrined in the ICESCR. In General Comment No. 3, the Committee on ESCR clarifies that the progressive realization of the ESC-rights only covers the result, the realization of the respective rights. In contrast, the States have an obligation to act towards the fulfilment of the rights 'within a reasonably short time after the Covenant's entry into force'.[671] The Committee goes on explaining that this obligation to act covers, in particular, the adoption of legislative measures (see also Art. 2 (1)), especially in the area of discrimination. Discrimination, according to the Committee, 'may be difficult to combat … effectively in the absence of a sound legislative foundation for the necessary measures'[672] Discrimination is defined by the ESCR Committee in its General Comment No. 20 as 'any distinction, exclusion, restriction or preference or other differential treatment that is directly or indirectly based on the prohibited grounds of discrimination and which has the intention or effect of nullifying or impairing the recognition, enjoyment or exercise, on an equal footing, of Covenant rights'.[673] The Committee also points to the importance of adopting legislation to combat discrimination in para. 37 General Comment No 20. The ESCR Committee also reserves the right to consider, which measures are 'appropriate' in the meaning of

670 UN Committee on Economic, Social and Cultural Rights 'General Comment No 16: The Equal Right of Men and Women to the Enjoyment of all Economic, Social and Cultural Rights (Art. 3 of the Covenant)' (11 August 2005) ESCOR [2006] Supp 2, 116, para. 27.

671 UN Committee on Economic, Social and Cultural Rights 'General Comment No 3: The Nature of States Parties Obligations' (26 November–14 December 1990) ESCOR [1991] Supp 3, 83, para. 2.

672 UN Committee on Economic, Social and Cultural Rights 'General Comment No 3: The Nature of States Parties Obligations' (26 November–14 December 1990) ESCOR [1991] Supp 3, 83, para. 3.

673 UN Committee on Economic, Social and Cultural Rights 'General Comment No 20: Non-discrimination in economic, social and cultural rights (art. 2, para. 2, of the International Covenant on Economic, Social and Cultural Rights)' (2 July 2009) ESCOR [2009], 118 para. 1.

Art. 2 (1) and calls on States parties to indicate in their reports not only the legislative measures towards the realization of ESC rights, but also to show why these measures are the most appropriate (see para. 4). General Comment No 20 additionally offers clarification on the evolving definition on 'sex' as a prohibited ground for discrimination. It states that since the ICESCR was adopted, the notion of the term has evolved to cover not only 'physiological characteristics but also the social construction of gender stereotypes, prejudices and expected roles, which have created obstacles to the equal fulfilment of economic, social and cultural rights'.[674] This again can be helpful specifically for persecution on gender ground which is punishable pursuant to the Rome Statute. The considerations by the ESCR Committee might be helpful in order to determine whether a State policy of systematic discrimination rising, e.g., to the level of a crime against humanity of persecution, is or has been taken place. The failure of a State to adopt legislation shielding specific groups from discrimination can also, in some exceptional instances, be seen as a State policy which is 'consciously aimed at encouraging' an attack against a civilian population. [675]

However, it is important to note that '[t]he existence of such a policy cannot be inferred solely from the absence of governmental or organizational action'.[676] The ESCR Committee's General Comment No. 3 contains more content which can be of help for the international criminal court or tribunals. While the ESCR Committee also elaborates on specific grounds of discrimination potentially relevant in the context of international criminal prosecutions, such as race, colour, religion or sex, the ESCR Committee's specific General Comment on discrimination (General Comment No. 20) is more concerned with the issues of special measures and direct v indirect discrimination in the area of economic, social and cultural rights. While these are no doubt important issues in the field of human rights law, the human rights abuses which trigger international

674 UN Committee on Economic, Social and Cultural Rights 'General Comment No 20 Non-discrimination in economic, social and cultural rights (art. 2, para. 2, of the International Covenant on Economic, Social and Cultural Rights)' (2 July 2009)ESCOR [2009], 118 para. 20.

675 See footnote no 6 Elements of Crimes of the Rome Statute of the International Criminal Court (adopted and entered into force 9 September 2002) Doc ICC-ASP/1/3 (Pt. II-B).

676 See footnote no 6 Elements of Crimes of the Rome Statute of the International Criminal Court (adopted and entered into force 9 September 2002) Doc ICC-ASP/1/3 (Pt. II-B).

criminal prosecution are so flagrant and the threshold for the crimes is so high that the subtleties of anti-discrimination law will probably not be of much assistance to practitioners in defining persecution as a crime against humanity.

c. Convention on the Elimination of All Forms of Discrimination against Women and the Committee on the Elimination of Discrimination against Women

In 1979, the CEDAW was adopted as the first of a number of major 'special' human rights conventions. CEDAW fulfils the initial intention by the drafters of the ICCPR and the IESCR to create a covenant which contains civil and political rights on the one hand and economic, social and cultural rights on the other. CEDAW therefore transcends the divide between those two areas and includes a far-ranging set of rights covering issues from political participation to education of healthcare.[677]

Art. 1 CEDAW contains a definition of the terms 'discrimination against women' which is held to mean

> any distinction, exclusion of restriction made on the basis of sex which has the effect or purpose of impairing or nullifying the recognition, enjoyment or exercise by women, irrespective of their marital status, on a basis of equality of men and women, of human rights and fundamental freedoms in the political, economic, social cultural, civil or any other field.

Taken the ICTY's jurisprudence on the crime of persecution, according to which persecution is 'the violation of the right to equality in some serious fashion that infringes on the enjoyment of a basic or fundamental right'[678] and Art. 7 (2) (g) Rome Statute which states that persecution is 'the intentional and severe deprivation of fundamental rights contrary to international law by reason of the identity of the group or collectivity', the definition set out in Article 1 CEDAW can provide a guideline for courts, in particular for the ICC, when faced with determining the core of persecution on gender grounds. In order to establish whether a 'violation of the right to

---

677 See also Hilary Charlesworth 'Inside/Outside: women and the International Human Rights System' in Aristotle Constantinides and Nikos Zaikos *The Diversity of International Law: Essays in Honour of Professor Kalliopi K Koufa* (Nijhoff Leiden 2009) 382–98, 386.

678 *Prosecutor v Tadić (Opinion and Judgment)* IT-94-1 (7 May 1997) para. 697.

equality in some serious fashion' has taken place, the ICC or any other court or tribunal recognizing the crime of persecution in gender grounds, can also resort to the list of State obligations set out in Art. 2 CEDAW. These obligations range from enshrining the principle of equality in national constitutions (Art. 2 (a) CEDAW) to repealing national penal provisions which discriminate against women (Art. 2 (g) CEDAW). However, it should not be forgotten that CEDAW is subject to more reservations than any of the other major human rights treaty and its content as well as the innovative interpretation by its treaty body has been looked upon with suspicion by many Member States, which makes is harder for practitioners who want refer to in the context of substantive international criminal law but are unsure about the customary nature of some of its provisions.[679]

A provision in CEDAW which is linked to crimes under international law is Art. 6, which provides that 'States Parties shall take all appropriate measures, including legislation, to suppress all forms of traffic in women and exploitation of prostitution of women'. This provision is connected to the crimes of sexual slavery and enforced prostitution as a crime against humanity under Art. 7 (1) (g) Rome Statute. It is important to note here that the term 'forced prostitution' in itself has been heavily criticised. For one, it has been argued that sexual slavery 'encompasses most, if not all forms of enforced prostitution'[680], a term which has been defined as 'conditions of control over a person who is coerced by another to engage in sexual activity'.[681] Additionally, the term 'prostitution' trivializes the experience of the victim, as 'prostitution' contains a connotation of an exchange (sexual acts against money) and downplays the suffering and the coercion involved. [682]

---

679 Henry J Steiner, Philip Alston and Ryan Goodman (eds) *International Human Rights in Context: Law Politics Morals* (3rd edition OUP Oxford 2008) 185.

680 UN Commission on Human Rights 'Systematic rape, sexual slavery and slave-like practices during armed conflict: Final report submitted by Ms. Gay J. McDougall, Special Rapporteur' (22 June 1998) UN Doc E/CN.4/Sub.2/1998/13 para. 31.

681 UN Commission on Human Rights 'Systematic rape, sexual slavery and slave-like practices during armed conflict: Final report submitted by Ms. Gay J. McDougall, Special Rapporteur' (22 June 1998) UN Doc E/CN.4/Sub.2/1998/13 para. 31.

682 Machtheld Boot, Rodney Dixon and Christopher K Hall 'Article 7: Crimes against Humanity' in Otto Triffterer Commentary on the Rome Statute of the International Criminal Court (2nd edition Beck Munich 2008) 159-273, 212; see

However, CEDAW does not address one of the most pressing issues, namely violence against women. This disregard of violence against women concerns domestic violence as well as violence committed in armed conflict or any other setting in which crimes under international law can be committed. According to Hilary Charlesworth, the causes for this neglect may lay in the fact that at the time CEDAW was adopted, 'the global extent of violence against women was not well-understood, or because violence was not analysed as a matter of discrimination'.[683] A contributing reason is within the group of State experts drafting the convention, the predominant was governed by the dichotomy between 'public' acts exercised by the State and regulated through international treaties and 'private' acts by individuals, which were generally seen as being detracted from the field of international law. This dichotomy is one of the main criticisms of feminist legal theory towards traditional international legal thinking, as it downgrades many of the experiences and actions of females to the realm of the 'private' and hence withdraw them of the control of the State as well as of the competent jurisdiction of the international community. [684] Be it as it may, violence against women has since then been addressed by the treaty body established under CEDAW, the CEDAW Committee. The CEDAW Committee issued two General Recommendations regarding violence against women. While General Recommendation No. 12 is very short and generally framed[685], General Recommendation No. 19 clarifies that gender-based violence is a form of discrimination coming under the realm of CEDAW 'which impairs or nullifies the enjoyment by women of human rights and fundamental freedoms under general international law or

---

also Women's Caucus for Gender Justice in the International Criminal Court 'Recommendations and Commentary for December 1997 PrepCom on the Establishment of an International Criminal Court' (1–12 December 1997) WC.5.6-9, 6–10.

683 Hilary Charlesworth 'Inside/Outside: women and the International Human Rights System' in Aristotle Constantinides and Nikos Zaikos *The Diversity of International Law: Essays in Honour of Professor Kalliopi K Koufa* (Nijhoff Leiden 2009), 382–98, 386.

684 See eg Hilary Charlesworth and Christine Chinkin *The Boundaries of Interantional Law: A Feminist Analysis* (Manchester University Press Manchester 2000).

685 UN Committee on the Elimination of Discrimination against Women 'General Recommendation No 12: Violence against Women' (1989) Compilation of General Comments and General Recommendations Adopted by Human Rights Treaty Bodies, U.N. Doc. HRI/GEN/1/Rev. 6 at 237 (2003).

under human rights conventions'.[686] As Alice Edwards puts it, this approach '[i]in many ways (…) transformed the CEDAW from an anti-discrimination treaty into a gender-based violence treaty'.[687] General Recommendation No. 19 included within the scope of these human rights and fundamental freedoms affected by gender-based violence:

> (a) The right to life;
>
> (b) The right not to be subject to torture or to cruel, inhuman or degrading treatment or punishment;
>
> (c) The right to equal protection according to humanitarian norms in time of international or internal armed conflict;
>
> (d) The right to liberty and security of person;
>
> (e) The right to equal protection under the law;
>
> (f) The right to equality in the family;
>
> (g) The right to the highest standard attainable of physical and mental health;
>
> (h) The right to just and favourable conditions of work.

Therefore, General Comment No. 19 refers to several issues of relevance to international criminal law and the protection of women against crimes under international law which primarily or frequently affect them. In the context of international criminal proceedings, albeit giving due consideration to the differences of the two regimes, judges would gain from referring to the jurisprudence of the CEDAW Committee to underline the fact that violence against women is seen not only as a crime against the women's physical integrity, but also as an indication and stemming from a system discrimination against women. In proceedings which deal with gender-based discrimination, the ICC can refer to the authority of the CEDAW Committee in order to establish grave violations of the prohibition of violence against women as one of the signs for the grave denials of human rights which constitutes persecution.

However, the fact that the single most important universal instrument on women's rights does itself not explicitly mention violence against

686 Para. 7 UN Committee on the Elimination of Discrimination against Women 'General Recommendation No 19: Violence against Women' (30 January 1992) GAOR 47th Session Supp 38, 1.

687 Alice Edwards ,Violence against Women as Sex Discrimination: Judging the Jurisprudence of the United Nations Human Rights Treaty Bodies' (2008) 18 Texas Journal of Women and the Law 1–54.

women does doubtlessly diminish its value for application by judges seeking to ensure they are on the safe ground of customary international law.

d. International Convention on the Elimination of all Forms of Racial Discrimination

In 2000, the Committee on the Elimination of Racial Discrimination published General Recommendation 25 which dealt with specific aspects of racial discrimination which do not affect men and women in the same way.[688] In it, the Committee ties in with sexual violence against women in the context of international criminal law, for instance sexual violence committed against women of a specific ethnic or racial group in armed conflict or during detention or forced sterilization of indigenous women.[689]

e. UNGA Declaration on the Elimination of Violence against Women

In 1993, the UNGA adopted the DEVW, which acknowledges in its preamble that 'violence against women is a manifestation of historically unequal power relations between men and women, which have led to domination over and discrimination against women by men and to the prevention of the full advancement of women, and that violence against women is one of the crucial social mechanisms by which women are forced into a subordinate position compared with men'.[690] Article 1 DEVWD states '[f]or the purposes of this Declaration, the term "violence against women" means any act of gender-based violence that results in, or is likely to result in, physical, sexual or psychological harm or suffering to women, including threats of such acts, coercion or arbitrary deprivation of

---

688 UN Committee on the Elimination of Racial Discrimination 'General Recommendation XXV on Gender-Related Dimensions of Racial Discrimination' (20 March 2000) GAOR 55th Session Supp 18, 152.

689 UN Committee on the Elimination of Racial Discrimination 'General Recommendation XXV on Gender-Related Dimensions of Racial Discrimination' (20 March 2000) GAOR 55th Session Supp 18, 152, para 2.

690 UNGA Res 48/104 'Declaration on the Elimination of Violence against Women' (20 December 1993) GAOR 48th Session Supp 49 vol 1, 217.

liberty, whether occurring in public or in private life.' [691] The Declaration includes a detailed description of its scope in Article 2 which provides that

> Violence against women shall be understood to encompass, but not be limited to, the following:
>
> (a) Physical, sexual and psychological violence occurring in the family, including battering, sexual abuse of female children in the household, dowry-related violence, marital rape, female genital mutilation and other traditional practices harmful to women, non-spousal violence and violence related to exploitation;
>
> (b) Physical, sexual and psychological violence occurring within the general community, including rape, sexual abuse, sexual harassment and intimidation at work, in educational institutions and elsewhere, trafficking in women and forced prostitution;
>
> (c) Physical, sexual and psychological violence perpetrated or condoned by the State, wherever it occurs.[692]

In 1994, the UN Commission on Human Rights adopted Resolution 1994/45, which established a Special Rapporteur on violence against women, including its causes and consequences,[693] who also reported specifically on violence against women committed within the context of armed conflict.[694]

f. African Charter on Human and Peoples Rights (Banjul Charter)

The African Charter on Human and Peoples' Rights (Banjul Charter) contains a very broad provision obliging Member States to 'ensure the elimi-

---

691 UNGA Res 48/104 'Declaration on the Elimination of Violence against Women' (20 December 1993) GAOR 48th Session Supp 49 vol 1, 217.

692 See Art. 2 UNGA Res 48/104 'Declaration on the Elimination of Violence against Women' (20 December 1993) GAOR 48th Session Supp 49 vol 1, 217; the same definitonal has been used in para. 113 UN World Conference on Women (4th) 'Beijing Declaration and Platform for Action'(17 October 1995) UN Doc A/CONF.177/20, 4 and later in UNGA Res 61/143 'Intensification of Efforts to Eliminate all Forms of Violence against Women' (19 December 2006) GAOR 61st Session Supp 49 vol 1, 326.

693 UN Commission on Human Rights Res 1994/45 (4 March 1994) ESCOR.

694 UN Commission on Human Rights, Special Rapporteur Ms. Radhika Coomaraswamy 'Violence against women perpetrated and/or condoned by the State during times of armed conflict (1997-2001)' (23 January 2001) Un Doc E/CN.4/2001/73.

nation of every discrimination against women and also ensure the protection of the rights of the woman and the child as stipulated in international declarations and conventions' (Art. 18 Banjul Charter).[695] Placing this provision in the context of Art. 18, which mainly deals with the protection of family life, outlining the family as the 'custodian of morals and traditional values recognized by the community' (Art. 18 (2) Banjul Charter) shows that the drafters of the Banjul charter drew on very traditional gender roles, portraying women as wives and mothers, and therefore as acting in the private sphere rather than in public life, as employees or in the political field for instance. This is also shown by the grouping together of 'women and children' emphasizing their vulnerability (as mothers) rather than portraying women as individuals claiming rights which they are correctly entitled to. As Hilary Charlesworth puts it '[v]iolations of women's human rights are typically presented as an aspect of women's inherent vulnerability, as if this attribute were a biological fact'.[696]

The provision is also extremely vague, defining neither the term 'discrimination' nor the conventions and declarations which protect the rights of women. It is therefore doubtful how much real authority can be drawn from such a stipulation. Nevertheless, the ICC could possibly escape some criticism of being Eurocentric in its applied and cited sources on the one hand and having neo-colonial tendencies, focussing solely on one continent, on the other hand, by citing this provision.

g. Beijing Declaration and Platform for Action

The outcome document of the Fourth World Conference on Women in Beijing in 1994 contains a part on violence against women which systematically defines and describes modes and circumstances of violence against women. [697] The language of the Beijing Platform for Action frames violence against women in terms of systematic and widespread hu-

---

695 African Charter on Human and Peoples' Rights (adopted 27 June1981, entered into force 21 October 1986) 1520 UNTS 217 (Banjul Charter).

696 Hilary Charlesworth 'International human rights law: A portmanteau for feminist norms?' in Gülay Caglar, Elisabeth Prügl and Susanne Zwingel Feminist Strategies in International Governance (Routledge Abingdon, Oxon/New York 2013) 21-37, 27.

697 Fourth World Conference on Women 'Beijing Declaration and Platform for Action' in 'Report' (17 October 1995) UN Doc A/CONF.177/20, 4.

man rights violations which are a manifestation of unequal power relations and cultural patterns and happen throughout societies.[698] It differentiates between three kinds of violence: in the family, in the general community and condoned by the State[699] and highlights that women's human rights are particularly at risk in the context of armed conflict and/or when women belong to a minority group.[700] The Platform for Action also contains a section on women and armed conflict which highlights that violations of women's rights are violations of fundamental human rights and that the perpetrators of mass human rights violations such as genocide, crimes against humanity and war crimes have to be punished.[701] The actions to be taken by governments differ somewhat from the usual human rights approach to violence against women in that they do not only call for investigation and criminal prosecution of perpetrators but also undertake to change harmful perceptions of women in society in order to change the role of women and break the cycle of systematic subordination which promotes violence

2. Protection of Women against Gender-Based Violence in International Criminal Law

Sexual violence can be committed in many different forms. It can amount to different crimes, keeping in mind the specific circumstances of the case in question. Before the *ad hoc* tribunals and hybrid courts, sexual violence, including rape, has so far been classified as

- rape as a crime against humanity or a war crime;
- torture as a crime against humanity and as a war crime:

698 Fourth World Conference on Women 'Beijing Declaration and Platform for Action' in 'Report' (17 October 1995) UN Doc A/CONF.177/20, 4 paras 112-3, 117, 118.

699 Fourth World Conference on Women 'Beijing Declaration and Platform for Action' in 'Report' (17 October 1995) UN Doc A/CONF.177/20, 4 para 113.

700 Fourth World Conference on Women 'Beijing Declaration and Platform for Action' in 'Report' (17 October 1995) UN Doc A/CONF.177/20, 4 paras 114, 116.

701 Fourth World Conference on Women 'Beijing Declaration and Platform for Action' in 'Report' (17 October 1995) UN Doc A/CONF.177/20, 4 para 131.

- genocide (in the alternative of causing serious bodily or mental harm to members of the targeted group or by imposing measures intended to prevent births within the group);
- persecution as a crime against humanity;
- enslavement as a crime against humanity;
- Other inhumane acts as a crime against humanity;
- outrages upon personal dignity and inhumane treatment as war crimes.[702]

In 2008, the UN Security Council adopted Resolution 1820 dealing with violence against women in conflict, in which it stated that violence against women could constitute a threat to international peace and security, genocide, crimes against humanity or war crimes and that States have an obligations to protect their population against sexual violence as part of their responsibility to 'protect and ensure the human rights of their citizens'.[703]

a. Genocide

The acts amounting to genocide listed in Article 6 Rome Statute, Article 4(2) ICTY Statute and Article 2(2) ICTR Statute, are a verbatim copy of the ones listed in Article II of the Genocide Convention. The groups protected are national, ethnical, racial or religious groups, gender is not mentioned as a factor.

Even though opinions have been voiced during the Rome Conference and outside, to include other stable groups into the extent of protection[704]

---

702 See also United Nations Department of Peacekeeping Operations *Review of the Sexual Violence Elements of the Judgments of the International Criminal Tribunal for the Former Yugoslavia, the International Criminal Tribunal for Rwanda and the Special Court for Sierra Leone in the Light of Security Council Resolution 1820* (United Nations New York 2010), 25.

703 UNSC Res 1820 (2008) (19 June 2008) SCOR [1 August 2007–31 July 2008] 154.

704 It can be argued about how stable a group the term 'gender' denominates if one refers to the commonly used definition of gender being socially constructed. However, the definition used in Article 7(3) Statute, which is valid for the whole of the Rome Statute, refers to gender as 'the two sexes, male and female, within the context of society' and arguable conveys to the term more stableness than usually attributed to it; see more in detail under Part Two Chapter Three III 2 c. (2) below.

it is unlikely that gender will be seen as within its jurisdiction by the ICC or any other international criminal tribunal in the near future. However, 'femicide' or 'gendercide' are increasingly discusses, particularly in social sciences, but also for example by the World Health Organization, which discusses the term under four rough categories, intimate femicide, murders in the name of 'honour', non-intimate femicide and dowry-related femicide.[705]

Less controversial is the acknowledgement that sexual violence committed with genocidal intent against members of an explicitly protected group is genocide. Some of the acts of sexual violence fall under Art. 6 (d) Rome Statute as 'measures intended to prevent births within the group', when, for example, women are deliberately raped and impregnated to give birth to change the ethnic composition of a population or to break female members of a group to a point where, after the rape, they do not wish to have any children.[706] The ICTR's *Akayesu* judgment in 1998 explicitly acknowledged rape as such to be genocide under the modality of causing seriously bodily or mental harm, when committed with the necessary intent. [707] The Chamber held that rape was 'one of the worst ways of inflict harm on the victim as he or she suffers both bodily and mental harm.'[708]

705 World Health Organization: Understanding Violence against Women: Femicide (World Health Organization 2012) 1-3 http://apps.who.int/iris/bitstream/10665/77421/1/WHO_RHR_12.38_eng.pdf (28 July 2015).

706 *Prosecutor v Akayesu (Judgment)* ICTR-96-4-T (2 September 1998) paras 507-8.

707 *Prosecutor v Akayesu (Judgment)* ICTR-96-4-T (2 September 1998) para 731; see also *Prosecutor v Furundžija (Judgment)* IT-95-17 (10 December 1998) para 172; *Prosecutor v Gacumbitsi (Judgment)* ICTR-01-64-T (17 June 2004) para 292; *Prosecutor v Muhimana (Judgment)* ICTR-95-1B-T (28 April 2005) paras 513, 517; *Prosecutor v Rutaganda (Judgment)* ICTR-96-3-T (6 December 1999) paras 50, 280, 292.

708 *Prosecutor v Akayesu (Judgment)* ICTR-96-4-T (2 September 1998) para 731; *Prosecutor v Furundžija (Judgment)* IT-95-17 (10 December 1998) para 172; see also Catharine A MacKinnon 'Rape, Genocide and Women's Human Rights' (1994) 17 Harvard Women's Law Journal 5-16; Sherrie L Russell-Brown 'Rape as Genocide' (2003) 21 Berkeley Journal of International Law 350-374.

b. Crimes against Humanity

(1) Sexual Violence

Pursuant to Art. 7 (1) (g) Rome Statute a multitude of acts of sexual violence are punishable before the ICC. These are '[r]ape, sexual slavery, enforced prostitution, forced pregnancy, enforced sterilization, or any other form of sexual violence of comparable gravity', making the list non-exhausting. In this, the Rome Statute seeks to remedy omissions in the statutes of the ICTY/ICTR according to which rape could be charged under Art. 5 (g) ICTY Statute and Art. 3 (g) ICTR Statute but no other forms of sexual violence were explicitly mentioned under Art. 5, even though the ICTY indeed convicted persons for acts of sexual violence as crimes against humanity under the headings of torture[709], persecution,[710] enslavement[711] and inhumane acts.[712] The concept of 'forced pregnancy' has already been used in the Vienna Declaration and Programme of Action and subsequently in the 1995 Beijing Declaration and Platform for Action before it was incorporated in the Rome Statute and in the Statute of the Special Court for Sierra Leone.[713]

Additionally, the ICC can prosecute persecution on grounds of gender pursuant to Art. 7 (1) (h) or sexual violence as torture pursuant to Art. 7 (1) (f) Rome Statute.

(2) Persecution

Article 6 (c) MT Charter contained 'persecution on political, racial or religious grounds in execution of or in connection with any crime within the jurisdiction of the Tribunal, whether or not in violation of the domestic law of the country where perpetrated', Article 5 (c) Charter for the Inter-

---

709 *Prosecutor v Delalić et al (Celebići Case Judgment)* IT-96-21-T (16 November 1998).

710 Prosecutor v Delalić et al (Celebići Case Judgment) IT-96-21-T (16 November 1998).

711 *Prosecutor v Kunarac (Judgment)* IT-96-23 (22 February 2001).

712 *Prosecutor v Tadić (Opinion and Judgment)* IT-94-1 (7 May 1997).

713 William A Schabas *The International Criminal Court: A Commentary on the Rome Statute* (OUP Oxford 2010) 174.

national Military Tribunal for the Far East contained the same provision with the exception of religious grounds which were omitted.

Article 5 (h) ICTY Statute and Article 3 (h) ICTR Statute list persecution on persecutions on political, racial or religious grounds under crimes against humanity (with regards to the ICTY the crime has to be committed in the context of an armed conflict). However, as highlighted above, the ICTY also acknowledged persecution on gender grounds[714] and stated very early on that '[c]rimes against humanity may be committed on discriminatory grounds other than those enumerated in art 5(h) [of the Statute of the ICTY], such as physical or mental disability, age or infirmity, or sexual preference'[715]

Article 7(1)(h) Rome Statute makes persecution punishable as a crime against humanity. Article 7(2)(g) Rome Statute defines persecution as 'the intentional and severe deprivation of fundamental rights contrary to international law by reasons of the identity of the group or collectivity'. The Rome Statute is the first international criminal statute which defines the crime of persecution. It is also the first statute which provides for the possibility of a conviction for persecution on gender grounds, whereupon Art. 7 (3) clarifies that the term 'gender' 'refers to the two sexes, male and female, within the context of society. The definition in the Rome Statute is the product of a compromise in the drafting of Article 21 (3) which prohibits adverse distinction of the application and interpretation of the law on several grounds, including gender.[716] While some States insisted on such a clause, and argued that not including, in particular, gender, would be a step backwards as gender was included in numerous human rights and humanitarian law instruments[717]other States did not want such a non-adverse distinction clause to be included.[718] As a compromise, a definition of gender was included, which is applicable to the whole of the Rome

714 *Prosecutor v Delalić et al (Judgment)* IT-96-21 (16 November 1998) para 941.

715 *Prosecutor v Tadić (Appeal Judgment)* IT-94-1-A (15 July 1999) para 285.

716 Machtheld Boot, Rodney Dixon and Christopher K Hall 'Article 7: Crimes against Humanity' in Otto Triffterer Commentary on the Rome Statute of the International Criminal Court (2nd edition Beck Munich 2008) 159-273, 273.

717 See Cate Steains 'Gender Issues' in Roy S Lee (ed) *The International Criminal Court: The Making of the Rome Statute* (Kluwer Law International The Hague 1999) 357–390, 372.

718 Machtheld Boot, Rodney Dixon and Christopher K Hall 'Article 7: Crimes against Humanity' in Otto Triffterer Commentary on the Rome Statute of the International Criminal Court (2nd edition Beck Munich 2008) 159-273, 273.

Statute.[719] This definition is characterized by a 'constructive ambiguity'[720] that appeases a multitude of negotiation parties and has to be further specified by interpretation by the practitioners which apply it.

This definition seems to conflates the two terms 'gender' and 'sex', but 'within the context of society' leaves rooms for the differentiation between 'sex' as referring to biological differences between men and women and 'gender' as the socially constructed identities and roles. The definition commonly used in the UN refer to gender as a social construct and can be used by the ICC in the future to fill the wide definition in Article 7 (3) Rome Statute with legal content. For example, the Secretary-General, in his report 'Integrating the gender perspective into the work of United Nations human rights treaty bodies', defines 'gender' as 'the socially constructed roles of women and men that are ascribed to them on the basis of their sex, in public and in private life' whereas 'sex' refers to 'the biological and physical characteristics of women and men'.[721] Here, human rights law has a lot to offer to the development of international criminal law regarding the prosecution of gender crimes. Interestingly, the definition in Article 7(3) Rome Statute could, in contrast, also significantly change the approach to gender in international human rights law. As the definition employed in the Rome Statute is vague enough to serve as a compromise and not to agitate States fearing a too rapid or too progressive development in this field, the definition is more appealing to these States than the more specific notions usually employed at the United Nations.[722] As ob-

---

719 Machtheld Boot, Rodney Dixon and Christopher K Hall 'Article 7: Crimes against Humanity' in Otto Triffterer *Commentary on the Rome Statute of the International Criminal Court* (2nd edition Beck Munich 2008) 159-273, 273 citing Barbara Bedont and Katherine Hall-Martinez 'Ending Impunity for Gender Crimes under the International Criminal Court' (1999) 6 Brown Journal of World Affairs 65-85, 68.

720 Valerie Oosterveld 'The Definition of "Gender" in the Rome Statute of the International Court: A Step Forward of Back for International Criminal Justice?' (2005) 18 Harvard Human Rights Journal 55-84, 81, referring to Anthony Aust *Modern Treaty Law and Practice* (Cambridge University Press Cambridge 2000) 184.

721 United Nations International Human Rights Instruments 'Integrating the gender perspective into the work of United Nations human rights treaty bodies: Report by the Secretary-General' (3 September 1998) UN Doc HRI/MC/1998/6 para 16.

722 Valerie Oosterveld 'The Definition of "Gender" in the Rome Statute of the International Court: A Step Forward of Back for International Criminal Justice?' (2005) 18 Harvard Human Rights Journal 55-84, 83.

served by Oosterveld, the Rome Statute definition has already been employed to define the notion of 'gender' in the Durban Declaration and Platform of Action that is part of the Report on the 2001 World Conference Against Racism, Racial Discrimination, Xenophobia and Related Intolerance.[723] So far, the Rome Statute definition has, however, not prevailed, and most major UN agencies and programs, first and foremost UN Women, use a definition of gender which emphasizes its socially constructed nature.[724] As mentioned, the notion 'within the context of society' gives the court leeway for various interpretation. The question that poses itself is what constitutes the 'society' Art. 7(3) Rome Statute speaks of? One area international criminal law could draw guidance from in this respect is refugee law, which considers not only the domestic, but also the international construction of gender within the international community.[725] This provides the possibility for the Court to extensively refer to the standards in non-discrimination of women under CEDAW. As such, there is room for ICC jurisprudence to develop the vague definition in a more progressive direction in line with the definitions most commonly used at the United Nations.

Additionally, even if the Court may decide that a certain crime cannot be subsumed under persecution on gender grounds as the term is defined in the Rome Statute, the crime could still be characterized as within the

723 UN World Conference against Racism, Racial Discrimination, Xenophobia and Related Intolerance 'Report' (2001) UN Doc A/CONF.189/12 75 Note 1.

724 UN Women 'Concepts and Definitions' http://www.un.org/womenwatch/osagi/conceptsandefinitions.htm (31 October 2017).

725 UNHCR 'Guidelines on International Protection No 1: Gender-Related Persecution Within the Context of Article 1A(2) of the 1951 Convention and/or its 1967 Protocol Relating to the Status of Refugees' (2002) UN Doc HCR/GIP/02/01; UNHCR EXCOM Conclusion No 39 (XXXVI) 'Refugee Women and International Protection' (1985) UN Doc HRC/IP/2; UNHCR 'Guidelines on Refugee Women' (1991) UN Doc EC/SCP/67, all as cited in Valerie Oosterveld 'Gender, Persecution, and the International Criminal Court: Refugee Law's Relevance to the Crime against Humanity of Gender-based Persecution' (2006) 17 Duke Journal of Comparative and International Law 49–89, 76 and Valerie Oosterveld 'The Definition of "Gender" in the Rome Statute of the International Court: A Step Forward of Back for International Criminal Justice?' (2005) 18 Harvard Human Rights Journal 55-84, 59 (fn 25) and 67-8 (fn 70); UNHCR 'Sexual and Gender-Based Violence against Refugees, Returnees and Internally Displaced Persons: Guidelines for Prevention and Response' (United Nations High Commissioner for Refugees 2003).

jurisdiction of the Court as persecution on 'other grounds that are universally recognized as impermissible under international law'.[726]

(3) Enslavement/ Sexual Slavery

Enslavement and sexual slavery, albeit different provisions in the Rome Statute (Arts 7 (1) (c) and 7 (1) (g) are intrinsically related in that sexual slavery is a specific form of slavery.[727] The grouping of the crime with other crimes of sexual violence show that on top of exercising powers attached to ownership over a person, the perpetrator caused the person over whom he exercised those powers to engage in acts of a sexual nature.[728] Slavery, including sexual slavery, are a part of *ius cogens*.[729]

In the *Kunarac* Case before the ICTY, the accused were convicted for enslavement as a crime against humanity pursuant to Article 5 (c) and acts of sexual and non-sexual nature were likewise considered to fall under enslavement as a crime against humanity.[730] The court extensively referred to human rights instruments dedicated to eliminating slavery,[731] to general human rights treaties and instruments containing a ban of slavery[732] as well as to jurisprudence on the matter by the ECtHR and the ECommHR

726 Machtheld Boot, Rodney Dixon and Christopher K Hall 'Article 7: Crimes against Humanity' in Otto Triffterer *Commentary on the Rome Statute of the International Criminal Court* (2nd edition Beck Munich 2008) 159-273, 220.

727 Machtheld Boot, Rodney Dixon and Christopher K Hall 'Article 7: Crimes against Humanity' in Otto Triffterer *Commentary on the Rome Statute of the International Criminal Court* (2nd edition Beck Munich 2008) 159-273, 211.

728 See Elements of Crime of Art. 7 (1) (g) Rome Statute.

729 *Prosecutor v Brima et al (Trial Chamber Judgment)* SCSL–2004–16–T (19 July 2007) para. 705.

730 *Prosecutor v Kunarac (Judgment)* IT-96-23 (22 February 2001) paras 518-543, in particular para. 543.

731 Slavery Convention (adopted 25 September 1926, entered into force 9 March 1927) 60 LNTS 253; Supplementary Convention on the Abolition of Slavery, the Slave Trade, and Institutions and Practices Similar to Slavery (adopted 7 September 1956, entered into force 30 April 1957) 266 UNTS 3; ILO 'Convention No 29 concerning Forced or Compulsory Labour' (adopted 28 June 1930, entered into force 1 May 1932) 39 UNTS 55; ILO 'Convention No 105 concerning the Abolition of Forced Labour' (adopted 25 June 1957, entered into force 17 January 1959) 320 UNTS 291.

732 Art. 4 UDHR; Art. 8 ICCPR; Art. 4 ECHR; Art. 6 ACHR; Art. 5 ACHPR.

(and other international criminal tribunals).[733] The Court also made extensive reference to provisions under international humanitarian law.[734] The court did, however, not make any mention of instruments dealing explicitly with human rights.

c. War Crimes

The mentioned neglect of gender issues in the area of human rights protection was mirrored by a disregard of the gendered dimension international humanitarian law. The Hague Conventions did not explicitly mention any form of sexual or other gendered violence, even though it contains, in Article 46 of the regulations annexed to the 1907 Hague Convention the vague provision stating that '[f]amily honour and rights […] must be respected'.[735] At the 'cradle' of modern international criminal law, at the Nuremberg International Military Tribunal[736] ('NIMT') and the International Military Tribunal for the Far East[737] ('IMFE'), neither rape and other forms of sexual violence, nor gender-based persecution were mentioned in the respective statutes as crimes against humanity or war crimes. Subsequently, even though evidence of rape and other forms of sexual violence was introduced by the French and Russian prosecutors, these acts are not mentioned in the final judgment, which does not in great detail enlist the single acts that constituted wither crimes against humanity or war crimes, but, in contrary, generally emphasizes that 'war crimes […] were attended

733 *Van Droogenbroeck v Belgium (Decision of 5 July 1979 on the admissibility of the application)* (EComm App 7906/77) D/R 17, 59; *Van der Mussele v Belgium* (ECtHR) (*Judgment*) (1983) 6 EHRR 163; *Prosecutor v Kunarac (Judgment)* IT-96-23 (22 February 2001) paras 522-527.

734 *Prosecutor v Kunarac (Judgment)* IT-96-23 (22 February 2001) paras 528-532.

735 Convention with Respect to the Laws and Customs of War by Land and its Annex: Regulations Respecting the Laws and Customs of War on Land (signed 29 July 1899, entered into force 4 September 1900) (1898–99) 187 CTS 429; Convention respecting the Laws and Customs of War on Land and its Annex: Regulations concerning the Laws and Customs of War on Land (signed 18 October 1907, entered into force 26 January 1910) (1907) 205 CTS 277.

736 Charter of the [Nuremberg] International Military Tribunal (8 August 1945) 82 UNTS 284.

737 Charter of the International Military Tribunal for the Far East (19 January 1946) 4 Bevans 20.

by every conceivable circumstance of cruelty and horror'.[738] Even though not enlisted in the Statute, rape was repetitively referred to in the main judgement of the IMFE, under 'Chapter VIII: Conventional War Crimes (Atrocities)'. Most prominently, the judgement recapitulates the events following the Japanese capture of the Chinese city of Nanking in 1937, which have commonly become known as the 'Rape of Nanking'.[739] In the final findings, the majority of the judges does, however, only very generally state that crimes under Count 54 (ordering, authorising and permitting the commission of conventional war crimes) and Count 55 (to take adequate steps to secure the observance and prevent breaches of conventions and laws of war in respect of prisoners of war and civilian internees) have been committed without specifically demonstrating through which acts the crimes were committed.[740] Furthermore, the IMTFE failed to prosecute the abduction, enslavement and rape of approximately 200.000 Chinese women in brothels principally frequented by Japanese soldiers.[741]

Rape was included within the acts that could constitute crimes against humanity under Art. II (1) (c) Control Council Law No. 10, which was issued by the Control Council for Germany on 20 December 1945. [742]

In the following years, the awareness for gender issues and non-discrimination on account of sex rose, which is reflected in the inclusion of

---

738 *The United States of America et al v Göring et al (Judgment and Sentences of the International Military Tribunal) (Nuremberg)* (1 October 1946) (1947) 41 AJIL 172–333, 224.

739 *The United States of America et al v Araki et al (Judgment of the International Military Tribunal for the far East)* (12 November 1948) reprinted in BVA Röling and CF Rüter (eds) The Tokyo Judgment (APA University Press Amsterdam 1977) 389–93.

740 *The United States of America et al v Araki et al (Judgment of the International Military Tribunal for the far East)* (12 November 1948) available at http://www.worldcourts.com/imtfe/eng/decisions/1948.11.04_IMTFE_Judgment.htm (31 October 2017).

741 See eg AW Brown and L Greenfell 'The International Crime of Gender-Based Apartheid and the Taliban' (2003) 4 Melbourne Journal of International Law 347–75, 354.

742 Control Council Law No 10 'Punishment of Persons Guilty of War Crimes, Crimes against Peace and against Humanity' (done 20 December 1945) (1946) 3 Official Gazette of the Control Council for Germany 50.

non-discrimination provisions in the Geneva Conventions.[743] Article 27 (2) Geneva IV also prohibits sexual violence against women, stating that '[w]omen shall be especially protected against any attack on their honour, in particular against rape, enforced prostitution, or any form of indecent assault.' The focus of this provision was put on rape as a crime against honour, personal honour and that of the extended family, therefore coching it 'in terms of chasity and modesty of women'[744] and not in terms of violation of physical integrity or the infliction of physical or mental harm.[745] For this reason, and the failure to include rape within its 'grave breaches', the way the Geneva conventions address sexual violence has been heavily criticized.[746] This protection is supplemented by Art. 3(1)(c) Common to all Geneva Conventions, which protects against 'outrages upon personal dignity, in particular humiliating and degrading treatment'.

Finally, Art. 76(1) Protocol Additional to the Geneva Conventions of 12 August 1949, and relating to the Protection of Victims of International Armed Conflicts states that '[w]omen shall be the object of special respect and shall be protected in particular against rape, forced prostitution and

743 See Art. 12 Geneva Convention for the Amelioration of the Condition of the Wounded and Sick in Armed Forces in the Field (adopted 12 August 1949, entered into force 21 October 1950) 75 UNTS 31 (Geneva Convention I); Art. 12 Geneva Convention for the Amelioration of the Condition of Wounded, Sick and Shipwrecked Members of Armed Forces at Sea (adopted 12 August 1949, entered into force 21 October 1950) 75 UNTS 85 (Geneva Convention II); Art. 14 Geneva Convention relative to the Treatment of Prisoners of War (adopted 12 August 1949, entered into force 21 October 1950) 75 UNTS 135 (Geneva Convention III); Art. 27 Geneva Convention relative to the Protection of Civilian Persons in Time of War (adopted 12 August 1949, entered into force 21 October 1950) 75 UNTS 287 (Geneva Convention IV).

744 Helen Durham and Katie O'Byrne The Dialogue of DifferenceL Gender Perspectives on International Humanitarian Law (2010) 92 International Review of the Red Cross 31-52, 35.

745 Helen Durham and Katie O'Byrne The Dialogue of DifferenceL Gender Perspectives on International Humanitarian Law (2010) 92 International Review of the Red Cross 31-52, 35.

746 Judith Gardam and Michelle Jarvis, Women *Armed Conflict and International Law* (Kluwer Law International The Hague 2001) 96-97; see also Helen Durham and Katie O'Byrne The Dialogue of DifferenceL Gender Perspectives on International Humanitarian Law (2010) 92 International Review of the Red Cross 31-52, 35 fn 13 for further references.

any other form of indecent assault.'[747] Art. 4(2)(e) Protocol Additional to the Geneva Conventions of 12 August 1949, and relating to the Protection of Victims of Non-International Armed Conflicts prohibits 'outrages upon personal dignity, in particular humiliating and degrading treatment, rape, enforced prostitution and any form or indecent assault'[748]

However, rape in the Geneva Convention context did not rise to a 'grave breach' nor is it listed as a violation of the laws and customs of war in any of the Conventions.[749] Therefore, at the ICTY, which has jurisdiction over grave breaches of the Geneva Conventions pursuant to Article 2 and violations of the laws and customs of war under Article 3, rape was not explicitly mentioned as a violation of international humanitarian law. The ICTR, having international humanitarian law jurisdiction only over violations of Common Article 3 and Additional Protocol II, can charge rape as a particular outrage upon personal dignity explicitly mentioned in Article 4 (e) ICTR Statute.

In the beginning of the 1990s, momentum was gained for the recognition of rape as a war crime. Monumental in this change were the events in the former Yugoslavia and later in Rwanda, where rape and other forms of sexual violence were systematically used against women and men. The ICRC clarified in 1992 that the grave breach of 'wilfully causing great suffering or serious injury to body and health' in Article 147 Geneva Convention IV covers rape.[750] Influential States like the USA also categorized rape and sexual assault as grave breaches.[751] Around the same time, the international community as started paying more attention to violations of women's rights in conflicts and the gendered nature of crimes under inter-

---

747 Protocol Additional to the Geneva Conventions of 12 August 1949, and relating to the Protection of Victims of International Armed Conflicts (Protocol I) (adopted 8 June 1977, entered into force 7 December 1978) 1125 UNTS 3.

748 Protocol Additional to the Geneva Conventions of 12 August 1949, and relating to the Protection of Victims of Non-International Armed Conflicts (Protocol II) (adopted 8 June 1977, entered into force 7 December 1978) 1125 UNTS 609.

749 Sherrie L Russell-Brown 'Rape as Genocide' (2003) 21 Berkeley Journal of International Law 350-374, 357.

750 International Committee of the Red Cross 'Aide-Mémoire' (3 December 1992) as cited in Theodor Meron 'Rape as a Crime under International Humanitarian Law' (1993) 87(3) American Journal of International Law 424-428, 426.

751 US Department of State 'Letter from Robert A Bradtke, Acting Assistant Secretary for Legislative Affairs, to Senator Arlen Spector' (27 January 1992) as cited in Theodor Meron 'Rape as a Crime under International Humanitarian Law' (1993) 87(3) American Journal of International Law 424-428, 427.

national law. At the World Conference on Human Rights in Vienna in 1993, States spoke out against gender-based violence and systematic rape in conflict situations and) called for the integration of the 'equal status of women' into the mainstream of UN activity[752]. They also reaffirmed that sexual violence in conflict is a violation of fundamental human rights.[753] Two years later, at the Fourth World Conference on women in Beijing, the governments agreed on the undertaking to 'integrate a gender perspective in the resolution of armed conflict and foreign occupation'[754] in order to protect women living in situations of armed and other conflict and foreign occupation'.[755]

In the Rome Statute, the term 'war crime' is defined as 'traditional' grave breaches, which are listed (Article 8(2)(a) Rome Statute), and '[o]ther serious violations of the laws and customs applicable in international armed conflict, within the established framework of international law' (Article 8(2)(b) Rome Statute). In this list, 'rape, sexual slavery, enforced prostitution, forced pregnancy, as defined in article 7, paragraph 2 (f), enforced sterilization, or any other form of sexual violence also constituting a grave breach of the Geneva Conventions' are expressly listed in Article 8(2)(b)(xxii).

Traditionally, as Charlesworth (Copelon) points out, the dichotomy between peace time and conflict, between the applicability of human rights law and the applicability of humanitarian law, promoted IHL, as the law of war, to focus on the 'warrior caste' and to neglect persons traditionally outside that group.[756] World War II brought with it the realization that

752 Cate Steains 'Gender Issues' in Roy S Lee (ed) *The International Criminal Court: The Making of the Rome Statute* (Kluwer Law International The Hague 1999) 357–390, 360; see also UN World Conference on Human Rights 'Vienna Declaration and Programme of Action' (25 June 1993) UN Doc A/CONF.157/23 Part I, paras 18 and 28, and Part II, para. 37.

753 Vienna Declaration and Programme of Action' (25 June 1993) UN Doc A/CONF. 157/23 Part I, paras 18 and 28, and Part II, para. 38.

754 UN World Conference on Women (4th) 'Beijing Declaration and Platform for Action' (17 October 1995) UN Doc A/CONF.177/20, 4, para. 142(b.).

755 UN World Conference on Women (4th) 'Beijing Declaration and Platform for Action' (17 October 1995) UN Doc A/CONF.177/20, 4, strategic objective E.1; Cate Steains 'Gender Issues' in Roy S Lee (ed) *The International Criminal Court: The Making of the Rome Statute* (Kluwer Law International The Hague 1999) 357–390, 360.

756 Hilary Charlesworth 'Feminist Methods in International Law' (1999) 93 American Journal of International Law 379-394, 386.

rules on warfare must contain rules on the treatment of protected persons and non-combatants. The events in the 1990s together with the evolution of women's rights in human right law and in many nation States, brought this realization to a next level, acknowledging that men and women are affected differently in armed conflict, on the one hand, and, sexual violence, which women are the main victims of, can be used in a systematic and strategic manner in conflict. Therefore, in order to effectively protect both men and women, sexual violence has to be recognized as a war crime and its commission has to be effectively prosecuted.

IV. Concluding Remarks

The analyis of women's human rights in the context of sexual violence in international criminal lawn and humanitarian law give way to the following conclusions: in general, human rights law, particularly in the area of women's rights, presents itself as a rich field for international criminal law to benefit from. The language of CEDAW and its treaty body is, at times, very similar in fact to the language employed when defining crimes against humanity. Mention is made of structural and systematic actions which are enviornments similat to the ones in which crimes against humanity and other mass crimes are committed.

However, even though reference to human rights law in the context of gender-based crimes is frequently made, the references just as often scratch merely on the surface and an in-depth analysis of human rights law in the area is abandoned for the sake of dismissing human rights law as a helpful denominator of the law. Often, chambers then move on to comparative law which they deem more useful.

Several reasons for this phenomenon can be brought forward. Some lie in the nature of human rights law as such, whereas others can be contributed to a lack of understanding on part of the practitioners applying the law.

First, generally, the field of women's human rights, like minority protection but unlike the prohibition of torture, does not exclusively deal with areas which are of interest to criminal prosecution. Most of the provisions in CEDAW, for example, are centred on non-discrimination and equality of women in fields such as health, education and employment. Second, the biggest deficit of the women's rights scheme is the merely scarce protection of women from violence. As explained above, violence against women is not explicitly mentioned in the most prominent instrument for women's rights, namely in CEDAW. This is surely one of the reasons why the reference to women's rights instruments in the context of international criminal proceedings has been scarce. An explicit prohibition of violence against women, whether committed by private actors but with acquiescence of the State or by State actors themselves, whether in the state of 'peace' or within an armed conflict or whether committed inside a State or by State agents abroad, would have certainly made it easier for judges to refer to CEDAW. However, as indicated above, CEDAW is not the only instrument which can be cited in this context. Whereas the drafters of CEDAW can surely be criticised for their narrow reading of the term 'discrimination', a reading which did not cover physical or psychological violence against women, the CEDAW Committee made clear, in its General Comment No. 19, that CEDAW does in fact prohibit gender-based violence as a manifestation of discrimination. Such violence does also include sexual violence, therefore providing a valuable point of reference for judges in international criminal courts and tribunals.

Third, another hindrance to women's human rights instruments serving as sources of inspiration of supporting the authoritative findings of international courts and tribunal in the weakness of their language. Comparing it for example with ICERD, which entails many immediately binding obligations, CEDAW gives considerably more discretion to States, as most of the obligations enshrined therein require States parties simply to take 'all appropriate measures'.[757]

Another set of reasons for the Courts' and Tribunals' reluctance, however, can be countered or at least weakened by fostering understanding of the different concepts, aims and instruments in this area. When it comes to gender-based crime and sexual violence, international criminal law and international humanitarian law are often more sophisticated and further developed than international human rights law. Nevertheless, a tendency can be observed for judges to at least *pro forma* refer to human rights law. Due to the fragmentation in this field, the partly controversial subjects and the differing nature of the instruments and bodies dealing with the subject, judges tend to refer to human rights law in this area rather superficially and to not deal with the multitude of soft law that shapes this area of human rights law in particular. This is because when it comes to torture or

757 Hilary Charlesworth and Christine Chinkin *The Boundaries of International Law: A Feminist Analysis* (Manchester University Press Manchester 2000) 220.

even minority rights, the law is a 'classical' 1st generation right which deals with public participation of life, liberty and protection of physical integrity from State violence. These are more accessible and more obvious also to judges who are not human rights experts than the soft law instruments that set out women's human rights and their protection from violence. Also, the approach of subsuming gender-based violence under the heading of discrimination is innovative but at the same time, controversial and judges might not feel comfortable in terms of consulting these kinds of 'activist' human rights provisions.

When a crime which has no equivalent in national law (persecution) and is formulated very vaguely[758] meets a concepts which is not yet very established in human rights law (protection from gender-based violence as a human right) the biggest problems in terms of reference to human rights law can be expected because these sort of crimes pose problems to criminal law experts and public international law experts alike.

Nevertheless there is an undeniable potential in women's rights instruments to be untapped. Especially the ICC, with its newly included ground of gender-based persecution, has the opportunity to draw from CEDAW itself as well as the CEDAW Committee's General Recommendations regarding non-discrimination and equality of women. The question which remains is, of course, whether the court will be aware of this work and whether, if it is, it sees the potential which lies in it.

Chapter Four: Conclusions Drawn from Case-Law Analysis

The degree of recourse to international human rights law in international criminal law can generally be called scarce. Often, judges refer to human rights law in passing, almost as a box that has to be ticked before moving on to more promising fields of law in the search for sbstantive elements of crimes, for example comparative law. Sometimes, human rights law is referred to when it supports the Chamber's view rather than examining it as a mandatory step in the process or examining the available law. The examination of three areas of human rights and international criminal law shows that, despite vast crossovers in the selected areas, there is scarce

758 Jonas Nilsson 'The Principle of Nullum Crimen Sine Lege' in Olaoluwa Olusanya *Rethinking International Criminal Law: The Substantive Part* (Europa Law Publishing Groningen 2007) 35-64 at 39.

reference that follows no clear system or dogmatic approach. However, there are degrees of disctinction between the selected areas. From the three areas examined, it is the reference to torture that is the most elaborate in terms of the variety and depth of the dogmatic consideration the bench enganged in. A reference to minority rights in order to strengthen the legal argument is less common and women's rights and instruments dealing with gender issues are discussed most infrequently.

The sub-chapters above explored the reasons for a lack of reference stemming from the law itself and its development for each area as well as the, often unused, potential that human rights law offers. But what conclusions can be drawn generally from this examination?

First, the nature of the instrument is decisive. This means on the one hand its status in the international legal order (legally binding or not? universally applicable or not?) and on the other hand the (legal and otherwise) authority as well as the publicity of the body which decided on or adopted it.

Second, the nature of the norm itself is of crucial importance. Provisions (or instruments) containing legal sanctions or provisions which generally relate to actions falling under the realm of criminal law and have a counterpart in national criminal law, rather than purely public law/ constitutional law are much more likely to be used before international criminal courts and tribunals. This can be seen in the comparison of the frequent use of the CAT as compared to other provisions of human rights.

The third and fourth conclusion are intertwined: it is decisive whether the protection of the right in question is controversially discussed within the international community. As the protection of minorities has been somewhat abandoned as a project by the international community after World War II, it has become less of an obvious choice for practitioners of international criminal law that do not have an in-depth knowledge of international criminal law. Even where the existence of rights as well as the general potential connection to international criminal law can be assumed, as it is the case with women's rights and sexual crimes, the extend of the rights, the international instruments governing them and the bodies applying them are not always grasped. This is also partly due to the fragmentation of protection regimes which can be (like the regime governing women's rights) confusing and include various international and regional bodies that produce documents which are binding to varying degrees.

The analyzed examples show that currently, there exists no convincing doctrine and methodology dealing with the use of human rights law in international criminal law. A call for a solid methodology in this respect is not a mere theoretical undertaking. The unequal interpretation of the law has a pressing practical component, as it can lead to the problem that, as shown above, the same conduct is deemed punishable by one Trial Chamber and not punishable by another Trial Chamber of the same court/ tribunal.

As international criminal law is a rather new area of law, it is unsurprising that it entails gaps which have to be closed by taking recourse to other areas of law. Such a recourse without a solid methodology to follow, is problematic with regards to the principle of *nullum crimen sine lege*; it can, due to differing interpretation of the law and the extent to which recourse can be taken, result in conflicting definitions of crimes and ultimately criminal conduct, even before the same court.

This can jeopardize the already challenging undertaking of international criminal justice and opens it up to yet another criticism it needs to invalidate.

Furthermore, if international criminal courts and tribunals are said to themselves create customary international law as international organizations or organs of international organizations, contradicting case law impedes this creation.[759] A streamlined education for judges, including training in criminal law and human rights/humanitarian law, together with the establishment of a methodology which is driven by theoretical understanding of both concepts, their goals and values rather than by experimenting in a legal vacuum, would counter this problem.

However, it is difficult to see any forum that possesses the necessary authority for such an undertaking. In a relatively recent area, as international criminal law, the lack of a central authority and the decentralized norm interpretation and production poses a particular difficulty to the legitimacy and therefore the future of the whole project. To counter this, while realistically taking into account the lack of a solid legal and moral authority in international law in general and international criminal law in particular, it would at any rate be desirable to work towards an improved exchange and coordination between the different courts and tribunals, as well as between the different chambers within the courts. Such a mechanism of prevention of conflicting case law by prior checking of draft judg-

759 See also KS Gallant 'International Criminal Courts and the Making of Public International Law: New Roles for International Organizations and Individuals' 2010 The John Marshall Law Review 603–34, 609.

ments does, for example exist within the ECtHR.[760] Such a common network of knowledge would foster the understanding of different basic legal concepts and could in that way contribute to a more streamlined jurisprudence.

760 The Case Law Conflict Prevention Unit under the authority of Jurisconsult checks draft judgments and flags potential contradictions with existing case law; see further David Harris, Michael O'Boyle and Others *Law of the European Convention on Human Rights* (OUP Oxford 2014) 126-7.

Part Three: Perception of the Value of Human Rights Law from the View of Practitioners

Chapter One: Perceptions of Human Rights Law in a Diverse Professional Environment

The analysis of the cases of *ad hoc* tribunals throughout the earlier part of this work showed that the existing links between international criminal law and many parts of human rights law are at best rudimentarily used.[761] It also demonstrated the dangers and pitfalls of the decentralized production and diffusion of norms in international criminal law. Enormous freedoms and responsibilities are bestowed upon the judge in this field due its rudimentary nature. The variety of professional backgrounds and expertise of judges not only feeds into this fragmentation of norms but intensifies it. Because of the judges' preeminent role, interviews are crucial if one wants to understand what drives the actual practical application of human rights law or the lack thereof, how the preconceived perception of the relationship of human rights law in international criminal law shaped said application, the understanding of when judges are mandated to apply human rights law and to what benefit.[762] This part is predominantly based on a qualitative study including 14 semi-structured expert interviews conducted

---

761 An adapted version of this part of the research has been published in Mayeul Hiéramente and Patricia Schneider *The Defence in International Criminal Trials: Observations on the Role of the Defence at the ICTY, ICTR and ICC* (Nomos 2016). The contribution is entitled 'Arguing Human Rights from the Bench? How Judges in International Criminal Courts Perceive International Human Rights Law', 72-92.

762 Interviews with judges were chosen due to their distinguished role in the trial as envisaged by the Rome Statute and the ICTY Statute. In practice, judges also rely on the legwork done by their Legal Officers. The nature of the work and the degree to which Legal Officers shape the judges decisions varies from judge to judge. It would be interesting to focus on Legal Officers, their background and if judges choose Legal Officers with similar expertise and background as their own (as far as they have the opportunity to choose in the recruitment process) or if they chose Legal Officers with different, but complementing backgrounds. As, in any case, judges have the overall authority over their decision and the last say in them, coupled with the authority bestowed upon them by the Rome Statute,

with 12 judges at the International Criminal Tribunal for the Former Yugoslavia (ICTY) and the ICC between January 2010 and January 2012 (two judges agreed to be interviewed twice).[763] The questions on which these conversations were based can be found in the annex. As judges can sit in more than one Chamber, the seven of the judges were assigned to a Pre-Trial Chamber, five to a Trial Chamber and five to an Appeals Chamber. The selection of judges as interviewees was based on the following factors. The ICTY is the international criminal tribunal which assembled by far the largest body of case law (also exceeding the ICTR) and this case law fundamentally shaped international criminal law in the past and will continue to do so in the future. The ICC as the permanent forum of international criminal litigation will build up on this case law and further contribute to its development and sophistication. The research sought a balance between the two institutions, and includes judges with considerable experience acting as judges in international criminal courts and tribunals as well as those whose experience as judges in international criminal justice was fairly recent. In approaching the judges for an interview request, consideration was also paid to maximal possible diversity as to their professional background (academic, judge, prosecutor, diplomat etc), field of expertise (public international law/criminal law), national background, legal system in the country of origin or education as well as diversity in gender and age. That being said, the number of interview partners is comparably low as there are in fact only a limited numbers of judges practising international criminal law.[764] To these judges, access is restricted. There are a number of potential interview partners who generally declined to speak about the way their decision-making process is conducted. Given these

---

judges were deemed to be the appropriate interview partners for the terms of this study.

763 All interviews with ICC judges were conducted during a four months stay of the author as a visiting professional at the International Criminal Court from January 2010 until April 2010. This programme is specifically designed for professionals to do their own research project on international criminal law. Later on, the author worked at the International Criminal Court as a staff member. During her time as an ICC staff member, no interviews with ICC staff was conducted. The interviews with ICTY judges were conducted between January 2010 and April 2010 and between May 2011 and January 2012.

764 The ICC, for example, has 18 serving judges and 23 former judges. Of the 18 serving judges, six judges have only been appointed to the bench after the last round of interviews was conducted in 2012.

limitations, the present qualitative study does not claim to present a comprehensive picture of the perception of human rights law in international criminal law. However, the data can help identify major tendencies in how the background and experience of judges can influence their understanding and interpretation of legal problems surrounding the role and application of human rights law in international criminal law. Data from the interviews was analyzed in light of and juxtaposed with other sources, applying the concept of triangulation. These sources included the documents such as judgments, official court documents and records and participations, conversations with legal practitioners and other experts of international criminal law on formal and informal levels and trial observation. Furthermore, judges volunteered their assessment of the various approaches of their colleagues in relation to their backgrounds, which again allows more general inferences and tendencies. While the interviews were not tape-recorded, notes were made during the interviews. The interviewees were assured of their anonymity. Hence, the references to the anonymized interviews do not refer to transcribed records but to notes made during and immediately after the the interview. Particularly note-worthy statements, which are quoted directly in the following, were noted from memory.

A number of scholarly works, from legal, sociological and anthropological perspectives, have dealt with creation of prosecutorial and investigative strategies and judgments in courts and with the question what big a role a systematic exegesis really plays vs the role attributed to external factors.[765] Mainly, these works have been dealing with the interpretation of national constitutions, thus with legal norms that are by definition

765 Eg Christina Boyd, Lee Epstein and Andrew Martin 'Untangling the Causal Effects of Sex on Judging' (2010) 54 American Journal of Political Science 398-411; Nienke Grossmann 'Sex Representation on the Bench and the Legitimacy oft he International Criminal Courts‘ (2011) 11 Internationnal Criminal Law Review 643-653; John Hagan, Ron Levi and Gebrielle Ferrales 'Swaying the Hands of Justice: The Internal and External Dynamics of Regime Change at the International Criminal Tribunal for the Former Yugoslavia' (2006) 31(3) Law and Social Inquiry 585-616; John Hagan and Ron Levi 'War Crimes and the Force of Law' (2005) 83(4) Social Forces 1499-1534; Kimi Lynn King and Megan Greeing ‚Gender Justice of Just Gender? The Role of Gender in the Sexual Assault Decisions at the International Criminal Tribunal of the Former Yugoslavia‘ (2007) 88 Social Science Quarterly 1049-1071; 'Uwe Kranenpohl ‚Die Bedeutung von Interpretationsmethoden und Dogmatik in der Entscheidungspraxis des Bundesverfassungsgerichts' 48 (2009) Der Staat 387–409; Rüdiger Lautmann *Freie Rechtsfindung und Methodik der Rechtsanwendung* (C

rather broad in order to be flexible enough to be applied to a variety of cases. Naturally, the nature of a national constitutional court differs from that of an international criminal court. To name the most obvious difference, a criminal court has, at all times, to ensure that it operates within the limits imposed on it through the principle of legality. Whereas constitutional courts can, to a large extent, be self-referential in the way that they refer to principles of a constitutional order which the courts constructed themselves out of the constitution,[766] criminal courts, when concretising the given norms, need to refer to systems outside of their own legal discipline in a narrow sense. They consult, for instance, the answer found to similar questions posed to national legal systems or human rights law. Constitutional courts can deliberately maintain a certain dogmatic vagueness in their decision so as to keep the body of case law flexible enough for their predecessors to apply it to new situations and future challenges the court is faced with. Criminal courts, on the contrary, are faced with the obligation to define a certain text in light of what a person, at the time of his or her actions that lead to his/her indictment before the court, could have reasonably held to be legal or illegal.

However, as international criminal law is a rather new legal discipline, the judges can often not resort to a lot of scholarly literature, commentaries or preceding cases, but have to define the limits and the scope of a specific crime themselves. In order to make the general terms of the Rome Statute or the ICTY/ICTR Statute sufficiently concrete to work with them in criminal proceedings, the judges are obliged to interpret the terms, keeping in mind the principle of legality. The leeway that the courts naturally have with this new body of law, when examining its limits and the terms of its application, will decrease on its own due to the growing number of case law in the area. Even though the courts are not bound by precedents within their own institution, let alone by case law decided at another international criminal court or tribunal, they tend to either adhere to previ-

---

Schon München 1967); Rüdiger Lautmann *Justiz—Die stille Gewalt: Teilnehmende Beobachtung und entscheidungssoziologische Analyse* (Athenäum Verlag Frankfurt am Main 1972); Ernst Gottfried Mahrenholz 'Probleme der Verfassungsauslegung, Verfassungsinterpretation aus praktischer Sicht' in Hans-Peter Schneider (ed) *Verfassungsrecht zwischen Wissenschaft und Richterkunst: Konrad Hesse zum 70. Geburtstag* (Heideberg Müller 1990) 53–65;.

766 Uwe Kranenpohl ‚Die Bedeutung von Interpretationsmethoden und Dogmatik in der Entscheidungspraxis des Bundesverfassungsgerichts' 48 (2009) Der Staat 387–409, 398.

ous decisions or, if the arguments used previously are dismissed, usually do so with an explicit explanation of why the court or tribunal decided not to follow what has previously been decided.

Furthermore, as determined above, international criminal law derives from the most serious violations of human rights, and human rights law, like constitutional law, is generally formulated in a very broad manner, and, indirectly, protects basic rights of a human person and therefore subject to extensive acts of interpretation by the judges who apply the law.

Additionally, both constitutional courts and international criminal Courts and Tribunals (or rather their Appeals Chambers) have to exercise an increased degree of self-control, as their judgements are not subject to the control by any other court of higher instance. When it comes to the ICC, an aggravating factor, which called for a particularly high degree of interpretation by the practitioners, is, that the Rome Statute is a compromise which has been drawn up by the States Parties under time pressure and therefore, at occasions, contains contradictory passages.

Hence, the tools available to the judges in order to interpret the normative framework in which they operate are similar, as is the inconsistency when it comes to working with those tools and methods. As has been observed in relation to the interpretation of national constitutions by national constitutional courts, 'the court, in truth, aims for the result which seems right to it. On the way to this [result], it adheres to basic exegetical rules or other principles of constitutional interpretation as pilot lights, but not as guarantees for the right result; they are buoys rather than pilots' (translation by the author).[767]

Therefore, the question, in the context of this work, is to what extent it can be expected that the way a judge evaluates the use of human rights law within substantive international criminal law is shaped by his or her professional and other background.

Traditionally, the events leading to a judicial decision-making process are categorized in accordance with seven different phases.[768] In the first phase, the problem is identified and the judge familiarizes himself or her-

767 Ernst Gottfried Mahrenholz 'Probleme der Verfassungsauslegung, Verfassungsinterpretation aus praktischer Sicht' in Hans-Peter Schneider (ed) *Verfassungsrecht zwischen Wissenschaft und Richterkunst: Konrad Hesse zum 70. Geburtstag* (Heideberg Müller 1990) 53–65, 60.

768 Ernst Gottfried Mahrenholz 'Probleme der Verfassungsauslegung, Verfassungsinterpretation aus praktischer Sicht' in Hans-Peter Schneider (ed) *Verfassungsrecht*

self with the situation he or she is called upon to judge. In phase two, the judge explores the alternatives for a possible solution of the situation. In the third phase, the judge gathers the facts for the different alternatives, the judges explores the circumstances of the case out of the pleadings and hearings. In phase four, the judge looks at the normative framework applicable to the situation and explores whether the alternatives are legally correct. The judge chooses one of the alternatives in the fifth phase. In the sixth phase, the chosen alternative is explained, the judgment is reasoned and delivered. Finally, the post-decision process constitutes the seventh and last phase. The decision-maker receives criticism and learns for his or her decision in the future.[769] Even though this is simply a descriptive formula which does not apply to all cases, the phases cannot be clearly distinguished from each other and the decision-maker often does not consort to the different phases in a chronological order, the formula helps to categorize the different fundamental phases of judicial decision-making.[770]

In the following, phases four and five are primarily scrutinized in order to inquire to what extent the professional and or personal background of the judges can play a role in the decision-making process in relation to the judges perception of the importance of international human rights law in substantive international criminal law and the judges' general willingness to use human rights law in order to define crimes under international law. The most significant factors in relation to the background of the judges are highlighted and analysed based on the empirical data collected.

There are plenty of ways in which the composition of a bench can shape the outcome of the trial. This is not to assume that the individuals who serve as judges belong to different homogenous groups and can be defined or define themselves by belonging to this group first and foremost. This solitarist approach to groups of human beings ineligibly shortens the view on the individuals belonging to that group who, in fact, belong to different groups and do not exclusively define themselves as a member of a

---

zwischen Wissenschaft und Richterkunst: Konrad Hesse zum 70. Geburtstag (Heideberg Müller 1990) 53–65, 60.

769 Rüdiger Lautmann *Justiz—Die stille Gewalt: Teilnehmende Beobachtung und entscheidungssoziologische Analyse* (Athenäum Verlag Frankfurt am Main 1972) 15.

770 Rüdiger Lautmann *Justiz—Die stille Gewalt: Teilnehmende Beobachtung und entscheidungssoziologische Analyse* (Athenäum Verlag Frankfurt am Main 1972) 15.

single group.[771] Even less so, it would be possible for the individuals belonging to a certain group to define, in a fixed homogenous way, what are the components of which this group is made up.

Nevertheless, there are a number of dividing lines which could possibly be of relevance to the work of the ICC and the ad hoc tribunals and which could influence the decision-making of the judges. Apart from the professional or geographical background of the members of the bench, their understanding of the role of human rights law in their work of applying international criminal law could also be framed in terms of which basic legal system is used in their country of origin, whether it is Common Law or Civil Law and whether they have been working mostly as academics or practitioners.

I. Safeguarding Professional Diversity on the Bench at the ICC and the ICTY

Pursuant to Art. 36 (3) (b) Rome Statute, a judge at the International Criminal Court shall either

i) Have established competence in criminal law and procedure, and the necessary relevant experience, whether as judge, prosecutor, advocate or in other similar capacity, in criminal proceedings; or
(ii) Have established competence in relevant areas of international law such as international humanitarian law and the law of human rights, and extensive experience in a professional legal capacity which is of relevance to the judicial work of the Court;

At the ICC, the focus is, pursuant to Art. 36 (5) Rome Statute, explicitly put on the judges with a criminal law background. They shall, in the first election, make up the majority of at least nine judges whereas at least five of the judges shall have an international law background. In its first session between 3 and 7 February 2003, the Assembly of States Parties elected 18 judges for a term of office of three, six and nine years. Further ordinary elections took place in 2006, 2009, 2011 and 2014. At the time of the writing, the next ordinary election is scheduled for Deember 2017 at the

771 See Amartya Sen *Identity and Violence: The Illusion of Destiny* (WW Norton & Co New York 2006.).

17th session of the Assembly of State Parties.[772] Additionally, the Assemby of States Parties elected some judges in special elections, eg when a judge resigned or passed away. Currently, there are 13 judges from list A (criminal law) and five judges from list B (international law) serving at the ICC.[773] However, some of the individuals listed as experts under list A do also have considerable experience under international law, so the lists do not always clearly reflect the focus of a judge's experience.

The assessment of whether a judge has the necessary qualification is to a large degree driven by the Coalition for the International Criminal Court (CICC), an association of civil society organizations which, since 2006, asks candidates to fill in questionnaires establishing their competence and motivation and organizes public seminars with and debates amongst the candidates.[774] These measures seek to contribute to the raising the respective candidates' expertise and assist the Assembly of State Parties in deciding about the competence of a candidate.[775] The questionnaire provided to the judges asks them, inter alia, about the legal systems they were educated and have worked in.[776] It also asks in detail about the experience in either criminal law (for List A candidates) or international law (for List B candidates) and invites the candidates to share their experience which would qualify them for running on the list they are not appointed on.[777] Additionally the nomination process is addressed and the candidate is requested to lay down what qualification a person needs to have to be appointed to the highest judicial office in his or her respective country as stipulated in Art. 36 (3) (a) Rome Statute.[778] The CICC addresses the issue of further training and skill enhancement stating that at the ICC as 'unique

772 Further information can be found under < http://www.coalitionfortheicc.org/fight/icc-elections-2017> (31 October 2017).

773 See < https://www.icc-cpi.int/about/judicial-divisions/biographies/Pages/default.aspx#> (31 October 2017).

774 Coalition for the International Criminal Court 'Judges' <http://www.coalitionfortheicc.org/topics/judges> (31 October 2017); See for the 2017 election of judges http://www.coalitionfortheicc.org/fight/icc-elections-2017 (31 October 2017).

775 < http://www.coalitionfortheicc.org/topics/judges> (31 October 2017).

776 Questions 7 a) and b); the questionaires with the anwers of the candiates for the 2017 Elections can be accessed under Coalition of the ICC 'Questionnaire for ICC Judicial Candidates: December 2017 Elections' <http://www.coalitionfortheicc.org/fight/icc-elections-2017> (31 October 2017).

777 Ibid Questions 8 a) and b).

778 Ibid Question 4.

institution', 'even judges with significant prior experience ...may not necessarily possess requisite skills and knowledge to manage these challenges'.[779] The questionnaire therefore explores the candidates' attitude towards the idea of 'ongoing workplace training aimed at promoting legal innovation and coordination amongst all judicial chambers in adjudicating complex questions of the human rights relating to law and policy'.[780] Finally, the CICC questionnaire explicitly addresses advocating for, reference to and application of human rights law. Question 16 of the questionnaire asks 'Do you have any experience working with or within international human rights bodies or courts and/or have you served on the staff or board of directors of human rights or international humanitarian law organizations?'[781] Since 2011, Question 17 is included to specifically ask about the reference to human rights law: 'Have you ever referred to or applied any specific provision of international human rights or international humanitarian law treaties within any judicial decision you have issued within the context of your judicial activity or legal experience?'[782]

In addition, an independent high-expert panel was established by the CICC in 2010, which, for the first time, conducted assessments on whether each individual candidate matched the qualifications outlined in Art. 36 Rome Statute. Before the 2011 elections of judges during the Tenth Session of the Assembly of States Parties, the Independent Panel, consisting of experts of international law and criminal law, most of them former international criminal judges or prosecutors, found that four of the nineteen candidates lacked sufficient qualification to be elected as judges of the ICC.[783] None of the candidates assessed as 'not qualified' by the Independent Panel were under the six judges elected to the bench by Assembly of States Parties between 12 and 21 December 2011. In 2011, the Assembly of States Parties set up an Advisory Committee on the Nomination of Judges which builds on the work of the Independent Panel and which also

779 Ibid Question No. 11.

780 Ibid.

781 Ibid Question 15.

782 Ibid Question 16.

783 Coalition for the ICC http://iccnow.org/documents/CICC_Press_Release_Report_of_the_Independent_Panel_on_ICC_Judicial_Elections_271111_EN.pdf (1 October 2015).

evaluates candidates prior to elections to the ICC bench.[784] This goes to show the increasing influence and importance that NGOs have in the area of international criminal law, where civil society has continuously pushed for the improvement and enhanced implementation of international criminal law.[785]

The majority of current judges under list A (experts of criminal law and procedure) does have no or only limited experience of the other category of relevant law. The same holds true for judges under list B (relevant areas of international law) regarding their expertise in criminal law. However, some judges indicate extensive expertise in both categories and could therefore have appeared under a different list. Article 39 (1) of the Rome Statute states that 'the Trial and Pre-Trial Divisions are composed predominantly of judges with criminal trial experience.' Insofar the focus on criminal experience and expertise in the chambers is a deliberate move and mirrors the merit that the court attaches to criminal law as opposed to international law in its everyday work. One reason for this might be that some of the interviewed judges saw the real challenges for the court in its procedural aspects, for which an expertise in criminal law and procedure and a mindset for the potential pitfalls of criminal trials in this respect is vital.[786] As one judge formulated it: 'the devil is in the procedure'.[787] The group of international law experts is generally more heterogeneous than the criminal law group. Whereas some of the judges previously to serving at the bench, held high positions in international organizations pertaining to human rights or humanitarian law, others were scholars, diplomats or worked in fields related to international law which are, at first sight, more detached from international criminal law.

At the ICTY the situations is slightly different, as there is no explicit quota system dividing the bench into international law and criminal law

---

784 Coalition for the ICC < http://www.coalitionfortheicc.org/news/20141009/expert-panel-reports-qualifications-icc-judicial-candidates > (31 October 2017); http://www.coalitionfortheicc.org/news/20171011/asp-committee-all-12-icc-judicial-candidates-pass-test-six-are-particularly-well (31 October 2017).

785 A good example of this was the recent attempt by the Southern Africa Litigation Centre to prevent Sudanese President Omar al-Bashir, for who the ICC issued a standing arrest warrant, from leaving South Africa where he travelled for a meeting of the African Union.

786 Interview No 2.

787 Interview No 2, p. 1.

experts in a provision which is otherwise very similar to the one in the Rome Statute. The respective provision in the ICTY Statute reads:

The permanent and *ad litem* judges shall be persons of high moral character, impartiality and integrity who possess the qualifications required in their respective countries for appointment to the highest judicial offices. In the overall composition of the Chambers and sections of the Trial Chambers, due account shall be taken of the experience of the judges in criminal law, international law, including international humanitarian law and human rights law.

The ICTY is currently composed of 7 judges.[788] Compared to that of the ICC, the present composition of the ICTY is somewhat more homogenous. The majority of the present judges have served as judges in their respective national jurisdictions before being appointed as judges of the ICTY. Most of the judges additionally had experience with criminal trials and a certain expertise in criminal proceedings prior to coming to the ICTY.

1. General attitude of judges towards the importance of HRL in ICL

When asked about the general importance attributed to human rights law in international criminal law, most judges, at first sight, display a conviction that human rights law has a high degree of importance to their work. Many judges referred to the development of international criminal law and, the common roots of human rights, humanitarian law and international criminal law, as well as to crimes under international law as severe violations of human rights.[789] Some describe human rights as always present in the work of the court. Even if that might not always be visible in the decisions that are produced and might not be explicitly mentioned there, these judges claim human rights issues are always underlying and present in the internal discussions. [790]

However, even in this generally framed question on the importance of human rights law on international criminal law, one can already spot differences between judges whose expertise lays primarily in the area of in-

788 At the ICTY, the numbers of judges are declining due to the imminent conclusion up of trials of first instance.

789 Eg Interview No 6; Interview No 7; Interview No 12.

790 Interview No 13; Interview No 7.

ternational criminal law and those who are first and foremost international lawyers. Whereas several judges, no matter which background, emphasized that their courts are criminal courts and not human rights courts and that therefore human rights play a somewhat ancillary role as compared to aspects of criminal law and procedure,[791] the criminal law experts often explicitly emphasized that their foremost task is to sit on a criminal court and some argue that the 'international element' is given too much weight, at least at the ICC.[792] It has also been stated that cases should be dealt with in a less academic manner, that the primary tasks of the ICC is to punish the perpetrators and help the victims, not 'to write beautiful decisions for academics'.[793] One judge describes human rights issues as 'not very urgent'.[794]

Interestingly, some of the judges pointed to the reciprocal effects of an increase in the use of human rights law in international criminal law for the field of human rights law. One judge used the example of the UN Commissioner for Human Rights, Navanethem Pillay, who, as a former judge of the ICTY and the ICC, draws from her practical experience in international criminal law by stirring up discussions about the impunity of human rights violations in her work as UN High Commissioner for Human Rights[795]. However, the answer to questions regarding the mutual effect of an increased interlinkage between the areas of international criminal law and human rights law is not always positive. One judge, for example, wondered whether international criminal law could also have a negative influence on human rights law, as is attached to human rights an 'aura of punitivity' which could hamper practical human rights work and keep States from enter into human rights commitments in the first place.[796]

791 Interview No 2; Interview No 5; Interview No 8; Interview No 10, Interview No 11.
792 Interview No 5, Interview No 10.
793 Interview No 5.
794 Interview No 2, p 1.
795 Interview No 3.
796 Interview No 4.

2. Specific relevance of the recourse to human rights law in substantive international criminal law

When asked about what areas of international criminal law could be most appropriate for the use of human rights law, most judges, criminal and international law experts alike, first pointed to procedural points, mostly to the right to a fair and expeditious trial, including the right to defend oneself, questions regarding the disclosure of evidence or to procedural rules for the protection of victims.[797] Whereas the international law experts usually by themselves referred also to the relevance of human rights law in the substantial aspects of defining a crime and exploring the boundaries of customary international law on a certain crime, most of the criminal law experts agreed that human rights law could be used in such way after it had been suggested to them by the interviewer. Some, however, dismissed the importance of international human rights law in substantive international criminal law altogether and claimed that most of the problematic issues in these regard had already been solved.[798]

When asked about what parts of human rights law would be the most obvious to take recourse to in substantive matters, the prohibition of torture was one of the areas most often referred to.[799] Here, judges mentioned concrete and widely ratified conventions like the CAT[800] or the ICCPR.[801] Minority rights law was generally not mentioned by any of the judges initially. Some judges agreed, after the suggestion by the interviewer that international criminal law can draw from minority rights law.[802] Yet, a certain confusion regarding what the concept of minority rights entails could be observed: whereas one judge rightly pointed out that the recognition of genocide and apartheid were influenced by concerns about minority protection,[803] one judge incorrectly claimed that minority rights law also covers the protection of women and could therefore be of value to the Court.[804] One can easily see how such a confusion about what the concept

797 Eg Interview No 2; Interview No3; Interview No 7; Interview No 8; Interview No 9; Interview No 11; Interview No 12.

798 Interview No 2; Interview No 6; Interview No 7.

799 Interview No 7; Interview No 10; Interview No 12.

800 Interview No 10; Interview No 12.

801 Interview No 10.

802 Interview No 7; Interview No 10; Interview No 12.

803 Interview No 12.

804 Interview No 7.

could prevent the court from seeking assistance in the case extra-statutory human rights law would have to be consulted.

Women's rights were the issue, which was most often mentioned by judges when asked areas of human rights of interest to substantive international criminal law.[805] However, the judges seemed to have only a vague idea where to find helpful instruments in this area. One judge mentioned CEDAW, in all other cases, the mention of women's rights seemed to have been guided merely by a vague idea of usefulness without any concrete provisions or concepts to draw from.[806]

The question of how it can be used and what are the limits of a use of human rights law in light of the principle of legality is characterized by a certain dogmatic vagueness. Whereas basically all the judges mentioned Art. 21 (3) Rome Statute as the provision which allows them to use human rights so to a certain extent, the exact meaning of that provision and the possibilities it opens for judges to make reference to human rights seems to be rather unclear. In particular, no judge mentioned that Article 21 (3), as examined above, may not be the right provision for including human rights law into substantive international criminal law.[807] Many judges seemed to be satisfied with Art. 21 (3) Rome Statute as a sufficient legal basis for applying international human rights law. In particular, customary international law as a source seemed to not be of particular relevance to the judges and was rarely brought up. Asked about how human rights can be used in international criminal law, particularly with regard to Art. 21 (3) Rome Statute, the judges gave a variety of different answers many of which contradicted each other. Human rights were seen as 'underlying principles'[808], 'sources of inspiration'[809] 'almost binding principles'[810] 'persuasive, but non-binding inspiration'[811], 'sources of brainstorming on

805 Interview No 2; Interview No 7; Interview No 10; Interview No 11; Interview No 13.

806 Inerview No 7.

807 See Part One Chapter Three above.

808 Interview No. 7; one judge additionally mentioned Art. 21 (2).

809 Interview No. 10.

810 Interview No. 7.

811 Interview No. 8; Interview No. 12.

a legal issue'[812], 'guiding principles'[813] and 'underlying constitutional provision'[814].

Some judges saw it as 'two sides of the same coin'[815], others dismissed this rhetorical figure and instead insisted on a 'qualitative difference'[816] of the two regimes, which they saw as not being of equal value, but which 'complement and reinforce each other'[817] or 'complement and inform each other'.[818]

II. Professional and Personal Factors Contributing to the Attitude towards International Human Rights Law

1. Public International Law Experts/(National) Criminal Law Experts

As can be inferred from the analysis of the previous sections, the dividing line between public international law experts and experts of criminal law was found to be one of the most decisive factors regarding the attitude towards human rights law. Experts of criminal law often seemed to be somewhat dismissive of the 'international element' of international criminal law and stated that this element is given too much weight in international criminal practice.[819] Human rights law in international criminal law was for most of the criminal law experts mostly a procedural issue, though most, but not all,[820] agreed that human rights law could also be used in the substantive definitions of crime when so suggested.

Generally, the criminal lawyers seemed to have less of a dogmatic problem with recourse to international human rights law in order to define

812 Interview No. 9.
813 Interview No. 9.
814 Interviews No. 5, 7, 8 and 10; in Interviews Nos 5 and 7, the term 'underlying constitutional provision' was brought up by the interviewer who asked the judges whether this is a term they could agree to in relation to human rights in international criminal law.
815 Interview No. 10.
816 Interview No. 11.
817 Interview No. 11.
818 Interview No 12.
819 Interview No 5, Interview No 10.
820 Interview No 2; Interview No 6; Interview No 7.

crimes, which, in general, they saw as not problematic.[821] In particular, they did often not see a dogmatic difference in the application of human rights law in substantive as opposed to procedural law. This might partly be due to the fact that the criminal lawyers interviewed also tended to have a purely practical background, whereas many of the international law experts have been working as academics prior to becoming judges at the ICTY or the ICC. One judge simply held that if the ECtHR came up with a decision which 'can equally work for the ICC' and can be used there, it becomes part of international criminal law.[822] One judge suggested to narrow down the quota in Art. 36 (3) (b) (i) to experts of international criminal law as opposed to general criminal law and procedure as a way to ensure quality throughout the bench.[823] In light of the limited number of established experts in the field on the one hand coupled with geographical quota requirements on the other hand, this suggestion does not seem viable at this point in time.

One judge stated that 'reference to human rights law is made to support already existing convictions and views' on a certain topic.[824] In the same vein, another judge said that what she was interested in is the impact of her decisions 'on the people' and not so much where they stem from.[825] This is congruent with the sociological findings regarding the decision-making process of judges in national legal systems[826] and also confirms an observation made by Antonio Cassese regarding the use of comparative law as an extra-statutory source of law at the ICTY.[827]

---

821 Interview No 5; Interview No 6;Interview No 7; Interview No 9.

822 Interview No 9.

823 Interview No 7.

824 Interview No 1.

825 Interview No 9.

826 Rüdiger Lautmann Justiz—Die stille Gewalt: Teilnehmende Beobachtung und entscheidungssoziologische Analyse (Athenäum Verlag Frankfurt am Main 1972) 101.

827 'Mon experience est que souvent le droit comparé est utilisé pour confirmer une solution que l'on avait déjà trouvée' Antonio Cassese in Mireille Delmas-Marty and Antonio Cassese (eds) *Crimes Internationaux Et Jurisdictions Internationales* (Presses Unversitaires de France Paris 2002) 140.

2. Common Law/Civil Law

The question whether they were educated in a common or in a civil law system was explicitly posed to the interviewees and some expressed opinions on whether and how this background influenced their work and the collaboration with their colleagues. Pursuant to Art. 36 (8) (a) (i) Rome Statute, the principle legal systems of the world shall be taken into account in the selection of the judges. Several of the judges emphasized that they see a dividing line between judges coming from civil law countries and judges with a common law background in their work.[828] This perception is backed by analyses of the deciding attitude of judges at the ICTY, which found clear differences between civil and common law judges in the way they refer to sources outside of international criminal law in order to back their arguments.[829]

One judge mentioned that there is more 'separation' by judges from common law countries: the judge was of the opinion that judges educated in common law systems were generally more willing than their colleagues from civil law countries to apply human rights regarding procedural, formalistic issues (rights of the accused regarding deadlines for submissions etc.) but that the strive for 'clean, clear criminal law' without referring to extra-statutory provisions.[830]

For another judge, the common law/civil law divide was interlinked with question of whether a judge came from a country which was a former British colony. This judge was of the opinion that judges coming from former British colonies applied Common law in a more dogmatically strict fashion than colleagues from the United Kingdom.[831] For most judges, List A and List B judges alike, this issue did, however, not pose a particular problem, even though one could suspect that judges with an expertise in international law might be more used to a flexible approach in this respect.

828 Interview No 1, Interview No 6.

829 Michael Bohlander and Mark Findlay ‚The Use of Domestic Sources as a Basis for International Criminal Law Principles' (2002) 2 Yearbook of International Law and Jurisprudence 3–26.

830 Interview No. 1.

831 Interview No 6.

3. Academics/Practitioners

Closely related to whether judges are criminal law or international law experts is the question whether they have a theoretical, academic background or expert a purely practical one. This issue was brought up by several judges on their own account, as it was not part of a question put to the judges, and the ones who brought it up usually felt strongly about the subject.[832] All the judges who brought up this topic were appointed on List A as experts of criminal law and they were all practitioners who had served as judges or prosecutors in their respective countries. These judges emphasized that the courts and tribunals needed more practitioners and deemed work with practitioners easier than with 'professors'.[833] Two of these judges criticised the way of evaluation and decision-writing: judges were writing 'too much', [834]facts should be dealt with in a 'less academic manner'[835] but in a more practical way ('help victims, punish perpetrators'[836]) as it was not about 'writing beautiful decisions for academics'[837] or writing 'for the public'.[838] Additionally, a desire to 'write history' and 'lay down principles' at the expense of efficiency and goal-oriented action' was criticized.[839] Another List A judge, however, stressed the importance of keeping up with developments in academic scholarly literature in decision-making.[840] None of the judges appointed through List B did express any views on the distribution of practitioners and more theory-focused individuals on the bench.

4. Developing Country/Industrialized Country

Application of human rights law might also depend also on the geographical background of the judge. According to Art. 36 (8) (a) (iii) Rome Statute the Court shall take equitable geographical representation into ac-

832 Interview No 5; Interview No 6; Interview No 13.
833 Interview No 13.
834 Interview No 6.
835 Interview No 5.
836 Interview No 5.
837 Interview No 5.
838 Interview No 6.
839 Interview No 5.
840 Interview No 9.

count when selection the judges. One European judge argued that human rights did not play a major role in practical international criminal law, but since they, as he argued, gained importance in the European legal discourse they receive more attention.[841]

However, the geographical background of the judge might not necessarily play a role in whether or not human rights law is referred to but rather which system of human rights protection is referenced. Several judges from the global south stated that international courts and tribunals frequently refer to case law of the ECtHR and underused jurisprudence and provisions from other regional systems of human rights protection. One judge argued that in terms of usefulness to international criminal law, the American system of human rights protection was more advanced than the European one as the IACtHR and the Commission dealt with massive human rights violations on a regular basis and therefore, their case law had more to offer to international criminal law.[842] Another judge argued that due to the fact that all cases before the court dealt with situations in African countries (at the time of the interview), more reference should be made to the African system of human rights protection and the use of human rights jurisprudence and rules should generally be more diversified.[843]

Additionally, one judge saw age as another decisive matter in how open a judge was to extra-statutory sources or input from outside he or her initial area of expertise.[844] This judge saw a generational shift in international criminal law and argued that older judges from the same generation generally had a more conservative approach to applying human rights law. The same judge argued that judges, in their decision-making process, are influenced by their personal experiences. Examples of these factors which were mentioned by this judge to be of influence were gender, sexual orientation and disability.[845]

841 Interview No. 1.
842 Interview No 7.
843 Interview No 8.
844 Interview No. 1.
845 Interview No. 1.

Chapter Two: Concluding Remarks

The answers given by the judges in the interviews conducted were often characterized by a certain dogmatic vagueness. This vagueness is by no means surprising given the multitude of diverse education and professional experiences of the judges which lead to different priorities in their work and differing degrees of attention given to the issue of human rights in international criminal law. Furthermore, in an area as vast as international criminal law which combines a plurality of different fields, it is nearly impossible to possess the same degree of expertise on all up and coming issues in academia and practice. For this reason, a bench consisting of several individuals whose expertise complements each other is of higher importance than in national criminal law where education is streamlined. On the other hand, due to the immense freedom that judges possess in the still emerging discipline of international criminal law, judges are under enormous pressure and their judgements regularly come under critical scrutiny. Therefore, it is even more important that the presence of international law experts on the bench is ensured. Currently, there are four Trial Chambers at the ICC in which only judges appointed from List A (experts in criminal law and procedure) are serving (even though one has to observe that most of these Trial Chambers have judges amongst them that do indeed also possess expertise in human rights law). It is also not evident why the ICC explicitly states that in its Trial Chambers, criminal law expertise is focussed on, whereas in the Appeals Chamber, most judges are appointed from List B (experts in international law).

The judges with an expertise predominantly rooting in criminal law often pointed to the need for a more practical approach at ICC proceedings and to the fact that the court was not established to write 'beautiful decisions' which are well-reviewed in academic circles.[846] Whilst the truth within this perception is the fact that the ICC and the *ad hoc* and hybrid courts, like any other criminal courts, decide on the guilt of individuals for specific actions, the problem that these new sorts of courts face is that they, at the same time, have to constantly justify the existence of their area of law and need to bring their reasoning in line with the principle of legality. This requires an enormous effort of justification on behalf of the judges, which might be something that international lawyers, as opposed

846 Interview No 5.

to criminal lawyers coming from national criminal justice systems, are used to.

Several times, the judges seemed to harbour scepticism towards the usefulness of human rights for their substantive work, in helping them to define crimes under international law. Several judges emphazised the importance of human rights law in international criminal procedure while, at the same time, downplaying its significance in terms of substantive law. Judges mentioned that according to them, the big problems regarding the definition of crimes are solved and the ICC will not have to deal with this issue majorly.[847] From a defence perspective, these statements should trigger a substantive amount of skepticism. On the one hand, it should be received positively by defence teams that the human rights of the accused in the pre-trial and trial period seems to have such a prominent role in the perception of the judges. This is particularly true for the ICC which has a chance to avoid some of the mistakes the ad hoc tribunals made in this respect, for example concerning the length of the trials. However, when one looks at the numerous innovations that the Rome Statute brings in comparison to previous statutes, stating that human rights law does not have any more to contribute to the substantive definition of crimes seems to be inaccurate. Particularly with regard to 'treaty crimes' which have previously been enshrined in human rights treaties only (such as the crime of apartheid [crimes against humanity, Art. 7 (1) (j) Rome Statute] or intentional attacks on UN personnel or other personnel or material involved in an assistance or peacekeeping mission [war crimes, Art. 8 (2) (b) (iii) Rome Statute], and to a lesser degree, forced disappearance [crimes against humanity, Art. 7 (1) (i) Rome Statute]) or regarding gender-based persecution will the ICC have to result sources outside the Rome Statute itself and will not be able to resort to case law issued by any other international criminal court or tribunal. This can lead to serious collisions with the principle of legality to the detriment of the accused. The very nature of the ICC as an international court, seen by some purely as a court functioning like any other criminal court and portrayed by others as an international court established to protect victims against mass violations seems to be disputed amongst judges.. The vagueness and the conflicting ideas portrays a spectrum of divergent opinions and dogmatic murkiness that should be worrisome to the attorneys representing accused persons.

847 Interview No 2; Interview No 6; Interview No 7.

As such, the approach of the CICC to assess candidates and work towards a comprehensive skill enhancement of judges seems to be the way forward. Incoherence in jurisprudence and legal norms in international law stems mostly from increasingly more separate legal regimes with a limited mandate.[848] International criminal courts and tribunals are few in numbers and with the establishment of a permanent International Criminal Court the numbers are likely to stagnate or, with the completion of the trials before the ICTR and the ICTY go down. As such, by ensuring that the question of how extra-statutory sources, in particular human rights law, can be used in international criminal law and what he limits of such an application are, international criminal law is confronted with the unique opportunity to counteract incoherent or conflicting jurisprudence at least to a certain degree and thereby avoid the level of fragmentation prevalent in more established fields like the law of the sea, human rights law or world trade law.[849] This is particularly crucial in international criminal law as enhanced fragmentation is likely to undermine the defendant's right to a fair trial.

848 Oliver Diggelmann and Tilman Altwicker 'Is There Something Like a Constitution of International Law? A Critical Analysis of the Debate on World Constitutionalism' (2008) 68 ZaöRV 623-650, 630.

849 Oliver Diggelmann and Tilman Altwicker 'Is There Something Like a Constitution of International Law? A Critical Analysis of the Debate on World Constitutionalism' (2008) 68 ZaöRV 623-650, 630; see also as referenced by Diggelmann and Altwicker Gerhard Hafner 'Pros and Cons Ensuing from Fragmentation of International Law' (2004) 25 Michigan Journal of International Law 849-863; George Abi-Saab 'Fragmentation or Unification: Some Concluding Remarks' (1999) 31 NYU Journal of International Law and Politics 919-932.

Conclusion

The examination pursued in this work was divided into three encompassing parts, which led to results that can be used independently as well as in conjunction. They map out the relationship between human rights law and substantive international criminal law in terms of *de lege lata* and dogmatic conception; the chances, pitfalls and prerequisites for an application of human rights law in substantive international criminal law; areas which present themselves as particularly well-suited for said application as well as taken and missed opportunities in this respect in the current jurisdiction; and the understanding of human rights law and its use by practitioners of international criminal law and what shapes this understanding.

Part One examined the reciprocal relation between human rights law and international criminal law, a subject that despite a multitude of research in both areas is still largely under-researched and not dealt with conclusively. This part acts as the legal theory basis of the research project. It outlines the similarities of both areas as law, starting from M. Cherif Bassiouni's Five-Stages-theory of the emergence and development of human rights, the criticism voiced against it as well as its relevance for a practical application of human rights law. It further follows up on the developments in jurisprudence and scholarly work since Bassiouni's model was published. It is concluded that, as a whole, Bassiouni's model of the evolution of human rights leading to a core group of rights whose mass violation is sanctioned by means of international criminal law, is not necessarily incorrect, but of limited value to practitioners applying substantive international criminal law.

Hence, as a first step, this book delves into explaining the dogmatic framework of how human rights law emerged and where international law fits in. This is crucial as a first step in determining how the two areas relate, how they evolved and to what degree they overlap or can even be considered to be congruent. As a next step, it is examined how the two areas are framed differently from the standpoint of legal policy, the addressee of the areas as well as the rights and obligations the areas convey to or demand of the addressee. Structural differences and similarities here decide to what degree human rights law can legitimately be used in international criminal law. Surely, both fields of law complement each other and their cross-fertilization leads to further developments in both areas. On the other hand it is shown that international criminal law and human rights law are in some way exact opposites. Their way of development, the precision which its terms and instruments are defined, the legal principles which they have to adhere to, the behaviour (of States or individuals) which the law seeks to trigger (in terms of rights or obligations), all this differs to a substantive degree and has to be kept in mind by practitioners seeking to apply extra-statutory law. Furthermore, structural differences between the areas of human rights law and international criminal law do, without doubt, exist and have to be taken into account when recourse to human rights law is taken in international criminal law. The argument brought forward that for the sake of universality, no such differences should be acknowledged, is of particular importance when it comes to the application of human rights law in procedural international criminal law, where these differences could easily undermine the rights of the accused. In substantive international criminal law, however, there is already a different scope of protection due to the limited jurisdiction of international court and tribunals in cases of widespread mass commission of crimes.

However, while caution is advised against an uncritical application of human rights law in international criminal law in the judgments of its courts and tribunals, this study argues that the structural and dogmatic differences of both areas are often up for discussion and fewer in number than sometimes argued by scholars of both fields.

More than conceptional differences, it is a potential violation of *nullum crimen sine lege* which can make the application of human rights in substantive international criminal law a risky exercise.

This work also concludes that there exists confusion as to what are the valid provisions which allow the ICC to apply human rights in the first place. Whereas Art. 21 (3) Rome Statute is deemed to be an appropriate gateway for human rights to be applied before the court in procedural matters, substantive extra-statutory law, including human rights law, needs to be applied pursuant to Art. 21 (1) (b) Rome Statute. Reference to human rights as mere 'guidance' or 'inspiration', without a conclusive and methodologically coherent determination of the status of a concept under customary international law, is deemed problematic as it can violate *nullum crimen sine lege.*

The last section of Part One delves deeper into the significance and construction of the principle of *nullum crimen sine lege* in the area of international criminal law. International criminal law in this respect offers a unique field of research as it combines criminal law with elements of public international law and hence implants an area in which legal certainty is of utmost importance for any proceeding to be legitimate in an area which is characterized by gradual evolvement of the ways States' behaviour changes into legal norms. The concept of *nullum crimen sine lege* has to be construed conservatively and narrowly in international criminal law so as to not violate the defendant's rights. Therefore, judges may only apply extra-statutory substantive law if it is part of customary international law. This still gives judges enough flexibility to take into account developments of the law.

Part Two examines this practical application of extra-statutory human rights law. It must be emphasised that many of the judgments analysed do indeed lack a degree of critical examination of whether the part of human rights law that the chamber seeks to apply is applicable in international criminal law and is indeed part of customary international law. The depth of the analysis employed by the respective chambers in this respect varies greatly and there is no coherent methodology to determine the applicability of a certain area of human rights law in the definition of crimes under international law or said category's status under customary international law.

The case-law analysis focuses on aspects in jurisprudence concerning the prohibition of torture, minority rights law and sexual crimes/gender issues. These three areas of law were chosen because they exhibit differing degrees of elaboration in human rights law as well as different level of connections with crimes known to most national legal systems. The prohibition of torture as such is a universally accepted fundamental part of customary international law,[850] widely recognized as a *ius cogens* norm[851] and prohibited not only in major international conventions but also mirrored in many national laws.[852] The rights of minorities, while protected in major international and regional conventions, are frequently misunderstood, looked upon with suspicion by many States for reasons rooted in history or practical policy, which is mirrored by reservations issued to Ar-

850 C Tofan (ed) *Torture in International Criminal Law* (Wolf The Hague 2011) 1.

851 Machtheld Boot, Rodney Dixon and Christopher K Hall 'Article 7: Crimes against Humanity' in Otto Triffterer Commentary on the Rome Statute of the International Criminal Court (2nd edition Beck Munich 2008) 159-273, 205.

852 .

ticle 27 ICCPR.[853] The issue of hate crime, which, to some extent, is an instrument of minority protection on a national level, is controversial and not embraced by many national legislators. Finally, the topic of violence against women has not been addressed in a binding international human rights instrument so far. The CEDAW Committee took on the issue by declaring that violence against women falls under its auspice, but its recommendations are not legally binding and its elaborations on why violence against women is discrimination are not shared by many countries. Hence, in the area of sexual violence as a matter of international criminal law, courts and tribunal have mostly soft law instruments at their disposal, in an area which is also intertwined with social mores and unfavourable attitudes. Hence the three areas provide three excellent points of departure to see under what circumstances human rights law is most often and most convincingly invoked.

The study finds that the definition and subject-matter or torture under international human rights law is referred to regularly. Here, courts have not missed many opportunities where pointing to human rights law would have strengthened or facilitated their argument. The reasons for this are manifold. First, the high-profile nature of the prohibition of torture as a *ius cogens* norm and in the fact that the prohibition of torture in human rights is governed by a widely ratified, robust convention make the relevance of the concept obvious also to experts of criminal law which might not be entirely familiar with the intricacies of public international law. The crime also has counterparts in many national legislations as a sanctioned prohibition which makes it further accessible to practitioners of various backgrounds. Concerning torture, the problem lies in how human rights law is referenced. There is no coherent method within or across the tribunals to determine the status of customary law of the subject. This leads, in the worst case, to an unequal application of the law. In comparison, minority rights law is less frequently referred to. The concept itself is less clear and more controversial and many of the crimes that have a relevance to minority rights, such as persecution, do not or not often find an equivalent in national law. The issue of minority protection seems somewhat abstract and foreign to many of those practitioners, which are criminal lawyers and do

853 See the Declarations of France, Turkey Declarations and Reservations of the States Parties to the International Covenant on Civil and Political Rights https://treaties.un.org/Pages/ViewDetails.aspx?src=TREATY&mtdsg_no=IV-4&chapter=4&lang=en (27 July 2015).

not have academic or practical experience in an area of public international law that includes human rights. The role of accessibility is most clear in the case of women's rights: at first glance, judges in international criminal cases do relatively often refer to human rights in cases of gender-based violence. However, such references are often superficial and leave the impression that the judges feel obliged to mention human rights law before moving on to areas like comparative law in their search for extra-statutory sources. This is despite the fact that, in particular, the rhetoric of crimes against humanity and that of women's rights as enshrined in the CEDAW are often quite similar. Both, in their subject-matter, deal with systematic, structural oppression. However, in the case of women's rights, three problems come together which aggravate an application: controversy, fragmentation and the nature of the instruments in question. Many controversies surround gender issues and women's rights, so that often, judges do not feel like human rights law in this field can answer to their legal needs or be of any assistance at all. Additionally, there are many different bodies and instruments that deal with women's rights, which makes it difficult the one main instrument which deals with the subject. Often, gender issues are formulated in soft law documents in a variety of different forms.

Generally, this study concludes that the best and most appropriate preconditions for an application of human rights in substantive international criminal law are given when two elements come together: first, an area of human rights law is governed by a well-established, robust and widely ratified convention. Second, the area of human rights law is mirrored by a direct or indirect counterpart in national criminal law. 'Classic' first generation rights are generally more accessible then up and coming, yet to be established concepts. In contrast, crimes which do not have a national criminal equivalent (like persecution) and concepts which are controversial in nature and governed by soft law (violence against women as discrimination) most problems in terms of reference can be expected.

The analysis of the relevant case law leads to the conclusion that the jurisprudence offers a multitude of unrealised opportunities to raise the legal as well as, in some cases, the political weight of the judgments through reference to human rights law. This is particularly obvious in the jurisprudence on persecution as a crime against humanity regarding the definition of persecution[854] or the delimitation of the protected groups.[855] With a view to the definition of persecution the definition of persecution if international refugee law was considered and, due to systematic differences in the two areas of law, rejected, without even mentioning international minority rights law, which dogmatically is much closer.[856] In the cases in which human rights law was referred to, there is no systematic approach identifiable and no dogmatically sound methodology. It is exclusively up to each chamber if and to what extent they engage in a discussion about the status of customary international law regarding a specific issue. In the extreme case, this leads to the paradoxical result that one and the same crime is punishable according to different requirements in one and the same forum.[857]

Part Three dealt with the perception of this problem by the judges. This part examined the preconditions under which judges deem a reference to human rights law helpful or compelling and for which sort of crimes such recourse is appropriate in their opinion.

Connecting to Parts One and Two, Part Three scrutinized how the perception of the interplay between human rights law and international criminal law, which dominates the discourse amongst practitioners, determines the extent to which they are ready to seek recourse to human rights law. The interviews have drawn up a very broad spectrum of partly diametrically opposite views on the relation between human rights law and international criminal law.

The statements regarding the relation between the two areas of law move between two extreme, irreconcilable stances on the subject. One opinion voiced was that human rights law has no place in international criminal jurisprudence and that international criminal law 'does not apply human rights law, this court applies its statute'.[858] Another judge set up

854 Eg *Prosecutor v Duško Tadić, (Judgment)* IT-94-1 (7 Mai 1997) para 654; paras 695-697.

855 Eg *Prosecutor v Dragan Nikolić (Review of Indictment Pursuant to Rule 61 Decision of Trial Chamber I)* IT-94-2-R61 (20 Oktober 1995) para. 27; *Prosecutor v. Goran Jesilić (Judgment)* IT-95-10 (14 Dezember 1999) paras 70-72.

856 *Prosecutor v Zoran Kupreškić et. Al (Judgment)* IT-95-16 (14 Januar 2000) para 589.

857 Eg *Prosecutor v Delalić et al (Judgment)* IT-96-21 (16 November 1998) para 473 and *Prosecutor v Kunarac (Judgment)* IT-96-23 (22 February 2001).

858 Statement made during a presentation about judges as law makers by a former judge of an international criminal tribunal.

the equation Human Rights Law + Criminal Law = International Criminal Law, making human rights law the decisive factor which differentiates national criminal law from international criminal law and held the view that definitions enshrined in the international bill of human rights that is the Universal Declaration of Human Rights, the International Covenant on Civil and Political Rights and the International Covenant on Economic, social and Cultural Rights can be used in her court with no further dogmatic consideration..[859]

Several factors related to the professional background of the judges had an influence on how they viewed the reference of human rights law. Criminal law experts, in theory, had less dogmatic misgivings about using human rights law in both procedural and substantive international criminal law, but they were often weary of the potential benefits and advantages of doing so: Criminal law experts often complained that the 'international element' was given too much weight at the ICC and the ICTY and that decisions should be dealt with in a less academic manner. As a consequence, experts on criminal law and procedure were less ready to apply human rights law than their counterparts appointed as criminal law experts and several of them argued that substantive problems which could ask for the applications of extra-statutory law have all been solved. This result is not particularly surprising given that judges appointed on List B (or, with regards to the ICTY, judges with international law expertise) are, in general, more familiar to public international law including human rights law. However, there is a considerable number of judges who do have a certain expertise in both areas and could have been appointed on either list. Throughout the benches, a certain vagueness as to the relationship between human rights law and international criminal law and, intertwined with that, the legal basis of applying human rights law could be observed. Some judges openly admitted that they only to resort to international human rights law when it supports their opinion which they have already previously formed, showing that they do not see the undertaking as a mandatory part of their work. A lack of in-depth knowledge in human rights law that could be referred to as well as insecurity as to how far such recourse can go and what its advantages are common. Regarding minority rights, a particular reluctance has been observed. Other dividing lines which were explored concern the legal system in which the judge was ed-

859 Interview No. 7.

ucated, whether they follow an academic or a more practical approach due to their prior work experience and their geographic background

The research project mapped out the practical influence of human rights in the jurisprudence of international court and tribunals and the dogmatic framework applied in the application. It explored the reasons for the reference to human rights law as well as the reason for a lack thereof and as such points to areas of possible synergy between international human rights and international criminal law.

The importance of ongoing workplace training and skill enhancement for judges and the necessity for diverse chambers able to fall back on expertise in criminal law and relevant fields of international law is increasingly promoted. The CICC's Independent Panel as well as the Advisory Committee set up by the Assembly of States Parties assess the experience of candidates through interviews and questionnaires. The CICC, additionally, explores their attitude towards continuous training. Since 2011, the CICC explicitly asks candidates about their prior experience with the application of human rights law. The results of this study show that this increasing understanding of the necessity of a comprehensive training of judges is vital for the further success of international criminal law. International criminal law as it stands conveys upon judges an enormous freedom to apply extra-statutory sources. This freedom is mirrored by a huge responsibility for an emerging field faced with loud and consistent criticism. This criticism focuses, *inter alia*, on the selectivity of international criminal law in terms of situations, cases and charges.

On the other hand, there is probably no other area of international law which can resort to a group of highly experienced senior experts with such a vast number of different fields of expertise. As the Rome Statute brings about numerous legal innovations, there will be plenty of instances in the future where judges will be forced to consult extra-statutory sources.

One of the biggest challenges, but also, a unique opportunity of the ICC as the one single permanent handler of international criminal law will be to benefit from its array of expertise and channel and streamline it into a more comprehensive and methodological approach in international criminal law that takes into account relevant fields of international law. What is necessary to work towards a more coherent and methodologically sound application of extra-statutory sources? This study has identified three main elements: First, an understanding of the best preconditions for an application of human rights law (robust convention + equivalent in national criminal codes). Second, a balanced composition of chambers is necessary, including members with various backgrounds. Third, a more streamlined education or, at a minimum, continuous training for judges in the areas of extra-statutory law that might be of relevance. These factors will foster a correct application of human rights law in substantive international criminal law in the future and will guarantee that the synergies between the two areas are not left untapped.

As it stands, international criminal law feels like an unfinished mosaic in which all the needed parts are present, but have not yet been employed to reassemble a complete coherent picture.

Annex

Questions for ICC/ICTY Judges

1- General Questions:

1.1- *Last profession before entering the ICC?*

1.2- *Education in a common law or in a civil law system?*

1.3- *Expertise pursuant to article 36 (3) of the Statute?*

2- General questions regarding the relationship between international criminal law and human rights law

2.1- *How would you personally describe the general relationship between international criminal law and human rights law?*

2.2- *How much would you say human rights law influences the work of the ICC in general (in procedural and substantive jurisprudence)?*

2.3- *How much does human rights law influence your specific work in particular?*

2.4- *To what extent can the jurisprudence of international human rights courts and/or treaty bodies influence the work of the ICC?*

2.5- *To what extent can international human rights courts and/or treaty bodies benefit from the work of the ICC?*

3- Specific areas of human rights law and their influence on international criminal law

3.1- *Which areas of human rights law would you say have had a significant influence in the evolution of international criminal law?*

3.2- *Which areas of human rights law would you say have a significant impact on the practical work of the ICC today?*

3.3.1- *To what extent would you say that international minority rights law has influenced the development of international criminal law?*

3.3.2- *Which specific crimes would you say were influenced by the overriding concern of minority protection and by substantive minority rights law and how?*

3.3.3- *What practical role does international minority rights law play in the application of international criminal law today?*

3.4.1- *To what extent would you say women's rights influenced the development of international criminal law?*

3.4.2- *What practical role do women's rights and gender issues play in the practical application of international criminal law today?*

3.5.1- *To what extent would you say that children's rights have influenced the development of international criminal law?*

3.5.2- *What practical role do children's rights play in the application of international criminal law today?*

3.6.1- *To what extent would you say that the prohibition of torture has influenced the development of international criminal law?*

3.6.2- *What practical role does the prohibition of torture play in the application of international criminal law today?*

3.7- *To what extent would you say judges at the ICC are willing to consider international human rights law in their decisions/judgments?*

3.8- *To what extent would you say that judges at the ICC have the mandate to consider international human rights law in their decisions/judgments?*

4- Question regarding the Rome Statute

4.2- *Would you say that the specific mentioning of human rights law in article 21 (3) of the Rome Statute will further the consideration/ application of human rights law in the work of the ICC?*

Bibliography

Cases

Application of the Convention on the Prevention and Punishment of the Crime of Genocide (Bosnia and Herzegovina v Serbia and Montenegro) (Merits) [2007] ICJ Rep 43.

Asylum Case (Colombia/Peru) (Judgement) [1950] ICJ Rep 266.

Aksoy v Turkey (ECtHR) Reports 1996-VI 2260.

Armed Activities on the Territory of the Congo (Democratic Republic of the Congo v Uganda) [2005] ICJ Rep 168.

Aydin v Turkey (ECtHR) Reports 1997-VI <http://hudoc.echr.coe.int/eng?i=001-58371> (31 October 2017).

Barayagwiza v Prosecutor (Decision) ICTR-97-19-A (3 November 1999).

Continental Shelf (Libyan Arab Jamahiriya/Malta) [1985] ICJ Rep 13, 29.

Costello-Roberts v United Kingdom (ECtHR) Series A No 247 C.

CR v United Kingdom (Judgment) (ECtHR) Series A No 335 C.

Cyprus v Turkey (EComHR App 6780/74 and 6950/75) 4 EHRR 482.

Cyprus v Turkey (ECommHR App 8007/77) (1979) 13 DR 85.

Denmark, Norway and Sweden v Greece (ECommHR App 4448/70) (1970) 13 YECommHR 108.

Denmark, Norway, Sweden and the Netherlands v Greece (ECommHR App 3321-3323/67 and 3344/67) (1968) 11 YECommHR 690.

Van Droogenbroeck v Belgium (Decision of 5 July 1979 on the admissibility of the application) (EComm App 7906/77) D/R 17.

EK v Turkey (Judgment) appl 28496/95 <http://hudoc.echr.coe.int/sites/eng/pages/search.aspx?i=001-64586>.

Fernando and Raquel Mejia v Peru Case 10.970 IACommHR Report No 5/96 (1 March 1996).

Filártiga v Peña-Irala United States Court of Appeals (2nd Cir 1980) 630 F 2d 876, 878–79.

Greco-Bulgarian Communities (Advisory Opinion) PCIJ Series B No 17.

Greek Case (ECommHR App Nos 3321/67 [*Denmark v Greece*]; 3322/67 [*Norway v Greece*]; 3323 [*Sweden v Greece*]; 3344/67 [*Netherlands v Greece*]) (1969) 12 YECommHR.

International Criminal Court 'Decision Pursuant to Article 15 of the Rome Statute on the Authorization of an Investigation into the Situation in the Republic of Kenya' ICC-01/09-19 (31 March 2010).

Interpretation of the Agreement of 25 March 1951 between the WHO and Egypt (Advisory Opinion) [1980] ICJ Rep 73

Ireland v United Kingdom (ECtHR) Series A No 25.

Ireland v United Kingdom (ECommHR App 5310/71) (1976) Series B No 23-I.

Kadić v Karadžić United States Court of Appeals (2nd Cir 1995) 70 F 3d 232.

Kokkinakis v Greece (Judgment) (ECtHR) Series A No 260 A.

Laureano Atachahua v Peru' (26 March 1996) GAOR 51st Session Supp 40, vol 2, 42.

Legal Consequences of the Construction of a Wall in the Occupied Palestinian Territory (Advisory Opinion) [2004] ICJ Rep 136.

Legality of the Threat or Use of Nuclear Weapons (Advisory Opinion) [1996] ICJ Rep 226.

Mugenzi and Mugiraneza v Prosecutor (Appeal Judgment) ICTR-99-50-A (4 February 2013).

Prosecutor v. *Ahmad Muhammad Harun ("Ahmad Harun") and Ali Muhammad Ali Abd-Al-Rahman ("Ali Kushayb"),* 'Warrant of Arrest for Ahmad Muhammad Harun ("Ahmad Harun")' ICC-02-/05-01/07-2 (27 April 2007).

Van der Mussele v Belgium (ECtHR) (Judgment) (1983) 6 EHRR 163.

Prosecutor v Akayesu (Amended Indictment) ICTR-96-4-I (June 1997).

Prosecutor v Akayesu (Appeal Judgment) ICTR-96-4-A (1 June 2001).

Prosecutor v Akayesu (Judgment) ICTR-96-4-T (2 September 1998).

Prosecutor v. Aleksovski (Appeal Judgment) IT-95-14/1 (24 March 2000).

Prosecutor v Jean-Pierre Bemba Gombo (Judgment on the appeal of Mr Jean-Pierre Bemba Gombo against the decision of Trial Chamber III of 28 July 2010 entitled 'Decision on the review of the detention of Mr Jean-Pierre Bemba Gombo pursuant to Rule 118(2) of the Rules of Procedure and Evidence') ICC-01/05-01/08-1019 (19 November 2010).

Prosecutor v Blagojević (Judgment) IT-02-60-A (9 May 2007).

Prosecutor v Blaškić (Judgment) IT-95-14-T (3 March 2000).

Prosecutor v Brđanin (Judgment) IT-99-36-T (1 September 2004).

Prosecutor v Brđanin (Appeal Judgment) ICTY-99-36-A (3 April 2007).

Prosecutor v Brima et al (Trial Chamber Judgment) SCSL–2004–16–T (19 July 2007).

Prosecutor v Češić (Sentencing Judgment) IT-95-10/1-S (11 March 2004).

Prosecutor v Delalić et al (Celebići Case Appeal Judgment) IT-96-21-A (20 February 2001).

Prosecutor v Delalić et al (Celebići Indictment) IT-96-21 (19 March 1996).

Prosecutor v Delalić et al (Celebići Case Judgment) IT-96-21-T (16 November 1998).

Prosecutor v Delić (Judgment) IT-04-83-T (15 September 2008).

Prosecutor v Deronjić (Judgment) IT-02-61-S (30 March 2004).

Prosecutor v Erdemović (Sentencing Judgment) IT-96-22-T (29 November 1996).

Prosecutor v Erdemović (Appeal Judgment) IT-96-22-A (7 October 1997).

Prosecutor v Furundžija (Judgment) IT-95-17 (10 December 1998).

Prosecutor v Furundžija (Appeal Judgment) IT-95-17/1-A (21 July 2000).

Prosecutor v Gacumbitsi (Judgment) ICTR-01-64-T (17 June 2004).

Prosecutor v Galić (Judgment) IT-98-29-T (5 December 2003).

Prosecutor v Galić (Appeal Judgment) IT-98-29-A (30 November 2006).

Prosecutor v Halilović (Judgment) IT-01-48-T (16 November 2005).

Prosecutor v Hadžihasanović et al (Decision on Joint Challenge to Jurisdiction) IT-01-47-PT (12 November 2002).

Prosecutor v Hadžihasanović and et al (Judgment) IT-96-22-T (29 November 1996).

Prosecutor v Haradinaj (Judgment) IT-04-84-T (3 April 2008).

Prosecutor v Imanishimwe et *al (Appeal Judgment)* ICTR-99-46-A (7 July 2006).

Prosecutor v Jelisić (Judgement) ICTY-IT-95-10 (14 December 1999).

Prosecutor v Kajelijeli (Judgment) ICTR-98-44A-T (1 December 2003).

Prosecutor v Kajelijeli (Appeal Judgment) ICTR-98-44-A-A (23 May 2005).

Prosecutor v Kambanda (Appeal Judgment) ICTR-97-23-A (19 October 2000).

Prosecutor v Germain Katanga and Mathieu Ngudjolo Chui (Judgment on the appeal of Mr. Germain Katanga against the decision of Pre-Trial Chamber I entitled "Decision on the Defence Request Concerning Languages) ICC-01/04-01/07-522 (27 May 2008).

Prosecutor v Kayishema (Judgment) ICTR-95-1-T (21 May 1999).

Prosecutor v Kordić (Appeal Judgment) IT-95-14/2-A (17 December 2004).

Prosecutor v Krajišnik (Judgment) IT-00-39-T (27 September 2006).

Prosecutor v Krstić (Appeal Judgment) IT-98-33-A (19 April 2004).

Prosecutor v Krstić (Judgment) IT-98-33-T (2 August 2001).

Prosecutor v Krnojelac (Judgment) IT-97-25 (15 March 2002).

Prosecutor v Kunarac (Appeal Judgment) IT-96-23 & IT-96-23/1-A (12 June 2002).

Prosecutor v Kunarac (Judgment) IT-96-23 (22 February 2001).

Prosecutor v Kupreškić (Judgment) IT-95-16 (14 January 2000).

Prosecutor v Kvočka (Judgment) IT-98-30 (2 November 2001).

Prosecutor v Limaj (Judgment) IT-03-66-T (30 November 2005).

UN Ad Hoc Committee on Genocide 'Summary Record of Meetings 175-225' (1948) UNESCOR 3rd Year, 7th Session, Supp. No. 6 at 7 UN Doc E/3/SR.175-225 (1948).

Prosecutor v Thomas Lubanga Dyilo (Decision on the confirmation of charges) ICC-01/04-01/803-tEN (29 January 2007).

Prosecutor v Thomas Lubanga Dyilo (Decision on the consequences of non-disclosure of exculpatory materials covered by Article 54(3)(e) agreements and the application to stay the prosecution of the accused, together with certain other issues raised at the Status Conference on 10 June 2008) ICC-01/04-01/06-1401 (13 June 2008).

Prosecutor v Thomas Lubanga Dyilo (Decision on the Prosecutor's "Application for Leave to Reply to 'Conclusions de la defense en reponse au memoire d'appeal du Procureur'" Separate Opinion of Judge Georghios M. Pikis) ICC-01/04-01/06-424 (12 September 2006).

Prosecutor v Thomas Lubanga Dylio (Decision on the Prosecution's Urgent Request for Variation of the Time-Limit to Disclose the Identity of Intermediary 143 or Alternatively to Stay Proceedings Pending Further Consultations with the VWU) ICC-01/04-01/06-2517 (8 July 2010).

Prosecutor v Thomas Lubanga Dyilo (Decision on Victims' Participation) ICC-01/04-01/06-1119 (18 January 2008).

Prosecutor v Thomas Lubanga Dyilo (Judgment) ICC-01/04-01/06 (14 March 2012).

Prosecutor v. Thomas Lubanga Dyilo (Judgment on the Appeal of Mr. Thomas Lubanga Dyilo against the Decision on the Defense Challenge to the Jurisdiction of the Court pursuant to Article 19(2)(a) of the Statute of 3 October 2006) ICC-01/04-01/06-772 (14 December 2006).

Prosecutor v Thomas Lubanga Dyilo (Prosecution's Closing Brief) ICC-01/04-01/06-2748-Red.

Prosecutor v Milutinović et al (Decision on Dragoljub Ojdanic's Motion Challenging Jurisdiction–Joint Criminal Enterprise) IT-99-37-AR72 (21 May 2003).

Prosecutor v Milutinović (Judgment) IT-05-87-T (26 February 2009).

Prosecutor v Muhimana (Judgment) ICTR-95-1B-T (28 April 2005).

Prosecutor v Musema (Judgment) ICTR-96-13-T (27 January 2000).

Prosecutor v Nahimana (Judgment) ICTR-99-52-T (3 December 2003).

Prosecutor v Nikolić (Review of Indictment Pursuant to Rule 61of the Rules of Procedure and Evidence) ICTY IT-94-2-R61 (20 October 1995).

Prosecutor v Niyitegeka (Judgment) ICTR-96-14-T (16 May 2003).

Prosecutor v Mathieu Ngudjolo (Judgment) ICC-01/04-02/12 (18 December 2012).

Prosecutor v Ntakirutimana (Judgment) ICTR-96-10 and ICTR-96-17-T (21 February 2003).

Prosecutor v Ntawukulilyayo (Judgment) ICTR-05-82-T (3 August 2010).

Prosecutor v Perišić (Judgment) IT-04-81-T (6 September 2011).

Prosecutor v Rugambarara (Judgment) ICTR-00-59-T (16 November 2007).

Prosecutor v Rutaganda (Judgment) ICTR-96-3-T (6 December 1999).

Prosecutor v Semanza (Judgment) ICTR-97-20-T (15 May 2003).

Prosecutor v Sikirica et al (Judgement on Defence Motions to Acquit) IT-95-8-T (3 September 2001).

Prosecutor v Simić et al (Judgment) IT-95-9 (17 October 2003).

Prosecutor v Stakić (Judgment) IT-97-24-T (31 July 2003).

Prosecutor v Mićo Stanišić (Judgment) IT-08-91-T (27 March 2013).

Prosecutor v Tadić (Appeal Judgment) IT-94-1-A (15 July 1999).

Prosecutor v Tadić (Decision on the Prosecutor's Motion Requesting Protective Measures for Victims and Witnesses) IC-94-I-10 (10 August 1995).

*Prosecutor v Tadić (*Decision on the Defence Motion for Interlocutory Appeal on Jurisdiction) IT-94-1-AR72 (2 October 1995).

Prosecutor v Tadić (Opinion and Judgment) IT-94-1 (7 May 1997).

Prosecutor v Todorović (Judgment) IT-95-9/1-S (31 July 2001).

Prosecutor v Vasiljević (Judgment) IT-98-32-T (29 November 2002).

Regina v Bartle ex p Pinochet United Kingdom House of Lords (24 March 1999) (1999) 38 ILM 581.

Situation on the Democratic Republic of the Congo (Decision on the Applications for Participation in the Proceedings of VPRS 1, VPRS 2, VPRS 3, VPRS 4, VPRS 5 and VPRS 6) ICC-01/04 UN (17 January 2006).

Situation in the Democratic Republic of the Congo (Judgment on the Prosecutor's Application for Extraordinary Review of Pre-Trial Chamber I's 31 March 2006 Decision Denying Leave to Appeal) ICC-01/04-168 (13 July 2006)

Sunday Times v United Kingdom (ECtHR) Series A No 30.

SW v United Kingdom (Judgment) (ECtHR) Series A No 335 B.

Trials of War Criminals Before the Nuremberg Military Tribunals Under Control Council Law No 10 (US Government Printing Office Washington DC 1952) vol I 16, vol II 182.

UN Committee against Torture 'Communication No 262/2005, *VL v Switzerland*' (20 November 2006) UN Doc CAT/C/37/D/262/2005).

UN Committee against Torture 'General Comment No 2: Implementation of Article 2 by States Parties' (24 January 2008) UN Doc CAT/C/GC/2.

UN Committee against Torture 'Decision 212/2002, *Guridi v Spain*' (24 May 2005) UN Doc CAT/C/34/D/212/2002.

UN HRC 'Communication No. 74/1980, *Angel Estrella v Uruguay*' (29 March 1983) UN Doc Supp. No. 40 (A/37/40) at 114.

UN HRC 'Communication No 1780/2008, *Aouabdia v. Algeria*' (22 March 2011) UN Doc CCPR/C/101/D/1780/2008.

UN HRC 'Communication No. 147/83, *Arzuaga Gilboa v Uruguay*' (1 November 1985) UN Doc CCPR/C/OP/2 at 17.

UN HRC 'Communication No 1588/2007, *Benaziza v. Algeria* (26 July 2010) UN Doc CCPR/C/99/D/1588/2007.

UN HRC 'Communication 162/1983, *Berterretche Acosta v Uruguay*' (25 October 1988) UN Doc Supp. No. 40 (A/44/40) at 183.

UN HRC 'Communication No. 428/1990, *Bozize v Central African Republic*' (7 April 1994) UN Doc CCPR/C/50/D/428/1990.

UN HRC 'Communication No 775/97, *Brown v Jamaica*' (23 March 1999) UN Doc CCPR/C/65/D/775/1997.

UN HRC Communication No 159/1983, *Cariboni v Uruguay*' (27 October 1987) UN Doc Supp. No. 40 (A/43/40) at 184.

UN HRC 'Communications No 623/1995, 624/1995, 626/1995 and 627/1995, *Domukovsky et al. v. Georgia*' (6 April 1998), UN Docs CCPR/C/62/D/623, 624, 626 & 627/1995.

Communication No 1640/2007, *El Abani v The Libyan Arab Jamahiriya*' (26 July 2010) UN Doc CCPR/C/99/D/1640/2007.

UN HRC 'Communication No 1295/2004, *El Awani v. The Libyan Arab Jamahiriya,* (11 July 2007) CCPR/C/90/D/1295/2004.

UN HRC 'Communication No 440/1990, *El-Megreisi v Libyan Arab Jamahiriya* (23 March 1994) UN Doc CCPR/C/50/D/440/1990.

UN HRC 'Communication No. 11/1977, *Grille Motta v Uruguay*' (29 July 1980) UN Doc Supp. No. 40 (A/35/40) at 132.

UN HRC 'Communication No 161/1983, *Herrera Rubio v Colombia*' (2 November 1987) UN Doc CCPR/C/OP/2 at 192.

UN HRC 'Communication 366/89, *Kanana v. Zaire*' (2 November 1993) UN Doc CCPR/C/49/D/366/1989.

UN HRC 'Communication No 197/1985, *Kitok v Sweden*' (27 July 1988) GAOR 43rd Session Supp 40, 221.

UN HRC 'Communication No 176/1984, *Lafuente Peñarrieta et al v Bolivia*' (2 November 1987) UN Doc CCPR/C/OP/2 at 201.

UN HRC 'Communication No 511/1992, *Länsman v Finland*' (26 October 1994) GAOR 50th Session Supp 40 vol 2, 66.

UN HRC 'Communication No 540/1993, *Laureano Atachahua v Peru*' (26 March 1996) GAOR 51st Session Supp 40, vol 2, 42.

UN HRC 'Communication No. 52/1979, *Lopez Burgos v Uruguay*' (29 July 1981) UN Doc CCPR/C/OP/1 at 88.

UN HRC Communication 194/85, *Miango Muiyo v Zaire*' (27 October 1987) UN Doc CCPR/C/OP/2.

UN HRC 'Communication No. 449/1991, *Mojica v Dominican Republic*' (5 July 1994) UN Doc CCPR/C/51/D/449/1991.

UN HRC 'Communication No. 124/82, *Muteba v Zaire*' (25 March 1983) UN Doc CCPR/C/OP/2.

UN HRC 'Communication No 167/1984, *Ominayak, Chief of the Lubicon Lake Band v Canada*' (26 March 1990) GAOR 45th Session Supp 40 vol 2, 1.

UN HRC Communication 'No 577/1994 *Polaly Campos v Peru*' (6 November 1997) UN Doc CCPR/C/61/D/577/1994.

UN HRC 'Communication No 188/84, *Portorreal v Dominican Republic*' (5 November 1987) UN Doc Supp No 40 (A/43/40).

UN HRC 'Communication No. 950/2000, *Sarma v Sri Lanka*' (6 July 2003) UN Doc CCPR/C/78/D/950/2000.

UN HRC 'Communication No 63/1979, *Sendic v Uruguay*' (28 October 1981) UN Doc No Supp. No. 40 (A/37/40) at 114 (1982).

UN HRC 'Communication No. 458/1991, *Womah Mukong v Cameroon'* (21 July 1994) UN Doc. CCPR/C/51/D/458/1991.

The United States of America et al v Araki et al (Judgment of the International Military Tribunal for the far East) (12 November 1948) available at http://www.worldcourts.com/imtfe/eng/decisions/1948.11.04_IMTFE_Judgment.htm (31 October 2017).

The United States of America et al v Göring et al (Judgment and Sentences of the International Military Tribunal) (Nuremberg) (1 October 1946) (1947) 41 AJIL 172–333.

Velasquez Rodriguez v Honduras (Judgment) IACtHR Series C No 4 (29 July 1988).

Documents

Abschied des Augsburger Reichstages (Augsburger Friede) (25 September 1555) in K Zeumer (ed) *Quellensammlung zum Staats-, Verwaltungs- und Völkerrecht* vol 2.1 *Quellensammlung zur Geschichte der Deutschen Reichsverfassung in Mittelalter und Neuzeit* (2nd edn Siebeck Mohr Tübingen 1913) 341.

African Charter on Human and Peoples' Rights (adopted 27 June1981, entered into force 21 October 1986) 1520 UNTS 217 (Banjul Charter).

International Committee of the Red Cross 'Aide-Mémoire' (3 December 1992) as cited in Theodor Meron 'Rape as a Crime under International Humanitarian Law' (1993) 87(3) American Journal of International Law 424-428, 426.

Alien Tort Claims Act (1789) 28 USC § 1350.

American Convention on Human Rights (signed 22 November 1969, entered into force 18 July 1978) 1144 UNTS 123 (Pact of San José).

American Declaration of the Rights and Duties of Man (10 December 1948) (1949) 43 AJIL Supp 133.

Charter of the International Military Tribunal for the Far East (19 January 1946) 4 Bevans 20.

Charter of the [Nuremberg] International Military Tribunal (8 August 1945) 82 UNTS 284.

Charter of the United Nations (adopted 26 June 1945, entered into force 24 October 1945) 1 UNTS 16.

Coalition for the International Criminal Court 'Coalition for the International Criminal Court Announces Global Campaign on ICC Elections: Global Coalition Committed to Ensuring

Independent, Fair, Transparent, and Merit-based Elections' (27 January 2011) <http://www.iccnow.org/documents/CICCElectionsCampaign_2011.pdf> (1 October 2015).

Coalition for the International Criminal Court 'Judges' <http://www.coalitionfortheicc.org/topics/judges > (31 October 2017).

Coalition of the ICC 'Questionnaire for ICC Judicial Candidates: December 2017 Elections' <http://www.coalitionfortheicc.org/fight/icc-elections-2017> (31 October 2017).

COE 'Convention for the Protection of Human Rights and Fundamental Freedoms' (signed 4 November 1950, entered into force 3 September 1953) 213 UNTS 221.

COE 'European Convention for the Prevention of Torture and Inhuman or Degrading Treatment or Punishment' (done 26 November 1987, entered into force 1 February 1989) 1561 UNTS 363.

COE 'European Prison Rules' (2 January 2006) <https://wcd.coe.int/ViewDoc.jsp?id=955747> (31 October 2017).

COE 'Framework Convention for the Protection of National Minorities' (opened for signature 1 February 1995, entered into force 1 February 1998) 2151 UNTS 243.

COE 'Protocol No 12 to the Convention for the Protection of Human Rights and Fundamental Freedoms' (signed 4 November 2000, entered into force 1 April 2005) CETS No 177.

COE 'Vienna Declaration of the Heads of State and Government of the Member States of the Council of Europe on the Reform of the Control Mechanism of the ECHR, on National Minorities, and on a Plan of Action against Racism' (9 October 1993) (1993) 14 HRLJ 373–76.

Commission of the Responsibility of the Authors of the War and the Enforcement of Penalties 'Report Presented to the Preliminary Peace Conference' (March 1919) (1920) 14 AJIL 95–154.

Control Council Law No 10 'Punishment of Persons Guilty of War Crimes, Crimes against Peace and against Humanity' (done 20 December 1945) (1946) 3 Official Gazette of the Control Council for Germany 50.

ILO 'Convention No 29 concerning Forced or Compulsory Labour' (adopted 28 June 1930, entered into force 1 May 1932) 39 UNTS 55.

ILO 'Convention No 105 concerning the Abolition of Forced Labour' (adopted 25 June 1957, entered into force 17 January 1959) 320 UNTS 291.

Convention on Consent to Marriage, Minimum Age for Marriage and Registration of Marriages (adopted 7 November 1962, entered into force 9 December 1964) 521 UNTS 231 (Marriage Convention).

Convention against Discrimination in Education (adopted 14 December 1960, entered into force 22 May 1962) 429 UNTS 93.

Convention on the Elimination of All Forms of Discrimination against Women (adopted 18 December 1979, entered into force 3 September 1981) 1249 UNTS 13.

Convention respecting the Laws and Customs of War on Land and its Annex: Regulations concerning the Laws and Customs of War on Land (signed 18 October 1907, entered into force 26 January 1910) (1907) 205 CTS 277.

Convention on the Political Rights of Women (adopted 20 December 1952, entered into force 7 July 1954) 193 UNTS 135.

Convention on the Rights of the Child (adopted 20 November 1989, entered into force 2 September 1990) 1577 UNTS 3.

Convention on the Rights of Persons with Disabilities (adopted 13 December 2006, entered into force 3 May 2008) 2515 UNTS 12.

Convention with Respect to the Laws and Customs of War by Land and its Annex: Regulations Respecting the Laws and Customs of War on Land (signed 29 July 1899, entered into force 4 September 1900) (1898–99) 187 CTS 429.

Convention respecting the Laws and Customs of War on Land and its Annex: Regulations concerning the Laws and Customs of War on Land (signed 18 October 1907, entered into force 26 January 1910) (1907) 205 CTS 277.

Convention on the Prevention and Punishment of the Crime of Genocide (adopted 9 December 1948, entered into force 12 January 1951) 78 UNTS 277.

Convention for the Protection of Human Rights and Fundamental Freedoms (Council of Europe signed 4 November 1950, entered into force 3 September 1953) 213 UNTS 221.

Convention relating to the Status of Refugees (signed 28 July 1951, entered into force 22 April 1954) 189 UNTS 150.

Convention against Torture and Other Cruel, Inhuman or Degrading Treatment or Punishment (adopted 10 December 1984, entered into force 26 June 1987) 1465 UNTS 112.

CSCE 'Document of the Copenhagen Meeting of the Conference on the Human Dimension of the CSCE' (29 June 1990) (1990) 29 ILM 1305.

CSCE 'Helsinki Summit Document: The Challenges of Change' (10 July 1992) (1992) 31 ILM 1385.

Declarations and Reservations of the States Parties to the International Covenant on Civil and Political Rights https://treaties.un.org/Pages/ViewDetails.aspx?src=TREATY&mtdsg_no=IV-4&chapter=4&lang=en (31 October 2017).

Eighth United Nations Congress on the Prevention on Crime and the Treatment of Offenders 'Basic Principles on the Role of Lawyers' (18 December 1990) UN Doc A/CONF.144/28/Rev 1, 118.

Elements of Crimes (9 September 2002) Doc ICC-ASP/1/3 (Pt. II-B).

Fourth World Conference on Women 'Beijing Declaration and Platform for Action' in 'Report' (17 October 1995) UN Doc A/CONF.177/20, 4.

Geneva Convention for the Amelioration of the Condition of the Wounded and Sick in Armed Forces in the Field (adopted 12 August 1949, entered into force 21 October 1950) 75 UNTS 31 (Geneva Convention I).

Geneva Convention for the Amelioration of the Condition of Wounded, Sick and Shipwrecked Members of Armed Forces at Sea (adopted 12 August 1949, entered into force 21 October 1950) 75 UNTS 85 (Geneva Convention II).

Geneva Convention relative to the Protection of Civilian Persons in Time of War (adopted 12 August 1949, entered into force 21 October 1950) 75 UNTS 287 (Geneva Convention IV).

Geneva Convention relative to the Treatment of Prisoners of War (adopted 12 August 1949, entered into force 21 October 1950) 75 UNTS 135 (Geneva Convention III).

Independent Panel on ICC Judicial Elections 'Report on International Criminal Court Judicial Nominations 2011' (26 October 2011) http://www.iccindependentpanel.org/sites/default/files/Independent%20Panel%20on%20ICC%20Judicial%20Elections%20-%20Report%2026%20October%202011.pdf (1 October 2015).

Inter-American Convention to Prevent and Punish Torture (done 9 December 1985, entered into force 28 February 1987) (1986) 25 ILM 519.

International Commission of Jurists *States of Emergency—Their Impact on Human Rights: A Comparative Study by the International Commission of Jurists* (International Commission of Jurists Geneva 1983).

Inter-American Convention on Forced Disappearance of Persons (done 9 June 1994, entered into force 28 March 1996) (1994) 33 ILM 1529.

International Convention on the Elimination of all Forms of Racial Discrimination (opened for signature 7 March 1966, entered into force 4 January 1969) 660 UNTS 195.

International Convention for the Protection of All Persons from Enforced Disappearance (adopted 20 December 2006, entered into force 23 December 2010) GAOR 61st Session Supp 49 vol 1, 408.

International Convention on the Suppression and Punishment of the Crime of Apartheid (adopted 30 November 1973, entered into force 18 July 1976) 1015 UNTS 243.

International Covenant on Civil and Political Rights (adopted 19 December 1966, entered into force 23 March 1976) 999 UNTS 171.

International Covenant on Economic, Social and Cultural Rights (adopted 16 December 1966, entered into force 3 January 1976) 993 UNTS 3.

International Criminal Court Assembly of States Parties 'Report of the Advisory Committee on Nominations of Judges on the work of its second meeting' (29 October 2013) Twelfth Session (20-28 November 2013) ICC-ASP 12/47.

International Criminal Court Assembly of States Parties 'Report of the Bureau on the establishment of an Advisory Committee on nominations of judges of the International Criminal Court' (30 December 2011) Tenth Session (12-21 December 2011) ICC-ASP/10/36.

International Criminal Court Assembly of States Parties 'Rules of Procedure and Evidence' (3–10 September 2002) Official Records ICC-ASP/1/3.

International Criminal Court The Office of the Prosecutor 'Statement to the United Nations Security Council on the situation in Libya, pursuant to UNSCR 1970 (2011)' (2 November 2011) <http://www.iccnow.org/documents/StatementICCProsecutorLibyaReporttoUNSC021113.pdf> (31 October 2017).

Organization of African Unity, Assembly of Heads of State and Government 'Declaration on a Code of Conduct for Inter-African Relations' Thirtieth Ordinary Session, Tunis, Tunisia, 13-15 June 1994 available at <https://www1.umn.edu/humanrts/africa/INTAFN.htm> (31 October 2017).

Preparatory Committee on the Establishment of an International Criminal Court 'Report of the Inter-Sessional Meeting from 19 to 30 January 1998 in Zutphen, The Netherlands' (4 February 1998) UN Doc A/AC.249/1998/L.13.

Principles of International Law Recognized in the Charter of the Nuremberg Tribunal and the Judgment of the Tribunal UNILC 'Report on Principles of the Nuremberg Tribunal' (29 July 1950) GAOR 5th session Supp 12, 11 (Nuremberg Principles).

Law on the Establishment of Extraordinary Chambers in the Courts of Cambodia for the Prosecution of Crimes committed during the Period of Democratic Kampuchea (27 October 2004) S/RKM/1004/006 http://www.eccc.gov.kh/sites/default/files/legal-documents/KR_Law_as_amended_27_Oct_2004_Eng.pdf (31 October 2017).

Protocol Additional to the Geneva Conventions of 12 August 1949, and relating to the Protection of Victims of International Armed Conflicts (Protocol I) (adopted 8 June 1977, entered into force 7 December 1978) 1125 UNTS 3.

Protocol Additional to the Geneva Conventions of 12 August 1949, and relating to the Protection of Victims of Non-International Armed Conflicts (Protocol II) (adopted 8 June 1977, entered into force 7 December 1978) 1125 UNTS 609.

Report of the Preparatory Committee on the Establishment of an International Criminal Court Volume I: Proceedings of the Preparatory Committee during March-April and August 1996 UN Doc A/51/22 (1996).

Report of the Secretary-General Pursuant to Paragraph 2 of Security Council Resolution 808 (1993)' UN Doc S/25704.

Rome Statute of the International Criminal Court (adopted 17 July 1998, entered into force 1 July 2002) 2187 UNTS 90.

Slavery Convention (adopted 25 September 1926, entered into force 9 March 1927) 60 LNTS 253.

Second Optional Protocol to the International Covenant on Civil and Political Rights, aiming at the Abolition of the Death Penalty (adopted 15 December 1989, entered into force 11 July 1991) GAOR 44th Session Supp 49 vol 1, 207.

Seventh United Nations Congress on the Prevention of Crime and the Treatment of Offenders 'Basic Principles on the Independence of the Judiciary' (26 August–6 September 1985) UN Doc A/CONF.121/22/Rev. 1, 58.

Statute of the International Court of Justice (adopted 26 June 1945, entered into force 24 October 1945) 145 BSP 832.

Statute of the Special Court for Sierra Leone (concluded 16 January 2002; entered into force 12 April 2002) 2178 UNTS 145.

Supplementary Convention on the Abolition of Slavery, the Slave Trade, and Institutions and Practices Similar to Slavery (adopted 7 September 1956, entered into force 30 April 1957) 266 UNTS 3.

Treaty of Peace between the Holy Roman Empire and Sweden and the Treaty of Peace between France and the Holy Roman Empire (signed and entered into force 24 October 1648) (1648–49) 1 CTS 198, 319 (these two treaties form the Westphalian Peace Treaty).

UN Ad Hoc Committee on Genocide 'Summary Records of the Fifth Meeting' (8 April 1948) UN Doc E/AC.25/SR.5.

UN Commission on Human Rights 'Analysis of Various Draft International Bills of Rights' (1947) UN Doc E/CN.4/W.16.

UN Commission on Human Rights 'Basic Principles and Guidelines on the Right to a Remedy and Reparation for Victims of Gross Violations of International Human Rights Law and Serious Violations of International Humanitarian Law' (19 April 2005) ESCOR 61st Session Supp 3, 136.

UN Commission on Human Rights 'Preliminary report submitted by the Special Rapporteur on violence against women, its causes and consequences, Ms. Radhika Coomaraswamy, in accordance with Commission on Human Rights resolution 1994/45' (22 November 1994) UN Doc E/CN.4/1995/42.

UN Commission on Human Rights 'Question of the human rights of all persons subjected to any form of detention or imprisonment, in particular: torture and other cruel, inhuman or degrading treatment or punishment: Report of the Special Rapporteur, Mr. Nigel S. Rodley' (12 January 1995) UN Doc E/CNA/1995/34.

UN Commission on Human Rights 'Question of the Human Rights of All Persons Subject to any Form of Detention or Imprisonment: Question of Enforced or Involuntary Disappearances: Report of the Working Group on Enforced or Involuntary Disappearances' (21 January 1983) UN Doc E/CN.4/1983/14.

UN Commission of Human Rights Special Rapporteur of the Sub-Commission on Prevention of Discrimination and Protection of Minorities, Benjamin Whitaker, 'Revised and Updated Report on the Question of the Prevention and Punishment of the Crime of Genocide' (2 July 1985) E/CN.4/Sub. 2/1985/6.

UN Commission on Human Rights Special Rapporteur of the Sub-Commission on Prevention of Discrimination and Protection of Minorities, Francesco Capotorti 'Study on the Rights of Persons belonging to ethnic, religious and linguistic minorities' (1979) UN Doc E/CN.4/Sub.2/384/Rev. 1.

UN Commission of Human Rights Special Rapporteur of the Sub-Commission on Prevention of Discrimination and Protection of Minorities, Nicodème Ruhashyankiko 'Study on the Question of the Prevention and Punishment of the Crime of Genocide' (4 July 1978) UN Doc E/CN. 4/Sub. 2/ 416.

UN Commission on Human Rights Special Rapporteur Bacre Waly Ndiaye 'Report of the Special Rapporteur of the Commission on Human Rights on extrajudicial, summary or arbitrary executions (6 October 1996) UN Doc A/51/457.

UN Commission on Human Rights Special Rapporteur Radhika Coomaraswamy 'Preliminary report submitted by the Special Rapporteur on violence against women, its causes and consequences in accordance with Commission on Human Rights resolution 1994/45' (22 November 1994) Un Doc E/CN.4/1995/42.

UN Commission on Human Rights Special Rapporteur Radhika Coomaraswamy 'Report of the Special Rapporteur on violence against women, its causes and consequences, submitted in accordance with Commission on Human Rights resolution 2002/52, Addendum 1: International, regional and national developments in the area of violence against women 1994-2003' (27 February 2003) UN Doc E/CN. 4/2003/75/Add.1.

UN Commission on Human Rights, Special Rapporteur Ms. Radhika Coomaraswamy 'Violence against women perpetrated and/or condoned by the State during times of armed conflict (1997-2001)' (23 January 2001) Un Doc E/CN.4/2001/73.

UN Commission on Human Rights Special Rapporteur Sir Nigel Rodley 'Question of torture and other cruel, inhuman or degrading treatment or punishment' (3 July 2001) UN Doc A/56/156.

UN Commission on Human Rights Special Rapporteur Yakin Ertürk 'Integration of the human rights of women and the gender perspective: Violence against Women; The due diligence standard as a tool for the elimination of violence against women: Report of the Special Rapporteur on Violence against Women, its causes and consequences' (20 January 2006) E/CN.4/2006/61.

UN Commission on Human Rights 'Study of the Right of Everyone to be Free from Arbitrary Arrest, Detention and Exile' (1962) UN Doc E/CN.4/826.

UN Commission on Human Rights 'Systematic rape, sexual slavery and slave-like practices during armed conflict: Final report submitted by Ms. Gay J. McDougall, Special Rapporteur' (22 June 1998) UN Doc E/CN.4/Sub.2/1998/13.

UN Commission on Human Rights 'Torture and other Cruel, Inhuman or Degrading Treatment or Punishment: Report by the Special Rapporteur, Mr. P. Kooijmans, appointed Pursuant to Commission on Human Rights resolution 1985/33' (19 February 1986) UN Doc E/CN.4/1986/15.

UN Commission on Human Rights 'Torture or other cruel, inhuman or degrading treatment or punishment' Res 2003/32 (2003) UN Doc E/CN.4/RES/2003/32.

UN Committee on Economic, Social and Cultural Rights 'General Comment No 3: The Nature of States Parties Obligations' (26 November–14 December 1990) ESCOR [1991] Supp 3, 83.

UN Committee on Economic, Social and Cultural Rights 'General Comment No 16: The Equal Right of Men and Women to the Enjoyment of all Economic, Social and Cultural Rights (Art. 3 of the Covenant)' (11 August 2005) ESCOR [2006] Supp 2, 116.

UN Committee on Economic, Social and Cultural Rights 'General Comment No 20: Non-discrimination in economic, social and cultural rights (art. 2, para. 2, of the International Covenant on Economic, Social and Cultural Rights)' (2 July 2009) ESCOR [2009], 1.

UN Committee on the Elimination of Discrimination against Women 'General Recommendation No 12: Violence against Women' (1989) Compilation of General Comments and General Recommendations Adopted by Human Rights Treaty Bodies, U.N. Doc. HRI/GEN/1/Rev. 6 at 237 (2003).

UN Committee on the Elimination of Discrimination against Women 'General Recommendation No 19: Violence against Women' (30 January 1992) GAOR 47th Session Supp 38, 1.

UN Committee on the Elimination of Discrimination against Women 'Rules of Procedure of the Committee on the Elimination of Discrimination against Women' (2001) UN Doc A/56/38 Annex I.

UN Committee on the Elimination of Racial Discrimination 'Annual Report' (20 September 1995) GAOR 50th Session Supp 18.

UN Committee on the Elimination of Racial Discrimination 'Conclusions and recommendations of the Committee on the Elimination of Racial Discrimination on Azerbaijan' (2005) UN Doc CERD/C/AZE/CO/4.

UN Committee on the Elimination of Racial Discrimination 'Conclusions and recommendations of the Committee on the Elimination of Racial Discrimination on Romania' (2001) UN Doc CERD/C/304/Add.85.

UN Committee on the Elimination of Racial Discrimination 'General Recommendation XXV on Gender-Related Dimensions of Racial Discrimination' (20 March 2000) GAOR 55th Session Supp 18, 152.

UN Committee on the Elimination of Racial Discrimination 'General Recommendation XXVII on Discrimination against Roma' (16 August 2000) GAOR 55th Session Supp 18, 154.

UN Committee on the Rights of the Child General Comment No. 3 (2003) (17 March 2003) UN Doc CRC/GC/2003/3.

UN Committee against Torture 'Consideration of Reports Submitted by States Parties under Article 19 of the Convention: Conclusions and Recommendations of the Committee against Torture: China (12 December 2008) UN Doc CAT/C/CHN/CO/4.

UN Committee against Torture 'Report of the Committee against Torture 37th session (6-24 November 2006) 38th session (30 April-18 May 2007)' GAOR 62nd session Supp 44.

UN ECOSOC 'Commentary of the Working Group on Minorities to the United Nations Declaration on the Rights of Persons Belonging to National or Ethnic, Religious and Linguistic Minorities' (4 April 2005) UN Doc E/CN.4/Sub.2/AC. 5/2005/2.

UN ECOSOC Res 1996/12 (23 July 1997) UN Doc E/RES/1996/12.

UN ECOSOC Res 117 (VI) (3 March 1948) Sixth Session UN Doc E/734.

UN Department of Economic and Social Affairs 'Study on the right of everyone to be free from arbitrary arrest, detention and exile' (1965) UN Doc E/CN.4/826/Rev. 1.

UNGA 'Advancement of women: Note by the Secretary-General' (1 August 2011) UN Doc A/66/215.

UNGA 'Impact of Armed Conflict on Children: Report of the expert of the Secretary-General, Ms. Grac'a Machel, submitted pursuant to General Assembly resolution 48/157' (26 August 1996) UN Doc A/51/306.

UNGA 'Implementing the responsibility to protect: Report by the Secretary-General' (19 January 2009) UN Doc A/63/677.

UNGA 'In-Depth Study on All Forms of Violence against Women: Report of the Secretary-General' (6 July 2006) UN Doc A/61/122/Add.1.

UNGA 'In-Depth Study on All Forms of Violence against Women: Report of the Secretary-General' (Publication Version) (6 July 2006) http://www.un.org/womenwatch/daw/vaw/publications/English%20Study.pdf (31 October 2017).

UNGA 'Intensification of efforts to eliminate all forms of violence against women Report of the Secretary-General' (4 August 2008) UN Doc A/63/214.

UNGA Res 47/121 'The situation in Bosnia and Herzegovina' (18 December 1992) GAOR 47th Session Supp 49, 44.

UNGA Res 47/133 'Declaration on the Protection of All Persons from Enforced Disappearance' (18 December 1992) GAOR 47th Session Supp 49 vol 1, 207.

UNGA Res 54/263 'Optional Protocols to the Convention on the Rights of the Child on the Involvement of Children in Armed Conflict and on the Sale of Children, Child Prostitution and Child Pornography' (25 May 2000) GAOR 54th Session Supp 49 vol 3, 6.

UNGA Res 96 (I) 'The Crime of Genocide' (11 December 1946) GAOR 1st Session Part II Resolutions 188.

UNGA Res 217 A (III) 'Universal Declaration of Human Rights' (10 December 1948) GAOR 3rd Session Part I Resolutions 71.

UNGA Res 217 C (III) 'Fate of Minorities' (10 December 1948) GAOR 3rd Session Part I Resolutions 77.

UNGA Res 3452 (XXX) 'Declaration on the Protection of All Persons from Being Subjected to Torture and Other Cruel, Inhuman or Degrading Treatment or Punishment' (9 December 1975) 30th Session Supp 34, 91.

UNGA 'Interim report of the Special Rapporteur on torture and other cruel, inhuman or degrading treatment or punishment' (22 July 2008) UN Doc A/63/175.

UNGA Res 43/173 'Body of Principles for the Protection of All Persons under any Form of Detention or Imprisonment' (9 December 1988) GAOR 43rd Session Supp 49 vol 1, 297.

UNGA Res 47/135 'Declaration on the Rights of Persons Belonging to National or Ethnic, Religious and Linguistic Minorities' (18 December 1992) GAOR 47th Session Supp 49 vol 1, 210.

UNGA Res 48/104 'Declaration on the Elimination of Violence against Women' (20 December 1993) GAOR 48th Session Supp 49 vol 1, 217.

UNGA Res 49/146 'Third Decade to Combat Racism and Racial Discrimination' (23 December 1994) GAOR 49th Session Supp 49 vol 1, 162.

UNGA Res 60/1 '2005 World Summit Outcome' (16 September 2005) GAOR 60th Session Supp 49 vol 1, 3.

UNGA Res 61/295 'United Nations Declaration on the Rights of Indigenous Peoples' (13 September 2007) GAOR 61st Session Supp 49 vol 3, 15.

UNGA Res 61/143 'Intensification of Efforts to Eliminate all Forms of Violence against Women' (19 December 2006) GAOR 61st Session Supp 49 vol 1, 326.

UNGA Sixth Committee (25 October 1948) UN Doc A/C.6/SR.83.

UN Guidelines on the Role of the Prosecutors (1990) <http://www.ohchr.org/EN/ProfessionalInterest/Pages/RoleOfProsecutors.aspx> (31 October 2017).

United Nations Diplomatic Conference of Plenipotentiaries on the Establishment of an International Criminal Court 'Report of the Preparatory Committee on the Establishment of an International Criminal Court: Addendum' (15-17 July 1998) A/Conf. 183/2/Add.1.

United Nations Department of Peacekeeping Operations *Review of the Sexual Violence Elements of the Judgments of the International Criminal Tribunal for the Former Yugoslavia, the International Criminal Tribunal for Rwanda and the Special Court for Sierra Leone in the Light of Security Council Resolution 1820* (United Nations New York 2010).

United Nations International Human Rights Instruments 'Integrating the gender perspective into the work of United Nations human rights treaty bodies: Report by the Secretary-General' (3 September 1998) UN Doc HRI/MC/1998/6.

UNHCR EXCOM Conclusion No 39 (XXXVI) 'Refugee Women and International Protection' (1985) UN Doc HRC/IP/2.

UNHCR 'Guidelines on International Protection No 1: Gender-Related Persecution Within the Context of Article 1A(2) of the 1951 Convention and/or its 1967 Protocol Relating to the Status of Refugees' (2002) UN Doc HCR/GIP/02/01.

UNHCR 'Guidelines on Refugee Women' (1991) UN Doc EC/SCP/67.

UNHCR 'Sexual and Gender-Based Violence against Refugees, Returnees and Internally Displaced Persons: Guidelines for Prevention and Response' (United Nations High Commissioner for Refugees 2003).

UNHRC 'Consideration of Reports Submitted by States Parties under Article 40 of the Covenant: Israel' (28 July 1998) GAOR 53rd Session Supp 40 vol 1.

UNHRC 'General Comment No 15: The Positions of Aliens under the Covenant' (9 April 1986) GAOR 41st Session Supp 40, 117.

UN HRC 'General Comment No 18: Non-Discrimination' (9 November 1989) GAOR 45th Session Supp 40 vol 1, 173, para. 7.

UN HRC 'General Comment No 20: Replaces General Comment 7 concerning Prohibition of Torture and Cruel Treatment or Punishment (Art. 7)' (3 April 1992) GAOR 47th Session Supp 40, 193.

UNHRC 'General Comment No 23: The Rights of Minorities (Art. 27)' (8 April 1994) GAOR 49th Session Supp 40 vol 1, 106.

UNHRC 'General Comment No 24: Issues relating to Reservations Made upon Ratification or Accession to the Covenant or the Optional Protocols thereto, or in Relation to Declarations under Article 41 of the Covenant' (11November 1994) GAOR 50th Session Supp 40 vol 1, 119.

UNHRC 'General Comment No 28: Equality of Rights between Men and Women (Art. 3)' (29 March 2000) GAOR 55th Session Supp 40 vol 1, 133.

UN HRC 'General Comment No 29: Derogations from Provisions of the Covenant during a State of Emergency (Art. 4)' (24 July 2001) GAOR 56th Session Supp 40 vol 1, 202.

UNHRC 'General Comment No 31: The Nature of the General Legal Obligation Imposed on States Parties to the Covenant' (29 March 2004) GAOR 59th Session Supp 40 vol 1, 175.

UNHR Council 'Resolution 23/25: Accelerating efforts to eliminate all forms of violence against women: preventing and responding to rape and other forms of sexual violence (25 June 2013) UN Doc /HRC/RES/23/25.

UN HR Council 'Resolution 16/7: Mandate of the Special Rapporteur on violence against

women, its causes and consequences' (8 April 2011) UN Doc A /HRC/RES/16/7.

UNICEF and Coalition to Stop the Use of Child Soldiers *Guide to the Optional Protocol on the Involvement of Children in Armed Conflict* (UNICEF New York 2003).

UNIFEM 'CEDAW and Security Council Resolution 1325: A Quick Guide' <https://www.un.org/ruleoflaw/blog/document/cedaw-and-security-council-resolution-1325-a-quick-guide/> (31 October 2017).

UN ILC 'Draft Articles against the Peace and Security of Mankind' Yearbook of the International Law Commission [1991] vol II part II UNYBILC 79-107.

UN ILC 'Draft Articles on Responsibility of States for Internationally Wrongful Acts' (2001) GAOR 56th Session Supp 10, 43.

UN ILC 'Draft Code of Crimes against the Peace and Security of Mankind' in 'Report of the International Law Commission on the Work of Its Forty-Third Session' (29 April – 19 July 1991) (1991) vol II part II UNYBILC 79.

UN ILC 'Draft Code of Crimes against the Peace and Security of Mankind' (1996) GAOR 51st Session Supp 10, 9.

UN ILC 'Draft Statute for an International Criminal Court with commentaries' in 'Report of the International Law Commission on the Work of Its Forty-Sixth Session' (2 May–22 July 1994) GAOR 49th Session Supp 10.

UN ILC 'Principles of International Law recognized in the Charter of the Nürnberg Tribunal and in the Judgment of the Tribunal, with commentaries'in (1950) vol II UNYBILC 375-378.

UN ILC 'Report of the International Law Commission on the Work of Its Forty-Sixth Session' (2 May–22 July 1994) GAOR 49th Session Supp 10, 40.

UN International Criminal Tribunal for the Former Yugoslavia 'Rules of Procedure and Evidence' (as amended 10 December 2009) IT/32/Rev. 44.

UN 'Pamphlet No 8 of the UN Guide for Minorities' available at http://www.ohchr.org/Documents/Publications/GuideMinorities8en.pdf (31 October 2017).

UNSC 'Annex II: Final Report of the United Nations Commission of Experts established Pursuant to Security Council Resolution 780 (1992)' (27 May 1994) UN Doc S/1994/674.

UNSC 'Final Report of the Commission of Experts Established Pursuant to Security Council Resolution 935 (1994): Annex IX' (9 December 1994) UN Doc S/1994/1405, Section D.

UNSC 'Report of the Secretary-General pursuant to Paragraph 2 of Security Council Resolution 808 (1993)' (3 May 1993) UN Doc S/25704.

UNSC Res 808 (1993) (22 February 1993) SCOR 48th Year 28.

UNSC Res 827 (1993) (25 May 1993) SCOR 48th Year 29.

UNSC Res 955 (1994) (8 November 1994) SCOR 49th Year 15.

UNSC Res 1366 (2001) (30 August 2001) SCOR [1 January 2001–31 July 2002] 283.

UNSC Res 1674 (2006) (28 April 2006) UN Doc S/Res/1674.

UNSC Res 1820 (2008) (19 June 2008) SCOR [1 August 2007–31 July 2008] 154.

UN Secretariat 'First Draft of the Genocide Convention' (26 June 1947) UN Doc E/447.

UN Secretary-General 'Address to the Commission on Human Rights' (7 April 2004) <http://www.un.org/press/en/2004/sgsm9245.doc.htm> (31 October 2017).

UN Standard Minimum Rules for the Treatment of Prisoners (1955) <http://www.ohchr.org/Documents/ProfessionalInterest/treatmentprisoners.pdf> (31 October 2017).

UNSC 'Statute of the International Criminal Tribunal for the Former Yugoslavia' UNSC Res 827 (1993) (25 May 1993) SCOR 48th Year 29.

UNSC 'Statute of the International Tribunal for Rwanda' UNSC Res 955 (1994) (8 November 1994) SCOR 49th Year 13.

UNSC 'Statute of the Special Tribunal for Lebanon' UNSC Res 1757 (2007) (30 May 2007) SCOR [1 August 2006–31 July 2007] 21.

UN World Conference on Human Rights 'Vienna Declaration and Programme of Action' (25 June 1993) UN Doc A/CONF.157/23.

UN World Conference against Racism, Racial Discrimination, Xenophobia and Related Intolerance 'Report' (2001) UN Doc A/CONF.189/12.

UN World Conference on Women (4th) 'Beijing Declaration and Platform for Action' (17 October 1995) UN Doc A/CONF.177/20, 4.

US Department of Justice, Office of Legal Counsel 'Memorandum for Alberto R. Gonzales, Counsel to the President Re: Standard of Conduct for Interrogation under 18 U.S.C. §§ 2340-2340A' (1 August 2002) https://www.aclu.org (31 October 2017).

US Department of State 'Letter from Robert A Bradtke, Acting Assistant Secretary for Legislative Affairs, to Senator Arlen Spector' (27 January 1992) as cited in Theodor Meron 'Rape as a Crime under International Humanitarian Law' (1993) 87(3) American Journal of International Law 424-428, 427.

United States Representative to the International Conference on Military Trials Robert H Jackson 'Planning Memorandum' (US Government Printing Office Washington 1949).

Vienna Convention on the Law of Treaties (concluded 23 May 1969, entered into force 27 January 1980) 1155 UNTS 331.

Women's Caucus for Gender Justice in the International Criminal Court 'Recommendations and Commentary for December 1997 PrepCom on the Establishment of an International Criminal Court' (1–12 December 1997) WC.5.6-9.

World Health Organization: Understanding Violence against Women: Femicide (World Health Organization 2012) 1-3 <http://apps.who.int/iris/bitstream/10665/77421/1/WHO_RHR_12.38_eng.pdf> (31 October 2017).

Literature

---- *Le Refus de L'oubli: La Politique de Disparation Forcée de Personne*s (Editions Berger-Levrault Paris 1981).

Amal Alamuddin 'Collection of Evidence' in Karim A A Khan, Caroline Buisma and Christopher Gosnell (eds) *Principles of International Criminal Justice* (OUP Oxford 2010).

Gudmundur Alfredsson 'Minorities, Indigenous and Tribal Peoples: Definition of Terms as a Matter of International Law' in Nazila Ghanea and Alexandra Xanthaki (eds) *Minorities, Peoples and Self-Determination, Essays in Honour of Patrick Thornberry* (Nijhoff Leiden 2005).

Jessica Almqvist 'Complementarity and Human Rights: A Litmus Test for the International Criminal Court' (2008) 30 Loyola of Los Angeles International and Comparative Law Review 20 (2008) 336-366.

Philip Alston 'The Historical Origins of the Concept of "General Comments" in Human Rights Law' in Laurence Boisson de Chazournes and Vera Gowlland-Debbas *The International Legal System in Quest of Equity and Universality: Liber Amicorum Georges Abi-Saab* (Nijhoff The Hague 2001).

Noora Arajarvi 'Between Lex Lata and Lex Ferenda – Customary International (Criminal) law and the Principle of Legality ' (2010-11) 15 Tilburg Law Review 163-182.

Mahnoush H Arsanjani 'The Rome Statute of the International Criminal Court' (1999) 93 American Journal of International Law 22-43.

Andrew Ashworth *Principles of Criminal Law* (6th ed OUP Oxford 2009).

Anthony Aust *Modern Treaty Law and Practice* (Cambridge University Press Cambridge 2000).

M Cherif Bassiouni *Crimes against Humanity in International Criminal Law* (2nd ed Kluwer Law International The Hague 1999).

M Cherif Bassiouni and Peter Manikas *The Law of the International Criminal Tribunal for the Former Yugoslavia* (Transnational Publishers Irvington-on-Hudson 1996).

M Cherif Bassiouni, 'Accountability for Violations of International Humanitarian Law and Other Serious Violations of Human Rights' in M Cherif Bassiouni (ed) *Post-Conflict Justice* (Transnational Publishers Ardsley New York 2002).

M Cherif Bassiouni 'The Proscribing Function of International Criminal Law in the Process of International Protection of Human Rights' (1982-3) 9 Yale Journal of World Public Order 193-216.

Cesare *Beccaria On Crime and Punishment and Other Writings* (reprinted Cambridge University Press 1995).

Barbara Bedont 'Gender-Specific Provisions in the Statute of the International Criminal Court' in Flavia Lattanzi and William Schabas *Essays on the Rome Statute of the International Criminal Court* Volume I (Il Sirente Ripa Fagnano Alto 1999).

Barbara Bedont and Katherine Hall-Martinez 'Ending Impunity for Gender Crimes under the International Criminal Court' (1999) 6 Brown Journal of World Affairs 65-85.

Johannes Binder *The Human Dimension of the OSCE: From Recommendation to Implementation* (Verlag Österreich Vienna 2001).

Gilbert Bitti 'Article 21 of the Statute of the ICC and the treatment of sources of law in the jurisprudence of the ICC' in Carsten Stahn and Göran Sluiter (eds) *The Emerging Practice of the International Criminal Court* (Brill The Hague 2008) 286-304

Michael Bohlander and Mark Findlay ,The Use of Domestic Sources as a Basis for International Criminal Law Principles' (2002) 2 Yearbook of International Law and Jurisprudence 3–26.

Machtheld Boot, Rodney Dixon and Christopher K Hall 'Article 7: Crimes against Humanity' in Otto Triffterer Commentary on the Rome Statute of the International Criminal Court (2nd edition Beck Munich 2008) 159-273.

Machteld Boot *Genocide, Crimes Against Humanity, War Crimes-Nullum Crimen Sine Lege and the Subject Matter Jurisdiction of the International Criminal Court* (Intersenita Antwerp 2002).

Theo van Boven 'Categories of Rights' in Daniel Moeckli, Sangeeta Shah and Sandesh Sivakumaran (eds) *International Human Rights Law* (OUP Oxford 2010) 173-188.

Theo van Boven 'Distinguishing Criteria of Human Rights' in Karel Vasak and Philip Alston (eds) *The International Dimensions of Human Rights* (Greenwood Press Wetport 1982).

Christina Boyd, Lee Epstein and Andrew Martin 'Untangling the Causal Effects of Sex on Judging' (2010) 54 American Journal of Political Science 398-411.

Bruce Broomhall 'Art 22: *Nullum crimen sine lege'* Otto Triffterer *Commentary on the Rome Statute of the International Criminal Court* (2nd edition Beck Munich 2008) 713-729.

Bruce Broomhall *International Justice and the International Criminal Court* (OUP Oxford 2003).

A Widney Brown and Laura Grenfell 'The International Crime of Gender-Based Persecution and the Taliban' (2003) 4 Melbourne Journal of International Law 347–75.

Ian Brownlie *Principles of Public International Law* (6th ed OUP Oxford 2012).

J Herman Burgers and Hans Danelius *The United Nations Convention against Torture: A Handbook on the Convention against Torture and Other Cruel, Inhuman or Degrading Treatment or Punishment* (Nijhoff Dordrecht 1988).

Doris Buss 'Learning our lesions: The Rwanda Tribunal record on prosecuting rape' in Clare McGlynn and Vanessa Munro Rethinking Rape Law: International and Comparative Perspectives (Routledge Abingdon 2010) 61-75.

Antonio Cassese 'Crimes against Humanity' in Antonio Cassese, Paola Gaeta John RWD Jones (eds) *The Rome Statue of the International Criminal Court: A Commentary* vol 1 (OUP Oxford 2002) 353-78.

Antonio Cassese *International Criminal Law* (2nd edition OUP Oxford 2008).

Hilary Charlesworth and Christine Chinkin *The Boundaries of International Law: A Feminist Analysis* (Manchester University Press Manchester 2000).

Hilary Charlesworth, Christine Chinkin and Shelley Wright 'Feminist approaches to international law' (1991) 85(4) *American Journal of International Law* 613-45.

Hilary Charlesworth 'Feminist Methods in International Law' (1999) 93 American Journal of International Law 379-394.

Hilary Charlesworth 'Inside/Outside: women and the International Human Rights System' in Aristotle Constantinides and Nikos Zaikos *The Diversity of International Law: Essays in Honour of Professor Kalliopi K Koufa* (Nijhoff Leiden 2009).

Hilary Charlesworth 'International human rights law: A portmanteau for feminist norms?' in Gülay Caglar, Elisabeth Prügl and Susanne Zwingel Feminist Strategies in International Governance (Routledge Abingdon, Oxon/New York 2013) 21-37.

Alison Cole 'International criminal law and sexual violence: an overview' in Clare McGlynn and Vanessa Munro *Rethinking Rape Law: International and Comparative Perspectives* (Routledge Abingdon 2010) 47-60.

Rhonda Copelon, 'Recognizing the egregious in the everyday: domestic violence as torture' (1994) 25 *Columbia Human Rights Law Review*, 291-367.

Georg Dahm, Jost Delbrück and Rüdiger Wolfrum *Völkerrecht* Volume I/1: *Die Grundlagen; die Völkerrechtssubjekte* (2nd edition De Gruyter Berlin 1989).

Georg Dahm, Jost Delbrück and Rüdiger Wolfrum *Völkerrecht* Volume I/2: *Der Staat und andere Völkerrechtssubjekte; Räume unter internationaler Verwaltung* (2nd edition De Gruyter Berlin 2002).

Georg Dahm, Jost Delbrück and Rüdiger Wolfrum *Völkerrecht* Volume I/3: *Die Formen des völkerrechtlichen Handelns; Die inhaltliche Ordnung der internationalen Gemeinschaft* (2nd edition De Gruyter Berlin 2002).

Mirjan Damaška 'What is the Point of International Criminal Justice?' (2008) 83 Chicago-Kent Law Review 329-369.

Mireille Delmas-Marty and Antonio Cassese (eds) *Crimes Internationaux Et Jurisdictions Internationales* (Presses Unversitaires de France Paris 2002).

Oliver Diggelmann and Tilman Altwicker 'Is There Something Like a Constitution of International Law? A Critical Analysis of the Debate on World Constitutionalism' (2008) 68 ZaöRV 623-650.

Louise Doswald-Beck and Sylvain Vité 'International Humanitarian Law and Human Rights Law' (1993) 293 International Review of the Red Cross 94-119.

Helen Durham and Katie O'Byrne 'The dialogue of difference: gender perspectives on international humanitarian law' 92 (2010) International Review of the Red Cross 31–52.

George E Edwards 'International Human Rights Challenges to the New International Criminal Court: the Search and Seizure Right to Privacy' (2001) 26 Yale Journal of International Law 323-412.

Alice Edwards 'Everyday rape: International human rights law and violence against women in peacetime' in Clare McGlynn and Vanessa Munro *Rethinking Rape Law: International and Comparative Perspectives* (Routledge Abingdon 2010) 92-108.

Alice Edwards *Violence against Women under International Human Rights Law* (CUP Cambridge 2011).

Alice Edwards ,Violence against Women as Sex Discrimination: Judging the Jurisprudence of the United Nations Human Rights Treaty Bodies' (2008) 18 Texas Journal of Women and the Law 1–54.

Asbjörn Eide and Rianne Letschert, 'Institutional Developments in the United Nations and at the Regional Level' (2007) 14(2) International Journal on Minority and Group Rights 299-332.

William J Fenrick 'The crime against humanity of persecution in the jurisprudence of the ICTY' (2001) 32 Netherlands Yearbook of International Law 81-96.

Peter Finell *Accountability under Human Rights Law and International criminal law against Minority Groups Committed by Non-State Actors* (Åbo Akademi Institute for Human Rights, Åbo/Turku May 2002).

Gerald G Fitzmaurice 'The Law and Procedure of the International Court of Justice: Treaty Interpretation and Certain Other Treaty Points' (1951) 28 *British Yearbook of International Law* 28 1-28.

Sir Gerald G Fitzmaurice 'The Law and Procedure of the International Court of Justice 1951-4: Treaty Interpretation and Other Treaty Points' (1957) 33 *British Yearbook of International Law* 203-38.

Joan Fitzpatrick *Human Rights in Crisis: The International System for Protecting Rights during States of Emergency* (University of Pennsylvania Press Philadelphia 1994).

Wolfgang Friedmann 'The North Sea Continental Shelf Cases – A Critique' (1970) 64 American Journal of International Law 229-240.

Kenneth S Gallant 'International Criminal Courts and the Making of Public International Law: New Roles for International Organizations and Individuals' (2010) 43 The John Marshall Law Review 603–34.

Judith Gardam and Hilary Charlesworth 'Protection of Women in Armed Conflicts' (2000) 22(1) *Human Rights Quarterly* 148-166.

Judith Gardam and Michelle J Jarvis *Women Armed Conflict and International Law* (Kluwer Law International The Hague 2001).

Juila Gebhard 'Arguing Human Rights from the Bench? How Judges in International Criminal Courts Perceive International Human Rights Law' in Mayeul Hiéramente and Patricia Schneider *The Defence in International Criminal Trials: Observations on the Role of the Defence at the ICTY, ICTR and ICC* (Nomos 2016), 72-92.

Julia Gebhard 'A Race between Education and Catastrophe? The Role of Minority Issues in the Prevention of Crimes under International Law' (Master Thesis University of Lund 2006) available at http://lup.lub.lu.se/luur/download?func=downloadFile&recordOId=1555279&fileOId=1563606 (31 October 2017).

Christine Gray 'The use of force and the international legal order' in Malcolm D Evans (ed) *International Law* (3rd ed OUP Oxford 2006) 615-650.

Nienke Grossmann ‚Sex Representation on the Bench and the Legitimacy oft he International Criminal Courts' (2011) 11 Internationnal Criminal Law Review 643-653.

Gerhard Hafner and Christina Binder 'The Interpretation of Article 21 (3) ICC Statute, Opinion Reviewed' (2004) 9 Austrian Review of International and European Law 163-190.

Gerhard Hafner 'Pros and Cons Ensuing From Fragmentation of International Law' (2004) 25 Michigan Journal of International Law 849-863.

John Hagan, Ron Levi and Gebrielle Ferrales 'Swaying the Hands of Justice: The Internal and External Dynamics of Regime Change at the International Criminal Tribunal for the Former Yugoslavia' (2006) 31(3) Law and Social Inquiry 585-616.

John Hagan and Ron Levi 'War Crimes and the Force of Law' (2005) 83(4) Social Forces 1499-1534.

Lotta Harbom and Peter Wallensteen *Patterns of Major Conflicts 1997-2008- Stockholm International Peace Research Institute Yearbook 2007: Armaments, Disarmaments and International Security* (OUP Oxford 2007).

David Harris, Michael O'Boyle and Others *Law of the European Convention on Human Rights* (OUP Oxford 2014).

Wolff Heintschel von Heinegg 'Criminal International Law and Customary International Law' in Andreas Zimmermann (ed) *International Criminal Law and the Current Development of Public International Law* (Duncker and Humblot Berlin 2003) 27-46.

Laurence R Helfer 'Forum Shopping for Human Rights' (1999) 148 University of Pennsylvania Law Review 285-400.

Tamás Hoffmann 'The Gentle Humanizer of Humanitarian Law – Antonio Cassese and the Creation of the Customary Law of Non-International Armed Conflict' in Carsten Stahn and Larissa van den Herik (eds) *Future Perspectives on International Criminal Justice* (Asser Press Leiden 2010). 58-80.

Rainer Hofmann 'The Framework Convention for the Protection of National Minorities: An Introduction' in Marc Weller (ed) *The Rights of Minorities: A Commentary on the European Framework Convention for the Protection of National Minorities*, (Oxford University Press, Oxford/New York 2005) 1-24.

Brigid Inder 'Reflection: Gender Issues and Child Soldiers – The Case of Thomas Lubanga Dyilo' The Lubanga Trial at the International Criminal Court (31 August 2011) http://www.lubangatrial.org/2011/08/31/reflection-gender-issues-and-child-soldiers-the-case-of-prosecutor-v-thomas-lubanga-dyilo-2/ (31 October 2017).

Segun Jegede 'The Right to A Fair Trial in International Criminal Law' in Chile Eboe-Osuji *Protecting Humanity: Essays in International Law and Policy in Honour of Navanethem Pillay* (Nijhoff Leiden 2010).

Hans-Heinrich Jeschenk 'The General Principles of International Criminal Law Set out in Nuremberg, as Mirrored in the ICC Statute' (2004) 2 Journal of International Criminal Justice 38-55.

Adam Jones *Genocide* (Routledge London 2006).

Annika Jones 'Insights into an Emerging Relationship: Use of Human Rights Jurisprudence at the International Criminal Court' (2016) 16 Human Rights Law Review, 701-29.

Christiane Kamardi *Die Ausformung einer Prozessordnung sui generis durch das ICTY unter Berücksichtigung des Fair-Trial Prinzips* (Springer Berlin 2009).

Jacob Katz Cogan 'International Courts and Fair Trials: Difficulties and Perspectives' (2002) 27 Yale Journal of International Law 111-140.

Hans Kelsen *Principles of International Law* (Rinehart and Company New York 1952).

Hans Kelsen 'Will the Judgment of the Nuremberg Tribunals Constitute a Precedent in International Law?' (1947) 1 International Law Quarterly 153-71.

Hunjoon Kim and Kathryn Sikkink 'Explaining the Deterrence Effect for Human Rights Prosecutions for Transitional Countries' (2010) 54(4) International Studies Quarterly 939-963.

Kimi Lynn King and Megan Greeing ‚Gender Justice of Just Gender? The Role of Gender in the Sexual Assault Decisions at the International Criminal Tribunal of the Former Yugoslavia‘ (2007) 88 Social Science Quarterly 1049-1071

Kriangsak Kittichaisaree *International Criminal Law* (OUP Oxford/New York 2001).

Uwe Kranenpohl ‚Die Bedeutung von Interpretationsmethoden und Dogmatik in der Entscheidungspraxis des Bundesverfassungsgerichts' 48 (2009) Der Staat 387–409.

Claus Kreß 'Nulla poena nullum crimen sine lege' in Rüdiger Wolfrum (ed) *Max Planck Encyclopedia of Public International Law* 2nd ed (OUP 2012) vol VII 889-899.

Claus Kreß 'On the Outer Limits of Crimes against Humanity: The Concept of Organization within the Policy Requirement: Some Reflections on the March 2010 ICC *Kenya* Decision' (2010) 23 Leiden Journal of International Law 855–73.

Thomas Kruessmann (ed) ICTY: Towards a Fair Trial? (Vienna Neuer Wissenschaftlicher Verlag 2008).

Julian Ku and Jide Nzelibe 'Do InternationalCriminal Tribunals Deter or Exacerbate Humanitarian Atrocities?' (2006) 84(4) WashingtonUniversity Law Review 777-833.

Will Kymlicka *Multicultural Citizenship: A Liberal Theory on Minority Rights* (OUP Oxford 1996).

Hersch Lauterpacht 'Codification and Development of International Law' (1955) 49(1) American Journal of International Law.

Hersch Lauterpacht *International Law and Human Rights* (FA Praeger London 1950).

Rüdiger Lautmann *Freie Rechtsfindung und Methodik der Rechtsanwendung* (C Schon München 1967).

Rüdiger Lautmann *Justiz—Die stille Gewalt: Teilnehmende Beobachtung und entscheidungssoziologische Analyse* (Athenäum Verlag Frankfurt am Main 1972).

Fleur van Leeuwen *Women's Rights are Human Rights: The Practice of the United Nations Human Rights Committee and the United Nations Committee on Economic, Social and Cultural Rights* (Intersentia Antwerp 2010).

Franz von Liszt ‚Die deterministischen Gegner der Zweckstrafe‘ (1893) 3 Zeitschrift für die gesamte Strafrechtswissenschaft 325-70.

Catharine A MacKinnon 'Rape, Genocide and Women's Human Rights' (1994) 17 Harvard Women's Law Journal 5-16.

Ernst Gottfried Mahrenholz 'Probleme der Verfassungsauslegung, Verfassungsinterpretation aus praktischer Sicht' in Hans-Peter Schneider (ed) *Verfassungsrecht zwischen Wissenschaft und Richterkunst: Konrad Hesse zum 70. Geburtstag* (Heideberg Müller 1990) 53–65.

Chad G Marzen 'The Furundzija Judgment and its Continued Vitality in International Law' (2010) 43 Creighton Law Review 505–27.

Margaret McAuliffe deGuzman 'Art. 21: Applicable law' in Otto Triffterer *Commentary on the Rome Statute of the International Criminal Court* (2nd edition Beck Munich 2008) 701-712.

Robert McCorquodale 'Non-state actors and international human rights law' in Sarah Joseph and Adam McBeth (eds) *Research Handbook on International Human Rights Law* (Elgar Cheltenham 2010).

G McIntryre 'Defending Human Rights in the Area of International Humanitarian Law: Human Rights in the Jurisprudence of the ICTY' in Gideon Boas and William A Schabas (eds) *International Criminal Law Developments in the Case Law of the ICTY* (Brill Leiden 2003).

Warwick A McKean *Equality and Discrimination in International Law* (Clarendon Oxford 1983).

Theodor Meron 'The Geneva Conventions as Customary Law' 1987 81(2) American Journal of International Law 348-370.

Theodor Meron 'Human Rights Marches into New Territory: The Enforcement of International Human Rights in International Criminal Tribunals' Fourth Marek Nowicki Memorial Lecture (28 November 2008) <http://web.ceu.hu/legal/pdf%20documents/Nowicki/Meron_Enforcement%20of%20HRwarsawnowicki13nov 08.pdf > (last accessed on 10 June 2013; speech no longer accessible online).

Theodor Meron 'Rape as a Crime under International Humanitarian Law' (1993) 87(3) American Journal of International Law 424-428.

Theodor Meron 'Revival of Customary Humanitarian Law' (2004) 99(4) American Journal of International Law 817-834.

Minority Rights Group International 'Briefing: Why a minority rights approach to conflict? The case of Southern Sudan' (2008) <http://www.academia.edu/3622460/Why_a_minority_rights_approach_to_conflict_The_case_of_Southern_Sudan> (31 October 2017).

Christopher W Mullins and Dawn L Rothe 'The Ability of the International Criminal Court to Deter Violations of International Criminal Law: A Theoretical Assessment' (2010) 10(5) International Criminal Law Review 771-785.

Vesna Nikolic-Ristanovic 'Sexual Violence, International Law and Restorative Justice' in Doris Buss and Ambreena Manji (eds) *International Law-Modern Feminist Approaches* (Hart Portland 2005).

Jonas Nilsson 'The Principle of Nullum Crimen Sine Lege' in Olaoluwa Olusanya *Rethinking International Criminal Law: The Substantive Part* (Europa Law Publishing Groningen 2007).

Manfred Nowak and Elisabeth McArthur *The United Nations Convention against Torture: A Commentary* (OUP Oxford 2008).

Manfred Nowak *U. N. Covenant on Civil and Political Rights: CCPR Commentary* (N P Engel Kehl 2005).

Stefan Oeter 'Der Schutz nationaler Minderheiten im Völkerrecht' in Rüdiger Wolfrum (ed) *Gleichheit und Nichtdiskriminierung im nationalen und internationalen Menschenrechtsschutz*

(Springer Berlin 2003) 187-214.

Valerie Oosterveld 'The Definition of "Gender" in the Rome Statute of the International Court: A Step Forward of Back for International Criminal Justice?' (2005) 18 Harvard Human Rights Journal 55-84.

Valerie Oosterveld 'Gender, Persecution, and the International Criminal Court: Refugee Law's Relevance to the Crime against Humanity of Gender-based Persecution' (2006) 17 Duke Journal of Comparative and International Law 49–89.

Jaime Oraá *Human Rights in States of Emergency in International Law* (Clarendon Press Oxford 1992).

Angela Paul *Kritische Analyse und Reformvorschlag zu Art. II Genozidkonvention* (Springer Berlin 2008).

Alain Pellet 'Applicable Law' in Antonio Cassese, Paola Gaeta John RWD Jones (eds) *The Rome Statue of the International Criminal Court: A Commentary* vol 2 (OUP Oxford 2002) 1051-1084.

Anne Peters 'Article 24' in Bruno Simma, Daniel Khan and others *The Charter of the United Nations: A Commentary* (3rd ed OUP Oxford 2012) 761-786.

Anne Peters 'Humanity as the A and Ω of Sovereignty' (2009) 20 EJIL 513-544.

Navanethem Pillay 'Protection of the Health of Women through International Criminal Law: Can International Criminal Law contribute to Efforts to Improve the Health of Women?' (2008) 22 Emory International Law Review 15–28.

Giulia Pinzauti 'The European Court of Human Rights' Incidental Application of International Criminal Law and Humanitarian Law- A Critical Discussion of *Kononov v. Latvia*' (2008) 6 Journal of International Criminal Justice 1043-1060.

Fausto Pocar 'International Criminal Tribunals and Serious Violations of International Humanitarian Law against Civilians and Prisoners of War' in Manoj Kumar Sinha (ed) *International Criminal Law and Human Rights* (Manak Delhi 2010) 1-26.

Helen Quane 'Rights in Conflict? The Rationale and Implications of using Human Rights in Conflict Prevention Strategies' (2007) 47 Virginia. Journal of International Law 463-523.

Amy E Ray, 'The Shame of it: Gender-Based Terrorism in the Former Yugoslavia and the Failure of International Human Rights Law to Comprehend the Injuries' (1997) 46 *American University Law Review* 793-840.

Darryl Robinson Defining "Crimes against Humanity" at the Rome Conference' (1999) 93 American Journal of International Law 43-57.

Patrick Robinson 'The Right to a Fair Trail in International Law, with Specific Reference to the Work of the ICTY' (2009) 3 Berkeley Journal of International Law Publicist 1-11.

Sherrie L Russell-Brown 'Rape as Genocide' (2003) 21 Berkeley Journal of International Law 350-374.

George Abi-Saab 'Fragmentation or Unification: Some Concluding Remarks' (1999) 31 NYU Journal of International Law and Politics 919-932.

Jean-Paul Sartre 'On Genocide' in Richard A Falk, Gabriel Kolko and Robert Jay (eds) *Crimes of War* (Random House New York 1971) 534-49.

Damien Scalia 'Long-term sentences in international criminal law: Do they meet the standards set out by the European Court of Human Rights?' (2011) 9(3) Journal of International Criminal Justice 669-687.

William A Schabas 'Article 6: Genocide' in O Triffterer *Commentary on the Rome Statute of the International Criminal Court* (2nd edition Beck Munich 2008) 143-157.

Wiliam A Schabas 'Developments relating to Minorities in the Law of Genocide' in Kristin Henrard and Robert Dunbar *Synergies in Minority Protection: European and International Law Perspectives* (CUP Cambridge 2008).

William A Schabas *Genocide in International Law: The Crime of Crimes* (CUP Cambridge 2009).

William A Schabas *The International Criminal Court: A Commentary on the Rome Statute* (OUP Oxford 2010).

William A. Schabas *Preventing Genocide and Mass Killing: The Challenge for the United Nations* (Minority Rights Group International London 2006) https://eprints.mdx.ac.uk/7840/1/MRGGenocideReport.pdf (31 October 2017).

William A Schabas 'Prosecuting Dr Strangelove, Goldfinger, and the Joker at the International Criminal Court: Closing the Loopholes' (2010) 23 Leiden Journal of International Law 847–53.

William A Schabas 'Article 6: Genocide' in Otto Triffterer *Commentary on the Rome Statute of the International Criminal Court* (2nd edition Beck Munich 2008) 143-157.

William A Schabas 'Article 67: Rights of the Accused' in Otto Triffterer *Commentary on the Rome Statute of the International Criminal Court* (2nd edition Beck Munich 2008) 1247-1274.

Egon Schwelb 'Crimes against Humanity' (1946) 23 British Yearbook of International Law 178-226.

Anja Seibert-Fohr *Prosecuting Serious Human Rights Violations* (OUP Oxford 2009).

Amartya Sen *Identity and Violence: The Illusion of Destiny* (WW Norton & Co New York 2006).

Mohamed Shahabuddeen, 'Does the Principle of Legality Stand in the Way of Progressive Development of Law?' (2004) 2 Journal of International Criminal Justice 1007-1017.

Malcolm N Shaw *International Law* (6th edition CUP Cambridge 2008).

Scott Sheeran 'Reconceptualizing States of Emergency under International Human Rights Law' (2012-13) 34 Michigan Journal of International Law 491-557.

Dinah Sheldon 'The Human Rights Judgments: The Jurisprudence of Regional Human Rights Tribunals – Lex Specialis or Lex Regionis?' in William A. Schabbas ans Shannonbrooke Murphy Research Handbook on International Courts and Tribunals (Edward Elgar Cheltenham/Northampton 2017).

Daniel Sheppard 'The International Criminal Court and "Internationally Recognized Human Rights": Understanding Article 21(3) of the Rome Statute' (2010) 10 International Criminal Law Review 43-71.

Bruno Simma and Andreas L Paulus 'The Responsibility of Individuals for Human Rights Abuses in Internal Conflict: Toward a World Public Order of Human Dignity' (1999) 93 American Journal of International Law 302-315.

Sandesh Sivakumaran 'Torture in International Human Rights and International Humanitarian Law: The Actor and the *Ad hoc* Tribunals' (2005) 18 Leiden Journal of International Law 541-556.

Robert D Sloane 'The Expressive Capacity of International Punishment: the Limits of the National Law Analogy and the Potential of International Criminal Law' (2007) 43(1) Stanford Journal of International Law 39-94.

James Sloan 'The International Criminal Tribunal for the Former Yugoslavia and Fair Trial Rights: A Closer Look' (1996) 9(2) Leiden Journal of International Law 479-501.

Göran Sluiter ,Human rights protection in the ICC pre-trial phase' in Carsten Stahn and Göran Sluiter (eds) *The Emerging Practice of the International Criminal Court* (Nijhoff Leiden 2009) 459-476.

Alette Smeulers and Fred Grünfeld *International Crimes and Other Gross Human Rights Violations* (Nijhoff Leiden 2011).

Carsten Stahn 'Internationaler Menschenrechtsschutz und Völkerstrafrecht' (1999) 3 Kritische Justiz 343-355.

Carsten Stahn and Sven-R. Eiffler 'Über das Verhältnis von Internationalem Menschenrechtsschutz und Völkerstrafrecht anhand des Statuts von Rom' (1999) 82(1) Kritische Vierteljahresschrift für Gesetzgebung und Rechtswissenschaft 253-277.

Cate Steains 'Gender Issues' in Roy S Lee (ed) *The International Criminal Court: The Making of the Rome Statute* (Kluwer Law International The Hague 1999) 357–390.

Lyal S Sunga 'International Criminal Law: Protection of Minorities' in Zelim A Skurbaty (ed) *Beyond a One-Dimensional State: An Emerging Right to Autonomy?* (Nijhoff Leiden 2005) 255-275.

Henry J Steiner, Philip Alston and Ryan Goodman (eds) *International Human Rights in Context: Law Politics Morals* (3rd edition OUP Oxford 2008).

Mia Swart 'Judicial Lawmaking at the ad hoc Tribunals: The Creative Use of the Sources of International Law and "Adventurous Interpretation"' (2010) 70 ZAöRV 459-486.

Immi Tallgren 'The Sensibility and Sence of International Criminal Law' (2002) 13(3) European Journal of Public International Law 561-595.

Claire de Than and Edwin Shorts *International Criminal Law and Human Rights* (Sweet &Maxwell London 2003).

Patrick Thornberry *International Law and the Rights of Minorities* (Clarendon Press Oxford 1991).

Patrick Thornberry 'The UN Declaration on the Rights of Persons Belonging to National or Ethnic, Religious and Linguistic Minorities: Background, Analysis, Observations, and an Update' in Alan Phillips and Allan Rosas (eds) *Universal Minority Rights* (Åbo Akademi University Institute for Human Rights/Minority Rights Group International Turku/Åbo and London 1995)13-76.

C Tofan (ed) *Torture in International Criminal Law* (Wolf The Hague 2011).

Otto Triffterer *Dogmatische Untersuchungen zur Entwicklung des materiellen Völkerstrafrechts seit Nürnberg* (E. Albert 1966) 1

United Nations War Crimes Commission *History of the United Nations War crimes Commission and the Development of the Laws of War* (HMSO London 1948).

Joe Verhoeven 'Article 21 of the Rome Statute and the Ambiguities of Applicable Law' (2002) 33 Netherlands Yearbook of International Law 3-22.

Wolfgang Graf Vitzthum (ed) *Völkerrecht* (5 ed De Gruyter Berlin/New York 2010).

David S Weissbrodt 'The Approach of the Committee on the Elimination of Racial Discrimination to Interpreting and applying International Humanitarian Law' (2010) 19 Minnesota Journal of International Law 327–62.

Gerhard Werle ‚Menschenrechtsschutz durch Völkerstrafrecht' (1997) 109(4) Zeitschrift für die gesamte Strafrechtswissenschaft 808-829.

Gerhard Werle *Völkerstrafrecht* (2. Auflage Mohr Siebeck 2007).

Gerhard Werle and Florian Jeßberger *Principles of International Criminal Law* (3rd ed OUP Oxford 2014).

HG van der Wilt, J Vervliet and others (eds): *The Genocide Convention: The Legacy of 60 Years* (Martinus Nijhoff Leiden 2012).

David Wippman 'Atrocities, Deterrence and the Limits of International Justice' (1999-2000) 23 Fordham International Law Journal 473-488.

Robert K Woetzel 'International Criminal Law and Human Rights: The Sharp Edge of the Sword' (1968) 62 Proceedings of the American Society of International Law at Its Annual Meeting (1921-1969) 117-123.

Rüdiger Wolfrum 'The Decentralized Prosecution of International Offences Through National Courts' in Yoram Dinstein and Mala Tabory *War Crimes in International Law* (Martinus Nijhoff The Hague 1996) 233-249.

Rüdiger Wolfrum '"New Minorities" as a Result of Migration' in Caterine Brölmann, Rene Lefeber and Marjoleine Zieck *Peoples and Minorities in International Law* (Nijhoff Dordrecht 1993).

Rüdiger Wolfrum 'The Prohibition of Discrimination in International Human Rights Treaties: The Development from an Accessory Norm to an Independent One' in Dirk Hanschel and Others *Mensch und Recht: Festschrift für Eibe Riedel* (Duncker und Humblot Berlin 2013) 2009-2019.

Rüdiger Wolfrum 'Prosecution of International Crimes by International and National Criminal Courts: Concurring Jurisdiction' *Studi di Diritto Internazionale in Onore di Gaetano Arangio-Ruiz* vol 3 (Editoriale scientifica Naples 2004) 2199-2209.

Rüdiger Wolfrum 'Das Verbot der Diskriminierung aufgrund von Rasse, Herkunft, Sprache oder Hautfarbe im Völkerrecht' in Rüdiger Wolfrum (eds) Gleichheit und Nichtdiskriminierung im nationalen und internationalen Menschenrechtsschutz (Springer Berlin 2003) 215-231.

Rebecca Young '"Internationally Recognized Human Rights" Before the International Criminal Court' (2011) 60 International and Comparative Law Quarterly 189-208.

Alexander Zahar and Göran Sluiter *International Criminal Law: A Critical Introduction* (OUP Oxford 2008).

Andreas Zimmermann 'Article 5: Crimes within the jurisdiction of the Court' in Otto Triffterer (ed) *Commentary on the Rome Statute of the International Criminal Court* (2nd ed Beck Munich 2008) 129-142.

Danilo Zolo 'Peace through Criminal Law?' (2004) 2 Journal of International Criminal Justice 727-734.

Boštjan Zupančič 'The Binding Nature of the Judgments of the ECHR and the Universality of Human Rights' (14 April 2014) available at http://www.cd-n.org/index.php?the-binding-nature-of-the-judgments-of-the-echr-and-the-universality-of-human-rights (31 October 2017).